Dr. Shaan Patel is a bestselling author with fifteen ~~published.~~
Below is early praise for his sixteenth book:

PREP EXPERT DIGITAL SAT PLAYBOOK

"This playbook is the ultimate companion for every student aspiring to ace their SATs. With a focus on fostering efficient study habits, this playbook isn't just about scoring higher—it's about helping you study smarter and transforming your approach to learning. Dr. Patel's unique strategies and insights empower you to tackle the SATs with confidence and ease, helping you not only improve your scores but also develop lifelong skills for academic excellence. Discover proven practices to enhance your productivity, boost your performance, and minimize stress along the way. Your SAT success story starts here!"

—**JESSICA HOLSMAN**, bestselling author of
The High School Survival Guide and founder of Study With Jess

"As a two-time National College Speaker of the Year who has spoken at over 100 universities, I know how important standardized tests still are to college admissions. This playbook enables students to excel in their college admissions tests, paving the way for academic and professional success. Shaan's methods are a game-changer that helps students achieve not only test prep success but also life success."

—**JAMES MALINCHAK**, bestselling author of *Chicken Soup for the College Soul* and star of ABC's hit TV Show *Secret Millionaire*

"Dr. Shaan Patel's *Prep Expert Digital SAT Playbook* brilliantly applies principles of habit formation and attentional focus. It's a fantastic guide that not only prepares students for the SAT but also teaches them how to study effectively. I recommend it to my own child and yours!"

—**NIR EYAL**, bestselling author of *Hooked* and *Indistractable*

"One of the great privileges of teaching undergraduate and graduate students at Yale is the opportunity to connect with talented, thoughtful, passionate people like Dr. Shaan Patel. It has been ten years since I first met Shaan when he matriculated at Yale, already a highly accomplished SAT tutor, entrepreneur, and individual committed to leveling the playing field for high school students preparing for college. Ten years hence, he is a highly successful clinician but still deeply committed to making the achievement of a high SAT score, and thus access to many schools, more realistic to everyone, not just those who would afford private tutors. Shaan brings *lux et veritas* (light and truth) to everything he touches."

—**DR. HOWARD P. FORMAN**, MD, MBA, Professor of Radiology and Public Health and Director of the MD/MBA Program at Yale University

"Having firsthand experience with Shaan's brilliance while he was in medical school at the University of Southern California, I'm thrilled to see his expertise shared in *Prep Expert Digital SAT Playbook*. As Shaan does so well, this guide is not just about mastering the SAT; it's about developing and nurturing a strategic, analytical mindset that you can apply in various areas. Shaan embodies the type of academic excellence and innovation we value at USC, and I know this guide will prove an invaluable resource for so many others striving for excellence when it comes to college and beyond."

—**DR. SHUBHA KUMAR**, PhD, MPH, Associate Vice Provost for Online Education and Associate Professor of Global Health at the University of Southern California

"Shaan's unique strength lies in his unwavering commitment to viewing tasks through the lens of the students. In this playbook, Shaan goes beyond the ordinary, ensuring that students are not only familiar with the nuances of the new digital SAT but are equipped with essential strategies and tools to navigate this journey. Having witnessed Shaan's impact, I can confidently say that this playbook is not only about acing a test; it's a guide that leads students toward academic and personal success."

—**GIOVANNI (JOHN) DURANTE**, host of *The College Admissions Process Podcast* and Principal of Syosset High School

"Having worked in elementary and higher education for years, I believe that hard work, determination, and merit play a significant role as students embark on their college journey—and throughout life. Dr. Shaan Patel's *Prep Expert Digital SAT Playbook* is a groundbreaking resource in the SAT prep landscape. The book brilliantly combines innovative educational strategies with practical, student-centered approaches.

This resource is not solely a guide for test preparation; it's a blueprint for academic empowerment, which resonates with my advocacy for transformative education that meets the needs of today's learners."

—**ROBYN SHULMAN**, LinkedIn's #1 Top Voice in Education (2018) and former writer at *Forbes*

"As an admissions counselor and director of the admissions consulting team at Prep Expert, I admittedly enjoy a front-row seat to the unparalleled success of Shaan's test preparation strategies. In *thousands* of meetings with families over the past six years, I've personally heard student after student enthusiastically attest to radical score improvements, in addition to countless expressions of gratitude from parents. Whether a student starting at 950 or a student starting at 1480 on the SAT, Shaan's superior techniques and deft explanations will improve the scores of all students. In the highly competitive world of college admissions, standardized testing remains a critical component of the application process—and one of the easiest ways to stand out from other students with high grades and many activities. Now, once again, Shaan has set the standard for test preparation with his new *Prep Expert Digital SAT Playbook* with clear and concise strategies for the digital SAT. I have no doubt students will continue to achieve remarkable score improvements, earn admission to top universities, and win millions of dollars of scholarships. Quite simply, there is no substitute for Shaan's new book and strategies to conquer the SAT."

—**AKBAR RAHEL**, Esq., Admissions Director at Prep Expert

"This book is so much more than proven strategies to help your child ace the digital SAT. It's a book that will give your child the confidence they need to believe they can actually do it. Just read the testimonials from real students who have used Dr. Patel's strategies over the past ten years to attain 300-, 390-, 500-point increases and full-ride scholarships as high as $500,000. I've seen this happen firsthand. Does it take hard work? Of course. But if your child knows their SAT score will make a difference in getting into their school of choice or getting that needed scholarship, this book is your golden ticket."

—**HENRY MITTELMAN**, Founder of CEO Advisory Partners and Forbes Coaches Council Member

"Prep Expert Digital SAT Playbook is a must-read to launch your collegiate and professional career! Dr. Patel shares his proven success tips to enable you to maximize your SAT scores—the first huge step in your post-high school career!"

—**DR. ROB YONOVER**, bestselling author of *Hardcore Inventing* and inventor of SeeRescueStreamer (as seen on *Shark Tank*)

"To any family who believes that 'test scores are optional and don't really matter,' you're wrong. Students with strong PSAT and SAT scores are statistically far more likely to get into the colleges they want. Shaan Patel and this book will lead your high schooler through the procedures, insights, and practice needed to catapult your student to the finish line: the university they've always dreamed of attending!"

—**DR. CAMILLE MOODY MCCUE**, PhD, Principal at The Sheldon Adelson Educational Campus and bestselling author of *Coding for Kids for Dummies*

PREPEXPERT

DIGITAL
SAT
PLAYBOOK

Winning Strategies to
Achieve Your Dream Score

Dr. Shaan Patel, MD, MBA

prepexpert.com

PREPEXPERT

PREP EXPERT DIGITAL SAT PLAYBOOK
Winning Strategies to Achieve Your Dream Score
First Edition

ISBN   978-1-5445-4528-8   *Hardcover*
         978-1-5445-4527-1   *Paperback*
         978-1-5445-4526-4   *Ebook*
         978-1-5445-4525-7   *Audiobook*

Published by Patel Educational Services Inc. DBA "Prep Expert."

To my brother, Sunny,

Your unwavering belief in my dreams has been my guiding light. Our countless conversations, filled with your supportive words and genuine faith in my abilities, have shaped not only this book but also the person I am today. You have always been my biggest supporter, celebrating each step forward and encouraging me to reach for my highest aspirations. This book is a reflection of the confidence and hope you've always had in me, crafted to inspire and empower others as you have inspired and empowered me.

With love and gratitude,
Shaan

FREE BONUS GIFTS!

PRACTICE TESTS, CHEAT SHEETS, AND MORE!

 **PREP**EXPERT

Download Your Free Bonus Gifts at prepexpert.com/bonus

As a thank you for purchasing this book, we have prepared some *free* bonus gifts for you!

- **Practice Tests:** Want full-length practice tests with hundreds of additional SAT exam questions? Access free SAT Practice Tests at the link below.

- **Cheat Sheets:** We have created Cheat Sheets that are quick-reference guides for students to remember key material for the SAT. Download free Cheat Sheets at the link below.

- **Test-Day Checklist:** We have prepared a Test-Day Checklist that will make sure you are fully prepared for your SAT test day. Download the free Checklist at the link below.

- **Bonus Chapters:** Want even more SAT prep content and strategies? Download free Bonus Chapters at the link below.

- **Academic Masterclasses:** Prep Expert Masterclasses help students succeed in all areas of academics and studying. Access a free Academic Success Masterclass at the link below.

- **Live Webinars:** Dr. Shaan Patel, the author of this book and founder of Prep Expert, hosts a live webinar every month for parents and students on how to ace the SAT or ACT, get into top colleges, and win big scholarships. Attend a free webinar at the link below.

 Scan the QR code or visit
prepexpert.com/bonus

50,000,000

students have taken the SAT.

10,000

students have achieved a perfect SAT score.

1

student who improved from an average SAT score to a perfect SAT score has written a book on how to do it.

You are now reading that SAT prep book.

Note that the numbers on this page are approximate. The number of students who take the SAT will continue to increase as time goes on. Approximately 2 million students take the SAT each year. The probability of achieving a perfect SAT score is 0.02%. This is equivalent to about 400 students achieving a perfect SAT score each year. We hope you are next!

ABOUT THE AUTHOR

Dr. Shaan Patel, MD, MBA

- Prep Expert Founder & CEO
- Perfect SAT Scorer
- #1 Bestselling Author
- As Seen on *Shark Tank*
- Board-Certified Dermatologist
- Yale & USC Alumnus, BA, MD, & MBA
- *Inc. Magazine*'s 30 Under 30 Class of 2019

In high school, Shaan Patel was like many of the students reading this book. He was a good student who got As and Bs. However, he was a poor standardized test–taker. Shaan had a lot of test anxiety, had no idea how to prepare for standardized exams, and received only an average score on his first SAT.

After spending hundreds of hours studying for the SAT in high school, Shaan raised his SAT score 640 points from average to perfect. Only 0.02% of all high school students achieve a perfect SAT score. Shaan's perfect SAT score completely changed his life! He received admission to top universities and over $500,000 in scholarships and awards.

Now, Dr. Shaan Patel has created Prep Expert to help high school students achieve their own dreams. Prep Expert is an education company that has helped more than 100,000 students improve their SAT and ACT scores, get into top colleges, and win over $100 million in scholarships. Prep Expert offers online SAT and ACT courses, academic tutoring, and college admissions consulting.

Dr. Shaan Patel completed his Bachelor of Arts (BA) degree at the University of Southern California, Master of Business Administration (MBA) at Yale University,

Medical Degree (MD) at the University of Southern California, and dermatology residency at Temple University Hospital. Dr. Patel is a board-certified dermatologist who practices teledermatology.

Dr. Shaan Patel is the Founder and CEO of Prep Expert. On ABC's Shark Tank, Dr. Patel closed a deal with Mark Cuban for an investment in Prep Expert.

CONTENTS

PREP EXPERT READING STRATEGIES

SAT MATH INTRODUCTION

PREP EXPERT MATH STRATEGIES

PREP EXPERT SAT VOCAB WORD LISTS

SAT PRACTICE QUESTION ANSWERS

$1 BILLION
SCHOLARSHIP MISSION

JANE DOE
1234 APPLE LANE
BOSTON, MA 11223

100

DATE Your Graduation Year

PAY TO THE
ORDER OF **YOUR NAME**

$ **100,000.00**

ONE HUNDRED THOUSAND DOLLARS

YOUR BANK
1448 Joy Lane
Burbank, CA 91502

MEMO Full Scholarship From Your Dream College

⑆123456789⑆   012345678910⑈   ⑆100⑆

Prep Expert's motto is *Change Your Score, Change Your Life*. Over the past decade, Prep Expert has helped students win over $100 million in scholarships. Over the next decade, Prep Expert has an even bigger mission: help students win over **$1 billion in scholarships**!

College tuition costs continue to skyrocket. The average cost of attendance for a public in-state university is over $100,000 and a private out-of-state university is over $200,000. Student loan debt is also at an all-time high, nearing $2 trillion in the United States.

But there is good news! You can reduce or even eliminate your college costs with scholarships. There are over 1.7 million private scholarships awarded each year worth over $7.4 billion. Achieving good grades and a high SAT score will help you get a share of those scholarships.

If you receive a scholarship after using Prep Expert books or courses, please let us know! You can drop us a note at the link below. This will help us keep track of our $1 Billion Scholarship Mission. You can also see what scholarships other students are winning at the link below.

Scan the QR code or visit
prepexpert.com/scholarships

FOREWORD
by MARK CUBAN

As an investor in Prep Expert, I am excited about our $1 Billion Scholarship Mission! Reducing your college costs is a critical step to securing your financial future.

Let me take you back to my college days. When I was your age, I had the opportunity to attend several good colleges. But I chose to attend Indiana University for one key reason: affordability. It was the least expensive option among the top ten business schools in the country. This early decision was one of my first lessons in financial practicality.

There are many similarities between my making my college decision and my experience as an owner of the Dallas Mavericks. Owning an NBA team isn't just about enjoying basketball; it's a serious business involving strategic decisions, just like choosing the right college is. Each player on the Mavericks represents a significant investment, much like your investment in your education. We scout for talent, potential, and a good fit for our team, similar to how you should evaluate universities for their ability to enhance your potential.

When I chose Indiana University, I made a decision similar to drafting a player. It wasn't the most obvious choice, but it was the right one for me financially, academically, and socially. Your college decision is like drafting your future. You need to pick a school that will add value to your life and help you in achieving your goals.

Choosing a college is a significant financial decision, one that will impact you for years to come. I'm not suggesting that you should consider only the cheapest option, but be mindful of the financial impacts. A dream college can turn into a financial nightmare if you're not careful.

Your journey through education is a long-term investment. Much like how I have evaluated potential investments on *Shark Tank*, you must evaluate your college options. It's not just about the brand name prestige or the campus vibe; it's about where you'll get the best return on your investment. Think about the education quality, the network you'll build, and, most importantly, the debt you might get into.

Here's something I firmly believe: student loan debt is a trap. It's absurd that teenagers are allowed to sign up for loans that can follow them for decades. This broken system of student loans can cripple your financial independence before you've even started. That's why I hate all forms of debt—be it credit card debt, business debt, or auto loan debt. But student loan debt? It's the worst of them all.

Student debt is a flawed system, and until it's fixed, your best defense is to be proactive about scholarships and financial aid. There are billions of dollars in scholarships out there, just waiting for students like you to claim them. Good grades and high test scores are your ticket, and this book will help you get there. Just by picking up this book, you're already ahead of the curve.

But scholarships aren't just handed out; they're earned. This is where your hard work comes into play. Grades, test scores, extracurriculars—they all count. Like the entrepreneurs I have invested in on *Shark Tank*, you need to present yourself as the best candidate, the one worth investing in.

Achieving good grades and test scores is nonnegotiable. It's like preparing for a pitch on *Shark Tank*. You need to know your stuff, be at the top of your game, and leave no stone unturned. Hard work, dedication, and a smart strategy are key. This book is a part of that strategy—it's your prep guide. By using it, you're already showing the kind of initiative that leads to success.

Just as I look for entrepreneurs who are hardworking, are dedicated, and have a strong desire to succeed, you need to embody these qualities in your educational journey. Strive for high grades and test scores, much like entrepreneurs who strive to improve their businesses. This book is a tool to help you achieve those scores, similar to how a coach helps an athlete improve.

Think of your college decision as a business. In business, the goal is to increase revenue and decrease expenses. The same applies to your college decision. Increase your revenue by winning scholarships. Apply to colleges that offer merit-based scholarships, and research outside scholarships from private companies. Decrease your expenses by choosing a college with lower tuition costs. Sometimes, the smarter choice is the more affordable one, even if it means turning down a more prestigious but expensive college.

I want to emphasize that this isn't just about saving money. It's about making informed, strategic choices that will set the foundation for your financial future. Education is an investment, and like any investment, it requires careful consideration of the return on investment. Making the right choices now can set the tone for your future success.

Remember, winning scholarships and choosing the right college is like assembling a championship team. It requires careful selection, hard work, and a focus on the end goal. And when you win those scholarships, thanks to this book, let us know at Prep Expert. Your victories are our victories. I would love to hear about it.

Good luck!

—M

THE JOURNEY

"It's not about the destination,
it's about the journey."

—RALPH WALDO EMERSON

MY SAT PREP JOURNEY

Welcome! My name is Dr. Shaan Patel, and I am the Founder and CEO of Prep Expert. Prep Expert's slogan is *Change Your Score, Change Your Life.* Our goal is to help you improve your SAT score so you get accepted into your dream university, win thousands in scholarships, and build effective study habits. To begin, I will explain how I got here in the first place.

I grew up in Las Vegas, Nevada, in my parents' budget motel, far from the glamor of the Las Vegas Strip. I went to inner-city public schools in the worst school district in the nation, with a 40% dropout rate. I was a regular high school kid who enjoyed eating fast food, surfing the web, and hanging out with friends.

I did not have a clue about standardized tests. When I took the SAT for the first time, I only scored around average. This was devastating to me because I wanted to apply to competitive colleges and universities. So I began studying for the most famous standardized test of all time.

After hundreds of hours of studying, I discovered many powerful strategies that helped raise my SAT score 640 points to a perfect score! Of the 50 million students who have taken the SAT, approximately 10,000 have achieved a perfect score—equal to about 0.02%. I am sure many of those 10,000 perfect scorers are natural geniuses, but I am not a genius. I learned how to ace the SAT—going from average to perfect.

My perfect SAT score changed my life. I received admission into prestigious universities like Brown, Northwestern, and Johns Hopkins. I received over twenty scholarships totaling more than $500,000 from companies like Coca-Cola, Toyota, and McDonald's. I received academic awards such as valedictorian, National Merit Finalist, and Presidential Scholar.

Ultimately, I chose to attend the University of Southern California for three reasons. First, USC offered me a full-ride scholarship, so I did not have to pay a dime for tuition, housing, books, or any other expenses. Second, I received admission into USC's BS/MD program, which was a competitive direct medical program. Third, USC is in Los Angeles, California, which is close to my home in Las Vegas, Nevada.

After completing my bachelor's degree in biology at USC, I also earned my medical degree at USC through the BS/MD Medical Program. During medical school, I took a two-year leave of absence to complete my MBA at Yale University. After medical school, I completed my residency in dermatology at Temple University Hospital. I now practice teledermatology as a board-certified dermatologist.

My SAT Score Made All of the Above Possible

If I had never studied for the SAT in high school, I would not have been admitted to competitive colleges and medical programs. If I had never studied for the SAT in high school, I would not have been paid to go to college. If I had never studied for the SAT in high school, I would not have developed the discipline needed to succeed in college, graduate school, and my career.

Studying for the SAT now, in high school, will compound your life success both directly and indirectly. Your SAT prep will produce direct success in the form of college acceptances and scholarship money. It will also produce indirect success by helping you to develop the habits required to succeed. Developing habits like hard work and self-control now will serve you well throughout your life. These habits will ultimately contribute to your future academic and career success.

Now, it is time to start your SAT prep journey!

YOUR SAT PREP JOURNEY

I told you about my own SAT prep journey to inspire your upcoming SAT prep journey. Sure, the SAT is only one test, but this one test changed my life. And it can change yours too.

I know how busy you are in high school because I was once in your shoes. You are likely trying to balance high school coursework, extracurriculars, sports, AP exams, a social life, and more. In addition to all these activities, you must still make time for SAT prep. And I am here to tell you that it will all be worth it.

You Need a Specific Reason That You Want a High SAT Score

No one wants a high SAT score just for the sake of having one. When I was in high school, I wanted a high SAT score because I wanted to get accepted into a combined medical program (known as "BS/MD" or "BA/MD" programs). Combined medical programs guarantee students a seat in medical school directly out of high school. It is a great opportunity for high school students who are looking to become physicians! The problem with direct BS/MD medical programs is that they are highly competitive. Direct medical programs often have acceptance rates that are lower than most Ivy League universities—sometimes lower than 5%. In addition, combined medical programs often only accept students who have SAT (or ACT) scores in the 99th percentile. My desire to get into a combined medical program was my specific reason for wanting a high SAT score.

What Is Your Specific Reason to Study for the SAT?

Studying for the SAT without a reason rarely works. Studying for the SAT because your parents want you to do well is okay, but your parents' will is an external motivator. I encourage you to find an internal motivator that will keep you going.

You must have a goal you want to achieve with your SAT score. This will serve as a powerful motivator to spend the time it takes to improve your SAT score. Try answering these questions:

- What are a few universities you dream of attending (e.g., Harvard, Stanford, Yale, etc.)?
- What career(s) would you like to pursue in the future (e.g., doctor, lawyer, pharmacist, engineer, tech entrepreneur, etc.)?
- Are there combined programs that would help fast-track your success in the future career that you would like to pursue (such as BS/MD medical programs, BA/JD law programs, BA/DDS dental programs, BA/MBA business programs, etc.)?
- How much scholarship money would you like to receive (e.g., $250,000, $100,000, etc.)?
- Are there specific scholarships or awards you would like to receive (such as National Merit, Presidential Scholar, etc.)?

Answering these questions will help you identify your goals. After identifying your goals, write them down. There is something powerful about writing your goals down and visualizing them. Doing so makes your goals much more likely to become reality. Write down the exact SAT score you would like to achieve. For example, you might want to write down something like the following:

"I have achieved a 1500 out of 1600 on the SAT, received admission to Yale University, and won $250,000 in college scholarships."

Notice how I wrote the above goals as if they had already been achieved. You are much more likely to achieve your goals if you feel like you have already achieved them—no matter how big your dreams are!

Write Your Goals Down Here

You should also write your goals down somewhere you often look (such as your phone). They will serve as a reminder of why you are embarking on this SAT prep journey in the first place.

PREP EXPERT'S JOURNEY

How can Prep Expert help you achieve your goals? To be honest, I never considered starting a test prep company...it just kind of happened. After I achieved a perfect SAT score in high school, I always wanted to write an SAT prep book. After my own life changed for the better thanks to my high SAT score, I wanted to help other students change their own lives by improving their test scores.

When I got to college, I created a book proposal to pitch to literary agents on the first SAT prep book written by a perfect SAT scorer. Unfortunately, over one hundred literary agents and publishers rejected my book proposal. They said that I lacked the platform to write such a book and that the SAT prep market was too competitive. One publisher even said she "didn't find [my] writing or persona particularly engaging," adding that I'm "not a great writer, no matter what [my] score is."

As you can imagine, I was pretty discouraged at this point. So I had two options. Plan A was to continue to hope for a book-publishing deal. Plan B was to quit. But when life gives you two options, create a third. I decided to leverage the material I had written for the book to teach SAT courses the summer before I started medical school. I worked tirelessly to launch Prep Expert.

In the first Prep Expert SAT course I ever taught, my students experienced an average score improvement of 376 points! This is equivalent to taking a student's SAT score from the 50th percentile to the 90th percentile. Of course, I had parents and students asking for more courses. I began training other instructors to teach my curriculum, and the rest is history.

Prep Expert has now helped more than 100,000 students improve their SAT and ACT scores, get into top colleges, and win over $100 million in scholarships. The highlight of the company was when I pitched Prep Expert on ABC's *Shark Tank* for an investment in 2016. We ended up closing an investment deal with Mark Cuban for $250,000 in exchange for 20% equity in Prep Expert. Mark Cuban has been an amazing investor, partner, and advocate for the company ever since.

McGraw-Hill, the world's largest education publisher, had initially rejected my book proposal. But when they saw what I was building with Prep Expert, they ended up offering me a book deal after all. The SAT prep book I wrote for McGraw Hill sold over 50,000 copies and became a #1 Amazon Best Seller. Ironically, what I originally wanted (to author a book) did not happen until I decided to take a completely different path (starting a company)!

Here are some testimonials from a few former Prep Expert parents and students:

"We were all floored when his scores came in last month, and he scored perfect. This SAT preparation book was the only one he used."
—Carolyn B. (parent of Neil B.—perfect SAT score)

"Hey Shaan! I know we don't know each other personally, but I just want you to know that your book got me a perfect score. I got the score solely because of reading and the writing strategies. Thanks so much; you were a lifesaver. I'll be attending Harvard this fall, and I'm sure your book helped me get there!"
—Abhinav S. (perfect SAT score)

"My name is Celina and I was in your August–September class. I received my scores for the October exam and I got a perfect score! I wanted to thank you for your guidance in helping me achieve my goal."
—Celina P. (perfect SAT score)

"Today, the scores came out, and I found out I got a perfect score. I really have to thank you for helping people like me. I never dreamed that I would actually get a perfect score. Your strategies gave me a smooth path to walk on. College seems much less intimidating now."
—Shirley Y. (perfect SAT score)

"I wanted to thank you for all the guidance that you gave me during this course! I'm very grateful to have had such a great instructor!"
—Michelle M. (perfect SAT score)

"My SAT score has improved by over 500 points from the first week of class!"
—Alexandar T. (500-point SAT score improvement)

"The Prep Expert curriculum combines expertise and passion for the SAT, along with top-notch teaching materials that inspire even the most unmotivated to succeed. I have now achieved confidence and proficiency on the SAT that I never had. My family agrees that it was the best $999 we have ever spent."

—Madison S. (560-point SAT score improvement)

"I was recently admitted to Stanford University. My SAT score was much higher than I could have expected to gain without your assistance and raising my SAT score through your program made a world of difference."

—Julia E. (390-point SAT score improvement)

"After both my son and daughter took Prep Expert SAT courses, my son improved 260 points and my daughter 340 points, and both got full ride scholarships worth $500,000!"

—Ami V. (parent of two Prep Expert students)

"I improved my score 360 points! Not only was the course informational, but also fun. In addition to incredible test advice, I also came away with great life advice."

—Audrey R. (360-point SAT score improvement)

"After taking Prep Expert, my SAT score improved 300 points and I got a full tuition scholarship offer to the University of San Diego worth over $100,000! I highly recommend Prep Expert!"

—Alexis H. (300-point SAT score improvement)

After going through Prep Expert's curriculum, if you end up achieving a high SAT score, getting into top universities, or winning college scholarships, please let us know. My favorite part of my job is hearing from successful students like the ones above. I hope you are next and are now inspired to ace the SAT yourself!

DIGITAL SAT INTRODUCTION

"The secret to getting ahead is getting started."

—MARK TWAIN

DIGITAL SAT OVERVIEW

Welcome to Prep Expert! The time you invest in Prep Expert will yield immense returns. You will learn many strategies, techniques, and tips to help you achieve the highest score possible on the Digital SAT. Let's get started.

DIGITAL SAT TEST FORMAT

Section	Questions	Time
SAT Reading & Writing Module 1	27 questions	32 minutes
SAT Reading & Writing Module 2	27 questions	32 minutes
Break	N/A	10 minutes
SAT Math Module 1	22 questions	35 minutes
SAT Math Module 2	22 questions	35 minutes
Total SAT Exam	**98 Questions**	**2 hours, 24 minutes**

Digital SAT Test Format

The Digital SAT includes four modules, presented in a specific sequence. The first module is an SAT Reading and Writing module that consists of 27 questions in 32 minutes. The second module is also an SAT Reading and Writing module that includes 27 questions in 32 minutes. Depending on how well you performed on the first Reading and Writing module, the second Reading and Writing module will include easier or harder questions. This is the "adaptive" feature of the Digital SAT, which we will discuss shortly.

After completing two modules, the Digital SAT will offer you a 10-minute break. This is a good opportunity to give your brain a chance to relax. Make sure you take this break in full.

Once the 10-minute break period is over, you will start the second half of the exam with the first SAT Math module. This module consists of 22 questions in 35 minutes. After completing this first SAT Math module, you will then be presented with a second SAT Math module that also includes 22 questions in 35 minutes. Depending on how well you performed on the first Math module, the second Math module will include easier or harder questions.

The total time to take the Digital SAT is 2 hours and 24 minutes. This includes the 10-minute break period in the middle of the test. Thus, the actual testing time is 2 hours and 14 minutes. There are a total of 98 questions on the Digital SAT. This is great news for students because this is the shortest version of the SAT ever created!

DIGITAL SAT SCORING

Section	Scaled Score
SAT Reading & Writing	200–800 Points
SAT Math	200–800 Points
Total SAT Exam	**400–1600 Points**

Digital SAT Scoring

The Digital SAT is scored out of a total of 1600 points. You will receive two subscores: an SAT Reading and Writing score between 200 and 800 points, and an SAT Math score between 200 and 800 points. Added together, these two subscores determine your total score out of 1600 on the Digital SAT. Note that SAT scores are always rounded to the nearest ten.

The "Adaptive" Nature of the Digital SAT

Now, let's discuss the adaptive nature of the Digital SAT. You should know that the Digital SAT adapts module by module, not question by question. This means the second module's difficulty level is based on your performance in the first module. If you perform well in the first module (on either SAT Reading and Writing *or* SAT Math), the second module related to that subject will present *more difficult* questions. This will give you the opportunity to attain a higher score overall. Conversely, if you perform poorly in the first module (on either SAT Reading and Writing *or* SAT Math), the second module related to that subject will present *less difficult* questions. This will limit your opportunity to achieve a higher score overall.

In other words, the first modules in both SAT Reading and Writing and SAT Math assess your baseline performance level. Based on your answers, the second modules related to these subjects adapt their difficulty to your skill level. This allows for a more precise measurement of your abilities. This also allows the Digital SAT to calculate an accurate score with fewer questions than traditional paper-based standardized tests.

The Digital SAT is a sophisticated, adaptive examination designed to accurately gauge your skills. Understanding the structure, scoring system, and adaptive nature we just discussed is critical for effective SAT preparation.

Digital SAT Intro

DIGITAL SAT TEST IMPORTANCE

Recently, you may have seen articles in the media stating that SAT or ACT scores are no longer important. Many journalists cite the trend of colleges going test-optional for admissions. However, you should ignore these arguments. By the end of this chapter, you will understand why the SAT is actually more important than ever for both college admissions and scholarships.

Is the SAT Still Important?

The SAT is still important for three key reasons.

Reason #1: SAT Scores Impact College Admissions

Even at test-optional colleges, SAT scores help you gain admission. Although these universities claim to be "test-optional," the data suggests otherwise. Acceptance rates at almost every test-optional college are significantly higher for students who submit test scores than for students who do not submit test scores. In fact, median SAT scores have increased for almost every Ivy League university after the implementation of test-optional college admissions policies. Now, almost every Ivy League university has a median SAT score of 1500 or above for their most recently accepted classes. SAT scores still help you get into college, period.

Reason #2: SAT Scores Impact Scholarships

SAT scores also help you secure scholarships. Every year, colleges and private companies give out billions of dollars in merit-based financial aid to students. If you do not have a test score, you will not be considered for a significant number of these scholarship opportunities. Many universities that are "test-optional" for admissions still give out big scholarships based on SAT or ACT scores! Scholarship eligibility is an important reason alone to take the SAT.

Reason #3: The Resurgence of Standardized Testing Requirements

Many universities have already reinstated standardized testing for admission. MIT, the most data-driven university in the world, has stated that their "ability to accurately predict student academic success...is significantly improved by considering standardized testing. Our research shows that good grades in high school do not themselves necessarily translate to academic success at MIT if you cannot account for testing." Harvard has also announced it will bring back standardized testing for high school seniors graduating in 2027. Once Harvard brings back standardized testing requirements, most other universities will follow.

The Truth about "Test-Optional" Colleges

Below is a table of the SAT score ranges for the top 100 Best National Universities, according to *US News & World Report*. The table uses the latest data available as of this writing. Notably, the SAT score ranges represent data for the 25th to the 75th percentile of students.

Most of these colleges have "test-optional" standardized testing policies. Examine the SAT score ranges for each college's admitted class. The students who actually get into these universities have high SAT scores.

An example highlighting this reality is that of New York University (NYU). NYU received a record 120,000 applications for first-year admission for its undergraduate class of 2027. But NYU admitted only 8% of all high school students who applied. The admitted class to NYU represented a median SAT score of 1540, nearly a perfect SAT score. Despite proclaiming a test-optional policy, NYU's actual admissions data reveals that the university is overwhelmingly accepting students with high SAT scores.

College admission is more competitive than ever. A high SAT score will help you get into your dream university—even if that college says that it is "test-optional."

Rank	University	SAT Score Range
1	Princeton University	1500–1580
2	Massachusetts Institute of Technology	1520–1580
3 (Tie)	Harvard University	1490–1580
3 (Tie)	Stanford University	1500–1580
5	Yale University	1500–1580
6	University of Pennsylvania	1500–1570
7 (Tie)	California Institute of Technology	Not reported
7 (Tie)	Duke University	1490–1570
9 (Tie)	Brown University	1490–1580
9 (Tie)	Johns Hopkins	1520–1570
9 (Tie)	Northwestern University	1490–1570
12 (Tie)	Columbia University	Not reported
12 (Tie)	Cornell University	1470–1570
12 (Tie)	University of Chicago	1500–1580
15 (Tie)	University of California, Berkeley	Not reported
15 (Tie)	University of California, Los Angeles	Not reported
17	Rice University	1490–1570
18 (Tie)	Dartmouth College	1500–1580
18 (Tie)	Vanderbilt University	1490–1570
20	University of Notre Dame	1420–1550
21	University of Michigan—Ann Arbor	1350–1530
22 (Tie)	Georgetown University	1390–1560
22 (Tie)	University of North Carolina at Chapel Hill	1350–1530
24 (Tie)	Carnegie Mellon University	1490–1570
24 (Tie)	Emory University	1430–1550
24 (Tie)	University of Virginia	1400–1540
24 (Tie)	Washington University in St. Louis	1500–1570
28 (Tie)	University of California, Davis	Not reported
28 (Tie)	University of California, San Diego	Not reported
28 (Tie)	University of Florida	1300–1490
28 (Tie)	University of Southern California	1450–1550
32	University of Texas at Austin	1230–1500

33 (Tie)	Georgia Institute of Technology	1370–1550
33 (Tie)	University of California, Irvine	Not reported
35 (Tie)	New York University	1470–1570
35 (Tie)	University of California, Santa Barbara	Not reported
35 (Tie)	University of Illinois Urbana-Champaign	1340–1530
35 (Tie)	University of Wisconsin—Madison	1350–1510
39	Boston College	1435–1540
40 (Tie)	Rutgers University—New Brunswick	1270–1480
40 (Tie)	Tufts University	1450–1550
40 (Tie)	University of Washington	1300–1520
43 (Tie)	Boston University	1350–1500
43 (Tie)	The Ohio State University	1310–1480
43 (Tie)	Purdue University—Main Campus	1200–1470
46	University of Maryland, College Park	1360–1520
47 (Tie)	Lehigh University	1340–1490
47 (Tie)	Texas A&M University	1150–1390
47 (Tie)	University of Georgia	1220–1420
47 (Tie)	University of Rochester	1390–1540
47 (Tie)	Virginia Tech	1220–1420
47 (Tie)	Wake Forest University	1380–1510
53 (Tie)	Case Western Reserve University	1410–1540
53 (Tie)	Florida State University	1210–1370
53 (Tie)	Northeastern University	1440–1550
53 (Tie)	University of Minnesota, Twin Cities	1290–1500
53 (Tie)	William & Mary	1375–1520
58 (Tie)	Stony Brook University—SUNY	1320–1500
58 (Tie)	University of Connecticut	1220–1440
60 (Tie)	Brandeis University	1340–1520
60 (Tie)	Michigan State University	1100–1340
60 (Tie)	North Carolina State University	1245–1440
60 (Tie)	The Pennsylvania State University, University Park	1210–1390
60 (Tie)	Rensselaer Polytechnic Institute	1360–1520
60 (Tie)	Santa Clara University	1290–1480
60 (Tie)	University of California, Merced	Not reported

67 (Tie)	George Washington University	1330–1490
67 (Tie)	Syracuse University	1260–1430
67 (Tie)	University of Massachusetts, Amherst	1260–1480
67 (Tie)	University of Miami	1310–1480
67 (Tie)	University of Pittsburgh	1280–1470
67 (Tie)	Villanova University	1380–1500
73 (Tie)	Binghamton University—SUNY	1340–1510
73 (Tie)	Indiana University Bloomington	1180–1400
73 (Tie)	Tulane University	1370–1510
76 (Tie)	Colorado School of Mines	1330–1490
76 (Tie)	Pepperdine University	1285–1480
76 (Tie)	Stevens Institute of Technology	1380–1510
76 (Tie)	University at Buffalo—SUNY	1190–1380
76 (Tie)	University of California, Riverside	Not reported
76 (Tie)	University of Delaware	1190–1360
82 (Tie)	Rutgers University–Newark	1030–1270
82 (Tie)	University of California, Santa Cruz	Not reported
82 (Tie)	University of Illinois Chicago	1110–1340
82 (Tie)	Worcester Polytechnic Institute	Not reported
86 (Tie)	Clemson University	1220–1410
86 (Tie)	Marquette University	1170–1360
86 (Tie)	New Jersey Institute of Technology	1190–1450
89 (Tie)	Fordham University	1320–1480
89 (Tie)	Southern Methodist University	1370–1510
89 (Tie)	Temple University	1120–1370
89 (Tie)	University of South Florida	1140–1330
93 (Tie)	Auburn University	1240–1390
93 (Tie)	Baylor University	1230–1410
93 (Tie)	Gonzaga University	1210–1410
93 (Tie)	Loyola Marymount University	1300–1460
93 (Tie)	University of Iowa	1130–1340
98 (Tie)	Drexel University	1230–1430
98 (Tie)	Illinois Institute of Technology	1220–1410

98 (Tie)	Rochester Institute of Technology	1270–1450
98 (Tie)	Rutgers University–Camden	1030–1280
98 (Tie)	Texas Christian University	1140–1360
98 (Tie)	University of Oregon	1140–1370
98 (Tie)	University of San Diego	Not reported

The Truth about "Test-Blind" Colleges

What about colleges with "test-blind" college admissions policies? This means that they will not consider SAT or ACT scores for admission even if students submit them. The University of California (UC) system has this type of college admissions policy.

However, the University of California website states, "Test scores could still be considered for other purposes such as course placement, certain *scholarships*, and eligibility for the statewide admissions guarantee." Some UC scholarships pay $80,000-plus over the course of four years of college! This is an example of how colleges may accept students without test scores for admission, but *not* award them scholarships. The UC system is not the only place this is happening. If you want to be eligible for major scholarships for hundreds of colleges across the nation, you will need an SAT or ACT score.

Is College Worth It?

Is college worth it? This question has been a topic of major public debate. Browsing social media, you will find thousands of influencers who claim that college is no longer worth it.

These internet gurus will often showcase their own lives as examples of how to become a millionaire in your twenties without college. They usually state that you can learn all the skills you need to succeed online, and that college is a waste of time and money. Do not buy what these internet peddlers are selling.

Sure, a small minority of people may become successful without a college degree. But the vast majority of college-educated people end up being more successful. Here is the data to prove it.

COLLEGE DATA

- **$1.2 million**: According to the Georgetown University Center on Education and the Workforce, the average college graduate earns $1.2 million more over their lifetime than a high school graduate.

- **Higher earnings**: According to the US Bureau of Labor Statistics, the median weekly earnings for workers with a bachelor's degree were $1,432, compared to $853 for workers with only a high school diploma.

- **Lower unemployment**: As of this writing, the unemployment rate for workers with a bachelor's degree is 2.1%, compared to 3.9% for workers with only a high school diploma.

- **Career success**: According to the Georgetown University Center on Education and the Workforce, college graduates were more likely to be employed, have higher salaries, and have more opportunities for advancement than non-college graduates.

- **Health**: According to a study by the National Bureau of Economic Research, attaining a college education actually reduces risk of mortality from deaths due to cancer and heart disease.

- **Longevity**: A study by the Brookings Papers on Economic Activity found that college graduates in 2021 had a life expectancy of eighty-three years, compared to seventy-five years for non-college graduates.

The Truth about College Costs

Now that we have established that college is worth attending, let's consider whether the cost of college is worth it. After all, the cost of college is increasing more quickly than ever. Here is the data to prove it.

COLLEGE COSTS DATA

- **Public university cost of attendance**: As of this writing, the Education Data Initiative estimates that the average cost to attend a public in-state university is $104,108 over four years.

- **Private university cost of attendance**: As of this writing, the Education Data Initiative estimates that the average cost to attend a private out-of-state university is $223,360 over four years.

- **Student loan debt**: As of this writing, the Education Data Initiative estimates student loan debt in the United States totals $1.77 trillion.

- **College affordability crisis**: According to a report from the Georgetown University Center on Education and the Workforce, college costs have increased by 169% from the years 1980 to 2019—while earnings for workers between the ages of twenty-two and twenty-seven have increased by only 19% during that same time period.

Do Not Pay the Sticker Price for College

Statistics like the ones above are often startling. Media articles and influencers often cite this data to make the argument that college is not worth the cost of attending. But what many people miss is that the numbers above are the *sticker* price. Most high-achieving students *do not pay* the sticker price. Instead, you can reduce or even eliminate your college costs with merit-based scholarships and financial aid. Here is the data to prove it.

MERIT-BASED FINANCIAL AID DATA

- **58% reduction in costs**: The US Department of Education found that on average, high-merit students have 58% of their tuition paid for by merit-based financial aid at very selective institutions.

- **1.7 million scholarships**: According to ThinkImpact, in the United States, more than 1.7 million fellowships and private scholarships are awarded each year, with 25% of college students receiving money from these scholarships and grants.

- **$7.4 billion in scholarship money**: Public and private companies award over $7.4 billion in scholarship money annually in the United States. Some of the most well-known companies that offer merit-based scholarships include Coca-Cola, Google, Intel, Microsoft, National Merit Scholarship Corporation, QuestBridge, and Walmart.

High school students receive merit-based financial aid based on their academic achievements. These include GPA, test scores, leadership, community service, or athletic talents.

One of the most important factors in determining whether you will receive merit-based financial aid is your SAT score. Most scholarship applications are due between December and April of your senior year of high school. You should aim to achieve a high SAT score before then. Once you achieve a high SAT score, you will have a much higher probability of receiving merit-based scholarship offers. Prep Expert will help you with the most important step in receiving thousands of dollars in scholarships: achieving a high SAT score.

Is the SAT Worth Taking?

As the media continues to dismiss the importance of the SAT, you must ignore the noise. These journalists often lack expertise in college admissions, scholarships, or test preparation.

Prep Expert will help you achieve a high Digital SAT score. This will maximize your opportunities for college admissions and scholarships. Your preparation for the Digital SAT will grant you access to incredible academic opportunities.

HOW THIS DIGITAL SAT PLAYBOOK WORKS

Your path to acing the Digital SAT begins here. First, let's understand the structure of the *Prep Expert Digital SAT Playbook* to maximize its benefits.

What You Will Learn

The *Prep Expert Digital SAT Playbook* will teach you everything you need to know to ace the Digital SAT. It covers the most important concepts you need to master related to every section of the SAT, including these:

- Prep Expert General Strategies
- Prep Expert Math Strategies
- Prep Expert Reading Strategies
- Prep Expert Writing Strategies

Teaching Methodology

The *Prep Expert Digital SAT Playbook* follows four important teaching principles to maximize learning retention.

1. **Prep Expert Strategy**: First, this playbook will teach you the key concepts related to a specific strategy.

2. **Prep Expert Example**: Second, this playbook will show you examples of that strategy in action.

3. **Prep Expert Practice**: Third, this playbook will have you practice applying the strategy to SAT questions.

4. **Prep Expert Review**: Fourth, this playbook will review the concepts related to the strategy to solidify your knowledge.

This structured design of the *Prep Expert Digital SAT Playbook* will ensure that you ace the Digital SAT!

PREPEXPERT

GENERAL STRATEGIES

"General knowledge is the foundation upon which all other learning is built."

—UNKNOWN

PREP EXPERT GENERAL STRATEGIES OVERVIEW

Prep Expert General Strategies are a collection of techniques designed to improve not only your SAT score, but also your study habits and test scores on other academic exams. These strategies include test-taking approaches, time management techniques, and test anxiety reduction methods. They are designed to equip students with the confidence and skills necessary to tackle any exam with confidence. *Prep Expert General Strategies* are applicable to a wide variety of standardized tests, including the PSAT, ACT, and AP Exams.

Learning how to study effectively is a key theme among these strategies. The adaptability of *Prep Expert General Strategies* means they will work for every student. Regardless of your current level of performance, these strategies offer a path to improvement. We will address how to overcome procrastination, improve study habits, and refine test-taking skills. You will see significant improvements not only to your SAT score, but also in your overall study approach for other high school courses and exams.

Prep Expert General Strategies are a comprehensive guide for academic success. They provide a blueprint for you to follow, ensuring that your study time is optimized and that you enter test day fully prepared. These strategies will instill habits in you that will foster lifelong learning and achievement. With the right mindset and tools, every student has the potential to excel. Apply these strategies to transform your academic aspirations into reality!

 **PREP**EXPERT

GENERAL STRATEGY #1

USE COLLEGE BOARD SAT QUESTIONS

PREP EXPERT STRATEGY

Practice with College Board SAT Questions **Only**

The first *Prep Expert General Strategy* is to practice exclusively with College Board SAT questions. This is the simple secret to achieving a high SAT score.

College Board is the company that creates the SAT. Therefore, College Board SAT practice questions are going to be the most accurate and similar to what you will encounter on test day. Practicing with real test questions is crucial. Many of the questions that you see on your actual SAT test day will be so similar to College Board practice SAT questions that you will think that you have seen them before. Consequently, you will be able to easily solve those questions!

Every high-scoring student I have prepped over the years has practiced with official SAT questions. If you would like to be a high-scoring SAT student, it is important that you practice with College Board SAT questions too.

Creating high-quality practice SAT questions is difficult. The College Board spends millions of dollars on statistical analysis and testing to create perfect test questions. Most companies do not have the budget or resources to create perfect test questions.

Third-party companies try to recreate real SAT questions, but often end up creating subpar questions riddled with issues. If you practice with test questions produced by third-party companies other than the College Board, then you are practicing with sub-par questions. Avoid third-party SAT questions as much as you can.

Maximize your SAT score by practicing with the gold standard: official SAT questions produced by the College Board.

Use College Board SAT Questions to maximize your SAT score.

PREP EXPERT EXAMPLE

Where to Find College Board SAT Questions

You might be wondering: Where do I find College Board SAT questions? Here are some resources to get you started with practicing with official test questions.

1. **Prep Expert SAT Courses**

   Visit Prep Expert's website: prepexpert.com

   If you enroll in a Prep Expert SAT Course, then you do not need to worry about hunting down College Board SAT practice questions. We use official College Board SAT practice questions already.

2. **College Board Bluebook App**

   Download the College Board's testing app: Bluebook

   This application contains multiple full-length College Board practice SAT exams that contain official test questions.

3. **The Official Digital SAT Study Guide**

   Purchase the College Board's book: The Official Digital SAT Study Guide

   If you prefer to practice with questions in a physical book, we recommend purchasing the College Board's *Official Digital SAT Study Guide*. This book contains multiple full-length College Board practice SAT exams. However, these practice exams are almost identical to the ones found in the College Board's Bluebook app.

4. **College Board's Website**

   Visit the College Board's official website: www.collegeboard.org

Navigate to the section of the website that is dedicated to "Digital SAT Practice and Preparation." Here you will find College Board SAT questions that you may not have seen before.

5. **Khan Academy's Website**
   Visit the Khan Academy's official website: www.khanacademy.org
   Navigate to the section of the website that is dedicated to "Digital SAT." Here you will find College Board SAT questions that you may not have seen before.

PREP EXPERT PRACTICE

Already Completed All College Board SAT Questions?

Because the Digital SAT is relatively new, there are not as many official practice questions available from the College Board for this digital version of the SAT compared to the old paper-based SAT. Therefore, some students reading this book may have already completed all available Digital SAT questions produced by the College Board. If you have already completed all of the College Board's practice SAT questions, I recommend doing them again.

Although it may seem repetitive, redoing the same questions has many benefits:

1. **Opportunity to apply strategies**
   Use your second attempt at the official College Board Digital SAT practice questions as an opportunity to apply the Prep Expert strategies you learn in this book. Determine if your test-taking approaches have significantly changed or not.

2. **Deepens your understanding**
   Identify why you got certain questions right or wrong to deepen your understanding. Document personal mistakes, insights, and breakthroughs. Become so familiar with official College Board SAT questions that nothing will surprise you on test day.

3. **Reduces test anxiety**
   A 2013 study found that retesting with the same questions significantly

reduces test anxiety. Retesting acclimates students to the test structure, types of questions, and timing constraints.[1]

Future Standardized Exams

When preparing for other standardized exams in the future, always practice using questions from the test creator. Apply this foundational principle to all standardized tests in your academic journey. If you are preparing for the ACT, use official questions produced by the company that creates the ACT (i.e., ACT, Inc.).

I have used this principle for every standardized exam that I have ever taken, including these:

- SAT
- PSAT
- AP Exams
- MCAT
- GMAT
- USMLE
- American Board of Dermatology Board Certification Exams

As you can see, I have taken a lot of standardized exams. But no matter the subject of the exam, one theme never changes: I always go to the test creator for my practice questions. This has resulted in high scores in almost every standardized exam that I have ever taken. Make sure you follow this principle on any future standardized test that you take.

PREP EXPERT REVIEW

Key Takeaways

- **Prep Expert General Strategy #1—*Use College Board SAT Questions***:
  Practicing with official College Board questions is crucial for a high SAT score.

---

1   Laura Iossi, "Strategies for Reducing Math Anxiety in Post-Secondary Students," Florida International University, 2007, https://digitalcommons.fiu.edu/cgi/viewcontent.cgi?article=1257&context=sferc&httpsredir=1&referer=.

- **Avoid third-party questions**: Third-party companies can only try to mimic real SAT questions. College Board's questions represent the real exam most accurately.

- **Where to find College Board questions**: You can find official SAT questions in a variety of resources including Prep Expert SAT Courses, College Board's Bluebook App, *The Official Digital SAT Study Guide*, College Board's website, and Khan Academy's website.

- **Retesting benefits**: Even if you have already completed all of the College Board SAT questions before, we recommend doing them again. This helps you master applying strategies, understanding previous mistakes, and reducing test anxiety.

GENERAL STRATEGY #2

SAT® is a trademark registered and owned by the College Board, which was not involved in the production of, and does not endorse, this product.

DON'T USE COLLEGE BOARD SAT STRATEGIES

PREP EXPERT STRATEGY

My SAT preparation advice may now seem contradictory. On the one hand, I recommend practicing with the College Board's SAT questions. On the other hand, I recommend avoiding the College Board's test-taking strategies. This might sound paradoxical, but by the end of this chapter, my rationale will be clear.

The College Board and Khan Academy "Strategies" Are Ineffective

The College Board and Khan Academy provide excellent SAT practice questions. However, the College Board and Khan Academy provide inadequate SAT "strategies." I am not even sure that you can call what they teach "strategies."

The College Board and Khan Academy state that the SAT measures only what students learn in their high school curriculums. Therefore, they teach students only what they have already learned in high school. They do not provide real SAT test-prep strategies.

Do you believe that the SAT measures only what you have already learned in high school? If that were true, students who excel in high school would not have to study for the SAT. Students who get As in high school would automatically get SAT scores in the 99th percentile. Students who perform well in their high school classes would always perform well on the SAT.

Of course, we know that is not the case.

The College Board's primary agenda is to tell school administrators that the SAT measures what students learn in high school. Therefore, the College Board's and Khan Academy's "strategies" simply regurgitate traditional high school problem-solving techniques. While this may sound like a good idea, high school approaches to SAT problems are often not the most effective way to solve SAT problems. For most students, traditional high school methods do not produce high SAT scores.

Don't Use College Board SAT Strategies to maximize your SAT score.

PREP EXPERT EXAMPLE

Prep Expert Unlocks the SAT Exam

Prep Expert's approach differs significantly from the College Board's approach. We know that there are specialized strategies, tips, and tricks you can use to maximize your SAT score.

Your high school curriculum does not cover these techniques. The College Board would not endorse Prep Expert strategies. These approaches challenge the College Board's contention that the SAT aligns with the curriculum taught in high schools.

For example, would the College Board teach you how to bypass traditional algebra by simply plugging in numbers on the SAT Math section? Would the College Board teach you the five specific words that are always incorrect on the SAT Reading section? Unlikely. These techniques undermine the College Board's assertion that the SAT measures what students learn in high school. The College Board and Khan Academy do not teach strategies to take advantage of the test.

Prep Expert, on the other hand, *does* teach these powerful strategies to help students maximize their SAT scores.

PREP EXPERT PRACTICE

The Best of Both Worlds

In *Prep Expert General Strategy #1—Use College Board SAT Questions*, I stressed the importance of using official practice questions in your SAT preparation. However, completing practice questions alone will not significantly improve your SAT score. You must apply new, innovative test-taking techniques as you practice. This is where Prep Expert comes in. We will teach you how to apply effective strategies to official SAT questions step by step.

The ideal SAT prep method combines College Board *questions* with Prep Expert *strategies*. *College Board questions* are the most authentic SAT questions available. *Prep Expert strategies* are the most effective SAT strategies available.

Apply Prep Expert strategies to College Board SAT questions for the most effective SAT preparation possible.

PREP EXPERT REVIEW

Key Takeaways

- **Prep Expert General Strategy #2—*Don't Use College Board Strategies***: While we do advise students to use College Board's SAT exams for practice questions, we do not recommend using the College Board's or Khan Academy's test-taking strategies.

- **Inefficiency of College Board strategies**: While College Board's practice questions are top-tier, their test preparation "strategies" are subpar. The College Board and Khan Academy teach only traditional high school methods, which are not effective in maximizing SAT scores.

- **College Board's motive**: The College Board's motive is to demonstrate to school administrators that the SAT tests only what students already learn in their high school classrooms. Of course, we know that is not the case. But this is why the College Board and Khan Academy teach students only traditional high school methods.

- **Prep Expert's motive**: Prep Expert's motive is to teach you unique strategies, tips, and tricks to maximize your SAT score. These test-taking techniques are not taught in standard high school classes, by the College Board, or by Khan Academy. Prep Expert methods are designed for one purpose only: to significantly improve your SAT score.

- **Optimal approach**: For the highest possible SAT score, practice applying effective Prep Expert Strategies to real College Board SAT questions.

 **PREP**EXPERT

GENERAL STRATEGY #3

FOLLOW THE 1,000 QUESTION RULE

PREP EXPERT STRATEGY

When preparing for the SAT, *Follow The 1,000 Question Rule*. Following this rule exponentially increases your probability of achieving a top SAT score.

The rule is straightforward: before taking the SAT, complete 1,000 practice questions.

But mastering the SAT is not just about the number of practice questions you complete. You must also understand *why* you got certain questions wrong. With every practice exam, you must understand your mistakes. Simply practicing without improving your approach based on previous mistakes is a waste of time.

The College Board does not have an infinite number of concepts it can test on the SAT. In reality, there are about thirty to fifty concepts tested per module. By practicing 1,000 questions, you will encounter the same concepts over and over again. This will foster familiarity and allow you to achieve a top SAT score.

Follow The 1,000 Question Rule to maximize your SAT score.

PREP EXPERT EXAMPLE

Described in the book *Outliers*, Malcolm Gladwell's "10,000 Hour Rule" states that mastery in any domain (sports, music, etc.) requires 10,000 hours of practice. Think of legends like the Beatles or Michael Jordan; their mastery arose from relentless dedication.

The good news is that you do not need to spend 10,000 hours to master the SAT. Instead, Prep Expert's data has shown that the number to aim for is 1,000. By working through 1,000 practice SAT questions, students can maximize their success on the SAT.

Prep Expert SAT Courses keep this principle in mind. By completing the exams and assignments in our SAT Courses, Prep Expert students surpass this 1,000-question target. But the emphasis is not just on completion. Review sessions help students comprehend their weak areas, thereby improving SAT scores even further.

The *1,000 Question Rule* also applies to other standardized exams. Whether you are preparing for the MCAT, LSAT, GRE, or any other standardized test in the future, this strategy will remain relevant. Practice with at least 1,000 official questions and review each question thoroughly. This will surely maximize your score on any standardized exam.

PREP EXPERT PRACTICE

This strategy is not based on mere theory. It is backed by significant research. A comprehensive meta-analysis of forty different research studies revealed that students who engage in significant practice markedly improve their test scores.[2] Three key conclusions emerged from this analysis:

1. **Score improvements were larger when identical tests were used for practice**. This is why Prep Expert recommends you *Use College Board SAT Questions*.

2. **The size of the score improvement increased with the number of practice tests given**. This is why Prep Expert recommends you *Follow The 1,000 Question Rule*.

---

2   James A. Kulik, Chen-Lin C. Kulik, and Robert L. Bangert, "Effects of Practice on Aptitude and Achievement Test Scores," *American Educational Research Journal* 21, no. 2 (1984): 435–47, https://doi.org/10.3102/00028312021002435.

3. **The ability level of the students studied influenced the degree of score improvement. Gains were larger for students of "high ability," a trait that can be cultivated**. This is why Prep Expert teaches you strategies to help you become "high ability."

PREP EXPERT REVIEW

Key Takeaways

- **Prep Expert General Strategy #3—*Follow The 1,000 Question Rule***: The 1,000 Question Rule emphasizes practicing with 1,000 real SAT questions and thoroughly reviewing them before test day.

- **Importance of review**: Simply practicing is insufficient. Understanding the reasons behind your incorrect answers is essential to avoid repeated mistakes.

- **Recurring patterns**: The SAT has a limited number of concepts it can test (about thirty to fifty per module). By practicing and reviewing 1,000 official SAT questions prior to test day, you will familiarize yourself with recurring patterns and question types.

- **10,000 Hour Rule**: Malcolm Gladwell's 10,000 Hour Rule from the book *Outliers* suggests that mastery in any field requires significant practice. With respect to SAT prep, Prep Expert recommends completing 1,000 practice SAT questions for maximum score improvement.

- **Scientific research**: Scientific research supports the effectiveness of the 1,000 Question Rule. The following three factors contribute to the largest score improvements on standardized tests: (1) practicing with identical forms of a test, (2) increasing the number of practice tests, and (3) elevating your ability level.

 **PREP**EXPERT

GENERAL STRATEGY #4

CHANGE YOUR HABITS TO CHANGE YOUR SCORE

PREP EXPERT STRATEGY

When preparing for the SAT, changing your habits is the key to changing your score. The SAT presents challenges that often differ from conventional high school tests. By adopting new test-taking strategies, you can optimize your SAT performance.

The Need for Habit Change

We are creatures of habit. Breaking established patterns is challenging. Whether the habit is scrolling social media or brushing your teeth, we often do not even realize we are engaging in these automatic behaviors.

The same goes for test-taking habits cultivated since elementary school. They have become so ingrained in our brains that we deploy them without much thought. But the SAT demands that you change these old test-taking habits. Even when it feels uncomfortable, embracing new strategies is the path to achieving a top SAT score.

Even if you are a straight-A student in high school, remember that the SAT is not another high school test. It is structured differently, tests concepts in unique ways, and requires a specialized approach.

If you have been approaching the SAT the same way you approach your high school exams, you will hit a performance ceiling.

Change Your Habits To Change Your Score to maximize your SAT score.

PREP EXPERT EXAMPLE

Sometimes students learn *Prep Expert Strategies*, but then fail to apply those strategies on test day on the real SAT exam.

For example, many students fail to apply the *Prep Expert Reading Strategy #1— Build Your Own Simple Solution (BOSS)* to SAT Reading questions. Students who have not ingrained the BOSS method into their test-taking habits might revert to their old habit of relying on the given answer choices. In contrast, students who have changed their habits and made BOSS a natural part of their test-taking habits will simplify the answer in their own words and arrive at the correct answer more efficiently.

Students often understand the concept behind many Prep Expert strategies, but then neglect to apply these strategies when practicing on their own. This disconnect between learning and application presents a significant barrier to score improvement.

Learning a strategy versus actually employing it are two very different things. To truly benefit from any strategy, you must apply it. Replace your old test-taking habits with new *Prep Expert Strategies* to significantly improve your SAT score.

PREP EXPERT PRACTICE

Try the following:

1. **Practice without applying *Prep Expert Strategies*.** Take a practice SAT test without applying any of the new *Prep Expert Strategies*. Write down your SAT score.

2. **Practice applying Prep Expert Strategies.** Take a different practice SAT test, this time actively applying the new Prep Expert Strategies you have learned. Write down your SAT score.

3. **Compare results**. Compare the results. How did the scores differ? Did some strategies feel more natural than others? Were there any questions for which you fell back into old test-taking habits?

The goal is to not only know what the new *Prep Expert Strategies* are, but also to integrate them so deeply into your approaches that they become automatic, second-nature habits during the test.

PREP EXPERT REVIEW

Key Takeaways

- **Prep Expert General Strategy #4—*Change Your Habits To Change Your Score***: Taking the test as you always have will not improve your score. Changing test-taking habits is crucial for improving your SAT score.

- **Implementation gap**: Many students learn strategies but fail to implement them on the actual SAT test day.

- **Breaking old habits**: It is essential to break old, ingrained test-taking habits and fully adopt the new *Prep Expert Strategies* that you learn. This requires you to consistently apply the strategies when you complete practice exams on your own. This is the only path to maximum SAT score improvement.

Prep Expert
General Strategies

 **PREP**EXPERT

GENERAL STRATEGY #5

HARNESS SELF-MOTIVATION

PREP EXPERT STRATEGY

To master any discipline, you must be self-motivated. One of the most powerful forces driving success in SAT prep is self-motivation.

External versus Internal Motivation

While there are many strategies to improve your SAT test-taking skills, none will yield results without motivation. There are two types of motivation: external and internal.

- **External motivation** comes from outside sources, such as parents or teachers, who want you to do well. While this might initiate action, external motivation is ineffective over the long term.

    versus

- **Internal motivation**, on the other hand, is a self-generated force. It is the innate desire to achieve a personal goal, such as aiming for a particular college or scholarship. This self-motivation works much better to sustain consistent effort over the long term.

Harness Self-Motivation (internal motivation) to maximize your SAT score.

PREP EXPERT EXAMPLE

Crafting Your Personal "Why"

To develop internal motivation, identify your personal "why." Simply wanting a high SAT score is an abstract goal. A score in itself is not motivating. It is what that score can produce for you that lights the fire of self-motivation.

- Do you dream of attending a top university?
- Do you envision yourself receiving a full-ride scholarship?
- Do you aspire to join the athletic team of a top college?

Identifying your "why" will serve as the internal motivation you need to complete your SAT prep journey.

PREP EXPERT PRACTICE

Visualizing Your Goals

Goals become more tangible when they are visual.

- **Is your dream to go to Yale?** Place a picture of its campus on your study wall.
- **Do you dream of getting a big scholarship?** Write a fictitious check with a large scholarship amount made payable to you.
- **Is your dream to be on the athletic team of a specific college?** Create a picture of yourself on the team and look at it often.

Visual reminders like these will enhance your self-motivation.

Practical Steps to Increase Self-Motivation

1. **Create a vision board**. Place photos of your dream colleges, scholarships, potential future careers, and inspiring quotes on a vision board.

2. **Goal list**. Alongside the board, list the target SAT score you need for each college or scholarship you are pursuing. This ties your aspirations to concrete numbers you can aim for.

3. **Regular reflection**. Spend a few minutes each day before studying to reflect on these visual goals.

A Personal Anecdote

Let me share a personal story from my high school years. On the first page of my SAT prep notebook, I wrote the following goals:

- *Achieve a perfect SAT score*
- *Gain admission to a combined BS/MD medical program*
- *Receive a full-ride scholarship to college*

Every time I opened my SAT prep notebook, those goals stared back at me. These aspirations reminded me why I was prepping for the SAT. I ended up achieving all of these goals.

It was not just luck that led to my success. It was the combination of hard work and this constant visual reminder in my SAT prep notebook. This created the self-motivation I needed to study for the SAT.

PREP EXPERT REVIEW

Key Takeaways

- **Prep Expert General Strategy #5—*Harness Self-Motivation***: Internal motivation, in which you want to do well for your own success, is more effective than external motivation, such as pressure from your parents.

- **Define your "why"**: You must establish your reasons for wanting a high SAT score. Perhaps you want to get into a dream university, earn big scholarships, or qualify for college athletics. Whatever your reasons are, make sure you are clear about them.

- **Visualization and goal setting**: Writing down and visualizing goals, like attending a specific university or earning a particular scholarship, can significantly enhance self-motivation.

- **Practical recommendations**: Create visual reminders, such as pictures of your dream colleges or a desired scholarship amount. Place these visuals in locations you will see most frequently. They will serve as a constant reminder and motivation booster.

- **Personal success story**: I achieved my goals in high school by keeping my goals visually present at the front of my SAT prep notebook. This constantly reminded me of what I aimed to achieve and why I was putting in the time and effort to study.

 **PREP**EXPERT

GENERAL
STRATEGY #6

MAKE THE SAT A
HIGH PRIORITY

PREP EXPERT STRATEGY

As a busy high school student, you are likely flooded with responsibilities such as classes, extracurriculars, and sports. Nevertheless, carving out time for SAT prep is important.

Ranking Priorities: Where Does the SAT Stand?

Consider your list of priorities. Perhaps you have ranked your GPA, sports, social life, and club activities above the SAT. Should SAT preparation be behind these? The answer is no.

You may want to gain admission into a top university, win thousands in scholarships, or secure your position in college athletics. With goals like these, the SAT must be a high priority.

Test Preparation: A Necessity, Not a Nice-to-Have

Many students believe SAT prep is an optional activity. This perspective handicaps your SAT score before you even start your preparation.

You may compare yourself with other students at your high school. But remember that most students at your high school will not be doing SAT prep. Not all students have ambitions of attending top universities or winning big scholarships.

You are among the elite few who recognize the importance of the SAT. Give the SAT its deserved attention by making SAT prep a high priority in your busy schedule.

Make The SAT A High Priority to maximize your SAT score.

PREP EXPERT EXAMPLE

"Work like there is someone working twenty-four hours a day to take it all away from you."
—MARK CUBAN

The above quote is from Prep Expert investor Mark Cuban. This quote should motivate you to work hard by reminding you of the other people who are working just as hard as you are. Of course, this quote is referring to business and entrepreneurship. But it also applies to college admissions and scholarships. You do need to work like there is someone working twenty-four hours a day to take it all away from you...because it is true!

There are other students who are working hard to get into the same colleges that you are going to be applying for, win the same scholarships that you are going to be applying for, and get a job in the same career that you are going to be aiming for. College, scholarships, and job applications are more competitive than ever. With the increasing competition for top colleges, scholarships, and careers, you must stay ahead of the curve.

Develop the determination to work harder than others to achieve your goals. This is the correct mindset to have: outwork everyone to get the high SAT score you deserve. Your high SAT score will then help you achieve your ultimate goals, whether they be college, scholarship, or career related.

PREP EXPERT PRACTICE

Here are some practical techniques you can use to *Make The SAT A High Priority*:

1. **Use organizational tools**. Use planners, checklists, or digital tools. Include daily time slots dedicated to SAT prep.

2. **Avoid comparison.** It is easy to look around and feel complacent if your peers are not doing SAT prep. Remember, everyone has their own unique journey.

3. **Consistency over intensity.** It is more effective to study consistently every single day than to cram occasionally.

4. **Mimic real test conditions.** Once a week, take a full-length SAT practice test. This not only helps track your progress, but also helps you build the stamina needed for test day.

To truly prioritize the SAT, integrate it into your daily routine. When I was in high school, I would put SAT prep tasks in my planner next to school assignments and deadlines. This ensured that I prioritized SAT preparation alongside my other high school responsibilities.

PREP EXPERT REVIEW

Key Takeaways

- **Prep Expert General Strategy #6—*Make The SAT A High Priority*:** Even with a busy high school schedule, it is essential to prioritize SAT preparation. The SAT should be just as important as your high school classes, and more important than sports, clubs, and social activities.

- **Test preparation is crucial:** SAT prep is not an "extra" activity. It is a necessity, especially for those pursuing competitive colleges and scholarships. Avoid comparing yourself to students who are not doing test prep.

- **Motivation from Mark Cuban:** Work as hard as if someone is trying to take away your opportunities. This mindset is applicable to college admissions, scholarship applications, and career aspirations.

- **Competition is high:** College and scholarship applications are getting increasingly competitive. You can stand out by working harder than other students.

- **Practical application:** Integrate SAT prep into daily planners and checklists. Treat SAT prep as equally important as your regular high school courses to ensure success.

Prep Expert
General Strategies

PREPEXPERT

GENERAL STRATEGY #7

KEEP AN SAT INSIGHT NOTEBOOK

PREP EXPERT STRATEGY

Creating an SAT Insight Notebook is essential for any student who wants to ace the SAT. Let's discuss its significance, organizational structure, and utility.

What Is an SAT Insight Notebook?

An SAT Insight Notebook is a simple notebook dedicated to documenting your personal insights and revelations regarding the SAT. By creating such a notebook, you will significantly improve your SAT score. Think of it as a personalized strategy book, tailored to your unique SAT prep insights. No generic SAT prep book can ever be as personalized to your individual challenges and breakthroughs as this notebook can be.

When I was in high school, I jotted down questions that particularly challenged me in my SAT Insight Notebook. This self-curated notebook was invaluable, allowing me to pinpoint exact areas of difficulty. For example, if I stumbled on a particular question on the SAT Math section, I would write down the question, why I answered it incorrectly, and how to answer similar questions correctly in the future.

Furthermore, this notebook is not just about writing down what you got wrong. It is about filling in knowledge gaps, even small ones. For example, if you have difficulty with the concept of conditional probability, dedicate a page in the Math section of your SAT Insight Notebook to clarifying this topic. This ensures that you understand the concept and minimizes future mistakes.

While it won't be the best SAT prep book for everyone, your SAT Insight Notebook will undoubtedly be the best one for you. Standard SAT prep books are designed for a broad audience. These do not cater to your unique needs. However, your SAT Insight Notebook, crafted from your own personal breakthroughs, will be your most valuable resource during your SAT prep journey.

Keep An SAT Insight Notebook to maximize your SAT score.

PREP EXPERT EXAMPLE

Imagine a student named Jane, a high school junior. While she performed well on the SAT Math modules, she struggled with reading comprehension.

Using her SAT Insight Notebook, Jane noted specific passages that troubled her, analyzed why she misunderstood them, and jotted down strategies to better understand similar texts in the future.

As she revisited the notes in her SAT Insight Notebook, Jane recognized a pattern: she often misinterpreted main idea questions. By documenting this personal insight, Jane was able to focus her efforts on improving this specific skill.

Over time, Jane was able to improve her interpretation of main idea questions on the SAT Reading section. She would have never noticed this deficiency if she did not document it in her SAT Insight Notebook.

Keep An SAT Insight Notebook to document your personal SAT insights, challenges, and breakthroughs. Keeping such a notebook will significantly improve your overall SAT score.

PREP EXPERT PRACTICE

Let's discuss how to create your own SAT Insight Notebook.

First, start your SAT Insight Notebook with a clear visualization of your goals. On the very first page, list out your dream colleges, universities, and scholarship amounts. Add visuals if they inspire you, such as pictures of specific college campuses or scholarship checks.

Second, set an SAT score goal with a plan to get there. For example, if your goal is to score 1500 out of 1600, write out an actionable plan. Perhaps, to reach that target, you will dedicate ten hours a week to SAT prep for the next ten weeks. Writing this at the front of your notebook not only serves as motivation, but also provides an actionable road map.

Third, divide your SAT Insight Notebook into four sections:

1. **SAT Math**. In the SAT Math section of your notebook, record challenges, insights, and other notes regarding math concepts.

2. **SAT Reading**. In the SAT Reading section of your notebook, note any difficulties and strategies for improving reading comprehension.

3. **SAT Writing**. In the SAT Writing section of your notebook, highlight grammar rules, writing styles, and related insights.

4. **Extra section**. In the Extra section of your notebook, document any notes about other related topics, such as college or scholarship applications.

PREP EXPERT REVIEW

Key Takeaways

- **Prep Expert General Strategy #7—*Keep An SAT Insight Notebook***: The SAT Insight Notebook is a notebook in which you jot down your personal insights, notes, and moments of realization during your SAT preparation journey.

- **Organization**: Organize the notebook into four sections: (1) SAT Math, (2) SAT Reading, (3) SAT Writing, and (4) Extra section (for related topics like college admissions or scholarships).

- **Personalization**: The SAT Insight Notebook is a personalized tool, more tailored to your needs than general SAT prep books. This makes it the best SAT resource specifically for you.

- **Goal setting**: On the notebook's first page, set clear goals and actionable plans to achieve those goals. For example, you may want to write your desired SAT score, planned hours of study per week, and aspirational colleges or scholarships.

 **PREP**EXPERT

GENERAL STRATEGY #8

LIMIT MEMORIZATION

PREP EXPERT STRATEGY

For effective SAT preparation, limit the amount of rote memorization you do. Traditional study models rely on memorization, which is often an inefficient preparation method. For many students, the word "study" conjures up notions of tedious memorization sessions. This can be a very anxiety-inducing idea.

Good news! The SAT requires a limited amount of memorization. In particular, there are not as many obscure vocabulary words on the Digital SAT as there were on previous older versions of the paper-based SAT exam.

If studying for the SAT does not require extensive memorization, how should students study? The answer is *practice*.

Instead of attempting to memorize each strategy word for word, students should apply strategies to practice questions. The goal is to apply strategies to real test questions so often that the strategies become unconscious habits.

Once *Prep Expert Strategies* become second nature to you, then you will see substantial SAT score improvements.

Limit Memorization to maximize your SAT score.

PREP EXPERT EXAMPLE

Memorization versus Review

It is important to distinguish the difference between memorization and review:

- **Memorization** involves trying to embed every detail of a concept into one's memory, a process that can be strenuous.

  versus

- **Review** involves revisiting previous strategies, problems, and insights, which is much less strenuous.

Effective SAT prep emphasizes review rather than memorization. This ensures new test prep strategies become second-nature test-taking habits.

Prep Expert often circles back to previous content for this reason. For example, have you noticed the *Prep Expert Review* section that follows every *Prep Expert Strategy* with summarized key takeaways?

By regularly reviewing previous knowledge, Prep Expert books and courses do not strain students with hard-core memorization. Instead, students have often reviewed the same concepts multiple times in different formats (books, lectures, practice exams, tutoring, etc.). This converts the test-taking strategies from abstract concepts to second-nature habits, which is when true SAT score improvement happens.

PREP EXPERT PRACTICE

The Myth of Test Day Amnesia

A common concern among students is the concept of "test day amnesia." This is the fear of forgetting everything you have learned on the day of the test. This anxiety can result in a vicious cycle: the more you fear forgetting, the greater your test anxiety, which leads you to actually forget.

I have good news for you: test day amnesia is not real. The test questions themselves serve as reminders of which particular strategies you need to apply. If you have practiced enough, there is no risk of "test day amnesia."

Do not worry about the dreaded test day amnesia.

What Do *You Need to Memorize?*

While the majority of SAT prep is review oriented, there are a couple of items you will need to memorize:

1. **Vocabulary**. Although the Digital SAT has fewer obscure vocabulary words than previous versions of the SAT, there are still some you need to know. Prep Expert provides vocabulary lists of the most common SAT words. You are likely already familiar with many of these words, so memorizing *Prep Expert SAT Vocab Word Lists* should be a manageable task. You can find these lists in the back of this book.

2. **Math formulas**. The SAT Math modules do require you to memorize a few math formulas. However, Prep Expert simplifies this process by providing all of the required formulas in the SAT Math section of this book.

PREP EXPERT REVIEW

Key Takeaways

- **Prep Expert General Strategy #8—*Limit Memorization***: The SAT does not require extensive rote memorization, especially in its digital format. Instead, effective SAT prep emphasizes review over memorization.

- **Emphasis on practice**: Studying for the SAT is primarily about practice. It is more beneficial to repeatedly practice strategies until they become second nature, rather than trying to memorize every detail of every strategy.

- **Review versus memorization**: While memorization can be painful and is not the main focus for SAT prep, review is essential. Reviewing strategies, problems, and insights regularly is more effective and less stressful than memorizing.

- **Test day amnesia myth**: The fear of forgetting everything on test day is not based in reality, especially if you have practiced the strategies enough. The test questions themselves will serve as the reminders for the strategies you need to apply. Ultimately, this will reduce any test anxiety you may have.

- **Key item to memorize**: The only significant memorization required for the SAT are the *Prep Expert SAT Vocab Word Lists*. These lists contain the most common words that regularly appear on the SAT. Almost everything else in SAT prep involves review, not memorization. You can find these lists in the back of this book.

 **PREP**EXPERT

GENERAL STRATEGY #9

IMPROVE YOUR PHYSICAL & BRAIN HEALTH

PREP EXPERT STRATEGY

This *Prep Expert General Strategy* might surprise you: your physical health plays a crucial role in your SAT prep. This is a concept that few other SAT prep books or courses discuss, but it is an important part of effective SAT preparation.

At first glance, achieving a high SAT score might appear unrelated to maintaining a fit lifestyle. But research has consistently shown how exercise benefits the brain and enhances its performance.

Many high school students find themselves in a sedentary routine. This is especially true if you are busy with high school courses, clubs, and SAT prep.

Your physical health is closely linked to your cognitive function. Aerobic exercise enhances memory, improves learning abilities, and improves brain performance. This connection between physical health and brain health is crucial.

Improve Your Physical & Brain Health to maximize your SAT score.

PREP EXPERT EXAMPLE

The summer before my senior year of high school, I would spend an hour a day on the elliptical. I was in the best shape of my life. In October of my senior year, I got a perfect SAT score. This peak in both my physical health and academic achievement was not coincidental. There is significant research pointing to the connection between exercise and cognitive ability.

The Physiological Evidence: Why Exercise Matters

Many studies reveal the connection between physical health and brain health:

1. **Gray matter growth**. One study found that physical activity can lead to increased gray matter in the brain.[3] Primarily composed of neuronal cell bodies, gray matter plays a pivotal role in memory.

2. **White matter growth**. Another study found that people who walked for forty minutes at least three times a week (a total of 120 minutes per week) experienced an increase in their brain's white matter.[4] Made of myelinated axons, this white matter solidifies neural connections and ensures a sharper mind. These same researchers also found that the walks improved memory. In addition, study participants' brains looked about a year or two younger than their chronological age when scanned by an MRI machine.

3. **Hippocampal growth**. Another study found people who did aerobic exercise had an average increase in their memory scores of 47% compared to those who did not exercise.[5] Researchers also found increased blood flow into the

---

3 Kirk I. Erickson, Regina L. Leckie, and Andrea M. Weinstein, "Physical Activity, Fitness, and Gray Matter Volume," *Neurobiology of Aging* 35, supplement 2 (September 2014): S20-S28, https://doi.org/10.1016/j.neurobiolaging.2014.03.034.

4 Andrea Mendez Colmenares et al., "White Matter Plasticity in Healthy Older Adults: The Effects of Aerobic Exercise," *NeuroImage* 239 (October 2021): 118305, https://doi.org/10.1016/j.neuroimage.2021.118305.

5 Binu P. Thomas et al., "Brain Perfusion Change in Patients with Mild Cognitive Impairment after 12 Months of Aerobic Exercise Training," *Journal of Alzheimer's Disease* 75, no. 2 (May 2020): 617–31, https://doi.org/10.3233/JAD-190977.

hippocampus. This region of the brain, responsible for memory, grows in individuals who engage in aerobic exercise. Physically active individuals also showed slower hippocampal decline, ensuring longevity in memory.

4. **Improved learning with BDNF**. One study found that people were able to learn vocabulary words 20% faster after they had exercised compared to people who did not exercise.[6] Exercise resulted in increased levels of brain-derived neurotrophic factor (BDNF), a protein linked to short-term learning success (i.e., faster and more efficient learning).

These studies (and thousands more) provide physiological evidence as to why improving your physical health will improve your brain health, and ultimately your SAT score.

PREP EXPERT PRACTICE

Integrating Exercise into Your Routine

Many students reading this book may be thinking, *I am too busy to exercise!* Here are some practical ways you can incorporate more activity into your busy daily routine:

1. **Sports engagement**. If you already participate in sports, continue. The physical activity you do through sports is more than adequate for brain health.

2. **Aerobic activities**. For students who do not participate in sports, try walking, running, or biking for at least thirty minutes a few times a week.

3. **Routine habits**. Take regular breaks during study sessions to stand, walk, or stretch. Simple habits, such as standing up and walking every hour or taking seven thousand to ten thousand steps daily, can be game changers.

4. **Tracking tools**. Use a device like an Apple Watch or a Fitbit to track your daily physical activity.

---

6   Bernward Winter et al., "High Impact Running Improves Learning," *Neurobiology of Learning and Memory* 87, no. 4 (May 2007): 597–609, https://doi.org/10.1016/j.nlm.2006.11.003.

Prep Expert
General Strategies

You will see the benefits of regular exercise in the form of improved memory and learning capabilities. This will improve your recall and problem-solving during the actual SAT.

PREP EXPERT REVIEW

Key Takeaways

- **Prep Expert General Strategy #9—*Improve Your Physical & Brain Health*:** Your physical health significantly impacts your brain health, which in turn impacts your SAT score.

- **Brain matter growth:** Exercise can increase both gray and white matter in the brain, directly improving memory capabilities essential for studying.

- **Memory boost:** Consistent physical activity increases blood flow to critical brain regions, slowing the breakdown of the hippocampus and boosting memory by an average of 47%.

- **Cognitive enhancement:** Studies show that those who exercise regularly have enhanced cognitive function, including a 20% faster rate of learning new vocabulary due to increased levels of BDNF.

- **Aerobic exercise benefits:** Aerobic exercises, such as walking, running, and biking, should be done at least three to four times a week for a minimum of thirty minutes to maximize brain health and improve SAT performance.

PREPEXPERT

GENERAL STRATEGY #10

KEEP YOUR PENCIL GLUED TO THE SCRATCH PAPER

PREP EXPERT STRATEGY

Prep Expert General Strategy #10 uncovers the important role of the scratch paper on the Digital SAT. You might wonder, *On a digital test, why revert to paper and pencil?* Let's discuss the scratch paper's unmatched importance.

In the era of the Digital SAT, it is easy to assume that everything you need is on the screen in front of you. This misconception can be costly. Despite the shift to a digital platform, scratch paper remains an invaluable tool.

On test day, you may notice other test-takers engrossed in their screens, barely using the provided scratch paper. But relying solely on the computer screen will stifle your critical thinking ability.

Keep Your Pencil (or Pen) Glued to the Scratch Paper

Engaging with the scratch paper helps streamline your thoughts, making problem-solving more efficient. Most of your best thinking will happen with paper and pencil. You will be surprised at how much easier the Digital SAT becomes when you start working out problems for Math modules as well as Reading and Writing modules on paper.

Your SAT Score Is Directly Correlated to How Much You Write Down

The more you write down on your scratch paper, the higher your SAT score will go. If a student does not have a pencil in hand while taking the Digital SAT, that student is unlikely to achieve a high score.

Keep Your Pencil Glued To The Scratch Paper to maximize your SAT score.

PREP EXPERT EXAMPLE

The Science of Working Memory

Working memory and critical thinking ability are inversely related. The more you use your working memory, the less critical thinking ability you will have. If you do not write anything down on paper, you end up overloading your working memory. When you overload your working memory, you reduce your critical thinking ability. If you limit your critical thinking ability during the SAT, you will answer many questions incorrectly.

Standardized tests become very difficult if you try to remember everything in your head. Instead, get the details out of your working memory and onto your scratch paper. This will free up lots of thinking power—immediately boosting your score.

Consider a reading comprehension passage in which you are trying to keep track of multiple characters, events, and themes. Rather than taxing your brain to remember every detail, jot down short notes on the provided scratch paper to help retain key points. Similarly, on math problems, instead of trying to remember complex equations, write them down on your scratch paper. These written notes are invaluable when answering questions.

The Power of Pencil and Paper

Each scribble, note, or doodle on your scratch paper symbolizes your active engagement with the test. The more you have written down on your scratch paper, the more critical thinking you were doing during the SAT, and thus, the higher your SAT score will be.

The end result of your scratch paper will not be a work of art. Instead, it will be messy and often illegible. But it is a tangible representation of your thought processes during the test. Don't be shy about filling up that scratch paper! Remember, your scratch paper will not be entering a beauty contest. Get your cognitive power onto the scratch paper no matter how messy it gets!

PREP EXPERT PRACTICE

This strategy can be applied to all sections of the SAT. Here are some examples of items you may want to write on your scratch paper as you are solving questions on the SAT:

- **Reading questions**: While reading passages, jot down your BOSS solution, the main idea, or any other details. This will save you from frequently revisiting the passage.

- **Math questions**: Always work out problems on paper. From algebraic formulas to geometric diagrams, writing out your work will help you find the correct solution.

- **Writing questions**: Before selecting an answer, write down how the corrected sentence should appear or any applicable grammar rules.

Keep Your Pencil Glued To The Scratch Paper during all the SAT practice tests you complete. Doing so will make this *Prep Expert Strategy* a natural part of your test-taking habits.

CAUTIONARY NOTE: ANNOTATE FUNCTION

While the Digital SAT comes with several features aimed at assisting test-takers, not all are worth using. One such tool is the "Annotate" function. At first glance, it might seem beneficial that it allows you to make notes directly on the digital test. However, in practice, it is clunky and ineffective. Here is what the Annotate function looks like on the Digital SAT:

Section 1, Module 1: Reading and Writing   31:44   ✏️ Annotate   ⋮ More

Directions ⌄   (Hide)

After clicking the "Annotate" button in the upper right-hand corner, you will see the following box pop up at the bottom of your screen:

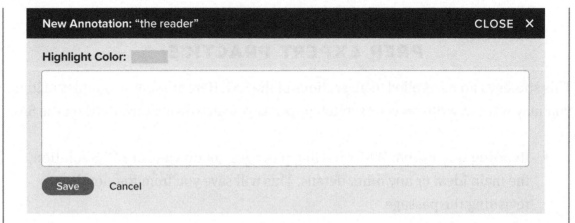

New Annotation: "the reader"   CLOSE ✕

Highlight Color:

[Save]   Cancel

The Digital SAT Annotate function requires you to complete four steps:

- **Step 1**: Highlight the part of the passage/question you are interested in.
- **Step 2**: Click the "Annotate" button at the top right of your screen.
- **Step 3**: Create a new annotation in the pop-up box and type out your notes.
- **Step 4**: Save your annotation to view later.

That is a lot of steps and wasted time. Instead, save time by simply writing down your notes on the provided scratch paper. There is a unique synergy that is achieved when you jot down your thoughts on paper. It is almost magical how the more you write on scratch paper, the higher your SAT score will go!

PREP EXPERT REVIEW

Key Takeaways

- **Prep Expert General Strategy #10—*Keep Your Pencil Glued To The Scratch Paper***: Despite the fact that the SAT is now digital, it is still crucial to use the provided scratch paper for most of the work.

- **Benefits of writing**: Physically writing down notes, solutions, and problem-solving steps boosts critical thinking. There is a direct correlation between increased scratch paper usage and higher SAT scores.

- **Limited working memory**: Relying solely on your working memory limits critical thinking ability. Transferring your thoughts onto paper frees up cognitive space, which enhances your problem-solving abilities.

- **Avoid the Annotate function**: The Digital SAT's Annotate function is clunky, time-consuming, and less effective than simply using scratch paper.

- **Magic advantage**: There is a seemingly magical improvement in SAT scores when students actively write on the provided scratch paper throughout the test.

Prep Expert
General Strategies

 **PREP**EXPERT

GENERAL STRATEGY #11

CROSS OUT ANSWER CHOICES

PREP EXPERT STRATEGY

One of the most effective ways to optimize your SAT performance is by crossing out incorrect answer choices. By doing so, you can focus your attention on the remaining options. This will streamline your decision-making process and increase the accuracy of your answers.

At first glance, taking the time to cross out answer choices on a digital test might seem counterintuitive. After all, if you mentally *think* an option is incorrect, why bother crossing it out? There are two primary reasons:

1. **Free up working memory**. Our working memory is limited. Every piece of information we store in our head, including incorrect answer choices, occupies our working memory. By crossing out incorrect answer choices, we free up our working memory.

2. **Enhance critical thinking**. The SAT is designed to assess your critical thinking skills. By crossing out incorrect answers, you can think critically about the remaining options.

Cross Out Answer Choices to maximize your SAT score.

PREP EXPERT EXAMPLE

On the Digital SAT, the College Board provides a unique tool designed specifically for this purpose. You can see how crossing out answer choices works here:

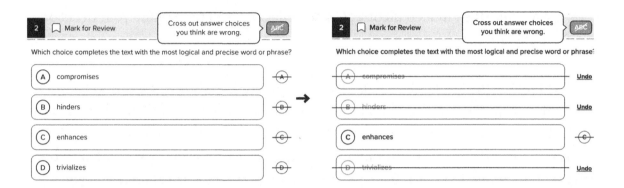

In the upper right-hand corner of each question, you will find an icon depicting "ABC." Hovering over this icon will reveal its function: "Cross out answer choices you think are wrong."

Clicking the ABC button activates the feature, presenting you with small circular icons next to each answer choice. By clicking on these buttons, you can cross out options you believe are incorrect. If you mistakenly cross out an option, there is an "Undo" button to reverse the action.

This tool helps you visually eliminate incorrect answers so that you can more easily identify the correct answer.

PREP EXPERT PRACTICE

During your SAT preparation, practice with the College Board's Digital SAT platform to get accustomed to the cross-out feature.

1. **Start with one module from each SAT section**. Practice with an SAT Math module and an SAT Reading and Writing module to determine how to most effectively *Cross Out Answer Choices* on both module types.

2. **Practice crossing out answer choices**. As you answer each question, actively use the cross-out feature to eliminate the choices you believe are incorrect.

3. **Time yourself**. Initially, it may seem like you are spending more time using this tool. But as you become adept, you will notice an increase in both speed and accuracy.

4. **Reflect on crossed-out answer choices**. Reflect on the choices you crossed out. Were they indeed incorrect? This reflection will help refine your decision-making skills.

A common concern is that using the cross-out tool might be too time consuming. After all, it requires two clicks: one click to activate the feature and another click for each choice you want to eliminate. But these actions take mere seconds.

The clarity provided by visually eliminating wrong answers leads to faster decision-making in the long run. By focusing only on potential correct answers, you also improve the accuracy of your responses.

The benefits in speed, clarity, and accuracy are well worth the initial time investment in crossing out answers on the Digital SAT.

PREP EXPERT REVIEW

Key Takeaways

- **Prep Expert General Strategy #11—*Cross Out Answer Choices***: Crossing out incorrect answer choices is a powerful strategy for acing the SAT.

- **Digital feature**: Use the specific Digital SAT feature provided by the College Board: a crossed-out ~~ABC~~ icon in the top right-hand corner of the question that allows users to eliminate wrong answers.

- **Time versus accuracy**: While it might seem time consuming, crossing out answers can actually save time and boost accuracy by clearly displaying which answer choices remain.

- **Working memory**: Eliminating incorrect answers frees up working memory and enhances critical thinking ability.

PREPEXPERT

LET YOUR SUBCONSCIOUS WORK

PREP EXPERT STRATEGY

Your subconscious mind is your secret weapon on the SAT.

- **Conscious mind:** The part of your brain that you actively use to solve questions.

    versus

- **Subconscious mind:** The part of your brain that passively processes information without your active awareness.

There is one situation in particular when the subconscious mind is most valuable on the SAT: when you are faced with a challenging problem and are unsure how to solve it.

Use your subconscious mind to solve these challenging problems you do not immediately know how to solve with your conscious mind.

Let Your Subconscious Work to maximize your SAT score.

PREP EXPERT EXAMPLE

How Most Students *Approach Problems*
They Do Not Know How to Solve

Students tend to spend a lot of time on challenging problems that they do not know how to solve immediately. They spend excessive time, energy, and effort trying to solve these problems. This approach has two significant drawbacks:

1. **It wastes time**. This approach consumes precious time that could be better spent on other questions. Working on a difficult question for two, three, or four minutes does not make sense. There are easier questions that can be solved more quickly in the same module and are equally valuable to your SAT score.

2. **It leads to frustration**. Grappling with a tough problem will also lead to frustration, which will negatively affect your performance on subsequent questions. Your mind will not be as sharp if you are still flustered by the previous difficult question.

How You *Should Approach Problems*
You Do Not Know How to Solve

How can your subconscious mind help you break the cycle described above? Instead of becoming frustrated because you cannot solve a question, pull yourself away from that question and move on.

You should have the willpower to think, *That's okay, I'll come back to this problem at the end of this module*. If you have been struggling with a problem for a while without making progress, pull yourself away from the problem and come back to it at the end of the module.

When you have been working on a question for an extended period with no clear solution in sight, mark it for review and move on. Your subconscious mind will continue to process the problem in the background as you actively tackle other questions.

The Magic of the Subconscious Mind

You will find something magical happens when you return to the difficult question: you will suddenly be able to solve the question with ease! Students often find that upon returning to a previously challenging question, they find it noticeably easier to solve. This is not because the problem changed or they suddenly became smarter. It is the magic of the subconscious at work! While you were consciously working on other problems, your subconscious mind was subtly processing the challenging question in the background.

Of course, this is not going to work every single time. There will obviously be some difficult questions that you are just unable to solve no matter what. But you will be surprised at how often this strategy works once you try it.

PREP EXPERT PRACTICE

The Digital SAT provides a practical tool to implement this strategy: a "Mark for Review" feature. You can see how it appears on the Digital SAT here:

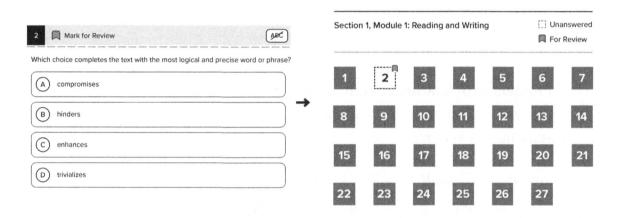

When you encounter a challenging question, click on the "Mark for Review" flag icon in the upper left-hand corner next to the question number. This will change the flag's color from white to red, labeling it as a problem to revisit later.

Once you have completed the module, you can easily return to the questions with red flags. This process allows you to quickly mark the difficult questions that you need to pull yourself away from and come back to later. This will give your subconscious mind plenty of time to process these problems.

To practice this strategy, do the following:

1. **Flagging system**. Familiarize yourself with the Digital SAT "Mark for Review" feature.

2. **Simulated tests**. During practice tests, mark challenging questions for review and proceed. Return to these questions after completing other questions in the module.

3. **Reflect**. Upon returning, spend a few moments gauging whether the problem seems easier. If so, it is a testament to the work of your subconscious mind.

PREP EXPERT REVIEW

Key Takeaways

- **Prep Expert General Strategy #12—*Let Your Subconscious Work***: Leverage the subconscious mind for problem-solving during the SAT.

- **Subconscious mind's role:** The subconscious mind works covertly in the background, helping to solve questions that the conscious mind finds challenging.

- **Problem with fixating on difficult questions**: Grappling with challenging questions for too long can waste precious time and negatively impact your subsequent answers.

- **Effective approach**: If you are stuck on a challenging question, flag it for review and return to it later. This will allow your subconscious mind to process it in the background. You will often find that the problem becomes much easier when you return to it at the end of the module.

- **"Mark for Review" feature**: Use the "Mark for Review" flag feature on the Digital SAT to easily navigate back to questions you intend to come back to at the end of a module.

PREPEXPERT

GENERAL STRATEGY #13

HIDE THE TIMER

PREP EXPERT STRATEGY

Taking the SAT can create a significant amount of stress. A constantly ticking timer on the Digital SAT only adds to this test anxiety.

The Digital SAT provides a visible timer at the top of the screen, ticking down as you proceed through each module. This feature is designed to help students keep track of the time. However, the timer can also have the unintended consequence of increasing test anxiety. Every second that ticks away can amplify stress, especially when tackling challenging questions. This heightened anxiety can hinder comprehension, slow down problem-solving, and lead to errors.

The solution? The "Hide" feature on the Digital SAT interface. By clicking the "Hide" button underneath the timer, it will disappear. This will allow you to focus on questions without the constantly ticking clock.

The key point of this strategy is simple: remove the persistent visual reminder of the ticking clock to reduce test anxiety. This will increase your focus on the content and boost your overall SAT score.

Hide The Timer to maximize your SAT score.

PREP EXPERT EXAMPLE

The Digital SAT provides a practical tool to implement this strategy: a "Hide" button directly underneath the timer at the top of the screen. You can see how it appears on the Digital SAT here:

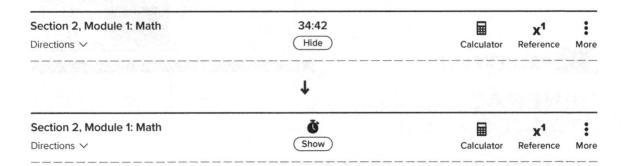

Click the "Hide" button at the top of your screen to hide the time remaining in the module. Click the "Show" button to show the time remaining.

You might wonder, *How will I know if I'm running out of time if I hide the timer?* Not to worry: the Digital SAT has you covered. When there are only five minutes left in a module, an alert will pop up on the screen to notify you, even if you have hidden the timer. This emulates the old paper-based SAT, in which proctors used to give a five-minute warning to alert students.

For effective pacing, periodically check the timer, especially at the halfway point of each module.

- **Reading and Writing Modules: 27 Questions in 32 Minutes**. When you get to the halfway point of a Reading and Writing module, which is *question 14*, show the timer to see if you have approximately *16 minutes remaining*.

- **Math Modules: 22 Questions in 35 Minutes**. When you get to the halfway point of a Math module, which is *question 12*, show the timer to see if you have approximately *17–18 minutes remaining*.

If you are significantly ahead of or behind these benchmarks, adjust your speed accordingly. For instance, if you reach the midway point in a module and find you have considerably more than the ideal time left, consider slowing down to ensure accuracy. Conversely, if you are behind, you may need to pick up the pace.

Let's consider two students: Alice and Bob. Alice chooses to keep the timer visible throughout her Digital SAT. As she progresses, she finds herself constantly glancing at the timer, especially when she encounters challenging questions. This frequent distraction causes her to second-guess her answers and rush through problems, resulting in careless mistakes.

Bob, on the other hand, decides to hide the timer. He only occasionally checks the timer, primarily at the halfway mark, and waits for the five-minute warning. Bob feels more relaxed and methodical in his approach, ensuring he understands each question before answering.

The outcome? Bob performs significantly better than Alice on the SAT. This is primarily because he managed his test anxiety by hiding the timer and fully concentrated on answering questions.

PREP EXPERT PRACTICE

Practice hiding the timer on Digital SAT practice exams. Here is a suggested approach:

1. **Simulation**. Familiarize yourself with hiding and un-hiding the timer on the Digital SAT platform.

2. **Pacing practice**. As you work through a module, intentionally show the timer only at the halfway point. Then continue until the five-minute warning pop-up alert goes off.

3. **Reflection**. After completing the module, reflect on how you felt. Did hiding the timer reduce your test anxiety? Did it allow for better concentration on each question?

By practicing to hide the timer, students will minimize distractions and reduce their test anxiety on the actual SAT test day.

PREP EXPERT REVIEW

Key Takeaways

- **Prep Expert General Strategy #13—*Hide The Timer***: Use the Digital SAT feature to hide the timer. This will reduce test anxiety and allow you to focus on each question without having to worry about a timer ticking down.

- **Pacing without the timer**: Check your progress at the module halfway points—around question 14 for SAT Reading and Writing modules and question 12 for SAT Math modules.

- **Five-minute warning**: You will receive a five-minute-warning pop-up even if the timer is hidden from view.

- **Outcome**: Ultimately, hiding the timer will reduce test anxiety and improve overall performance during the exam. With strategic time checks at the halfway points of each module and the five-minute-warning pop-up, you will still effectively manage your time during the SAT.

GENERAL STRATEGY #14

READ EVERYTHING LITERALLY

PREP EXPERT STRATEGY

Prep Expert General Strategy #14 emphasizes the importance of reading everything on the SAT in a completely literal manner. This technique is crucial in reshaping how you interpret information on standardized exams.

The Literal Approach

At its core, this strategy is about adopting a strict approach to interpretation. You should take the information on a standardized test exactly as it appears without making any assumptions.

In high school English classes, students are often rewarded for finding deeper meaning in poems, novels, and literary works. However, the SAT actually penalizes students for such interpretation.

The SAT requires a direct approach: the meaning of the text is only what is written on the page and nothing more. Making assumptions or trying to find deeper meanings will lead to incorrect answers.

On the SAT, you must read every passage, every question, and every answer choice literally!

Read Everything Literally to maximize your SAT score.

PREP EXPERT EXAMPLE

Everyday Language versus SAT Language

In everyday interactions, language is full of ambiguities. We often make assumptions to fill in gaps or comprehend the intent behind what others are saying. We have a natural inclination to make assumptions in daily conversations. This can make it challenging for students to adopt a strategy of reading everything literally on the SAT.

Consider the following statement:

> *"Mike said he should wear sunscreen when he goes outside to prevent getting a sunburn."*

In everyday language, we would not question this statement. We would likely make an unconscious assumption to understand who and what Mike is talking about.

But on the SAT, you should be critical of a sentence like this. Ask yourself, who does "he" refer to? Is Mike giving someone else advice, or was someone else advising Mike? The SAT demands precision and clarity, and understanding these nuances is critical. Make no assumptions on the SAT.

Let's try another statement:

> *"I was so thirsty, I drank the water bottle quickly."*

At a casual glance, this seems like an accurate statement. But on closer inspection, you should realize that you cannot physically drink a bottle, just the water *inside* of a bottle. You must read literally to spot discrepancies such as this. Our daily language skill of reading between the lines can actually negatively impact our SAT performance.

PREP EXPERT PRACTICE

As you practice with real SAT questions, take each word and phrase literally. Over time, you should aim to naturally spot discrepancies or ambiguities in statements.

Look back at previous SAT problems or tests you have attempted. Can you spot instances where a literal approach would have helped you identify the correct answer? Reflect on why you made certain mistakes. Reinforce the importance of face-value reading as you review.

It is not enough to understand this strategy in theory. Consistent practice with literal interpretation will embed this approach into your test-taking habits. This will help you with not only the SAT, but also other standardized tests that value precise language.

Practice reading with a literal approach on every Digital SAT practice question that you complete from here on out.

PREP EXPERT REVIEW

Key Takeaways

- **Prep Expert General Strategy #14—*Read Everything Literally***: Read everything on the SAT literally. This improves scores across all sections, especially SAT Reading.

- **High school versus SAT**: High school English classes reward finding deeper meanings in texts. The SAT penalizes finding deeper meaning that goes beyond the text. Always take questions, answer choices, and passages at face value on the SAT.

- **Everyday language pitfalls**: Daily language is ambiguous. On the SAT, avoid over-interpreting or filling in gaps as you would normally do in everyday language.

- **Avoid assumptions**: Making assumptions means going beyond the scope of what is literally said or written. These assumptions negatively impact SAT scores. Practice to train your brain to read without making assumptions.

PREPEXPERT

GENERAL STRATEGY #15

REDUCE TEST ANXIETY

PREP EXPERT STRATEGY

The SAT often creates test anxiety. Whether you feel it intensely or as a subtle undercurrent, test anxiety affects nearly all students. Let's discuss how to manage it.

What Is Test Anxiety?

Test anxiety refers to the experience of feeling nervous, worried, or fearful before or during an exam. It can manifest in physical symptoms, such as a rapid heartbeat, sweating, or nausea. It can also manifest in psychological symptoms like a negative mindset, racing thoughts, or difficulty concentrating.

Individuals at all levels of academic achievement can experience test anxiety. Even if they are well prepared, it can interfere with their ability to perform well on exams. If not managed, this anxiety can negatively impact even the best-prepared students. Despite achieving a perfect SAT score and now owning a test prep company, even I have had my own battles with test anxiety.

Why Is Test Anxiety Bad for Your SAT Score?

Anxiety activates your body's stress response. This can interfere with your ability to focus, think, and process and recall information, which can impact your score.

By creating a negative mindset, test anxiety can reduce your confidence in your abilities. These thoughts and emotions can further exacerbate your anxiety and reduce your performance.

Test anxiety can also lead to avoidance behaviors like procrastination or skipping questions, which can result in lower scores. It is essential to manage test anxiety effectively to ensure that it does not interfere with your academic performance.

Stay Calm During the SAT

Staying calm during the SAT is the key to a high score. If your heart is racing due to test anxiety, caffeine, or some other pressure you feel while you are taking the SAT, you will not achieve your best score. Do not make the SAT a bigger deal than it is—it is just one exam of many.

You will likely take many more exams, including AP Exams and standardized exams for graduate school (i.e., GRE, GMAT, MCAT, LSAT, etc.). You should actually be worry free, because the SAT is one of the few standardized exams that you can take multiple times without admissions committees seeing all of your scores. So you have nothing to lose! Remember this fact to help take the edge off any test-day anxiety you may have.

Let Go of the Outcome

Let go of the outcome of the test to reduce your anxiety. Letting go of the outcome allows you to focus on the process rather than the result. When you become overly focused on the outcome of the SAT, such as the score you will receive or the consequences of not doing well, it will create pressure.

By letting go of the outcome, you can shift your focus to the process of taking the SAT. This means focusing on the steps you need to take to answer each question, managing your time effectively, and staying focused. By focusing on the process, you can reduce test anxiety and improve your performance.

Letting go of the outcome can help reduce the fear of failure. If you place too much emphasis on the outcome, you may feel like your self-worth is tied to your performance on the SAT. This will create more pressure and increase your test anxiety. By letting go of the outcome, you can view the test as an opportunity to learn and grow rather than a measure of your worth.

Reduce Test Anxiety to maximize your SAT score.

PREP EXPERT EXAMPLE

A Tale of Two SATs

Drawing from personal experience, consider two of my SAT attempts that went very differently.

The first time I took the SAT I was wracked with test anxiety. I couldn't sleep the night before. I had a Red Bull energy drink the morning of, which caused my heart to race. I was very attached to the outcome. I felt like my SAT score was tied to my self-worth. The SAT was going to be so important to my college and scholarship applications. I felt so much pressure that I couldn't focus on the process. I couldn't focus on taking one question at a time and answering it step by step. My mind was racing, my heart was racing, and I couldn't concentrate. Of course, I didn't score well—my first SAT score was fairly average.

The last time I took the SAT, in October of my senior year of high school, my experience was completely different. I slept well the night before. I did not have any caffeine on the morning of the SAT. I knew it was the last time I had the opportunity to take the SAT. I had the mindset of "Whatever score I get is what I get, and that's what I'm going to submit to colleges and scholarships." I completely let go of the outcome. Because I had let go of the outcome, I was calm during the exam. I focused on answering each question one by one, solving each problem step by step. My heart was not racing. Guess what happened? I got a perfect SAT score.

Clearly, reducing my test anxiety had a major positive impact on my performance on the SAT!

PREP EXPERT PRACTICE

Here are some practical approaches you can use to reduce your test anxiety:

1. **Preparation**. Regularly take practice SAT tests under timed conditions. Familiarize yourself with the format, types of questions, and pacing.

2. **Positive mindset**. During these practice tests, actively challenge and reframe any negative thoughts that arise. Write a list of positive affirmations and review them before each test.

3. **Relaxation techniques**. Integrate short meditation or deep breathing sessions before starting your practice tests. This can set a calm tone.

4. **Time management**. Practice hiding the timer and pacing yourself during practice SAT exams. Note any modules where you took longer than expected and aim to improve pacing.

5. **Visualization**. Spend a few minutes before each practice test visualizing a high score.

6. **Let go of the outcome**. Do not make the SAT a bigger deal than it is. Focus on the process of answering each question, step by step, rather than worrying about the final outcome.

PREP EXPERT REVIEW

Key Takeaways

- **Prep Expert General Strategy #15—*Reduce Test Anxiety***: Reduce your test anxiety to significantly improve your test day performance and overall SAT score.

- **Test anxiety defined**: Test anxiety is a common experience in which students feel nervous, worried, or fearful before or during tests. It can manifest both physically (e.g., rapid heartbeat) and psychologically (e.g., negative mindset).

- **Impact on performance**: Test anxiety can hinder focus, clarity of thought, and information recall, leading to a lower SAT score.

- **Strategies to overcome test anxiety**: Thoroughly prepare yourself by setting study schedules, practicing with sample tests, employing relaxation techniques, managing your time effectively, and visualizing success.

- **The power of letting go**: Your performance on the SAT is not tied to your worth as a human being. Focusing on the process, rather than obsessing over the outcome, can reduce test anxiety and lead to better results.

PREPEXPERT

GENERAL STRATEGY #16

CAPITALIZE ON COMPLEXITY

PREP EXPERT STRATEGY

As a general rule, if you are unsure of the answer to an SAT question, you want to make a random guess. Why? The College Board's test-question writers design incorrect choices to appear appealing to uncertain students. Thus, unsure students who guess with a bias often select the wrong choice. You should eliminate as much bias from your guess as possible. But there is an exception to this rule: *Prep Expert General Strategy #16—Capitalize On Complexity*. This method guides your guessing based on the order of difficulty of the questions.

Understanding Order of Difficulty on the SAT

The SAT organizes its questions in modules based on their difficulty level. *On most modules:*

- The first third of questions are of **easy difficulty**.
- The middle third of questions are of **medium difficulty**.
- The last third of questions are of **hard difficulty**.

Now, how do we distinguish between these levels of difficulty?

- **Easy difficulty**: More than half of all students answer these questions correctly.
- **Medium difficulty**: Approximately half of all students answer these questions correctly.
- **Hard difficulty**: Less than half of all students answer these questions correctly.

Understanding where a question lies within a module can help guide your guessing. Adjusting your guessing to the complexity of questions will improve your SAT score. Use the order of difficulty to your advantage and navigate the SAT with greater precision.

Capitalize On Complexity to maximize your SAT score.

PREP EXPERT EXAMPLE

Capitalizing on Complexity on SAT Math Modules

EASY SAT MATH QUESTIONS

Easy SAT Math questions generally have straightforward, simple, or obvious answers. For example, if a math problem at the beginning of a module includes the numbers 2 and 3, the answer might be 6, a solution easily derived from the numbers in the problem.

HARD SAT MATH QUESTIONS

Hard SAT Math questions generally have obscure, ugly, or less-than-obvious answers. For example, if a math problem at the end of a module includes the numbers 2 and 3, the answer might be $\sqrt{19}$, a solution not easily derived from the numbers in the problem.

STUDENT-PRODUCED RESPONSE SAT MATH QUESTIONS

For these fill-in-the-blank SAT Math questions, even if it is a tough question, it is advisable to guess an answer that can be derived from the problem's numbers. For example, let's say that the question includes the numbers 50 and 2. Then you might guess 100 (50 multiplied by 2), 25 (50 divided by 2), or 12.5 (50 divided by 2^2).

Capitalizing On Complexity on SAT Reading and Writing Modules

EASY SAT READING AND WRITING QUESTIONS

Easy SAT Reading and Writing questions generally have straightforward, simple, or obvious answers. For example, you might find a straightforward vocabulary word such as "physical" in the correct answer for an easy question.

HARD SAT READING AND WRITING QUESTIONS

Hard SAT Reading and Writing questions have obscure, ugly, or nonobvious answers. For example, a difficult vocabulary word such as "clandestine" might be within the correct answer choice to a hard question.

Of note, the Reading and Writing modules do not follow the easy, medium, and hard question organization exactly. However, you will generally find that the questions progress from easier to harder on Reading and Writing modules, with some exceptions in between.

PREP EXPERT PRACTICE

If an easy SAT question that is located at the beginning of a module is consuming too much time, pause and re-evaluate your approach. It is possible you are not using the most efficient method to solve the problem.

If a hard SAT question that is located at the end of a module seemed like it was very easy to solve, pause and re-evaluate your approach. It is rare for difficult questions to have simple solutions, so make sure that you did not make a mistake.

Capitalize On Complexity guides guessing based on the difficulty of a question. Instead of pure random guessing, your guesses are guided by the order of difficulty of the modules on the SAT.

By understanding the order of difficulty, you can make more informed guesses when needed, and thus improve your SAT score.

PREP EXPERT REVIEW

Key Takeaways

- **Prep Expert General Strategy #16—*Capitalize On Complexity*:** Use the inherent order of difficulty in SAT modules (easy to hard) to guide your guessing.

- **Order of difficulty**: SAT questions typically progress from easiest at the beginning of a module to hardest at the end.

- **Guided guessing**: For easy questions, the answers often relate directly to numbers in the problem on SAT Math modules or easier vocabulary words on SAT Reading and Writing modules. For hard questions, the answers are typically more obscure, less obvious, or made up of more difficult vocabulary.

- **Re-evaluation**: If an easy question seems too difficult or a hard question seems too easy, reconsider your approach to ensure accuracy.

- **Application**: This strategy is more useful on the SAT Math modules, but also applies to SAT Reading and Writing modules.

 **PREP**EXPERT

GENERAL STRATEGY #17

TURN OFF THE TECH

PREP EXPERT STRATEGY

We are almost all increasingly attached to technology. Your brain is wired to pay attention to new information. Now, thousands of years later, every time your phone dings with a new notification, your brain squirts out dopamine. Dopamine is the neurotransmitter responsible for pleasure in the brain. We love that feeling, but it can be a distraction. Distraction is the enemy of studying.

Our phones beep, buzz, and provide unexpected information as we scroll...just like a slot machine, keeping us waiting for the next dopamine hit. Slot machines steal our money, and our devices steal our focus. And just like sitting at a slot machine, it can be hard to recognize the hours spent spinning the wheels (or in technology's case, scrolling social media, playing video games, watching YouTube videos, etc.).

To Improve Focus, Turn Off the Tech When Studying for the SAT

There are so many technological distractions that can pull you away from studying for the SAT. Some examples include text messages, social media, YouTube, video games, etc.

Disconnect from the internet, phone, or any other tech that may distract you from studying. Because notifications are pinging us at all times of the day, it is hard to find time to concentrate without interruption.

Nir Eyal's book *Hooked* explains that we are all "hooked" on technology because things like smartphones and apps are actually designed to become habits that our brains become habitually hooked to checking. Because these hardwired dopamine habits are hard to resist, it is better just to avoid the urge altogether.

Turn Off The Tech to maximize your SAT score.

PREP EXPERT EXAMPLE

The Mere Presence of Your Phone Reduces Brain Power

A 2017 study followed a group of people taking a test. Half of the participants were asked to place their turned-off phones on their desks as they took the test. The other half of the participants were asked to leave their turned-off phones in another room.

The results: participants with their phones in another room scored 20% higher on average on the test than the group that had their phones on their desks.[7]

Our phones can be that distracting! Just seeing your phone on your desk reduces brain power. This can be enough to make your brain wonder what you're missing. Did you just get a text message, a social media notification, or an email? These micro-distractions impede brain performance.

Key takeaway: put your phone in a different room when studying for the SAT.

PREP EXPERT PRACTICE

You may be wondering how you can turn off the technology when the SAT itself is *digital*. Although the SAT is now a digital exam, you can still minimize tech distractions while you study for the SAT. Here are a few strategies you can use to *Turn Off The Tech* when studying:

---

7   Adrian F. Ward et al., "Brain Drain: The Mere Presence of One's Own Smartphone Reduces Available Cognitive Capacity," *Journal of the Association for Consumer Research* 2, no. 2 (April 2017): 140–54, https://doi.org/10.1086/691462.

1. **Physical separation**. Place your phone and/or smartwatch in another room while studying. This ensures you do not experience visual or auditory distractions.

2. **Offline study**. Download necessary materials or documents, disconnect from the internet, and focus. This prevents the temptation to browse the web or check social media.

3. **Paper practice**. Even in the era of the Digital SAT, practicing on paper has value. Print out practice SAT exams and complete them with your pencil. This gives you a break from screen time and still allows you to practice efficiently.

4. **Set boundaries**. If you must be online (for example, to complete a practice Digital SAT), do not leave other tabs open with social media apps, YouTube, or other distracting websites.

The strategy goes beyond the SAT. *Turning Off The Tech* is a valuable study method for any academic study, professional task, or other focused work.

This strategy might initially be challenging to implement, but its benefits are limitless. Not only can it boost SAT performance, but it can also prove transformative for your broader academic and professional goals.

PREP EXPERT REVIEW

Key Takeaways

- **Prep Expert General Strategy #17—Turn Off The Tech**: Constant notifications from smartphones and other technology create dopamine-driven distractions that reduce the effectiveness of your studying.

- **App design and addiction**: Tech platforms like social media and YouTube are designed to be addictive. They divert our attention away from productive study tasks.

- **Impact on test performance**: A 2017 study found that even a visible turned-off smartphone on the desk while taking a test can lower scores by 20%.

- **Recommended strategies:** To effectively prepare for the SAT, place your phone in another room, silence your smartwatch, and download study materials to minimize online distractions.

- **Long-term implications:** Beyond the SAT, reducing tech distractions is critical for academic and professional success.

GENERAL STRATEGY #18

STUDY AT THE LIBRARY

PREP EXPERT STRATEGY

The right study environment plays a crucial role in your SAT prep. One highly effective strategy that I have consistently relied upon is studying at the library. This approach proved invaluable during my own SAT prep, transforming my score from average to perfect.

The magic of the library has extended to success on other exams for me too, including the PSAT, AP Exams, GMAT, MCAT, United States Medical Licensing Exams, and the American Board of Dermatology board certification exams.

The common thread? Studying at the library has elevated my performance, and it will do the same for you.

Why the Library?

The first question you might ask is, "Why the library?" The answer is focused attention. Your home is typically full of distractions. Tech distractions such as computers, phones, TVs, and smart speakers often derail our best intentions to study. Non-tech distractions such as family members, pets, and household activities can be equally disruptive.

Contrast this with the library. It is an oasis of concentration. Libraries offer limited tech and non-tech distractions. There are usually no loud TVs or chatty family members to destroy your focus at the library.

The library is one of the most boring places on Earth. This is what makes it the perfect place to study.

Study At The Library to maximize your SAT score.

PREP EXPERT EXAMPLE

Study Challenge

If you are skeptical about the difference in your productivity that working at the library could make, consider doing the following challenge:

- **Home study**: Study at home for two hours.

    versus

- **Library study**: Study at the library for two hours.

The studying does not need to be on the same day. In fact, it is preferable if the two hours of study time at each location takes place on different days.

Afterward, ask yourself the following questions:

- In which environment were you more effective studying?
- In which environment were you less distracted?
- In which environment were you more absorbed in the material?

Most students find the library offers a superior learning environment compared to home.

PREP EXPERT PRACTICE

Of course, not everyone has an easily accessible public library. In such cases, the goal should be to create a library-like atmosphere at home. This makeshift "home library" should do the following:

1. **Ensure quiet**. Use earplugs or headphones to block out noise if sharing space with others.

2. **Provide ample desk space**. This makes it easy to spread out all your study materials, whether they are laptops, books, or printouts.

3. **Use comfortable seating**. Opt for a chair that offers support and comfort. Refrain from studying in bed, which can make you sleepy.

4. **Have good lighting**. Prolonged reading requires optimal lighting to avoid eye strain.

5. **Maintain a no-talking rule**. As in a library, ensure minimal disturbances. Make sure family members are aware of your focused study sessions.

6. **Keep the area tidy**. A clutter-free workspace helps you cultivate a clear mind, allowing for more efficient study sessions.

7. **Limit technology**. Keep your phone in a different room to avoid unnecessary distractions. Avoid having a TV on in the background.

Creating a library-like environment at home can significantly improve your study efficiency. By minimizing distractions, you are setting yourself up for study success.

PREP EXPERT REVIEW

Key Takeaways

- **Prep Expert General Strategy #18—*Study At The Library***: The library offers an optimal study environment for the SAT, your high school coursework, and future standardized exams.

- **Home versus library:** Homes often have numerous technological and non-technological distractions, which reduce study efficiency. In contrast, libraries limit distractions, encourage focus, and enhance study efficiency.

- **Study challenge**: Compare a two-hour study session at home against a two-hour study session at the library. Evaluate your productivity, distractions, and information retention. Determine which location to study at after completing this challenge.

- **Creating an at-home library**: If accessing a library is difficult, emulate its environment at home by ensuring quietness, ample workspace, sufficient lighting, limited distractions, and that you have an organized study area.

- **Limit technology**: Regardless of your study location, limit technological interruptions by putting phones and other devices away and emphasizing focused study sessions.

Prep Expert
General Strategies

 **PREP**EXPERT

GENERAL STRATEGY #19

USE THE POMODORO TECHNIQUE

PREP EXPERT STRATEGY

Many students hate the idea of studying because they have no idea how to structure their time. Some students think that studying involves sitting at a desk for many hours without any breaks.

My guess is that *most teachers have not taught you how to study effectively*. Instead, teachers just tell you to study the course material. But *how* do you study?

There are many techniques you can use to study more effectively. One of the most powerful techniques is called the "Pomodoro Technique."

What Is the Pomodoro Technique?

The Pomodoro Technique is a time management method developed by Francesco Cirillo in the late 1980s. The technique breaks down work into twenty-five-minute intervals, called "Pomodoros," separated by short breaks of five minutes. After three or four Pomodoros, you take a more extended break of thirty to sixty minutes. The Pomodoro Technique is based on the idea that working in focused intervals increases your productivity.

Breaking down work into intervals can make it easier to stay focused and avoid burnout. The Pomodoro Technique can be used for any type of work, including studying, writing, or project work. In this case, we will apply it to SAT prep.

The key is to set a specific goal for each Pomodoro interval and eliminate any distractions during that time. By doing this, you can increase productivity and improve overall time management.

The Modified Pomodoro: The 50/10 Rule

The standard Pomodoro Technique involves working for twenty-five minutes, then taking a five-minute break. A modified version of the Pomodoro Technique involves double that: working for fifty minutes, then taking a ten-minute break. This is known as the "50/10 Rule."

At Prep Expert, many of our high-achieving students prefer the 50/10 Rule because it allows for longer work periods and longer breaks. In fact, Prep Expert SAT Courses have three-hour classes that are structured after this rule: fifty minutes of class time followed by ten-minute breaks, repeated three times (three hours total).

Of course, if you prefer to have more frequent breaks, there is nothing wrong with structuring your time using the standard 25/5 Rule.

Why The Pomodoro Technique Works

It is nearly impossible to study for one hour straight with no breaks. Taking breaks will help your brain recharge and raise your SAT score.

SAT studying does not count if you are scrolling social media, text messaging friends, or eating. But you can do these things between your twenty-five-minute or fifty-minute study periods.

During your break, you are free to message your friends, respond to emails, scroll social media, etc. You can grab a snack or use the restroom. Then you should go back to focused studying for the next twenty-five or fifty minutes.

What you will discover is that after your break, your mind will be refreshed. If you regularly schedule breaks into your study periods, then you can manage your time more effectively.

Use The Pomodoro Technique to maximize your SAT score.

PREP EXPERT EXAMPLE

Below is an example of how you can apply the Modified Pomodoro Technique to SAT studying. I have written out a schedule for how you might want to structure your SAT studying on a weekend morning.

Weekend Morning

9:00 a.m.–9:50 a.m.	Read new SAT strategies
9:50 a.m.–10:00 a.m.	Break
10:00 a.m.–10:50 a.m.	Review old SAT exams
10:50 a.m.–11:00 a.m.	Break
11:00 a.m.–11:50 a.m.	Complete practice SAT questions
11:50 a.m.–12:00 p.m.	Break
12:00 p.m.–1:00 p.m.	Lunch break

This is the Modified Pomodoro Technique in action. You are doing a specific study task every fifty minutes, then you are taking a ten-minute break. Notice how from 9:00 a.m. to 9:50 a.m., you read new SAT strategies, then you take a ten-minute break. Then during the study block from 10:00 a.m. to 10:50 a.m., you review old SAT exams, then you take a ten-minute break. From 11:00 a.m. to 11:50 a.m., you complete practice SAT questions, and then take another ten-minute break. Finally, after you have done three Pomodoros, you can take a lunch break, which is a full hour to completely relax.

If you are ambitious, you can also structure an afternoon study session after your lunch break in the same way, with three "50/10" hours of studying (whether it be for the SAT, an AP Exam, or something else).

Time Boxing

Notice how each fifty-minute period in the above example contains a specific goal or task to complete. This is called "time boxing." Time boxing is another proven technique for improving productivity, time management, and studying. The essence of this technique is to dedicate each time interval to a single task. During each time box, there should be no multitasking—just pure, focused study.

The goal is to get accustomed to this method during your SAT prep, ensuring you make the most of your time. Once you can effectively apply the Pomodoro Technique to your SAT prep, you can apply it to other studying (e.g., AP Exams). You can customize this method by incorporating other subjects, practice tests, or review sessions. It takes practice, but once you get good at estimating how much time a particular task will take, you will be a master of time management.

PREP EXPERT PRACTICE

Make Sure to Take Full Breaks during the Digital SAT

On your SAT test day, do not skip the break time that you are given. You will be given a ten-minute break after the first two SAT Reading and Writing modules. Take full advantage of this break by going to the restroom, eating a snack, and giving your brain a chance to relax.

You will find that if you fully relax during this ten-minute break from the Digital SAT, your brain will be refreshed. Then you will be ready to ace the next two SAT Math modules.

BONUS: HOW TO SNEAK EXTRA BREAK TIME DURING THE DIGITAL SAT

If you finish a module early on the SAT, *do not* click forward to the next module. If you start the next module, the timer for the next module will automatically start.

Instead, if you finish a module a few minutes early, sit and wait for the timer for that module to expire. This will give your brain some extra break time during the SAT so that it can recharge for the next module.

PREP EXPERT REVIEW

Key Takeaways

- **Prep Expert General Strategy #19—*Use The Pomodoro Technique*:** The Pomodoro Technique is a time management method that structures study

---

time into intervals: twenty-five minutes of focused work followed by a five-minute break.

- **Modified version**: A modified version, known as the 50/10 Rule, involves a fifty-minute work session followed by a ten-minute break. This method is preferred by some for its longer work periods and longer breaks.

- **Emphasis on focus**: Both versions emphasize the importance of single-tasking during the focused intervals and taking full advantage of breaks to recharge. This method can be applied to various tasks, including SAT prep, academic studies, and even professional work.

- **Significance of breaks**: Breaks are crucial not just for relaxation, but also for mental rejuvenation. Even during the SAT, it's vital to capitalize on the provided breaks to enhance performance. Properly timed breaks can prevent distractions, reduce the urge for multitasking, and elevate the overall efficiency of study sessions.

- **Time boxing**: For optimal results, each focused interval ("time box") should have a clear, specific goal, and potential distractions should be minimized.

 **PREP**EXPERT

GENERAL STRATEGY #20

USE THE SECRET TO SUCCESS

PREP EXPERT STRATEGY

Self-Control Is the Most Accurate Predictor of Success

The secret to achieving incredible success is self-control. While attributes like IQ, emotional intelligence, and grit are important, research has consistently shown that self-control is the main factor that shapes a person's success.

Good news! Self-control is not an innate trait you must be born with. Self-control is a skill you can learn. For most students, high school is the perfect time to develop this attribute. Why? Because high school is often the first time in your life that you need to study intensely. For SAT prep, this means resisting distractions, committing to schedules, and practicing discipline.

However, tech distractions like social media, YouTube, and video games make developing self-control challenging. I previously discussed the need to limit technology in *Prep Expert General Strategy #17—Turn Off The Tech*.

Let me share my personal journey to developing self-control with you. During elementary and middle school, I did not have self-control. I was often distracted by technology, particularly TV. But in high school, I spent hundreds of hours studying

---

for the SAT. Studying for the SAT inadvertently taught me the habit of self-control. Developing self-control not only led to my perfect SAT score, but also to my subsequent academic success in college, medical school, and business school. This self-control has also led to my professional success as an entrepreneur, author, and dermatologist.

If you wish to achieve a top SAT score and build a foundation for lifelong success, **self-control is your secret weapon**. Self-control can propel you to unparalleled heights both academically and professionally.

Use The Secret To Success (self-control) to maximize your SAT score.

PREP EXPERT EXAMPLE

The Stanford Marshmallow Experiment

The Stanford Marshmallow Experiment, led by psychologist Walter Mischel in the late 1960s and early 1970s, studied self-control in children.

In the experiment:

- Researchers placed children between the ages of four and six years old in a room alone with a single marshmallow.
- Each child was given an option: eat the marshmallow immediately or wait fifteen minutes to receive a second marshmallow as a reward for patience.
- The choice was essentially between an immediate reward or a larger, delayed reward.
- Researchers observed each child's decision and behavior during the waiting period.

Research Findings

Only about one-third of the children managed to wait the full fifteen minutes to receive the second marshmallow. The others consumed the first marshmallow before the time was up.

The experiment itself was a simple test of a child's ability to use self-control to delay gratification. But its most notable findings came from longitudinal follow-up studies many years later, when the researchers found that the children who had shown self-control were more successful by almost every measure! These outcomes included:

- Higher SAT scores (i.e., 210 points higher on average)
- Better careers and higher salaries
- Healthier lifestyles (i.e., lower body mass index)
- Fewer substance-abuse problems
- Better social and emotional skills (i.e., more popular with peers and teachers)

The experiment showed that having self-control predicts future success in almost every aspect of life.

PREP EXPERT PRACTICE

Here is how you can develop self-control as you study for the SAT:

1. **Set clear boundaries**. Dedicate specific hours to study without distractions. This means no phone, no social media, and an environment that is conducive to studying.

2. **Time management**. Use timers to simulate the SAT environment. Try studying in focused time intervals to gradually build stamina for test day.

3. **Seek accountability**. Having a study buddy or another figure you are accountable to can remind you of your goals and keep you on track.

4. **Limit technology**. As emphasized in the *Turn Off the Tech* strategy, reduce your dependence on tech gadgets during study hours. This not only helps improve concentration, but also builds self-control.

PREP EXPERT REVIEW

Key Takeaways

- **Prep Expert General Strategy #20—*Use The Secret To Success***: Self-control is the secret to success, significantly influencing SAT scores as well as overall life achievements.

- **Evidence**: The Stanford Marshmallow Experiment tested kids' ability to delay gratification. Those who waited for a second marshmallow (demonstrating self-control) were later found to have better life outcomes by almost every measure, including higher SAT scores.

- **Learnability**: Self-control is not innate; it can be developed. High school is an optimal time to develop self-control due to its academic demands and challenges.

- **Personal Experience**: I did not have self-control when I was five years old. I developed self-control in high school, when I spent hundreds of hours studying for the SAT. Developing self-control led to my perfect SAT score. In addition, developing self-control in high school also led to my subsequent success in college, medical school, business school, dermatology residency, and as an author and entrepreneur!

SAT WRITING INTRODUCTION

"Grammar is a piano I play by ear.
All I know about grammar is its power."

—JOAN DIDION

DIGITAL SAT WRITING OVERVIEW

Let's discuss the SAT Writing section. Remember, SAT Writing and SAT Reading questions are combined into the same module.

DIGITAL SAT READING & WRITING FORMAT

Section	Questions	Time
SAT Reading & Writing Module 1	27 questions	32 minutes
SAT Reading & Writing Module 2	27 questions	32 minutes
TOTAL SAT READING & WRITING	54 QUESTIONS	64 MINUTES

Digital SAT Writing Format

The first module on the Digital SAT will be an SAT Reading and Writing module that contains 27 questions in 32 minutes. The second module on the Digital SAT will also be an SAT Reading and Writing module that contains 27 questions in 32 minutes.

The first 13 to 14 questions on each module are typically SAT Reading questions. In other words, the first half of each module includes SAT Reading questions, such as passage-based questions. The second 13 to 14 questions on each module are typically SAT Writing questions, meaning that the second half of each module includes SAT Writing questions, such as grammar questions.

Essentially, SAT Writing questions appear in the second half of each SAT Reading and Writing module.

Digital SAT Writing Content

The SAT tests the following writing skills and knowledge areas:

SAT WRITING CONTENT

Domain	Knowledge Testing Point	# Of Questions	%
Standard English Conventions	• Boundaries • Form, structure, and sense	11–15 questions	~26%
Expression of Ideas	• Rhetorical synthesis • Transitions	8–12 questions	~20%

The first domain is *Standard English Conventions*, which includes 11 to 15 questions on the SAT. This makes up about 26% of all questions on the SAT Reading and Writing modules. The knowledge testing points within this domain include *Boundaries* as well as *Form, Structure, and Sense*. *Boundaries* questions measure a student's ability to use punctuation properly. *Form, Structure, and Sense* questions measure a student's ability to use Standard English grammar properly.

The second domain is *Expression of Ideas*, which includes 8 to 12 questions on the SAT. This makes up about 20% of all questions on the SAT Reading and Writing modules. The knowledge testing points within this domain include *Rhetorical Synthesis* and *Transitions*. *Rhetorical Synthesis* questions measure a student's ability to selectively extract information from bullet point notes to achieve a writing goal. *Transitions* questions measure a student's ability to use logical transitions properly.

Right now, it is not super important to understand all of the above knowledge testing points. We will discuss them in more detail as we cover *Prep Expert Writing Strategies*. For now, know that these knowledge testing points test grammar. Essentially, the second half of the SAT Reading and Writing modules is primarily going to contain grammar-based questions.

We will teach you *Prep Expert Writing Strategies* to ace these questions. In summary, 46% of the questions on an SAT Reading and Writing module will relate to Writing. The other 54% of the questions relate to Reading.

Why Separate Writing and Reading?

Reading and writing questions are combined together into the same modules on the SAT. Why does Prep Expert separate out SAT Reading versus SAT Writing? Because the strategies you need to succeed on SAT Reading are different from the strategies you need to succeed on SAT Writing. SAT Reading contains primarily passage-based questions, while SAT Writing contains primarily grammar-based questions. These are two separate skill sets, so we separate out the *Prep Expert Strategies* for SAT Reading and SAT Writing.

SAT Writing
Introduction

Why Separate Writing and Reading?

PREPEXPERT
WRITING STRATEGIES

"The great enemy of clear language is insincerity."

—GEORGE ORWELL

PREP EXPERT WRITING STRATEGIES OVERVIEW

Prep Expert Writing Strategies are a collection of techniques designed to improve your SAT Writing score. These strategies will help you refine grammar skills, ensure clarity, use effective transitions, and maintain concise writing. Through these strategies, you will learn how to ace complex prompts and eliminate common errors.

Within the SAT Reading and Writing modules, the second half of questions focus on grammar and writing skills. *Prep Expert Writing Strategies* help you tackle these last 13 to 14 questions that test writing mechanics and coherence. These strategies will teach you how to apply appropriate Standard English conventions. These skills are not only vital for the SAT, but also for clear and effective writing in academic and professional contexts.

Prep Expert Writing Strategies are adaptable, which makes them an ideal resource for students at all levels of proficiency. Whether you are struggling with grammar basics or looking to polish your writing expertise, these strategies will address your goals.

The foundation of Prep Expert's approach to SAT Writing is practice. Applying these strategies to actual SAT questions will help you develop habits to express ideas succinctly.

These writing skills will also set you up for academic and professional success. If you aspire to write with clarity and coherence, mastering these strategies is a key step on your journey.

Personally, learning how to write well was the most important skill that I learned in high school. My ability to write clearly has produced tremendous positive results in high school, college, graduate school, business, and beyond. The ability to write well

Prep Expert
Writing Strategies

will help you succeed in any future career you choose. Why? Because you will be able to communicate your ideas with clarity, accuracy, and precision.

Prep Expert Writing Strategies pave the path to SAT Writing excellence. By integrating these strategies into your preparation, you can elevate your writing skills. They are a road map to success on SAT Writing.

Master and apply all of the *Prep Expert Writing Strategies* to maximize your SAT Writing score.

 **PREP**EXPERT

WRITING STRATEGY #1
DO NOT TRUST YOUR EAR

PREP EXPERT STRATEGY

Most students approach SAT Writing questions by selecting the answer choice that *sounds correct*. Do not make this mistake. *Do Not Trust Your Ear* on SAT Writing questions.

If you trust your ear to select an answer, you will get many SAT Writing questions wrong. Why? Incorrect answers often *sound* good. Correct answers often *sound* bad.

Instead, select answers based on known grammatical rules. Learn the grammatical rules that are tested on the Digital SAT. Then figure out which grammatical rule applies to each SAT Writing question.

Learn the *Prep Expert Writing Strategies* that we cover in this book. This will help you identify which grammar category each question falls into. It is important that you understand all the nuances of the grammar strategies and rules. Once you have learned these, you will no longer need to rely on your ear for SAT Writing questions. Instead, you will be able to categorize each question by grammatical error.

Here are a few examples of grammar concepts tested on the SAT:

- **Idioms**: You need to identify when there is an idiomatic error.
- **Singular-plural mismatches**: You need to identify when there is a singular-plural error.
- **Parallelism**: You need to identify when there is a parallel structure error.
- **Verb tense**: You need to identify when there is a verb tense error.

Select answer choices based on the category of grammatical error the question is testing, rather than what sounds good to you. The only way to be well prepared for all the grammatical rules that can be tested on the Digital SAT is to learn all the *Prep Expert Writing Strategies* covered in this book.

Do Not Trust Your Ear to maximize your SAT Writing score.

PREP EXPERT EXAMPLE

Consider the following *Prep Expert Examples*.

Be Literal When Reading SAT Writing Questions

One bad habit that many students have is *not* reading literally. This is due to our daily conversations. In everyday communication, we cut our family, our friends, and ourselves slack.

We tend to know what people mean when they are speaking or writing. Therefore, we are not huge sticklers, even if they do not have perfect grammar. But do not let this habit carry over to the SAT. With respect to the SAT Writing questions, you must take everything you read literally.

EXAMPLE 1: *"Do you remember that time where Jason hiked to the top of the mountain?"*
If your friend said the above sentence to you in everyday conversation, you would not notice the grammatical error because it *sounds* fine. But you should be able to identify the grammar error in this sentence on the SAT! You should notice that "where" is a relative pronoun that can only refer to geographic locations. You cannot use "where" to refer to time. Instead, you should use the relative pronoun "when." We will learn this specific grammatical rule later. For now, remember: *Do Not Trust Your Ear*. Instead, read the sentences on the SAT Writing section literally. This will make it much easier to spot grammatical errors.

EXAMPLE 2: *"It is amazing how colorful the sky is."*

Again, in everyday language, the above sentence *sounds* fine. But think literally about the sentence and ask yourself the following question: What is "it" referring to? There is actually no noun in this sentence that the pronoun "it" can logically refer to. The sentence may be improved by clearly stating: "The colorful sky is amazing." We will learn more about pronoun errors later. For now, just remember: *Do Not Trust Your Ear* on SAT Writing questions.

EXAMPLE 3: *"I hope to win the art contest next year like Sarah's masterpiece did this year."*

Once again, in everyday language, the above sentence *sounds* fine. But remember: *Do Not Trust Your Ear*. Think literally about the sentence. The sentence is comparing a person ("I") to a work of art ("Sarah's masterpiece"). On the SAT, you cannot compare a person to a thing. We must compare a person to a person (or a work of art to a work of art). We will learn more about making consistent comparisons later.

Hopefully, you now see that trusting your ear does not work on SAT Writing questions.

PREP EXPERT PRACTICE

Try applying this *Prep Expert Strategy* yourself to the following SAT practice questions:

1

In 1895, engineer Alfred Lawson designed the first gasoline-powered airplane. He attached a small engine to a lightweight frame and connected it to a propeller using a series of _____. These mechanisms allowed the engine's power to be efficiently transferred to the propeller, enabling the aircraft to generate thrust and achieve flight.

Which choice completes the text so that it conforms to the conventions of Standard English?

A) gear's teeth
B) gears' teeth
C) gear's teeths
D) gears teeth'

## 2

In 1066, King Harold II led the English army into the Battle of Hastings against the Normans, only to fall during the conflict. As a result, the English Council appointed Edgar II, a member of the House of Wessex with a strong claim to the English throne, to rule. However, upon William the Conqueror's arrival in London later that year, _____ leading to the coronation of the first Norman king of England.

Which choice completes the text so that it conforms to the conventions of Standard English?

A) Edgar's reign was deposed,

B) the deposition of Edgar took place,

C) it was Edgar who was deposed,

D) Edgar was deposed,

The answers to these SAT practice questions can be found in the back of this book.

PREP EXPERT REVIEW

Key Takeaways

- **Prep Expert Writing Strategy #1—*Do Not Trust Your Ear***: Avoid relying on what "sounds correct" to your ear when answering SAT Writing questions. Incorrect answers often sound good, while correct answers often sound awkward.

- **Grammatical rules**: Focus on applying grammatical rules to select correct answers. Categorize each question based on the grammatical error that is being tested.

- **Common grammar concepts**: Familiarize yourself with common grammar concepts tested on the SAT, like idioms, singular-plural mismatches, parallelism, and verb tense.

- **Expert strategies**: Practice the *Prep Expert Writing Strategies* this book provides to enhance your identification of grammar categories and improve answer selection.

- **Literal reading:** Take a literal approach to reading SAT Writing questions to effectively spot grammatical errors. This is a different approach than your typical informal interpretation of everyday language.

 **PREP**EXPERT

WRITING
STRATEGY #2

SKIP READING
THE DIRECTIONS

PREP EXPERT STRATEGY

Skip Reading The Directions on the SAT Reading and Writing Modules to save time. Do not waste time on your test day reading directions.

Many students waste time reading the directions for the SAT. This is precious time that they could instead use to answer questions.

Familiarize yourself with the directions for the SAT Reading and Writing modules well before test day so that you do not need to read them on your SAT test day.

Below, we have reproduced the directions to the SAT Reading and Writing modules as you will see them on your Digital SAT test day. Read these directions now so that you do not have to read them on test day.

Read the directions now so that you do not waste time on test day reading the directions.

These directions can be summarized as follows:

- This module tests reading and writing skills
- Each question has an associated passage

- You should read carefully
- Every multiple-choice question has four answer choices
- Choose the single best answer

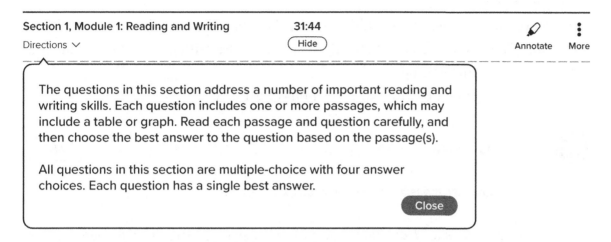

Section 1, Module 1: Reading and Writing — 31:44 — Hide — Annotate — More

The questions in this section address a number of important reading and writing skills. Each question includes one or more passages, which may include a table or graph. Read each passage and question carefully, and then choose the best answer to the question based on the passage(s).

All questions in this section are multiple-choice with four answer choices. Each question has a single best answer.

Close

The directions are standard and straightforward. You do not need to read them again on test day.

Skip Reading The Directions to maximize your SAT Writing score.

PREP EXPERT EXAMPLE

Consider the following *Prep Expert Examples*.

Standard English Conventions Questions

To save even more time, you should also *Skip Reading The Directions* for Standard English Conventions questions. These questions specifically test grammar on the Digital SAT Reading and Writing modules.

Below are the directions for the Standard English Conventions questions:

23   Mark for Review   ABC

Which choice completes the text so that it conforms to the conventions of Standard English?

Read the directions for Standard English Conventions now so you do not need to read them on test day. You will typically encounter 5 to 8 Standard English Conventions questions in the middle of an SAT Reading and Writing module. When you get to these

Prep Expert
Writing Strategies

questions, you do not need to read the directions over and over. This will save you even more time during the Digital SAT.

Transitions Questions

To save even more time, you should also *Skip Reading The Directions* for *Transitions* questions. These questions specifically test logical transitions on the Digital SAT Reading and Writing modules.

Below are the directions for the *Transitions* questions:

Read the directions for *Transitions* questions now so you do not need to read them on test day. You will typically encounter 2 to 5 *Transitions* questions in the middle of an SAT Reading and Writing module. When you get to these questions, you do not need to read the directions over and over. This will save you even more time during the Digital SAT.

PREP EXPERT PRACTICE

Try applying this *Prep Expert Strategy* yourself to the following SAT practice questions:

3

According to etiquette experts, it is best to avoid discussing politics and religion at the dinner table. When hosting a dinner party, the host should make an effort to steer the conversation toward neutral topics. For example, the host could ask guests whether _____ enjoyed any good books or movies recently.

Which choice completes the text so that it conforms to the conventions of Standard English?

A) they

B) one

C) you

D) it

## 4

In recent years, climate change has become a topic of growing concern. _____ many organizations are taking steps to reduce their carbon footprint and promote sustainability in their operations.

Which choice completes the text with the most logical transition?

A) As a result,
B) On the other hand,
C) For example,
D) Accordingly,

The answers to these SAT practice questions can be found in the back of this book.

PREP EXPERT REVIEW

Key Takeaways

- **Prep Expert Writing Strategy #2—*Skip Reading The Directions***: To conserve time on test day, skip reading the directions on the SAT Reading and Writing modules. Familiarize yourself with the instructions well in advance.

- **Familiarize yourself with certain question types**: Review and understand the directions for different question types (e.g., *Standard English Conventions*, *Transitions*) before the test day to avoid unnecessary reading.

- **Time management**: Reallocate the time saved by not reading directions to critically think about the answer to each question. This will improve your overall SAT score.

- **Bluebook app**: Use the College Board's Bluebook app to read and understand the directions for SAT Reading and Writing modules well before test day.

Prep Expert Writing Strategies

WRITING STRATEGY #3

READ THE WHOLE PARAGRAPH

PREP EXPERT STRATEGY

Digital SAT Writing questions contain fill-in-the-blanks of a single sentence within a larger paragraph. Many students try to save time by reading only the sentence containing the fill-in-the-blank. They skip reading the larger paragraph that the sentence is a part of. This is not a good idea.

Do not try to save time by skipping the whole paragraph. This will increase your error rate on SAT Writing questions.

If you do not read the whole paragraph, you will often lose necessary context for the question. You will answer many SAT Writing questions incorrectly if you do not read the larger paragraph that the fill-in-the-blank sentence is part of.

Read The Whole Paragraph

You must read the entire paragraph of every SAT Writing question. Do not try to skip steps by reading only the single sentence with the fill-in-the-blank grammar issue.

Why? The other sentences in the paragraph often provide helpful context clues to the answer to the SAT Writing question. Therefore, it is useful to read the entire paragraph. Do not just read the fill-in-the-blank sentence.

Read The Whole Paragraph to maximize your SAT Writing score.

PREP EXPERT EXAMPLE

Consider the following *Prep Expert Example*:

Ex

The committee has finalized its decision after weeks of deliberation. _____ chosen the design submitted by a local artist for the town's new mural. The artwork, depicting the town's vibrant history and culture, will be painted on the large wall facing the town square.

Which choice completes the text so that it conforms to the conventions of Standard English?

A) They have
B) They has
C) It has
D) It have

If you attempt to answer this question without reading the whole paragraph, you might answer it incorrectly.

Let's imagine that you *did not* read the whole paragraph to answer this question. You might select answer choice (A) because "They have" *sounds* correct. But remember, *Do Not Trust Your Ear*. Answer choice (A) is actually incorrect.

Instead, you should *Read The Whole Paragraph* before selecting an answer. By reading the first sentence, you will have the necessary context that the subject is "committee." Therefore, the pronoun in the second sentence must refer back to "committee." A "committee" is a thing (not a person). The correct pronoun to refer to a "committee" is "it." "It" is a singular pronoun that requires the singular verb "has." Therefore, the correct answer is (C).

Read The Whole Paragraph to ensure you have the full context necessary to answer SAT Writing questions correctly.

Prep Expert
Writing Strategies

PREP EXPERT PRACTICE

Try applying this *Prep Expert Strategy* yourself to the following SAT practice questions:

5

In 1952, renowned British sculptor Henry Moore created two monumental sculptures: *Reclining Figure* and *King and Queen*. In 2018, _____ displayed at the Tate Modern gallery alongside several other works from Moore's prolific career.

Which choice completes the text so that it conforms to the conventions of Standard English?

A) it was
B) they were
C) this was
D) some were

6

In January 1965, Bob Dylan reached the pinnacle of his career as a folk singer-songwriter when he performed at the prestigious Newport Folk Festival. The audience was captivated by his poignant lyrics and unique vocal style. _____ Dylan decided to shift gears and explore a new musical direction that would surprise and challenge his fans.

Which choice completes the text with the most logical transition?

A) In addition,
B) Consequently,
C) In contrast,
D) Nevertheless,

The answers to these SAT practice questions can be found in the back of this book.

PREP EXPERT REVIEW

Key Takeaways

- **Prep Expert Writing Strategy #3—*Read The Whole Paragraph*:** For SAT Writing Questions, it is crucial to read the entire paragraph—not just the sentence with the blank—to understand the necessary context to answer questions correctly.

- **Avoid skimming:** If you skip reading the larger paragraph to save time on SAT Writing questions, this will lead to increased errors. Why? You will not have the full context necessary to answer every SAT Writing question correctly.

- **Context clues**: The surrounding sentences often provide helpful clues to answer fill-in-the-blank SAT Writing questions correctly.

- **Systematic approach**: Adopt a systematic approach by reading the whole paragraph before attempting to answer a grammar question. This method ensures you have all of the necessary context clues to help you select the correct answer.

PREPEXPERT

WRITING STRATEGY #4
IGNORE PREPOSITIONS

PREP EXPERT STRATEGY

Ignore Prepositions to effectively identify grammar errors. This *Prep Expert Writing Strategy* is crucial on the SAT. Use it to maximize your SAT Writing score.

When tackling SAT Writing questions, it is best to *Ignore Prepositions*. It is rare to find grammar errors in prepositional phrases. By ignoring prepositional phrases, we can more easily identify grammatical errors.

Typically, prepositional phrases in SAT questions only distract students from identifying grammar errors. To avoid being distracted from our task of identifying grammatical errors, we should ignore prepositional phrases.

To find writing errors, focus on the simplified sentence without prepositional phrases. Ignore prepositional phrases on SAT Writing questions to find grammatical errors more easily.

What Types of Grammatical Errors Become Easier to Spot When You Ignore Prepositions?

- Singular-plural mismatch errors (most common)
- Pronoun errors

Prep Expert Writing Strategies

- Transition errors
- Comparison errors
- Parallelism errors

We will cover all of these error types in more depth as we review the *Prep Expert Writing Strategies*. For now, understand that if you ignore prepositional phrases, it will be easier to find a wide variety of grammatical errors on SAT Writing questions.

Before you can learn how to *Ignore Prepositions*, you must first understand what prepositions are.

What Is the Formal Definition of a Preposition?

A preposition is a word that shows the relationship between subjects, objects, or actions. Prepositions can indicate a variety of relationships, such as these:

- Location
- Direction
- Time
- Manner
- Cause

Examples of common prepositions include these:

- In
- At
- To
- From
- With
- About
- Through
- Of

For instance, in the sentence "I am going to the store," the word "to" is a preposition indicating the direction of the action.

What Is the Informal Definition of a Preposition?

You can also remember what prepositions are by thinking about them as anything a squirrel can do with a log.

- **Above**: A squirrel can climb *above* a log.
- **Around**: A squirrel can run *around* a log.
- **Beside**: A squirrel can sit *beside* a log.
- **Inside**: A squirrel can hide *inside* a hollow log.

- **On**: A squirrel can sit *on* top of a log.
- **Under**: A squirrel can hide *under* a log.

These are just a few examples. Of course, there are many prepositions that cannot relate a squirrel to a log. But hopefully, these examples give you an idea of how prepositions can be used to describe the relationship between subjects, objects, and actions.

Here are some of the most common prepositions that appear on the SAT:

about	among	below	down	into
above	around	beneath	during	of
across	as	beside	for	off
after	at	between	from	on
against	before	beyond	in	onto
amid	behind	by	inside	out

You do not need to memorize this table, but this should give you a good idea of what prepositions are.

What Are Nonessential Appositives?

You should also *Ignore Nonessential Appositives*. An appositive is a noun or noun phrase that renames or explains another noun. It comes right after the noun in a sentence.

A "nonessential" appositive is not required to understand the meaning of a sentence. If you remove nonessential appositives, the sentence will maintain the same meaning.

Here is an example of a nonessential appositive:

My best friend, **a teacher at a local school**, invited me to her classroom.

In the sentence above, the phrase "a teacher at a local school" is not necessary. On the SAT, you should ignore this nonessential appositive and read it as follows:

My best friend invited me to her classroom.

When you ignore unnecessary appositives, sentences become much simpler.

By ignoring prepositional phrases and nonessential appositives, we can easily identify grammatical errors. When answering SAT Writing questions, focus on important details and ignore nonessential information to identify grammatical errors more quickly.

Ignore Prepositions to maximize your SAT Writing score.

PREP EXPERT EXAMPLE

Consider the following *Prep Expert Example*:

Original sentence: The sharp teeth, each longer than most people's fingers, of the ferocious lion is a threat to other animals.

In the sentence above, ignore the prepositions "of the ferocious lion" and "to other animals."

In addition, ignore the nonessential appositive "each longer than most people's fingers." The simplified sentence will then read as follows:

Simplified sentence: The sharp teeth **is** a threat.

When we ignore prepositions and unnecessary appositives, the sentence becomes simpler. This makes it easier to identify the singular-plural mismatch error in this sentence. The plural subject "teeth" is paired incorrectly with the singular verb "is." The corrected sentence should read as follows:

Corrected sentence: The sharp teeth **are** a threat.

The original sentence was long and convoluted due to prepositional phrases and a nonessential appositive. This made it difficult to spot the grammatical error. Ignoring prepositions and unnecessary appositives makes the grammatical error in the sentence much easier to identify.

Prep Expert
Writing Strategies

PREP EXPERT PRACTICE

Try applying this *Prep Expert Strategy* yourself to the following SAT practice questions:

<table>
<tr><td>

7

Archaeologists studying the ancient Egyptian pyramids, the monumental structures built as tombs for the country's pharaohs, were amazed to find that the arrangement of the pyramids, like the arrangement of the stars in Orion's belt, _____ identical.

Which choice completes the text so that it conforms to the conventions of Standard English?

A) are
B) is
C) were
D) have been

</td><td>

8

In Yellowstone National Park, the renowned Old Faithful geyser spews hot water and steam into the air periodically. Rhythmic eruptions from this _____ tourists from all over the world.

Which choice completes the text so that it conforms to the conventions of Standard English?

A) parks feature attract
B) park's feature attracts
C) park's feature attract
D) parks' feature attracts

</td></tr>
</table>

The answers to these SAT practice questions can be found in the back of this book.

PREP EXPERT REVIEW

Key Takeaways

- **Prep Expert Writing Strategy #4—*Ignore Prepositions*:** To effectively identify grammar errors, *Ignore Prepositions* on SAT Writing questions.

- **Definition of prepositions:** Prepositions are words that indicate relationships between words in sentences.

- **Types of grammatical errors:** When you *Ignore Prepositions*, it becomes easier to spot grammar errors, such as singular-plural mismatch errors, pronoun errors, transition errors, comparison errors, and parallelism errors.

- **Nonessential appositives**: Nonessential appositives are unnecessary to understand the meanings of sentences, so you should also ignore them while searching for grammar errors.

- **Simplify to identify errors more easily**: Ignoring prepositions and nonessential appositives simplifies sentences. This makes it easier to identify various grammatical errors, especially singular-plural mismatch errors.

Prep Expert
Writing Strategies

PREPEXPERT

WRITING STRATEGY #5

AVOID SINGULAR-PLURAL MISMATCHES

PREP EXPERT STRATEGY

As a basic grammatical rule, subjects and verbs must agree in number. A singular-plural mismatch error occurs when the subject and the verb in a sentence do not agree in number. This is a common error on SAT Writing questions.

A singular subject must be paired with a singular verb, and a plural subject must be paired with a plural verb. On SAT Writing questions, you must ask yourself, *Is the subject singular or plural?* Then ask, *Is the verb singular or plural?* Make sure that the subject and the verb agree in number.

How to Differentiate between Singular and Plural Verbs

Singular verbs usually end in *-s* or *-es*. Here are some examples:

- He **walks** to school.
- She **runs** in the park.
- He **plays** basketball.
- The dog **barks** at the mailman.

Plural verbs usually **do not** end in *-s* or *-es*. Here are some examples:

- They **walk** to school.
- We **run** in the park.
- He and his friends **play** basketball.
- The dogs **bark** at the mailman.

There are some exceptions in English verb conjugation, but these are good rules of thumb.

Ignore Prepositions to Easily Identify Singular-Plural Mismatches

SAT test-question writers often make singular-plural mismatch errors difficult to spot by using prepositional phrases to separate the subject from its associated verb.

Ignoring prepositions between the subject and verb can help you focus on the essential elements of the sentence. This makes it easier to identify disagreement in number between the subject and verb. Prepositions do not affect subject-verb agreement, so ignoring prepositions helps you focus on the subject-verb agreement.

Avoid Singular-Plural Mismatches to maximize your SAT Writing score.

PREP EXPERT EXAMPLE

Consider the following *Prep Expert Example*:

Original sentence: The group of students in the classroom are finishing their assignments.

Try ignoring the prepositional phrase "of students in the classroom." The sentence would then read as follows:

Simplified sentence: The group **are** finishing their assignments.

Ignoring prepositions makes it easy to identify that "group" (a singular subject) is incorrectly paired with "are" (a plural verb). Because "group" is a singular subject, it should be paired with a singular verb like "is."

Corrected sentence: The group **is** finishing their assignments.

Singular-plural mismatch errors are easier to spot when you *Ignore Prepositions* that are separating the subject and verb. This allows you to clearly identify the true subject and true verb in the sentence, and place them next to each other. Remember this strategy when assessing subject-verb agreement.

PREP EXPERT PRACTICE

Try applying this *Prep Expert Strategy* yourself to the following SAT practice questions:

9

In her culinary creations, chef Sarah Nguyen often combines contrasting flavors and textures. Interestingly, the combination of spicy and sweet in her signature dish _____ a harmonious balance of taste.

Which choice completes the text so that it conforms to the conventions of Standard English?

A) are
B) have been
C) were
D) is

10

The traditional Japanese game of Sugoroku, similar to the Western board game Backgammon, involves rolling dice and moving pieces along a board. The objective of the game is to reach the final space before the opponent does. Landing on certain spaces _____ a player to move their piece forward by a specific number of additional spaces.

Which choice completes the text so that it conforms to the conventions of Standard English?

A) enables
B) were enabling
C) has enabled
D) enable

The answers to these SAT practice questions can be found in the back of this book.

PREP EXPERT REVIEW

Key Takeaways

- **Prep Expert Writing Strategy #5—*Avoid Singular-Plural Mismatches*:** Ensure that subjects and verbs match in number to prevent singular-plural mismatch errors.

- **Singular and plural pairing:** Pair singular subjects with singular verbs. Pair plural subjects with plural verbs.

- **Verb characteristics:** Singular verbs often end in -s or -es. Plural verbs usually do not.

- **Ignore prepositions:** Ignoring prepositions helps to highlight the sentence's subject and verb, making it easier to identify singular-plural mismatches.

Prep Expert
Writing Strategies

 **PREP**EXPERT

WRITING STRATEGY #6

PRESERVE PARALLELISM

PREP EXPERT STRATEGY

SAT Writing questions must maintain parallel structure. Parallelism refers to the use of matching structures, forms, or patterns in a sentence. Parallelism makes sentences clearer and more aesthetically pleasing.

Here are a few examples of correct parallel structure:

- **Parallel structure with verbs**: I like to *run*, *swim*, and *bike*.
- **Parallel structure with nouns**: He is not only *my boss*, but also *my mentor*.
- **Parallel structure with adjectives**: She was *tired*, *hungry*, and *thirsty*.

Maintain parallel structure across verbs, nouns, and adjectives on the SAT. In addition, maintain parallel structure across lists, conjunctions, and related sentences.

Preserve Parallelism to maximize your SAT Writing score.

PREP EXPERT EXAMPLE

Consider the following *Prep Expert Examples*.

Parallelism in Lists

SAT Writing questions will sometimes contain lists of items. You must *Preserve Parallelism* in that list.

> *Incorrect example: My hobbies are **running**, **swimming**, and **to ride my bike**.*
> *Correct example: My hobbies are **running**, **swimming**, and **biking**.*

Parallelism across Conjunctions

SAT Writing questions may contain conjunctions. You must *Preserve Parallelism* across those conjunctions.

> *Incorrect example: She likes to **dance** salsa and **cooking** Italian food.*
> *Correct example: She likes to **dance** salsa and **cook** Italian food.*

Parallelism across Related Sentences

SAT Writing questions may contain two separate, but related, sentences. You must *Preserve Parallelism* across those sentences.

> *Incorrect example: She likes **playing** basketball. In addition, she enjoys **to watch** football.*
> *Correct example: She likes **playing** basketball. In addition, she enjoys **watching** football.*

PREP EXPERT PRACTICE

Try applying this *Prep Expert Strategy* yourself to the following SAT practice questions:

## 11

Jane Smith, the founder of an environmental organization, developed a groundbreaking recycling program in 2012 and a solar energy initiative in _____.

Which choice completes the text so that it conforms to the conventions of Standard English?

A) 2014: which led to significant energy savings

B) 2014, this led to significant energy savings

C) 2014, which led, to significant energy savings

D) 2014; this led to significant energy savings

## 12

In order to prevent soil erosion and improve the overall soil structure, agronomist Maya Gupta has proposed that a system of contour farming be implemented in the hilly regions of the country. This farming method would slow down water runoff and _____ a natural barrier that would prevent soil from being washed away.

Which choice completes the text so that it conforms to the conventions of Standard English?

A) creates

B) create

C) creating

D) created

The answers to these SAT practice questions can be found in the back of this book.

PREP EXPERT REVIEW

Key Takeaways

- **Prep Expert Writing Strategy #6—*Preserve Parallelism*:** Ensure parallel structure in sentences for clarity on SAT Writing questions.

- **Application:** Maintain parallelism across different sentence elements such as verbs, nouns, and adjectives.

- **Sentence elements:** Preserve parallelism in varied contexts, such as lists, conjunctions, and related sentences.

- **Benefits:** Consistent use of parallel structure will increase your SAT Writing score and improve your writing in general.

PREPEXPERT

WRITING STRATEGY #7

MAINTAIN VERB TENSE AGREEMENT

PREP EXPERT STRATEGY

Verb tenses must agree on SAT Writing questions. Verb tense disagreement occurs when the verb tense used in a sentence does not match the tense used in the rest of the sentence or the intended meaning. Keep verb tenses consistent within sentences on the SAT Writing section.

Verb Tense Names

There are many verb tenses used to indicate the time or duration of an action. For example, there are simple verb tenses like the present, past, and future tenses. There are also complex verb tenses such as the perfect, progressive, and continuous tenses.

Do not get caught up in learning the names of different verb tenses. For example, it is not important to know what the "perfect continuous" tense is for the SAT. Trying to memorize tense names will not add many (if any) points to your SAT score.

Prep Expert used to teach all the different tenses that you might see on the SAT. We would teach students all about the present tense, past tense, future tense, perfect tense, progressive tense, continuous tense, and perfect continuous tense. However,

Prep Expert
Writing Strategies

---

many students would get confused by all of the different tenses. It is not important to know the names of the tenses because the SAT will never ask you for the name of a particular verb tense. Instead, focus on keeping verb tenses consistent within sentences and paragraphs.

Maintain Verb Tense Agreement to maximize your SAT Writing score.

PREP EXPERT EXAMPLE

Consider the following *Prep Expert Examples*.

> *Incorrect example*: I **am studying** for my test **yesterday**.
> *Correct example*: I **studied** for my test **yesterday**.

The above sentence contains a disagreement in verb tense because "am studying" is in the present continuous tense, but "yesterday" indicates a past time. The sentence should be rewritten so that the verb tense is maintained within the context of the sentence.

> *Incorrect example*: **By next year, I am graduating** from college.
> *Correct example*: **By next year, I will have graduated** from college.

The above sentence contains a disagreement in verb tense because "am graduating" is in the present continuous tense, but "by next year" indicates a future time. The sentence should be rewritten so that the verb tense is maintained within the context of the sentence.

> *Incorrect example*: They **had eaten** dinner when we **arrive**.
> *Correct example*: They **had eaten** dinner when we **arrived**.

The above sentence contains a disagreement in verb tense because "arrive" is in the present tense, but "had eaten" indicates a past time. The sentence should be rewritten so that the verb tense is maintained within the context of the sentence.

Using simple logic like the above to deduce the correct verb tense can improve your SAT Writing score significantly.

PREP EXPERT PRACTICE

Try applying this *Prep Expert Strategy* yourself to the following SAT practice questions:

13

When creating her debut album, the singer-songwriter drew on her own experiences growing up in a small town. The critically acclaimed album is her first solo project, but her music _____ recognized in previous collaborations. Early in her career, she collaborated with renowned artists and received industry recognition for her contributions.

Which choice completes the text so that it conforms to the conventions of Standard English?

A) were

B) have been

C) has been

D) are

14

In her groundbreaking research on the structure of DNA, scientist Rosalind Franklin captured X-ray diffraction images that provided key insights into its helical nature. Today, Franklin _____ credited as a crucial contributor to the discovery of the DNA double helix.

Which choice completes the text so that it conforms to the conventions of Standard English?

A) will be

B) had been

C) was

D) is

The answers to these SAT practice questions can be found in the back of this book.

PREP EXPERT REVIEW

Key Takeaways

- **Prep Expert Writing Strategy #7—*Maintain Verb Tense Agreement***: On SAT Writing questions, ensure verb tenses are consistent within sentences to avoid disagreement and convey accurate meanings.

- **Variety of verb tenses**: Be aware of different verb tenses, like simple (present, past, future) and complex (perfect, progressive, continuous) tenses. However, focus more on their correct application than on their specific names.

Prep Expert
Writing Strategies

- **Disregard tense names**: Knowing the names of tenses (e.g., "perfect continuous") is not crucial for the SAT because questions will not ask for tense identification.

- **Consistency and logic**: Prioritize maintaining consistent verb tenses within sentences and paragraphs to optimize your SAT Writing score.

- **Practical application**: Apply simple logical reasoning, like ensuring temporal coherence, to improve your performance on verb tense SAT Writing questions.

PREPEXPERT

WRITING STRATEGY #8

CHECK PRONOUN PRECISION

Prep Expert
Writing Strategies

PREP EXPERT STRATEGY

Let's discuss the types of pronoun errors you may encounter on the SAT.

What Is a Pronoun?

A pronoun takes the place of a noun (or pronoun) mentioned earlier in a sentence.

   Pronoun errors occur when the pronoun does not match the noun in number, gender, or case. When answering SAT Writing questions, be sure to use pronouns that refer to their antecedent nouns.

Common Pronouns

he	him	it	our	they	we
her	I	me	she	us	you

   You don't have to memorize the list above, but it can help you understand which pronouns may be incorrect on SAT Writing questions.

Why Are Pronoun Errors Often Difficult to Spot?

In everyday language, most of us misuse pronouns all the time. For example, we might be talking about the author of a book and later refer to that author as "they." Of course, you should not refer to a singular "author" with the plural pronoun "they."

While misusing pronouns in everyday language is not a big deal, making this mistake on the SAT can cost you. When you come across a pronoun on an SAT Writing question, make sure it clearly refers to one and only one noun in the sentence.

Check Pronoun Precision to maximize your SAT Writing score.

PREP EXPERT EXAMPLE

Consider the following *Prep Expert Examples*.

Pronoun Error: Singular-Plural Pronouns

If a noun in a sentence is singular, the pronoun replacing it should also be singular. If a noun in a sentence is plural, the pronoun replacing it should also be plural.

> *Incorrect example: Jake and Andre want to become **a lawyer** when they grow up.*
> *Correct example: Jake and Andre want to become **lawyers** when they grow up.*

The noun phrase "Jake and Andre" is plural. Therefore, the pronoun, "a lawyer," should be plural as well and changed to "lawyers." Notably, "a lawyer" is not actually a pronoun in this example, but rather a noun phrase. Nevertheless, the same singular-plural principle applies to both pronouns and noun phrases.

Pronoun Error: Lost Pronouns

An SAT question may present a pronoun that does not refer to anything in the sentence. If this is the case, then rewrite the sentence so the pronoun refers to one noun. Or remove the pronoun altogether.

> *Incorrect example: **It** was bittersweet to see Courtney graduate.*
> *Correct example: Seeing Courtney graduate was bittersweet.*

The pronoun "it" does not refer to any noun in the sentence. Be cautious when you encounter "it" on the SAT. It is frequently a lost or an ambiguous pronoun with no clear reference. Make sure to double check!

Pronoun Error: Relative Pronouns

Relative pronouns add more information about a noun in specific contexts in sentences. The most common relative pronouns are "who/whom/whose," "when," "where," and "which."

Who/Whom/Whose	Must refer to people • **Who**: Use when you would use "he" • **Whom**: Use when you would use "him" • **Whose**: Use to indicate possession
When	Must refer to time
Where	Must refer to geographic locations • **Whereby**: This means "by which" and does not refer to geographic locations
Which	Must refer to inanimate objects

*Incorrect example: Remember the time **where** we played video games all night long?*

*Correct example: Remember the time **when** we played video games all night long?*

The above example refers to time. Instead of using the relative pronoun "where" that refers to geographic locations, use the relative pronoun "when" that refers to time.

Pronoun Error: Subject versus Object Pronouns

A subject pronoun actively completes the action of a verb. An object pronoun passively receives the action of a verb. Ask yourself whether a pronoun is doing or receiving the action in a sentence.

To tell subject and object pronouns apart, ask yourself whether a pronoun can fly a kite:

Subject Pronoun: A subject pronoun is any pronoun that can fly a kite.	[**Insert subject pronoun**] can fly a kite.
Object Pronoun: An object pronoun is any pronoun that a kite can be flown by.	A kite can be flown by [**insert object pronoun**].

Incorrect example: **Me** *can fly a kite.*
Correct example: **I** *can fly a kite.*

In the above example, the object pronoun "me" is used incorrectly. The pronoun is actively doing the action of flying a kite, so the sentence needs a subject pronoun. In this case, the correct pronoun should be the subject pronoun "I."

Here is a quick reference table of subject versus object pronouns.

Subject Pronouns	Object Pronouns	Subject Pronouns	Object Pronouns
I	me	it	it
you	you	we	us
he	him	they	them
she	her		

Pronoun Error: Ambiguous Pronouns

SAT questions will often be unclear about what or whom a particular pronoun is referring to. In other words, the noun that the pronoun is referring to is ambiguous. This is also the most common way we misuse pronouns in everyday language.

*Incorrect example: Mark and Michael were both excited to compete in the basketball tournament, but **he** was certainly the better player.*
*Correct example: Mark and Michael were both excited to compete in the basketball tournament, but **Michael** was certainly the better player.*

The pronoun "he" is ambiguous because it is unclear whether "he" is referring to "Mark" or "Michael." The sentence should be rewritten to remove this ambiguity.

PREP EXPERT PRACTICE

Try applying this *Prep Expert Strategy* yourself to the following SAT practice questions:

## 15

The early 20th-century German automobile engineer Ferdinand Porsche is renowned for designing some of the most iconic cars in history. In order to improve performance, Porsche rethought the arrangement of a traditional car engine, positioning it at the rear of the vehicle and making _____ more balanced overall.

Which choice completes the text so that it conforms to the conventions of Standard English?

A) those
B) one
C) them
D) it

## 16

Many ants, especially those belonging to the genus *Formica*, are known for their ability to carry objects that are many times their own weight. Ants accomplish this feat by using their strong mandibles and by having a powerful exoskeleton that can support _____ during transportation.

Which choice correctly completes the sentence and conforms to the conventions of Standard English?

A) they
B) one
C) it
D) themselves

The answers to these SAT practice questions can be found in the back of this book.

PREP EXPERT REVIEW

Key Takeaways

- **Prep Expert Writing Strategy #8—*Check Pronoun Precision*:** Pronoun errors happen when the pronoun does not match the noun in number, gender, or case.

- **Types of SAT pronoun errors:**
  - **Singular-plural pronouns:** Ensure that the pronoun's number (singular/plural) matches the noun it is replacing.
  - **Lost pronouns:** Every pronoun should have a clear, identifiable noun it refers to.
  - **Relative pronouns:** Use appropriate relative pronouns based on the context (e.g., "who" for people, "when" for time, "where" for place, etc.).

- **Subject versus object pronouns**: Subject pronouns perform an action, while object pronouns receive the action.
- **Ambiguous pronouns**: Ensure that the pronoun's reference is clear and not ambiguous.

- **Identifying pronoun errors**: Using pronouns incorrectly is common in everyday language. But it is important to find and fix these pronoun mistakes on the SAT to achieve the highest score possible.

WRITING STRATEGY #9

USE ACCURATE POSSESSIVES

PREP EXPERT STRATEGY

The Digital SAT tests possessive errors more frequently than the old paper-based SAT did. Therefore, it is crucial to thoroughly understand possessives and how they may appear on the Digital SAT Writing questions.

Possessives

A possessive is a grammatical construction used to indicate that one noun or pronoun belongs to another noun or pronoun. To show ownership, add an apostrophe (') and the letter "s" to a singular noun. For plural nouns that end in "s," simply add an apostrophe (') at the end.

Possessive Pronouns

A possessive pronoun is a type of pronoun that shows ownership. Unlike many other possessives, possessive pronouns typically do not have an apostrophe. Common possessive pronouns are "mine," "yours," "his," "hers," "its," "ours," and "theirs." A possessive pronoun typically replaces a noun in a sentence.

Prep Expert
Writing Strategies

Possessive Adjectives

A possessive adjective is a type of adjective that shows ownership and describes a noun. Common possessive adjectives are "my," "your," "his," "her," "its," "our," and "their." Like possessive pronouns, possessive adjectives typically do not contain an apostrophe. Unlike possessive pronouns, possessive adjectives do not replace nouns—they describe them.

Contractions

Possessives and contractions both use an apostrophe, but they have different grammatical functions. A contraction is formed when two words are combined into one using an apostrophe.

Use Accurate Possessives to maximize your SAT Writing score.

PREP EXPERT EXAMPLE

Consider the following *Prep Expert Examples*.

Possessive Examples

> *Singular possessive: The **dog's** collar*
> *Plural possessive (for a noun that ends in "s"): The **teachers'** lounge*

Possessive Pronoun Examples

> *Possessive pronoun ("mine" shows ownership of the noun "book"): This book is **mine**.*
> *Possessive pronoun ("hers" shows ownership of the noun "coat"): The coat is **hers**.*

Possessive Adjective Examples

> *Possessive adjective ("his" describes the noun "car"): **His** car is parked in the garage.*
> *Possessive adjective ("king's" describes the noun "palace"): The **king's** palace is grand.*

Expert tip: There is no "king" in the sentence above. Therefore, if the SAT test-question writers put the pronoun "he" later on in the sentence, it would be incorrect. Why?

Because the pronoun "he" must refer to a person (i.e., a noun), and "king's" is not a person. Instead, "king's" is simply a possessive adjective that describes the noun "palace."

Contraction Examples

I'll = I will   *can't = cannot*   *you're = you are*

Possessives versus Contractions

The table below shows possessives and contractions that commonly cause confusion on the Digital SAT. These words sound similar but have different meanings. Make sure you know the difference.

Possessive	Contraction	Possessive	Contraction
its	it's	their	they're
your	you're	whose	who's

PREP EXPERT PRACTICE

Try applying this *Prep Expert Strategy* yourself to the following SAT practice questions:

17

In her award-winning documentary *Voices of the Ocean*, filmmaker Maria Thompson explores the hidden world beneath the waves, weaving together scientific findings, personal interviews, and breathtaking footage to reveal the _____ that inhabit the deep sea.

Which choice completes the text so that it conforms to the conventions of Standard English?

A) mysteries; of the creatures
B) mystery's of the creatures
C) mysteries of the creatures
D) mysteries' of the creature's

18

The Wright brothers are often credited with inventing the first airplane, but _____ invention was actually the result of years of work by many pioneers in aviation.

Which choice completes the text so that it conforms to the conventions of Standard English?

A) they're
B) its
C) their
D) it's

The answers to these SAT practice questions can be found in the back of this book.

PREP EXPERT REVIEW

Key Takeaways

- **Prep Expert Writing Strategy #9—*Use Accurate Possessives***: The Digital SAT emphasizes possessive errors more than previous paper-based versions of the SAT.

- **Possessive formation**: Possessives are formed with an apostrophe ('s) to indicate ownership.

- **Possessive pronouns**: Possessive pronouns (e.g., "mine," "yours") lack apostrophes and *replace nouns*.

- **Possessive adjectives**: Possessive adjectives (e.g., "my," "your") also lack apostrophes and *describe nouns*.

- **Contractions**: Contractions use apostrophes to shorten phrases and combine them into one word (e.g., "I'll" for "I will").

- **Differentiating possessives and contractions**: Possessives (e.g., "its," "your") and contractions (e.g., "it's," "you're") may sound similar, but they have different functions and meanings. It is important to differentiate between the two on SAT Writing questions.

 **PREP**EXPERT

WRITING STRATEGY #10

COMPARE CORRECTLY

On the SAT, comparison errors occur when comparisons are inconsistent in their construction. Using clear and precise language is important to avoid incorrect comparisons. Make sure to use the correct forms of comparison. Always compare things that are similar enough to be comparable.

Comparison Error: Double Comparatives

Comparatives are used to compare two things. Comparatives usually end in "-er" or use the word "more." The most common type of comparative error occurs when the SAT uses two comparatives together (i.e., "double comparatives").

This comparison error occurs when a sentence uses both "more" and the "-er" suffix for the same adjective—for example, saying "more taller" instead of "taller" or "more faster" instead of "faster."

Comparison Error: Double Superlatives

Superlatives are used to compare three or more things. Superlatives usually end in "-est" or use the word "most." The most common type of comparison error related to superlatives occurs when the SAT uses two superlatives together (i.e., "double superlatives").

Prep Expert
Writing Strategies

This comparison error occurs when a sentence uses both "most" and the "-est" suffix for the same adjective—for example, saying "most tallest" instead of "tallest" or "most fastest" instead of "fastest."

Comparison Error: Unequal Comparisons

This comparison error occurs when a sentence compares things that are not comparable. For example, you cannot compare a person to an action.

Comparison Error: Misplaced Modifiers

This comparison error occurs when a sentence places a modifier in the wrong part of the sentence, leading to ambiguity in the comparison. We will go over this comparison error in more detail in the *Prep Expert Writing Strategy #14—Modify Appropriately*.

Compare Correctly to maximize your SAT Writing score.

PREP EXPERT EXAMPLE

Consider the following *Prep Expert Examples*.

Comparison Error: Double Comparatives

*Incorrect example: She is **more smarter** than her brother.*
*Correct example: She is **smarter** than her brother.*

You cannot use two comparatives together in comparisons.

Comparison Error: Double Superlatives

*Incorrect example: That was the **most easiest** test I've ever taken.*
*Correct example: That was the **easiest** test I've ever taken.*

You cannot use two superlatives together in comparisons.

Comparison Error: Unequal Comparisons

*Incorrect example: My new phone's **speed** is faster than my friend's **phone**.*
*Correct example: My new phone's **speed** is faster than my friend's phone's*
*   **speed**.*

You cannot compare an adjective ("speed") to a noun ("phone").

Comparison Error: Misplaced Modifiers

*Incorrect example: Like many famous **musicians**, Adele's **vocal talents** far surpass most people.*

*Correct example: Like many famous **musicians**, **Adele** has vocal talents that far surpass the vocal talents of most people.*

You cannot compare "musicians" to "vocal talents."

PREP EXPERT PRACTICE

Try applying this *Prep Expert Strategy* yourself to the following SAT practice questions:

19

Famed architect Sarah Whitman was renowned for her innovative designs that blended functionality with art. Recognized in 2015 as one of the most influential architectural achievements of the decade, _____ became a symbol of modern urban planning.

Which choice completes the text so that it conforms to the conventions of Standard English?

A) Whitman's creation of the Skylight Tower
B) the Skylight Tower was created by Whitman
C) in 2015 Whitman created the Skylight Tower, and it
D) the Skylight Tower; Whitman's creation

20

In 2020, botanist Dr. Emily Harris pioneered the use of a new plant grafting technique that increased crop yields without the use of chemicals. By enhancing the natural resilience of the plants, _____

Which choice completes the text so that it conforms to the conventions of Standard English?

A) the technique's success in boosting harvests and reducing dependency on pesticides has been demonstrated.

B) the technique has successfully boosted harvests and reduced dependency on pesticides.

C) both the harvests boosting and dependency on pesticides reducing have been demonstrated by the technique.

D) the boosting of harvests and the reducing of dependency on pesticides have been the technique's success.

Prep Expert
Writing Strategies

The answers to these SAT practice questions can be found in the back of this book.

PREP EXPERT REVIEW

Key Takeaways

- **Prep Expert Writing Strategy #10—*Compare Correctly***: Comparison errors on the SAT can occur when there are inconsistencies in the construction of comparisons.

- **Avoiding errors**: To avoid comparison errors, it is essential to use clear and precise language, employ correct comparative and superlative forms, and ensure that the things being compared are equal or comparable.

- **Common errors**: Common comparison errors include double comparatives (using "more" and the "-er" suffix together), double superlatives (using "most" and the "-est" suffix together), unequal comparisons (comparing incomparable things), and misplaced modifiers.

PREPEXPERT

WRITING STRATEGY #11

USE LOGICAL TRANSITIONS

PREP EXPERT STRATEGY

Many transition errors appear on SAT Writing questions. Therefore, you must understand this *Prep Expert Strategy* in depth.

What Is a Transition?

Transitions are words or phrases that connect ideas or sentences, making them flow smoothly. Transitions can show changes in topics, add details, compare or contrast, emphasize a point, or show the order of events.

Transition Questions

It is crucial to know how to use logical transitions because each SAT Reading and Writing module contains 2 to 5 *Transitions* questions. See the example below:

| 23 | 🔖 Mark for Review | | ABC |

Which choice completes the text with the most logical transition?

Prep Expert
Writing Strategies

Most Common Transitions That Appear on the SAT

additionally	despite	however	likewise	nonetheless
although	finally	in conclusion	meanwhile	similarly
as a result	furthermore	in contrast	moreover	therefore
consequently	hence	in summary	nevertheless	thus

You do not need to memorize the above list. But hopefully it gives you a good idea of the types of transitions that appear on SAT Writing questions.

Transition Errors

Transition errors can happen on the SAT when there is unclear or disorganized writing. These errors arise from missing or incorrect transitions between sentences or ideas. Transition mistakes can make writing hard to understand.

What Is a Conjunction?

A conjunction is a word that connects words, phrases, or clauses within a sentence. Conjunctions are used to join two or more ideas, thoughts, or actions.

Conjunction Errors

Conjunction errors on the SAT can occur when the conjunction is used incorrectly. This can diminish the clarity and meaning of a sentence. To avoid conjunction errors, use the appropriate conjunction for the context.

What Is the Difference between a Conjunction and a Transition?

While both conjunctions and transitions are types of linking words, they have different functions and uses.

- A **conjunction** is a word that is used to connect two or more words, phrases, or clauses to create a complete sentence (**one sentence**).

    versus

- A **transition** connects two or more sentences or ideas to create coherence and flow in a text (**two or more sentences**).

The same word can be both a conjunction and a transition (e.g., "although"). *Use Logical Transitions* to maximize your SAT Writing score.

PREP EXPERT EXAMPLE

Consider the following *Prep Expert Examples*.

Transition Error: Incorrect Transitions

Using the wrong transition leads to confusion and lack of coherence. For example, using "in conclusion" to introduce a new idea instead of concluding an argument can cause a transition error.

> *Incorrect example: She wanted to go to the park.* **As a result**, *she went to the movies.*
> *Correct example: She wanted to go to the park.* **However**, *she went to the movies instead.*

"As a result" is the incorrect transition in this example.

Transition Error: Flow of Ideas in Paragraphs

Using logical transitions is important for creating a smooth flow of ideas between sentences in a larger paragraph. Therefore, *Prep Expert Writing Strategy #3—Read the Whole Paragraph* is particularly important when answering *Transitions* questions. To answer these questions correctly, you need to understand how ideas flow from one sentence to the next.

> *Incorrect example: I am interested in pursuing a career in journalism. I have always enjoyed writing and researching.* **In conclusion**, *I am also interested in learning about international cultures and languages.*
> *Correct example: I am interested in pursuing a career in journalism. I have always enjoyed writing and researching.* **Additionally**, *I am also interested in learning about international cultures and languages.*

"In conclusion" is the incorrect transition for the flow of ideas between sentences in this paragraph.

Conjunction Error: Incorrect Conjunctions

Conjunctions join clauses, but they must be used correctly to avoid errors. For example, using "and" instead of "but" in a sentence that presents two contrasting ideas can create confusion.

> *Incorrect example: Cheryl was exhausted at mile twenty,* **and** *she continued running to finish the marathon.*
>
> *Correct example: Cheryl was exhausted at mile twenty,* **but** *she continued running to finish the marathon.*

"And" is the incorrect conjunction in this example.

Conjunction Error: Missing Conjunctions

This occurs when a sentence requires a conjunction to link two ideas, but the conjunction is missing altogether.

> *Incorrect example: I went to the store, bought some groceries.*
>
> *Correct example: I went to the store* **and** *bought some groceries.*

"And" is the missing conjunction in this example.

Conjunction Error: Correlative Conjunctions

Correlative conjunctions are used in pairs to join words or phrases, and they must always be paired together on the SAT. The most common correlative conjunctions on the SAT are:

- "both...and"
- "either...or"
- "neither...nor"
- "not only...but also"
- "not just...but also"
- "whether...or"

> *Incorrect example:* **Not only** *did she finish her project,* **but** *she presented it in class.*
>
> *Correct example:* **Not only** *did she finish her project,* **but** *she* **also** *presented it in class.*

"Not only" is part of a correlative conjunction that must be paired with "but also" later in the sentence.

Conjunction Error: Redundant Conjunctions

Using two conjunctions to connect phrases can create redundancy and make a sentence awkward. Common redundant conjunctions include these:

"BUT YET" OR "BUT STILL"

*Incorrect example: I wanted to go, **but yet** I couldn't.*
*Correct example: I wanted to go, **but** I couldn't.*

"AND ALSO"

*Incorrect example: She brought chips **and also** salsa.*
*Correct example: She brought chips **and** salsa.*

"OR ELSE"

*Incorrect example: You need to study, **or else** you will fail.*
*Correct example: You need to study, **or** you will fail.*

"BECAUSE SINCE"

*Incorrect example: I didn't go **because since** it rained.*
*Correct example: I didn't go **because** it rained.*

PREP EXPERT PRACTICE

Try applying this Prep Expert Strategy yourself to the following SAT practice questions:

## 21

Renowned musician Bob Dylan released his critically acclaimed album *Highway 61 Revisited* in 1965, featuring iconic songs such as "Like a Rolling Stone" and "Desolation Row." _____, Dylan followed up with *Blonde on Blonde* in 1966, which further solidified his status as a musical legend.

Which choice completes the text with the most logical transition?

A) On the other hand

B) As a result

C) In contrast

D) Furthermore

## 22

Plants have developed various mechanisms to cope with harsh environmental conditions. Some desert plants, _____, have evolved the ability to store water in their fleshy leaves and stems to survive in arid regions.

Which choice completes the text with the most logical transition?

A) on the other hand

B) similarly

C) in fact

D) for instance

The answers to these SAT practice questions can be found in the back of this book.

PREP EXPERT REVIEW

Key Takeaways

- **Prep Expert Writing Strategy #11—*Use Logical Transitions***: Transitions are words or phrases that connect ideas or sentences, ensuring a smooth flow. They are vital for showing changes in topics and for detailing, contrasting, emphasizing, and illustrating the sequence of events.

- **SAT Transitions questions**: Each SAT Reading and Writing module contains 2 to 5 *Transitions* questions. It is essential to use logical transitions to avoid unclear or disorganized writing.

- **Transition errors**: Using incorrect transitions can lead to confusion. For instance, "in conclusion" should not introduce new ideas, but rather should conclude paragraphs.

- **Conjunction errors**: Conjunction errors include the use of incorrect conjunctions, missing conjunctions, correlative conjunctions, and redundant conjunctions.

- **Conjunctions versus transitions**: Conjunctions connect elements within a single sentence, while transitions connect multiple sentences.

PREPEXPERT

WRITING STRATEGY #12

READ THE STUDENT'S GOAL FIRST ON NOTES QUESTIONS

PREP EXPERT STRATEGY

What Are* Notes *Questions?

The last few questions on SAT Reading and Writing modules are typically questions that present a student's notes. You must use relevant information from these notes to answer the questions.

The College Board refers to these questions as *Rhetorical Synthesis* questions. At Prep Expert, we keep it simple and refer to these questions as *Notes* questions. These questions test your ability to selectively integrate information from bullet points to achieve a specific writing goal.

The Structure of a Notes Question

While studying a famous musician, a student has taken the following notes:

- Ella Fitzgerald is a renowned jazz vocalist.

- She is often referred to as the "First Lady of Song."

- Fitzgerald's rendition of "Summertime" is considered one of her signature performances.

- Her album "Ella Fitzgerald Sings the Cole Porter Song Book" is a celebrated collection of jazz standards.

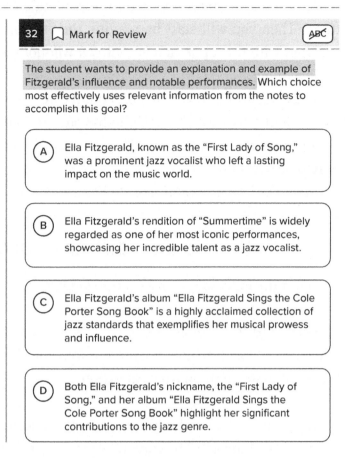

32 ☐ Mark for Review (ABC)

The student wants to provide an explanation and example of Fitzgerald's influence and notable performances. Which choice most effectively uses relevant information from the notes to accomplish this goal?

(A) Ella Fitzgerald, known as the "First Lady of Song," was a prominent jazz vocalist who left a lasting impact on the music world.

(B) Ella Fitzgerald's rendition of "Summertime" is widely regarded as one of her most iconic performances, showcasing her incredible talent as a jazz vocalist.

(C) Ella Fitzgerald's album "Ella Fitzgerald Sings the Cole Porter Song Book" is a highly acclaimed collection of jazz standards that exemplifies her musical prowess and influence.

(D) Both Ella Fitzgerald's nickname, the "First Lady of Song," and her album "Ella Fitzgerald Sings the Cole Porter Song Book" highlight her significant contributions to the jazz genre.

How to Approach Notes Questions

Many students work their way from top to bottom on Notes questions. But this is a flawed approach. Why? Because the key item you need to focus on (the student's goal) is at the bottom. So you should *Read The Student's Goal First*!

Here is the correct approach to Notes Questions:

- **Step 1:** Skip reading the blurb at the top as well as the question near the bottom because these items are almost always the same
- **Step 2:** Read the student's goal first
- **Step 3:** Read the bullet point notes (focusing on the notes that are relevant to the student's goal)
- **Step 4:** Select the answer choice that most effectively achieves the student's goal

Prep Expert
Writing Strategies

Why Read the Student's Goal First on Notes Questions?

What happens if you *do not* read the student's goal as the first item on Notes questions? Then you will start by reading the student's notes in bullet point form. The problem with this approach is that *you will not know which bullet points to focus on while reading.*

You can only know which bullet points are relevant to the student's goal if you read the student's goal *first*! This will help you zero in on which bullet points from the student's notes are most relevant. This method will also help you ignore the bullet points that are irrelevant.

Read The Student's Goal First On Notes Questions to maximize your SAT Writing score.

PREP EXPERT EXAMPLE

Consider the following *Prep Expert Examples.*

Examples of Student Goals

The student's writing goal is different for every Notes question. Here are some examples of student goals on Notes questions:

1. To present something (e.g., research, findings, studies, etc.)
   - *Example*: The student wants to present the study and its findings.

2. To provide an explanation or example (i.e., of a phenomenon, an event, etc.)
   - *Example*: The student wants to provide an explanation and example of _____.

3. To compare differences or similarities between two or more items
   - *Example*: The student wants to compare some characteristics of the two _____.

PREP EXPERT PRACTICE

Try applying this *Prep Expert Strategy* yourself to the following SAT practice questions:

While researching a topic, a student has taken the following notes:

- In the late 19th and early 20th centuries, Nikola Tesla made significant contributions to the development of alternating current (AC) electrical systems.

- Tesla's work laid the foundation for modern AC power systems and helped usher in the Second Industrial Revolution.

- He also conducted pioneering work in wireless communication and electromagnetism.

- The unit of magnetic field strength, the Tesla, is named in his honor.

- Despite his numerous contributions, Tesla died with little money and recognition.

23

The student wants to emphasize the most impactful aspects of Tesla's career. Which choice most effectively uses relevant information from the notes to accomplish this goal?

A) Tesla was a prominent scientist in the late 19th and early 20th centuries.

B) Tesla's work in AC power systems and electromagnetism was crucial to the Second Industrial Revolution.

C) The unit of magnetic field strength is named the Tesla in his honor.

D) Despite his significant contributions, Tesla died with little money and recognition.

While researching a topic, a student has taken the following notes:

- In 2017, paleontologists discovered ancient dog bone fragments in the site of Oberkassel, a German archaeological site.

- The fragments were estimated to be 14,000 years old.

- A genetic analysis of the fragments indicated that these dogs shared similarities with modern dog breeds.

- These genetic similarities provide evidence that the Oberkassel dogs may have been domesticated.

24

The student wants to present the Oberkassel study and its conclusions. Which choice most effectively uses relevant information from the notes to accomplish this goal?

A) In 2017, an exploration of dog domestication led to a genetic study of dog bone fragments discovered in Oberkassel, Germany.

B) A 2017 analysis of dog bone fragments found in Oberkassel, Germany, suggests that dogs there may have been domesticated 14,000 years ago.

C) In 2017, paleontologists studied the genetic lineage of dogs in Oberkassel, Germany, from more than 14,000 years ago.

D) Dog bone fragments estimated to be 14,000 years old were found in Oberkassel, Germany, in 2017.

The answers to these SAT practice questions can be found in the back of this book.

PREP EXPERT REVIEW

Key Takeaways

- **Prep Expert Writing Strategy #12—*Read The Student's Goal First On Notes Questions***: *Rhetorical Synthesis* (or *Notes*) questions on the SAT Reading and Writing modules test students' ability to integrate information from bullet points to achieve a specific writing goal.

- **Optimal approach**: The best way to tackle these questions is to first read the student's goal, then read the bullet point notes, and finally select the answer choice that aligns with the goal.

- **Importance of order**: Reading the student's goal first allows students to identify which bullet points are relevant to focus on.

WRITING STRATEGY #13

PUNCTUATE APPROPRIATELY

PREP EXPERT STRATEGY

What Is Punctuation?

Punctuation marks and symbols clarify sentence meaning and structure. Using punctuation correctly is crucial for clear and effective communication.

Most Common Punctuation That Appears on the SAT

Period (.)	Indicates the end of a sentence or an abbreviation
Comma (,)	Separates clauses within a sentence or items in a list
Colon (:)	Introduces an item or a list
Semicolon (;)	Connects two independent clauses that are closely related in meaning
Question Mark (?)	Appears at the end of a sentence to indicate a direct question
Exclamation Point (!)	Indicates strong emotion or emphasis
Quotation Marks ("")	Indicate direct speech or enclose titles of shorter works

Prep Expert
Writing Strategies

Parentheses ( )	Enclose additional information that is not essential to the sentence
Dash (—)	Indicates a break or interruption in thought or to set off an appositive

Punctuate Appropriately to maximize your SAT Writing score.

PREP EXPERT EXAMPLE

Consider the following *Prep Expert Examples*.

Punctuation Error: Misplaced Punctuation

This occurs when a punctuation mark is misplaced in a sentence, leading to a change in meaning.

> *Incorrect example: My mom said to get three items: from the grocery store milk, bananas, and cookies.*
> *Correct example: My mom said to get three items from the grocery store: milk, bananas, and cookies.*

The colon is misplaced in the incorrect example.

Punctuation Error: Missing Punctuation

This occurs when a punctuation mark is omitted from a sentence, creating ambiguity in the sentence.

> *Incorrect example: She walked into the room saw her friend and smiled.*
> *Correct example: She walked into the room, saw her friend, and smiled.*

Commas are missing from the incorrect example.

Punctuation Error: Inconsistent Punctuation

This occurs when punctuation is used inconsistently throughout a piece of writing, making it more difficult to understand.

Incorrect example: She walked the dog, went grocery shopping; and then, picked up the kids from school.

Correct example: She walked the dog, went grocery shopping, and then picked up the kids from school.

Commas should be used consistently to separate a list of items.

Punctuation Error: Fragments

A fragment is an incomplete sentence that is missing either a subject or a verb. The SAT often creates fragments by incorrectly changing a verb to the present participle form ending in "-ing."

*Incorrect example: The poem "Falling Leaves" **delivering** a powerful message about the fleeting nature of happiness.*

*Correct example: The poem "Falling Leaves" **delivers** a powerful message about the fleeting nature of happiness.*

There is no verb in the incorrect example; you must change "delivering" to "delivers."

Punctuation Error: Run-On Sentences

A run-on sentence is a sentence that contains two or more complete sentences that are not separated by appropriate punctuation. The SAT often creates run-on sentences by incorrectly separating two complete sentences with a comma rather than a period.

Incorrect example: I woke up early this morning, I went for a jog around the park.

Correct example: I woke up early this morning. I went for a jog around the park.

Separating two complete sentences with only a comma creates a run-on sentence.

PREP EXPERT PRACTICE

Try applying this *Prep Expert Strategy* yourself to the following SAT practice questions:

## 25

The first commercially successful graphical computer game, Pong, transformed the gaming industry not only by introducing visually stimulating graphics but also by facilitating competitive gameplay between users that depended on these _____ to Pong's release, playing games usually meant single-player text-based adventures which could be mundane.

Which choice completes the text so that it conforms to the conventions of Standard English?

A) innovations prior

B) innovations, prior

C) innovations. Prior

D) innovations and prior

## 26

In 1903, Orville and Wilbur Wright made history by achieving the first powered, controlled, and sustained flight with their aircraft, the Wright Flyer. The Wright brothers' invention would lead to more than just _____ as pioneers in aviation, they would revolutionize transportation and transform the world.

Which choice completes the text so that it conforms to the conventions of Standard English?

A) flight, though:

B) flight, though,

C) flight. Though,

D) flight though

The answers to these SAT practice questions can be found in the back of this book.

PREP EXPERT REVIEW

Key Takeaways

- **Prep Expert Writing Strategy #13—*Punctuate Appropriately***: Punctuation clarifies sentence meaning and structure. It plays a vital role in clear and effective communication.

- **Common SAT punctuation**: The SAT commonly tests your knowledge of various punctuation marks, including periods, commas, colons, semicolons, question marks, exclamation points, quotation marks, parentheses, and dashes.

- **Punctuation errors**: Punctuation errors can involve misplaced punctuation, missing punctuation, inconsistent punctuation, fragments, and run-on sentences.

- **Misplaced punctuation**: Misplaced punctuation can lead to ambiguity or changes in meaning in sentences.

- **Missing and inconsistent punctuation**: Missing or inconsistent punctuation can make sentences harder to understand.

- **Fragment and run-on sentences**: Fragments are incomplete sentences. Run-on sentences combine multiple sentences without proper separation, often due to incorrect punctuation.

 **PREP**EXPERT

WRITING
STRATEGY #14
MODIFY APPROPRIATELY

PREP EXPERT STRATEGY

What Is a Modifier?

A modifier is a phrase that provides more information about the noun that it is directly next to in a sentence. Modifiers can be placed before or after the phrase they modify. Using modifiers correctly is crucial to avoid confusion or unintended meanings in a sentence.

Why Are Modifier Errors Difficult to Spot for Most Students?

For students who have not studied for the grammar section of the SAT, modifier errors are hard to spot. This is because we often use modifiers incorrectly in everyday language. Modifier errors rarely "sound incorrect." Students who approach the SAT Writing section by searching for errors that "sound incorrect" will be at a disadvantage. By specifically looking for modifier errors on the SAT, you will have a huge advantage.

The Two-Step Process to Modify Appropriately

Use the following two-step process to *Modify Appropriately* on SAT Writing questions:

- **Step 1:** Determine what noun the modifier *should* be modifying.
- **Step 2:** Determine what noun is *actually* next to the comma of the modifier.

If the noun in Step 1 and the noun in Step 2 do not match, then you have a modifier error. Commonly on SAT Writing questions, the noun that is directly next to the comma is similar to the noun that should be modified, but it is not the exact noun that is needed. For example, there is a difference between the "office" and the "office manager" (one is a place and the other is a person).

Modify Appropriately to maximize your SAT Writing score.

PREP EXPERT EXAMPLE

Consider the following *Prep Expert Examples.*

Misplaced Modifiers at the Beginning *of a Sentence*

This occurs when the modifier is a phrase at the beginning of a sentence. If the beginning modifier is not describing the noun directly next to the comma, then it is a modifier error.

Incorrect example: After finishing my homework, **my phone** *rang with an important message to answer.*

Correct example: After finishing my homework, **I** *received an important message on my phone.*

"My phone" is not what finished the homework. Instead it was the person "I." Therefore, "I" needs to be directly next to the beginning modifier "after finishing my homework."

Misplaced Modifiers at the End *of a Sentence*

This occurs when the modifier is a phrase at the end of a sentence. If the ending modifier is not describing the noun directly next to the comma, then it is a modifier error.

Incorrect example: The Chicago Bulls had **Michael Jordan***, one of the most celebrated team franchises in NBA history.*

Correct example: Michael Jordan was on the **Chicago Bulls***, one of the most celebrated team franchises in NBA history.*

Prep Expert
Writing Strategies

Michael Jordan is not "one of the most celebrated team franchises in NBA history." Instead it is the Chicago Bulls. Therefore, "Chicago Bulls" needs to be directly next to the ending modifier "one of the most celebrated team franchises in NBA history."

PREP EXPERT PRACTICE

Try applying this *Prep Expert Strategy* yourself to the following SAT practice questions:

27

In evaluating the work of Mexican artist Frida Kahlo, _____ have overlooked her significant influence on the Surrealist movement.

Which choice completes the text so that it conforms to the conventions of Standard English?

A) the focus of many art historians has been on Kahlo's exploration of identity and suffering; they

B) there are many art historians who have focused on Kahlo's exploration of identity and suffering, but they

C) Kahlo's exploration of identity and suffering has been the focus of many art historians, who

D) many art historians have focused on Kahlo's exploration of identity and suffering but

28

Despite being healthy, tasty, and high in fiber, _____ they are high in sugars, and their caloric content can add up quickly if not moderated.

Which choice completes the text so that it conforms to the conventions of Standard English?

A) there are two drawbacks associated with eating fruits:

B) two drawbacks are associated with eating fruits:

C) fruits' two associated drawbacks are that

D) fruits have two associated drawbacks:

The answers to these SAT practice questions can be found in the back of this book.

PREP EXPERT REVIEW

Key Takeaways

- **Prep Expert Writing Strategy #14—*Modify Appropriately***: A modifier is a phrase that adds information about a noun in a sentence. It can be placed before or after the noun. Using modifiers correctly is essential to avoid confusion.

- **Why modifier errors are challenging**: Many students find it difficult to spot modifier errors because they often do not "sound incorrect" in everyday language. Students who search for errors based on how they sound may miss modifier errors completely on the SAT.

- **The two-step process**: Modifying appropriately is a two-step process: (1) Determine the noun the modifier should modify (intended noun), and (2) Ensure that the noun that is actually next to the modifier matches the intended noun. Mismatches between these nouns result in modifier errors.

- **Misplaced modifiers at the beginning**: Misplaced modifiers at the beginning of sentences occur when the noun adjacent to the comma is not the item the beginning modifier is describing.

- **Misplaced modifiers at the end**: Misplaced modifiers at the end of sentences occur when the noun adjacent to the comma is not the item the ending modifier is describing.

 **PREPEXPERT**

WRITING STRATEGY #15

APPLY APPOSITIVES APPROPRIATELY

PREP EXPERT STRATEGY

The Digital SAT tests appositive errors more often than the old paper-based SAT did. Therefore, it is crucial to understand appositives and how they may appear on Digital SAT Writing questions.

What Is an Appositive?

An appositive is a phrase that renames or explains another noun that comes immediately before or after it. Depending on the context, appositives can be set off by commas, parentheses, or dashes. Appositives are often used to provide additional information or clarify meaning.

Think of appositives as "middle modifiers." Appositives are very similar to the modifiers we learned about in the previous *Prep Expert Writing Strategy #14—Modify Appropriately*. Instead of appearing at the beginning or end of a sentence, appositives typically appear in the middle of a sentence.

Apply Appositives Appropriately to maximize your SAT Writing score.

PREP EXPERT EXAMPLE

Consider the following *Prep Expert Examples*.

Appositive Error: Missing Commas

Appositives that are set off by commas require commas both before and after the appositive. Failing to include one or both of these commas can create confusion or ambiguity.

> *Incorrect example: My friend the doctor will be visiting us tonight.*
> *Correct example: My friend, the doctor, will be visiting us tonight.*

To make the sentence clearer, add two commas to set off the appositive "the doctor."

Appositive Error: Incorrect Punctuation

The SAT will sometimes use parentheses or dashes instead of commas to set off appositives. While this is acceptable in some cases, it can sometimes be grammatically incorrect.

> *Incorrect example: The capital of France (Paris) is a beautiful city.*
> *Correct example: The capital of France, Paris, is a beautiful city.*

The appositive "Paris" should be set off using commas, not parentheses.

Appositive Error: Incorrect Order

When using multiple appositives in a sentence, it is important to keep the order clear and logical.

> *Incorrect example: The recipe called for sugar, **a cup**, flour, **two cups**, and eggs, **three**.*
> *Correct example: The recipe called for a cup of sugar, two cups of flour, and three eggs.*

To make the list clear, include each quantity within the list of items instead of using separate appositives.

Appositive Error: Incorrect Pronouns

An appositive does not need an additional pronoun next to it, given this often causes redundancy.

> Incorrect example: My parents, who are retired, **they** enjoy traveling around the world.
>
> Correct example: My parents, who are retired, enjoy traveling around the world.

The additional pronoun "they" next to the appositive is not necessary in the above example.

Appositive Error: Unnecessary Appositives

Appositives should provide useful additional information about the noun they refer to. Using unnecessary appositives can make the sentence wordy, redundant, or confusing.

> Incorrect example: The talented guitar player, **who is a musician,** performed a new song at the concert.
>
> Correct example: The talented guitar player performed a new song at the concert.

The appositive "who is a musician" is unnecessary because a guitar player is by definition a musician. This appositive does not add any useful additional information. Therefore, you should remove "who is a musician" altogether.

PREP EXPERT PRACTICE

Try applying this *Prep Expert Strategy* yourself to the following SAT practice questions:

## 29

Leonardo da Vinci is widely recognized for painting masterpieces such as *The Last Supper* (1498) and *Mona Lisa* (1503), but he also had a keen interest in anatomy, the study of _____ numerous detailed drawings of the human body and carrying out dissections to deepen his understanding.

Which choice completes the text so that it conforms to the conventions of Standard English?

A) bodies; creating
B) bodies. Creating
C) bodies creating
D) bodies, creating

## 30

Microtubules, components of the cell skeleton that maintain cell shape and aid in cell division, form when *tubulin proteins* polymerize into long chains. In a groundbreaking 2015 study, molecular _____ demonstrated that a protein called *tau* regulates the stability of *microtubules*.

Which choice completes the text so that it conforms to the conventions of Standard English?

A) biologist, John Smith
B) biologist John Smith,
C) biologist John Smith
D) biologist, John Smith,

The answers to these SAT practice questions can be found in the back of this book.

PREP EXPERT REVIEW

Key Takeaways

- **Prep Expert Writing Strategy #15—*Apply Appositives Appropriately***: The Digital SAT frequently tests appositive errors.

- **Definition of appositive**: An appositive is a phrase that renames or explains another noun. Appositives typically appear in the middle of a sentence and are set off by commas, parentheses, or dashes.

- **Common appositive errors**: Errors related to appositives include missing commas, incorrect punctuation (parentheses or dashes), incorrect order in sentences with multiple appositives, unnecessary pronouns, and unnecessary appositives.

Prep Expert
Writing Strategies

- **Impact of appositive errors**: These errors can result in confusion, ambiguity, redundancy, or wordiness in sentences.

- **Correcting appositive errors**: To correct appositive errors, use proper punctuation, maintain logical order, and eliminate unnecessary pronouns and appositives.

 **PREP**EXPERT

WRITING STRATEGY #16

AVOID PASSIVE VOICE

PREP EXPERT STRATEGY

The SAT Prefers the Active Voice over the Passive Voice

Active voice and passive voice are two different ways of structuring a sentence.

- **Active voice**: The subject of the sentence performs the action described by the verb. *Example:* The dog chased the cat.
- **Passive voice**: The subject of the sentence is acted upon by the verb. *Example*: The cat was chased by the dog.

The active voice is more direct and engaging, while the passive voice is more indirect and vague.

Two Clues to Identify Passive Voice

A sentence will often have at least one (if not both) of the following clues to help you identify that the sentence is using a passive voice construction:

- **Clue #1:** The sentence uses the word "by"

Prep Expert
Writing Strategies

- **Clue #2:** The sentence uses a form of "to be"
- **Examples:** am, is, are, was, were, been, or being

Passive voice can be constructed in other ways, but these two clues are the most helpful in identifying passive voice.

Avoid Passive Voice to maximize your SAT Writing score.

PREP EXPERT EXAMPLE

Consider the following *Prep Expert Examples*.

Active Voice	Passive Voice
I aced the SAT.	The SAT **was** aced **by** me.
She plays tennis.	Tennis **is** played **by** her.
They love to eat.	Eating **is** loved **by** them.
The dog fetched the bone.	The bone **was** fetched **by** the dog.

PREP EXPERT PRACTICE

Try applying this *Prep Expert Strategy* yourself to the following SAT practice questions:

31

Even though they provide rapid transportation and help bridge large distances, _____ they produce significant carbon emissions and can be a source of noise pollution.

Which choice completes the text so that it conforms to the conventions of Standard English?

A) there are two drawbacks with airplanes:

B) two drawbacks are associated with airplanes:

C) airplanes' two associated drawbacks are that

D) airplanes have two associated drawbacks:

While researching a topic, a student has taken the following notes:

- Sea otters are marine mammals that live in the Pacific Ocean.

- In a 2022 study, researcher Maria Gonzalez studied the impact of human activity on sea otter populations.

- She analyzed data from several coastal regions and found that human-caused habitat destruction and pollution were the primary threats to sea otters.

- Gonzalez suggested that efforts to reduce human activity in coastal regions could help preserve sea otter populations.

## 32

The student wants to present the study and its findings. Which choice most effectively uses relevant information from the notes to accomplish this goal?

A) Maria Gonzalez studied sea otters in a 2022 study and found that habitat destruction and pollution are major threats to their populations.

B) In a 2022 study, sea otters were found to be impacted by human activity.

C) Sea otters are marine mammals that live in the Pacific Ocean and were the subject of a 2022 study by Maria Gonzalez.

D) In a 2022 study, Maria Gonzalez analyzed data from several coastal regions and concluded that reducing human activity in these areas could help preserve sea otter populations.

The answers to these SAT practice questions can be found in the back of this book.

PREP EXPERT REVIEW

Key Takeaways

- **Prep Expert Writing Strategy #16—*Avoid Passive Voice*:** The English language prefers the active voice over the passive voice.

- **Active voice:** This is more direct and engaging. Active sentence constructions are when the subject performs the action described by the verb.

- **Passive voice:** This is more indirect and vague. Passive sentence constructions are when the subject is acted upon by the verb.

- **Identifying passive voice:** Look for clues such as the use of "by" and forms of "to be" (e.g., am, is, are, was, were, been, or being) in sentences to identify passive voice constructions.

Prep Expert
Writing Strategies

PREPEXPERT

WRITING
STRATEGY #17
AVOID INFINITIVES

PREP EXPERT STRATEGY

What Is an Infinitive?

An infinitive is the base form of a verb that often includes the word "to." Infinitives are not conjugated by tense. Infinitives do not indicate who or what is performing the action. Instead, they provide a general description of an action or state of being.

The SAT Dislikes Infinitive Verbs

If an answer choice contains the infinitive form of a verb, then it is most likely *not* the correct answer. You should avoid infinitives on the SAT. Once in a while, the correct answer will contain an infinitive verb. But as a general rule of thumb, *Avoid Infinitives* on SAT Writing questions.

Avoid Infinitives to maximize your SAT Writing score.

PREP EXPERT EXAMPLE

Consider the following *Prep Expert Examples.*

Examples of Infinitive Verbs

to be	to get	to know	to see
to come	to go	to make	to take
to do	to have	to say	to think

There are thousands of infinitives in the English language. Obviously, you do not need to memorize them. Simply recognize that they typically have "to" in front of the verb.

PREP EXPERT PRACTICE

Try applying this Prep Expert Strategy yourself to the following SAT practice questions:

33

In 2008, Bitcoin was introduced as the world's first decentralized cryptocurrency. While many people have invested in Bitcoin, its volatile value has raised questions about its long-term stability as an investment. Many analysts _____ that Bitcoin's rapid price fluctuations are a sign of an asset bubble, which occurs when the price of an asset is driven above its fundamental value.

Which choice completes the text so that it conforms to the conventions of Standard English?

A) claim
B) to claim
C) have claimed
D) claiming

34

In 1924, the first Winter Olympics were held in Chamonix, France. The Games featured six sports and sixteen events and were a huge success, _____ the foundation for the modern Winter Olympics that we know today.

Which choice correctly completes the text so that it conforms to the conventions of Standard English?

A) laying
B) laid
C) to lay
D) having laid

The answers to these SAT practice questions can be found in the back of this book.

PREP EXPERT REVIEW

Key Takeaways

- **Prep Expert Writing Strategy #17—*Avoid Infinitives*:** An infinitive is the base form of a verb, often with the word "to," and it is not conjugated for tense. It provides a general description of an action or state of being without specifying the doer.

- **SAT and infinitive verbs:** The SAT generally does not prefer infinitive verbs in answer choices for writing questions. While there may be exceptions, it is usually advisable to avoid choosing answer choices with infinitive verbs.

- **Examples of infinitive verbs:** Common examples of infinitive verbs include "to be," "to get," "to know," "to see," "to come," etc. There are many infinitives in the English language, and they typically have "to" before the verb.

PREPEXPERT

WRITING STRATEGY #18

AVOID THE "-ING" SUFFIX

PREP EXPERT STRATEGY

What Is the "-ing" Suffix?

The "-ing" suffix is commonly used in English to make verbs continuous, gerunds, or adjectives. Usually, we add "-ing" to a base verb to make a noun, verb, or adjective.

The SAT Dislikes "-ing" Suffixes

If an answer choice contains the "-ing" suffix, then it is most likely *not* the correct answer. You should avoid the "-ing" suffix on the SAT. In formal writing, there is often a preference for more clear and concise language. Overusing the "-ing" suffix can lead to wordiness and less direct communication.

Occasionally, the correct answer will contain an "-ing" suffix. Use this *Prep Expert Strategy* more as a general rule of thumb than a hard-and-fast rule.

Avoid The "-ing" Suffix to maximize your SAT Writing score.

Prep Expert
Writing Strategies

PREP EXPERT EXAMPLE

Consider the following *Prep Expert Examples*.

"-ing" Suffix Type	Function	Example
Continuous verb (present participle)	The "-ing" word acts like a **verb**.	I am **studying**.
Gerund	The "-ing" word acts like a **noun**.	**Studying** is boring.
Independent adjective	The "-ing" word acts like an **adjective**.	Studying is **boring**.

It is not necessary to memorize the "-ing" suffix types for the SAT. Just familiarize yourself with the different ways the "-ing" suffix can be used.

PREP EXPERT PRACTICE

Try applying this Prep Expert Strategy yourself to the following SAT practice questions:

35

In 1973, Katharine Graham became the first female Fortune 500 CEO, leading the *Washington Post*. Her fearless leadership and her habit of tackling controversial stories, even in the face of _____ revolutionize the traditionally male-dominated field of journalism.

Which choice completes the text so that it conforms to the conventions of Standard English?

A) adversity, helped
B) adversity, helping
C) adversity that helped
D) adversity to help

36

In the late 18th century, the Industrial Revolution began transforming economies worldwide. As factories sprang up and urban centers expanded, many scholars _____ that these technological advancements were both a blessing and a curse for society at large.

Which choice completes the text so that it conforms to the conventions of Standard English?

A) believing
B) believe
C) having believed
D) to believe

The answers to these SAT practice questions can be found in the back of this book.

PREP EXPERT REVIEW

Key Takeaways

- **Prep Expert Writing Strategy #18—*Avoid The "-ing" Suffix***: The "-ing" suffix is commonly added to base verbs in English to create continuous verbs, gerunds (noun forms), and adjectives. It essentially transforms base verbs into various linguistic forms.

- **SAT and "-ing" suffix**: The SAT typically does not prefer answer choices that contain the "-ing" suffix. The SAT prefers more clear language in formal writing, and overusing "-ing" can lead to a lack of clarity. Of course, there may be some exceptions.

- **Prep Expert Examples**: The "-ing" suffix can be used to create continuous verbs (present participles), gerunds (noun forms), and independent adjectives. Familiarity with these different uses can be helpful in recognizing when to avoid the "-ing" suffix.

PREPEXPERT
WRITING STRATEGY #19
AVOID EXCESS

PREP EXPERT STRATEGY

What Is Excess in English Grammar?

"Excess" refers to mistakes in language use that go beyond the acceptable norms of grammar, usage, and syntax. These errors often involve the overuse or misuse of certain words, phrases, or constructions. This leads to a lack of clarity, precision, or coherence in sentences. It is important to strive for clear, concise, and accurate language use. *Avoid Excess* on the SAT Writing answer choices.

Three Reasons to Avoid Excess on the SAT

REASON #1: CLARITY

Clear communication is one of the primary goals of grammar. Succinct language helps achieve this. Using fewer words can make your sentences easier to understand. Ultimately, the intended meaning is less likely to be misinterpreted.

REASON #2: EFFICIENCY

Succinct language is more efficient than wordy language. It allows a sentence to convey its message with minimal effort.

REASON #3: AESTHETIC

Succinct language can also be more aesthetically pleasing. The SAT values concision and precision. Test-question writers appreciate the elegance of well-crafted, succinct sentences.

Avoid Excess to maximize your SAT Writing score.

PREP EXPERT EXAMPLE

Consider the following *Prep Expert Examples*.

Three Types of Excess Errors on the SAT

EXCESS ERROR #1: REDUNDANCY

Redundancy refers to the repetition of words or ideas that are already implied or stated elsewhere in the sentence or paragraph.

> *Incorrect example: The two organizations **joined together** to form a partnership.*
> *Correct example: The two organizations **joined** to form a partnership.*

The word "together" is redundant because the word "joined" already implies "together."

EXCESS ERROR #2: WORDINESS

Wordiness refers to the use of long or convoluted sentences, with unnecessary words, phrases, or clauses that make the text harder to understand.

> *Incorrect example: **Due to the fact** it was raining outside, we decided to stay indoors instead of going for a walk.*
> *Correct example: **Because** it was raining outside, we decided to stay indoors instead of going for a walk.*

The phrase "due to the fact" is wordy, and you can convey the same idea more succinctly with one word: "because."

EXCESS ERROR #3: AWKWARD PHRASING

Awkward phrasing refers to the use of awkward or incorrect sentence structures, verb tenses, or prepositions that make the sentence sound unnatural or confusing.

*Incorrect example: Yesterday, I **have went** to the gym.*

*Correct example: Yesterday, I **went** to the gym.*

The phrase "have went" is awkward and excessive compared to succinctly using the verb "went."

PREP EXPERT PRACTICE

Try applying this *Prep Expert Strategy* yourself to the following SAT practice questions:

37

The preamble to the Constitution of the United States begins: "We the people of the United States, in Order to form a more perfect Union, establish Justice, insure domestic Tranquility, provide for the common defense, promote the general Welfare, and the Blessings of Liberty to ourselves and our Posterity, _____."

Which choice completes the text so that it conforms to the conventions of Standard English?

A) do ordain and establish this Constitution for the United States of America

B) do ordain and establish this Constitution for the United States of America we do

C) do hereby ordain and establish this Constitution for the United States of America we do

D) do hereby do ordain and establish this Constitution for the United States of America we do

38

In 2020, scientist John Bennett led the development of an advanced solar panel technology that increased the energy conversion efficiency by 15%. By converting more sunlight into usable energy, _____

Which choice completes the text so that it conforms to the conventions of Standard English?

A) the mitigation of reliance on non-renewable energy sources has been achieved by these solar panels.

B) these solar panels have mitigated reliance on non-renewable energy sources.

C) the solar panels' mitigation of reliance on non-renewable energy sources has been achieved.

D) reliance on non-renewable energy sources has been mitigated by these solar panels.

The answers to these SAT practice questions can be found in the back of this book.

PREP EXPERT REVIEW

Key Takeaways

- **Prep Expert Writing Strategy #19—*Avoid Excess***: "Excess" refers to writing errors that go beyond accepted grammar norms, leading to unclear and imprecise sentences.

- Reasons to avoid excess on the SAT:
  - **Clarity**: Concise language enhances clarity.
  - **Efficiency**: Succinct language is more efficient.
  - **Aesthetics**: The SAT values aesthetically pleasing sentences.

- Types of excess errors on the SAT:
  - **Redundancy**: Unnecessary repetition of words or ideas.
  - **Wordiness**: Use of long, convoluted sentences with unnecessary elements.
  - **Awkward phrasing**: Use of unnatural or confusing sentence structures.

Prep Expert
Writing Strategies

 **PREPEXPERT**

WRITING STRATEGY #20

AVOID THESE 5 KISS OF DEATH PHRASES ON SAT WRITING

PREP EXPERT STRATEGY

The Five Words That Are Always *Incorrect on SAT Writing Questions*

These five phrases are the "kiss of death" for any answer choice on SAT Writing questions. The presence of any of these phrases will automatically make an answer choice incorrect.

FIVE KISS OF DEATH PHRASES

- being
- is why / is because
- there is / there are
- it is
- very

Note: This is only true for SAT Writing questions that are typically located at the end of an SAT Reading and Writing module. SAT Reading questions that are typically located at the beginning of an SAT Reading and Writing Module may still have correct answers that contain these words.

Prep Expert
Writing Strategies

Five Kiss Of Death Phrases On SAT Writing

KISS OF DEATH PHRASE #1: "BEING"

"Being" is a form of "to be" that creates sentences with passive voice constructions. An answer choice that contains the word "being" is typically incorrect because this word can lead to weak or passive sentences. Therefore, the word "being" is almost always incorrect on SAT Writing questions.

KISS OF DEATH PHRASE #2: "IS WHY" OR "IS BECAUSE"

"Is why" and "is because" are colloquial phrases that are often used in everyday speech, but you should not use them in formal written English. An answer choice that contains the phrase "is why" or "is because" is typically incorrect because both phrases are informal and redundant. Therefore, the phrases "is why" and "is because" are almost always incorrect on SAT Writing questions.

KISS OF DEATH PHRASE #3: "THERE IS" OR "THERE ARE"

"There is" and "there are" are phrases that can make sentences vague and wordy. An answer choice that contains the phrase "there is" or "there are" is typically incorrect because these phrases are wordy and can lead to passive voice. Therefore, the phrases "there is" and "there are" are almost always incorrect on SAT Writing questions.

KISS OF DEATH PHRASE #4: "IT IS"

"It is" is another phrase that can make sentences vague and wordy. An answer choice that contains the phrase "it is" is typically incorrect because this phrase is wordy and often unclear. Therefore, the phrase "it is" is almost always incorrect on SAT Writing questions.

KISS OF DEATH PHRASE #5: "VERY"

"Very" is an imprecise adverb. An answer choice that contains the word "very" is typically incorrect because this word is excessively informal. Therefore, the word "very" is almost always incorrect on SAT Writing questions.

Avoid These 5 Kiss Of Death Phrases On SAT Writing to maximize your SAT Writing score.

Prep Expert
Writing Strategies

PREP EXPERT EXAMPLE

Consider the following *Prep Expert Examples*.

Five Kiss Of Death Phrases On SAT Writing

KISS OF DEATH PHRASE #1: "BEING"

"Being" often creates passive voice constructions.

> *Incorrect example:* **Being** *criticized by my manager, a mistake was made on the report.*
>
> *Correct example: My manager criticized me for making a mistake on the report.*

The use of "being" in the first sentence creates a passive construction, which makes the sentence unclear. Passive constructions are less effective when the subject performing the action is known or should be emphasized. The second sentence contains an active rather than passive construction, which is more direct and easier to understand. The phrasing clearly identifies the subject ("my manager") as the one performing the action ("criticized"). This makes the second sentence more straightforward.

KISS OF DEATH PHRASE #2: "IS WHY" OR "IS BECAUSE"

"Is why" and "is because" often create less formal sentences.

> *Incorrect example: The reason we are late* **is because** *we got stuck in traffic.*
>
> *Correct example: We are late because we got stuck in traffic.*

In the first sentence, "is because" adds unnecessary words, making the sentence less concise. In formal writing, you should use "because" by itself. Doing so makes the second sentence more direct and clear.

KISS OF DEATH PHRASE #3: "THERE IS" OR "THERE ARE"

"There is" and "there are" often create wordy sentences.

> *Incorrect example:* **There is** *a decision that needs to be made by the committee regarding the new project.*

Correct example: The committee needs to make a decision regarding the new project.

The first sentence is wordy and passive. The direct, active construction of the second sentence conveys the same meaning more efficiently.

KISS OF DEATH PHRASE #4: "IT IS"

"It is" often creates vague sentences.

*Incorrect example: **It is** important for us to attend the meeting tomorrow.*
Correct example: Attending the meeting tomorrow is crucial for us.

The first sentence is vague and wordy. What noun is the pronoun "it" referring to? This is unclear. But the more direct and concise construction of the second sentence conveys the same meaning more effectively.

KISS OF DEATH PHRASE #5: "VERY"

Using "very" often creates an overly informal tone.

*Incorrect example: The presentation was **very** good, and I learned a lot from it.*
Correct example: The presentation was excellent, and I learned a lot from it.

Replacing "very good" with "excellent" makes the description clearer and more specific. The second sentence is more professional and precise.

PREP EXPERT PRACTICE

Try applying this *Prep Expert Strategy* yourself to the following SAT practice questions:

Prep Expert
Writing Strategies

## 39

A forecast developed by economist Maria Sanchez suggests that the rate of inflation—the rate at which the general level of prices for goods and services is rising—in a country with high government debt _____ double the rate of inflation in a country with low government debt.

Which choice completes the text so that it conforms to the conventions of Standard English?

A) being
B) to be
C) to have been
D) will be

## 40

In evaluating the works of American author Mark Twain, _____ have often overlooked his serious social commentaries hidden within the humor.

Which choice completes the text so that it conforms to the conventions of Standard English?

A) many scholars have focused on Twain's humor but
B) Twain's humor has been the primary interest of many scholars, who
C) there are many scholars who have focused on Twain's humor, but they
D) the focus of many scholars has been on Twain's humor; they

The answers to these SAT practice questions can be found in the back of this book.

PREP EXPERT REVIEW

Key Takeaways

- **Prep Expert Writing Strategy #20—*Avoid These 5 Kiss Of Death Phrases On SAT Writing***: The five "kiss of death" phrases that are always incorrect on SAT Writing questions are "being," "is why/is because," "there is/there are," "it is," and "very."

- **Sentence issues**:
  - **"Being"**: Leads to weak or passive sentences
  - **"Is why" or "is because"**: Informal and redundant
  - **"There is" or "there are"**: Makes sentences wordy and can lead to passive voice
  - **"It is"**: Wordy and sometimes unclear
  - **"Very"**: Seen as less formal or professional

- **Exceptions**: This strategy works 99% of the time. Rarely, one of these phrases might appear in the correct answer to an SAT Writing question.

EARN A
$100 GIFT CARD

REFER A FRIEND TO PREP EXPERT

Earn a $100 Amazon Gift Card at prepexpert.com/refer

Do you know someone who might benefit from a Prep Expert SAT or ACT course? If so, you can earn a $100 Amazon gift card when you refer them to Prep Expert! Your friend will also earn a $100 Amazon gift card after they sign up for Prep Expert using your referral link.

Here's how the Prep Expert Referral Program works:

- **Step 1**: Sign up for a referral link at prepexpert.com/refer

- **Step 2**: Send your referral link to your friends.

- **Step 3**: Get a $100 Amazon gift card per friend you refer to Prep Expert! Your referral will also get a $100 Amazon gift card after they sign up for Prep Expert using your link.

You do not have to be enrolled in a Prep Expert SAT or ACT course to refer friends. There is no limit on the number of friends you can refer to Prep Expert! If you refer ten friends, you will earn $1,000 in Amazon gift cards. They will each get a $100 Amazon gift card too. See full terms and conditions at the link below.

**Scan the QR code or visit
prepexpert.com/refer**

SAT READING INTRODUCTION

"Reading is to the mind what exercise is to the body."

—JOSEPH ADDISON

DIGITAL SAT READING OVERVIEW

Let's discuss the SAT Reading section. Remember, SAT Writing and SAT Reading questions are combined into the same module.

DIGITAL SAT READING & WRITING FORMAT

Section	Questions	Time
SAT Reading & Writing Module 1	27 questions	32 minutes
SAT Reading & Writing Module 2	27 questions	32 minutes
TOTAL SAT READING & WRITING	54 QUESTIONS	64 MINUTES

Digital SAT Reading Format

The first module on the Digital SAT will be an SAT Reading and Writing module that contains 27 questions in 32 minutes. The second module on the Digital SAT will also be an SAT Reading and Writing module that contains 27 questions in 32 minutes.

The first 13 to 14 questions on each module are typically SAT Reading questions. In other words, the first half of each module includes SAT Reading questions, such as passage-based questions. The second 13 to 14 questions on each module are typically SAT Writing questions, meaning the second half of each module includes SAT Writing questions, such as grammar questions.

Essentially, SAT Reading questions appear in the first half of the questions on each SAT Reading and Writing module.

Digital SAT Reading Content

The SAT tests the following reading skills and knowledge areas:

SAT READING CONTENT

DOMAIN	KNOWLEDGE TESTING POINT	# OF QUESTIONS	%
Craft and Structure	• Words in context • Text structure and purpose • Cross-text connections	13–15 questions	~28%
Information and Ideas	• Central ideas and details • Command of evidence (textual, quantitative) • Inferences	12–14 questions	~26%

The first domain is *Craft and Structure*, which includes 13 to 15 questions on the SAT. This makes up about 28% of all questions on the SAT Reading and Writing modules. The knowledge testing points within this domain include *Words in Context*, *Text Structure and Purpose*, and *Cross-Text Connections*. *Words in Context* questions measure a student's ability to use vocabulary properly. *Text Structure and Purpose* questions measure a student's ability to analyze the organization and objectives of passages. *Cross-Text Connections* questions measure a student's ability to compare and contrast the viewpoints of two different authors who are writing about the same topic.

The second domain is *Information and Ideas*, which includes 12 to 14 questions on the SAT. This makes up about 26% of all questions on the SAT Reading and Writing modules. The knowledge testing points within this domain include *Central Ideas and Details*, *Command of Evidence*, and *Inferences*. *Central Ideas and Details* questions measure a student's ability to identify the main idea of a passage. *Command of Evidence* questions measure a student's ability to use both written and numerical data to draw conclusions. *Inferences* questions measure a student's ability to make logical deductions based on the text of a passage.

It is not all that important to understand what each of the above knowledge testing points are right now. We will discuss them in more detail as we cover *Prep Expert Reading Strategies*. For now, know that these knowledge testing points test reading comprehension. Essentially, the first half of the SAT Reading and Writing modules are going to contain comprehension-based questions.

We will teach you *Prep Expert Reading Strategies* to ace these questions. In summary, 54% of the questions on an SAT Reading and Writing module will be related to Reading. The other 46% of the questions will be related to Writing.

Why Separate Writing and Reading?

Reading and writing questions are combined together into the same modules on the SAT. Why does Prep Expert separate out SAT Reading versus SAT Writing? Because the strategies you need to succeed on SAT Reading are different from the strategies you need to succeed on SAT Writing. SAT Reading contains primarily passage-based questions, while SAT Writing contains primarily grammar-based questions. These are two separate skill sets, so Prep Expert separates out the strategies for SAT Reading and SAT Writing.

PREPEXPERT
READING STRATEGIES

"The man who does not read has no advantage over the man who cannot read."

—MARK TWAIN

PREP EXPERT READING STRATEGIES OVERVIEW

Prep Expert Reading Strategies are a collection of techniques designed to improve your SAT Reading score. These strategies will teach you how to improve passage-reading comprehension and question-answering accuracy.

Within the SAT Reading and Writing modules, the first half of questions focuses on reading comprehension and skills. *Prep Expert Reading Strategies* help you tackle these first 13 to 14 questions that test reading comprehension and inferential reasoning. The second half of each SAT Reading and Writing module consists of grammar-based writing questions. It is important to master the *Prep Expert Writing Strategies* to master the final 13 to 14 questions in each SAT Reading and Writing Module.

Prep Expert Reading Strategies are adaptable, which makes them an ideal resource for students at all levels of proficiency. Whether you are struggling with vocabulary or looking to ace the most advanced reading questions, these strategies will address your goals.

The foundation of Prep Expert's approach to SAT Reading is practice. Applying these strategies to actual SAT questions will help you develop habits to comprehend passages with precision.

These reading skills will also set you up for academic and professional success. If you aspire to ace any standardized test with passage-based comprehension questions in the future, mastering these strategies is a key step on your journey.

Personally, I used these same *Prep Expert Reading Strategies* to ace many standardized exams beyond the SAT, including the PSAT, AP Exams, MCAT, GMAT, United States Medical Licensing Exams, and American Board of Dermatology board-certification exams. Almost every standardized exam that you take in the future will include some kind of passage-based comprehension component. Therefore, learning these Prep Expert Reading Strategies now will help you on all standardized tests in the future.

Prep Expert Reading Strategies pave the path to SAT Reading excellence. By

---

integrating these strategies into your preparation, you can elevate your reading skills. They are a road map to success on SAT Reading.

Master and apply all of the *Prep Expert Reading Strategies* to maximize your SAT Reading score.

 **PREP**EXPERT

READING
STRATEGY #1

BUILD OWN SIMPLE
SOLUTION (BOSS)

PREP EXPERT STRATEGY

Build (Your) Own Simple Solution (BOSS)

The BOSS strategy is the key to mastering the SAT Reading section. *Build (Your) Own Simple Solution* means creating your own answer to the question *before* looking at answer choices (A), (B), (C), or (D).

You must write down your own answer on the provided scratch paper. After you have written down your BOSS solution, then look at the answer choices. Determine which answer choice best matches your BOSS solution.

How Most Students Approach SAT Reading Questions

Most students do not create BOSS solutions on SAT Reading questions. Instead, they simply go straight to reading the answer choices. The problem with this approach is that many students begin debating between answer choices. For example, has this thought process ever gone through your head while reading the answer choices for an SAT Reading question?

A) *Sounds good.*

B) *No.*

C) *Oh, I didn't think of this before. Maybe this is the answer?*

D) *Oh wow, I didn't see this before—this could be the answer?*

You end up selecting (D), when the answer was in fact (A), and get the question wrong!

BOSS Solves the Biggest Problem

The biggest problem most students have with the SAT Reading section is that they select enticing, but incorrect, answer choices. Having a specific BOSS solution written down on your scratch paper means you will not get distracted by incorrect answer choices.

If an answer choice does not closely match your BOSS solution, cross it out. If you do not have a BOSS solution written down to compare the answer choices to, you will likely fall for incorrect answer choices.

A Treasure Hunt

Imagine going on a treasure hunt without knowing what the treasure looks like. Let's say the treasure is a diamond, but you do not know that. Along the way, you would likely get distracted by platinum, gold, and silver on your treasure hunt and never find the diamond. If you do not know what you are looking for, then it is hard to find the correct item.

Similarly, reading through answer choices without knowing what you are looking for can make it hard to find the right answer. Having a BOSS solution is like having a drawing of the exact diamond you need to find on the treasure hunt!

If you know what the diamond you need to find looks like, you won't get distracted by platinum, gold, or silver (the incorrect answer choices). Instead, you will go straight for the diamond (the correct answer choice) that matches your drawing of the diamond (your BOSS solution).

Can You Just Think of a BOSS Solution?

No! You must write down your BOSS solution. It is not enough to only *think* of an answer in your head. If you only *think* of a BOSS solution, but do not write it down on scratch paper, then you are clogging up your limited working memory and reducing your critical thinking ability.

What If Your BOSS Solution Does Not Match an Answer Choice Perfectly?

It is fine if your BOSS solution does not perfectly match an answer choice. The important thing is to come up with a solution to which to compare the answer choices. By creating a BOSS solution, you are doing the critical thinking that the SAT wants you to do.

Even if your BOSS solution does not match any of the answer choices, you will likely still answer the question correctly. Why? Because you have thought critically about the concepts associated with the question, which will lead you to the correct answer.

Doesn't Writing a BOSS Solution Down on Paper Slow You Down?

No! It is true that creating a BOSS solution requires some extra time on the front end of a question, as you write an answer down on your scratch paper.

However, BOSS still saves a tremendous amount of time overall on the back end. Why? Because you don't waste time debating answer choices. The majority of your time is *not* spent reading passages, as most students believe. Deliberating over answer choices is actually how students spend the majority of their time during SAT Reading and Writing modules.

BOSS solves the biggest problem of the SAT Reading section: you no longer have to debate between answer choices. Just select the one that most closely matches your BOSS solution.

Why Most Students Don't Like Writing Down a BOSS Solution

Most students would prefer not to write down a BOSS solution on scratch paper. Why? Because it takes time and effort. Most students would prefer to be lazy and just start looking at the answer choices. Don't be like most students.

Instead, take the time and effort to write down a BOSS solution for every SAT Reading question before looking at the answer choices. Students who do this are rewarded with higher SAT Reading scores.

Does Your BOSS Solution Need to Sound Like an SAT Answer Choice?

No! You do not need to write down an academic or complex BOSS solution. Your BOSS solution can be as simple as the words "good" or "bad."

Of course, the more specific your BOSS solution is, the more likely it is to match one of the answer choices. But if you really can't think of a BOSS solution, write down something simple that makes sense, and then start comparing it to the available answer choices.

Getting good at coming up with BOSS solutions takes practice. So make sure you practice creating BOSS solutions for every SAT Reading question from here on out.

Build (Your) Own Simple Solution to maximize your SAT Reading score.

PREP EXPERT EXAMPLE

Consider the following *Prep Expert Example*.

Let's *Build (Our) Own Simple Solution* together on an SAT Reading question. On *Prep Expert Examples* such as the one below, I purposely do not show you the entire problem all at once. This is because I want to show you my step-by-step approach. That way, you can follow the same steps when you take the Digital SAT.

The most important step for every SAT Reading question is creating a BOSS solution before looking at the answer choices. Make it a habit to ignore answer choices on SAT Reading questions until after you have created a BOSS solution. Your BOSS solution may be different from the BOSS solution we create below, but they will likely be similar. The point of writing down a BOSS solution is not to create the perfect answer—it is to do the critical thinking necessary to prevent you from getting distracted by the incorrect answer choices.

Step 1: Read the Question

> **Ex**
>
> Which choice best states the main idea of the text?

Step 2: Read the Passage and Ignore Answer Choices

> **Ex.**
>
> In an attempt to revolutionize the concept of learning spaces, educators Sarah Thompson and Mike Johnson designed an innovative school environment. The school building features flexible classrooms with movable walls, comfortable seating options ranging from bean bags to standing desks, and interactive virtual reality learning stations. Thompson and Johnson believe that this dynamic and versatile design will encourage students to be more engaged, foster a love for learning, and enhance their academic performance.

Step 3: Write Down Your BOSS Solution on Scratch Paper

For our BOSS solution, let's write down the following on our scratch paper:

Unique features = good

The main idea of the passage is to describe how the design features of the school improve students' learning. Of course, we don't need to write all of that down on our scratch paper. Instead, we can simply write down "*Unique features = good.*" This gives us a specific BOSS solution to compare the answer choices to.

Step 4: Compare Your BOSS Solution to the Answer Choices

Ex.

A) The flexible design of the school building by Sarah Thompson and Mike Johnson is impractical and hinders students' learning experiences.

B) Creating an environment with virtual reality learning stations and movable walls is the most effective way to boost academic performance in schools.

C) Sarah Thompson and Mike Johnson, as educators, have always been passionate about designing innovative and dynamic learning spaces.

D) **Despite its unconventional features, the school environment designed by Sarah Thompson and Mike Johnson aims to improve student engagement, learning interest, and academic performance.**

Remember, our BOSS solution was "*Unique features = good.*" This solution most closely matches answer choice (D). If we did not have a BOSS solution written down, we may have been tricked by answer choice (B). It sounds like a good answer. However, the passage is about all of the school's innovative features, not just its virtual reality stations and movable walls.

Having a BOSS solution saved us a lot of time because we did not have to debate between answer choices (B) and (D). We can simply select answer choice (D), and move on. From now on, use BOSS to answer every SAT Reading question you come across.

PREP EXPERT PRACTICE

Try applying this *Prep Expert Strategy* yourself to the following SAT practice questions:

## 41

Dr. Jane Goodall, a primatologist and anthropologist, has dedicated her life to the study of chimpanzees. She has observed their behaviors for decades and has seen the many ways they are similar to humans. Based on her research, she _____ that chimpanzees possess a level of intelligence that was once thought to be unique to humans.

Which choice completes the text with the most logical and precise word or phrase?

A) discredits

B) assumes

C) postulates

D) ignores

## 42

The following text is adapted from F. Scott Fitzgerald's 1925 novel *The Great Gatsby*. Nick Carraway is attending one of Gatsby's extravagant parties.

Nick entered the party, feeling a mix of excitement and curiosity. As he glanced around, his eyes widened and a smile spread across his face. The dazzling lights, the lively music, and the glamorous atmosphere overwhelmed him. It was as if he had stepped into a vibrant and enchanting world. He felt a sense of wonder, as if he had discovered something extraordinary for the first time.

According to the text, what is true about Nick Carraway?

A) He has attended similar parties in the past.

B) He is indifferent toward Gatsby's extravagant lifestyle.

C) He is captivated and delighted by the party's ambiance.

D) He finds the party overwhelming and uninteresting.

The answers to these SAT practice questions can be found in the back of this book.

PREP EXPERT REVIEW

Key Takeaways

- **Prep Expert Reading Strategy #1—*Build (Your) Own Simple Solution (BOSS)*:** Come up with your own answer before reviewing the given answer choices to avoid getting distracted by incorrect choices.

- **Common student approach:** Many students read the given answer choices immediately. This leads them to get confused and select incorrect answers that have enticing language.

- **Solution to common mistakes:** Writing down a BOSS solution on the provided scratch paper gives you a clear point of reference. This helps you eliminate incorrect answer choices and improves your decision-making accuracy.

- **Advantages of using BOSS:** The BOSS method improves critical thinking, frees up working memory, and saves time typically lost to debating between answer choices.

- **Consistent practice is key:** Regularly practicing the BOSS strategy leads to better performance and higher scores in SAT Reading. Even if your initial BOSS solution is not perfect, you are still more likely to answer SAT Reading questions correctly.

PREPEXPERT

READING STRATEGY #2

READ THE QUESTION FIRST

PREP EXPERT STRATEGY

Read the Question First on SAT Reading

By reading the question first on SAT Reading, you will know exactly what the problem is asking for before reading the passage. This means you will have a goal in mind and will know what to look out for while reading the passage.

Reading the question first clarifies what you should focus on while reading the passage. Ultimately, this allows you to ignore details of the passage that are not relevant to the question at hand.

Do Not Read the Passage First on SAT Reading

Many students approach SAT Reading problems by reading the passage first. This is a mistake. If you read the passage first without reading the question, you will not know what to focus on as you read.

Without a specific goal to focus on, your mind will become overloaded with information. You will try to remember every detail of the passage, overburdening your working memory and decreasing your critical thinking ability.

Correct Order of Items to Read on SAT Reading

Read the components of an SAT Reading problem in the following order:

1. Question
2. Blurb (if applicable)
3. Passage
4. Answer choices (only after you create a BOSS solution)

Read The Question First to maximize your SAT Reading score.

PREP EXPERT EXAMPLE

Consider the following *Prep Expert Example*.

Below is the anatomy of a typical SAT Reading problem as it is presented on the Digital SAT testing application.

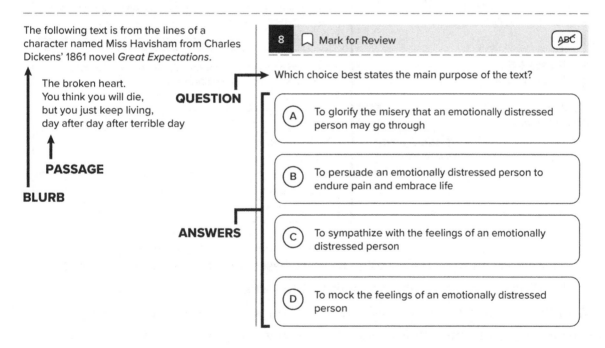

The *incorrect* approach to this SAT Reading problem would be to read the items in the following order:

1. Blurb
2. Passage

3. Question
4. Answer choices (without having created a BOSS solution)

The *correct* approach to this SAT Reading problem would be to read the items in the following order:

1. Question
2. Blurb
3. Passage
4. Answer choices (only after you have created a BOSS solution)

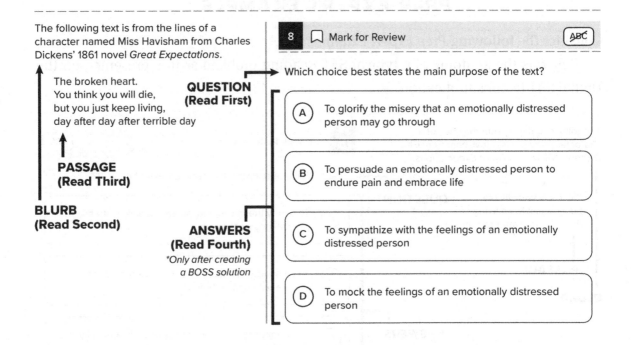

The following text is from the lines of a character named Miss Havisham from Charles Dickens' 1861 novel *Great Expectations*.

The broken heart.
You think you will die,
but you just keep living,
day after day after terrible day

QUESTION (Read First)

PASSAGE (Read Third)

BLURB (Read Second)

ANSWERS (Read Fourth)
*Only after creating a BOSS solution

8 Mark for Review ABC

Which choice best states the main purpose of the text?

A To glorify the misery that an emotionally distressed person may go through

B To persuade an emotionally distressed person to endure pain and embrace life

C To sympathize with the feelings of an emotionally distressed person

D To mock the feelings of an emotionally distressed person

In this case, the question is "Which choice best states the main purpose of the text?" Reading this question first prepares you to focus on the main idea of the passage. With this question about the main idea in mind while reading the passage, you can create a more accurate BOSS solution. Creating a better BOSS solution makes you more likely to answer the SAT Reading question correctly. In this way, *Prep Expert Reading Strategy #1—BOSS* and *Prep Expert Reading Strategy #2—Read The Question First* flow together.

PREP EXPERT PRACTICE

Try applying this *Prep Expert Strategy* yourself to the following SAT practice questions:

43

A study by a team of psychologists at a university found that people who spend more time on social media tend to have more negative views of their own bodies. The researchers surveyed 500 undergraduate students about their social media habits and their perceptions of their own bodies. They found that those who spent more time on social media tended to have more negative views of their own bodies, even when controlling for factors like gender and weight.

Which choice best states the function of the underlined sentence in the overall structure of the text?

A) To summarize the results of the study

B) To present a specific example that illustrates the study's findings

C) To explain part of the methodology used in the study

D) To call out a challenge the researchers faced in conducting their analysis

44

In the early 20th century, the Harlem Renaissance was a flourishing artistic and cultural movement among African Americans. In an essay for a history class, a student argues that the poetry of Langston Hughes was a significant contribution to the movement, reflecting both the struggles and the aspirations of the black experience in America.

Which finding, if true, would most directly support the student's claim?

A) Hughes was born in Joplin, Missouri, in 1902, and later attended Columbia University in New York City, where he became acquainted with other notable writers and intellectuals of the time.

B) Hughes's poetry was characterized by vivid and evocative language, often incorporating elements of African American culture, folklore, and music.

C) Despite facing discrimination and prejudice throughout his life, Hughes published numerous books of poetry, fiction, and nonfiction, and became one of the most prominent literary figures of the Harlem Renaissance.

D) Other prominent writers and poets of the Harlem Renaissance, such as Zora Neale Hurston and Countee Cullen, also addressed issues of race and identity in their work, but their writing did not resonate as widely with African American audiences as Hughes's poetry did.

The answers to these SAT practice questions can be found in the back of this book.

PREP EXPERT REVIEW

Key Takeaways

- **Prep Expert Reading Strategy #2—*Read The Question First***: Start SAT Reading problems by reading the question first to establish a clear goal before diving into the passage. This enables you to filter information more efficiently.

- **Avoid the passage-first approach**: Reading the passage before the question can overwhelm your working memory and hinder your critical thinking ability. This overloads your mind with details that are likely irrelevant to the question.

- **Follow a structured order**: Adhere to a specific, structured order when approaching SAT Reading problems: first the question, followed by the blurb and the passage, and finally the answer choices (but only after creating your own BOSS solution).

 **PREP**EXPERT

READING STRATEGY #3

UNDERSTAND THE MAIN IDEA

PREP EXPERT STRATEGY

Understand the Main Idea on SAT Reading

It's essential to understand the main idea of SAT Reading passages. This will help you understand the passage overall and increase your likelihood of answering the question correctly.

Where Is the Main Idea Located?

On an SAT Reading passage, the main idea is typically located toward the beginning of the passage (i.e., in the first, second, or third sentence of the paragraph). However, in some cases, the main idea may be located in the last sentence of the paragraph.

It is not important to highlight the exact sentence that contains the main idea. Instead, make sure to understand the main idea of the passage overall.

Do You Need to Write Down the Main Idea?

No! Unlike BOSS solutions, it is not necessary to write down the main idea of every SAT Reading passage. There is one exception to this rule: when the SAT Reading question specifically asks about the main idea of the passage.

Example question: Which choice best states the main purpose of the text?

When you see the above question on the SAT, you should write down the main idea of the passage before looking at the answer choices. This will serve as your BOSS solution for the question.

Understand The Main Idea to maximize your SAT Reading score.

PREP EXPERT EXAMPLE

Consider the following Prep Expert Example. Let's *Understand The Main Idea* together on an SAT Reading question.

Step 1: Read the Question

> **Ex**

Which choice best represents the main idea of the passage?

Step 2: Read the Passage and Ignore Answer Choices

> **Ex**

The following text is adapted from Charles Dickens' 1838 classic novel *Oliver Twist*. Oliver, a young boy, is left alone in the undertaker's shop.

> After being left alone in the undertaker's shop, Oliver sets the lamp on a workman's bench and looks around with a mixture of awe and dread. The sight of an unfinished coffin on black trestles in the middle of the shop fills him with cold trembles, and he imagines that he might see a terrifying figure emerging from it.

Step 3: Write Down Your BOSS Solution on Scratch Paper

For our BOSS solution, let's write down the following on our scratch paper:

Oliver is scared.

The main idea of the passage is that Oliver is terrified while in the undertaker's shop. Of course, we don't need to write all of that down on our scratch paper. Instead, we can simply write down *"Oliver is scared."* This gives us a specific BOSS solution to which to compare the answer choices.

Step 4: Compare Your BOSS Solution to the Answer Choices

A) Oliver is fascinated by the workman's bench in the undertaker's shop.
B) **Oliver feels a mixture of awe and dread while he is alone in the shop**.
C) Oliver is eager to finish the unfinished coffin on black trestles.
D) Oliver expects to find something cheerful in the undertaker's shop.

Remember, our BOSS solution was *"Oliver is scared."* This most closely matches answer choice (B).

In this case, the question was specifically asking about the main idea of the passage, so our BOSS solution matched the main idea. This will not always be the case.

Even for questions that do not specifically ask about the main idea, it is important to understand the main idea of the passage. Doing so will help you focus while reading the passage, so that you can answer more SAT Reading questions correctly.

PREP EXPERT PRACTICE

Try applying this *Prep Expert Strategy* yourself to the following SAT practice questions:

45

The invention of the World Wide Web revolutionized the way we access and share information today. Before its creation, accessing information on the internet was a tedious task. Tim Berners-Lee, a computer scientist, recognized the need for a system that would allow people to easily share information and documents. The result was the World Wide Web, a network of interlinked hypertext documents that could be accessed from anywhere in the world. With the creation of the web, the internet became more user friendly and accessible to the average person.

Which choice best states the main purpose of the text?

A) To discuss Berners-Lee's invention of the World Wide Web
B) To explain how hypertext documents work
C) To call attention to the benefits of the internet
D) To indicate how popular the World Wide Web is

## 46

In the early 20th century, mathematicians proposed the concept of fractals, intricate geometric shapes with self-similarity at different scales. However, it wasn't until the advent of computers and advanced mathematical algorithms that the true nature of fractals could be explored. In 1980, Benoit Mandelbrot introduced the Mandelbrot set, a specific fractal pattern generated by a simple mathematical equation. This breakthrough allowed for a deeper understanding and visualization of the complexity and beauty of fractals.

Which choice best states the main idea of the text?

A) The development of computers and mathematical algorithms enabled the exploration and understanding of the true nature of fractals.

B) Mathematicians in the early 20th century introduced the concept of fractals and their intricate self-similarity.

C) The Mandelbrot set is a specific fractal pattern that revolutionized the understanding of fractals.

D) Fractals are intricate geometric shapes that exhibit self-similarity at different scales and possess great complexity and beauty.

The answers to these SAT practice questions can be found in the back of this book.

PREP EXPERT REVIEW

Key Takeaways

- **Prep Expert Reading Strategy #3—*Understand The Main Idea***: Grasping the main idea of SAT Reading passages is crucial for answering questions correctly. Doing so guides your focus throughout the passage.

- **Main idea location**: Typically, the main idea can be found in the first few sentences of a passage or paragraph. Sometimes it may appear at the end of a passage though. Regardless, understanding the main idea is more important than knowing its exact location within the passage.

- **Writing down the main idea isn't usually necessary**: Unlike the case of BOSS solutions, writing down the main idea is usually not necessary. Of course, if a question is specifically asking about the main idea, then you should write it down. This main idea will also serve as your BOSS solution.

- **Improves focus and accuracy**: Even if the question does not directly ask for the main idea, understanding it enhances your focus while reading. Ultimately, this leads to more accurate answers on the SAT Reading section.

 **PREP**EXPERT

READING STRATEGY #4

MAKE INFERENCES, NOT ASSUMPTIONS

PREP EXPERT STRATEGY

Inferences versus Assumptions

There is a subtle yet important difference between inferences and assumptions:

- **Inferences**: Based on evidence from the SAT Reading passage
- **Assumptions**: *Not* based on evidence from the SAT Reading passage

Making assumptions that go beyond the scope of what is written in the passage is one of the biggest mistakes that students make. On SAT Reading questions, make inferences, not assumptions.

Identifying Assumptions in SAT Reading Answer Choices Is a Key Skill

Recognizing when SAT Reading answer choices contain assumptions that exceed the scope of what is written in the passage is a key skill that will help you eliminate incorrect answer choices.

SAT test-question writers love tricking students into making assumptions. Do not fall for their tricks. Avoid assumptions on answer choices. Doing so will help you avoid selecting incorrect answers on the SAT Reading section.

Make Inferences, Not Assumptions to maximize your SAT Reading score.

PREP EXPERT EXAMPLE

Consider the following *Prep Expert Examples*. Now let's illustrate the difference between inferences and assumptions.

Example 1: **Mark is tall and athletic.**

Imagine that an SAT Reading passage contained the statement above. Below is the difference between an *assumption* (which you are *not* allowed to make) and an *inference* (which you *are* allowed to make) on SAT Reading.

- **Assumption**: Mark plays basketball.
- **Inference**: Mark is physically in good shape.

Just because Mark is tall and athletic does not necessarily mean that he plays basketball. This is an *assumption* that goes beyond the scope of the passage text. However, you can make the *inference* that Mark is physically in good shape. The passage text contains evidence that supports the *inference*, but not the *assumption*.

Example 2: **The doctor speaks to patients harshly.**

Imagine that an SAT Reading passage contained the statement above. Below is the difference between an *assumption* (which you are *not* allowed to make) and an *inference* (which you *are* allowed to make) on SAT Reading.

- **Assumption**: The doctor is a man.
- **Inference**: The doctor has an aggressive demeanor.

Just because the doctor speaks harshly does not necessarily mean that the doctor is a man. This is an *assumption* that goes beyond the scope of the passage text. However, you can make the *inference* that the doctor has an aggressive demeanor. The passage text contains evidence that supports the *inference*, but not the *assumption*.

Example 3: The computer science student spends hours a day coding.

Imagine that an SAT Reading passage contained the statement above. Below is the difference between an *assumption* (which you are *not* allowed to make) and an *inference* (which you *are* allowed to make) on SAT Reading.

- **Assumption:** The student is intelligent.
- **Inference:** The student is dedicated.

Just because the student spends hours a day coding does not necessarily mean that the student is intelligent. This is an *assumption* that goes beyond the scope of the passage text. However, you can make the *inference* that the student is dedicated. The passage text contains evidence that supports the *inference*, but not the *assumption*.

PREP EXPERT PRACTICE

Try applying this *Prep Expert Strategy* yourself to the following SAT practice questions:

47

The following text is adapted from J. D. Salinger's novel *The Catcher in the Rye*.

> I'm the most terrific liar you ever saw in your life. It's awful.
> If I'm on my way to the store to buy a magazine, even, and
> somebody asks me where I'm going, I'm liable to say I'm going
> to the opera. It's terrible. So when I told old Spencer I had to go
> to the gym and get my equipment and stuff, that was a sheer lie.

What can be inferred about the speaker based on the text?

A) The speaker is an accomplished opera singer.

B) The speaker is generally truthful and doesn't lie often.

C) The speaker has a habit of lying about even the most mundane things.

D) The speaker is nervous and often makes up elaborate stories to impress people.

## 48

The following text is adapted from Charles Dickens' 1859 historical novel *A Tale of Two Cities*. A mob is formed outside a mansion belonging to the Evrémondes, a wealthy and influential aristocratic family.

> One woman, more impassioned than the rest, threw her scarf high into the sky and yelled (as much as I could discern) "Down with the Evrémondes!" Everyone bellowed, but whether it was against the Evrémondes or not, was hard to determine: some were shouting "Justice!" and some "Bread!", but no one seemed to understand what they were really demanding.
>
> All this I observed from the open balcony of the Evrémondes' dining room, looking over the shoulder of the family's patriarch.
>
> "What is the meaning of all this?" he kept muttering to himself. "I've never heard such a clamor before—and at this hour of the day! And with such concord!"

Based on the text, how does the patriarch of the Evrémondes family respond to the mob?

A) He questions the intention behind the mob's shouting, even though he pretends to understand their demands.

B) He shows interest in addressing the mob, despite the mob's apparent hostility toward his family.

C) He expresses empathy for the mob's grievances, despite being clearly annoyed by their shouting.

D) He perceives the mob as unified, even though the mob's demands are quite varied.

The answers to these SAT practice questions can be found in the back of this book.

PREP EXPERT REVIEW

Key Takeaways

- **Prep Expert Reading Strategy #4—*Make Inferences, Not Assumptions***: Inferences are evidence-based deductions drawn from the SAT Reading passage. Assumptions are conclusions not supported by evidence in the text that go beyond the scope of the passage.

Prep Expert
Reading Strategies

- **A common pitfall**: Avoid making assumptions that extend beyond the passage's content. This is a frequent error among students.

- **A critical skill**: Develop the ability to identify which answer choices contain assumptions rather than inferences. This is crucial for ruling out incorrect answer choices.

- **Test writers' traps**: Be aware that SAT test-question writers often try to bait students into making assumptions. Steer clear of these traps to choose correct answers on SAT Reading.

PREPEXPERT
READING STRATEGY #5

USE THE 7-REPETITION METHOD FOR VOCAB

PREP EXPERT STRATEGY

Is Vocabulary Important for SAT Reading?

Yes! Thankfully, the SAT no longer tests highly obscure vocabulary words like it did many years ago. However, it is still important to memorize certain vocabulary words for the SAT.

The SAT tests vocabulary *directly* via *Words in Context* questions. These are the questions that ask, "Which choice completes the text with the most logical and precise word or phrase?"

The SAT tests vocabulary *indirectly* via reading passages and answer choices. If you do not understand the meanings of the words in the passages or answer choices, then you will answer many questions incorrectly on SAT Reading.

You must have a good understanding of specific vocabulary words to score high on the SAT.

Which Vocabulary Words Should You Memorize for the SAT?

Refer to *Prep Expert SAT Vocab Word Lists*. These are data-driven lists of the vocabulary words that appear most frequently on SAT Reading.

Studying *Prep Expert SAT Vocab Word Lists* is one of the most effective ways to raise your SAT score. It will give you a huge advantage over other students on test day because you will have prepared with a list of actual, frequently appearing SAT vocabulary words.

How Should You Memorize SAT Vocabulary Words?

In high school, teachers often tell you to "memorize" vocabulary words, lists, and other study materials. The problem is that no one ever teaches you *how* to memorize.

Here is one technique that has worked well for me: **the 7-Repetition Method**. Repetition is an important aspect of memory formation. If you see something seven times, you are more likely to remember it. Use this fact to help you memorize SAT vocabulary words.

Repeat the definition or synonym of a vocab word seven times, whether in your mind or out loud. You can also use flash cards, practice word association, and create sentences with the vocabulary words. Do what works for you! But make sure that you use a systematic approach to memorizing the hundreds of words on *Prep Expert SAT Vocab Word Lists*.

What Are Some Benefits of Memorizing Vocabulary Words?

These are just some of the benefits of memorizing vocabulary words:

- You will comprehend SAT Reading passages, questions, and answer choices better
- You will comprehend SAT Writing passages, questions, and answer choices better
- You will write better college application essays
- You will write better scholarship application essays
- You will write better high school essays
- You will write better papers in college
- You will comprehend passages on other standardized tests better (i.e., AP Exams)
- You will improve your general reading comprehension
- You will improve your general writing ability

Prep Expert SAT Vocab Word Lists can be found in the back of this book. *Use The 7-Repetition Method For Vocab* to maximize your SAT Reading score.

PREP EXPERT EXAMPLE

Consider the following *Prep Expert Example*:

- *Memorize*: Promulgate = Broadcast

Suppose that you want to memorize that the word "promulgate" means "broadcast." *Use The 7-Repetition Method For Vocab* by repeating the following in your mind or out loud 7 times:

> *Promulgate means broadcast.*
> *Promulgate means broadcast.*
> *Promulgate means broadcast.*
> *Promulgate means broadcast.*
> *Promulgate means broadcast.*
> *Promulgate means broadcast.*
> *Promulgate means broadcast.*

While this repetition might seem like overkill, I bet that you will now forever remember what "promulgate" means! Try this method out for yourself when memorizing *Prep Expert SAT Vocab Word Lists*. Determine if it helps to embed the words in your long-term memory.

PREP EXPERT PRACTICE

Try applying this *Prep Expert Strategy* yourself to the following SAT practice questions:

## 49

During an excavation in Egypt, archaeologists uncovered a burial site containing the remains of a woman ruler from the New Kingdom period. The tomb was filled with elaborate treasures and symbols of power, suggesting the ruler's high status. This discovery may lead historians who have argued that pharaohs were exclusively male to _____ that women might have also held the title and ruled as pharaohs.

Which choice completes the text with the most logical and precise word or phrase?

A) persist

B) surmise

C) speculate

D) concede

## 50

Scientists have long struggled to explain the origin of Earth's magnetic field, which is crucial for protecting the planet's atmosphere from the solar wind. Recent research by Julien Aubert and his team has provided a more _____ explanation by simulating the conditions of Earth's core and mantle. Using advanced computer models, they were able to show how convection in the molten core generates electric currents that produce the magnetic field.

Which choice completes the text with the most logical and precise word or phrase?

A) ambiguous

B) circumstantial

C) convoluted

D) plausible

The answers to these SAT practice questions can be found in the back of this book.

PREP EXPERT REVIEW

Key Takeaways

- **Prep Expert Reading Strategy #5—*Use The 7-Repetition Method For Vocab***: Vocabulary is crucial for the SAT, especially for *Words in Context* questions. In addition, possessing an enhanced vocabulary is helpful for your overall comprehension of SAT Reading passages and answer choices.

- **Targeted vocabulary lists**: Use data-driven *Prep Expert SAT Vocab Word Lists* that contain common SAT vocabulary words to improve your test performance.

- **Memorization technique**: Employ the 7-Repetition Method to effectively memorize vocabulary. This method reinforces memory by repeating a word's definition or synonym seven times.

- **Multifaceted benefits**: Memorizing vocabulary not only aids in SAT success, but also improves general reading comprehension skills, essay writing skills, AP Exam performance, and more.

IGNORE ANSWER CHOICES

PREP EXPERT STRATEGY

You Must Ignore Answer Choices on SAT Reading

Recall that the most powerful Prep Expert Strategy for the SAT Reading section is BOSS (Build (Your) Own Simple Solution). In order for BOSS to be effective, you must Ignore Answer Choices.

You need to Build (Your) Own Simple Solution *before* looking at the answer choices. Therefore, you must Ignore Answer Choices until after you have written down a BOSS solution on your scratch paper.

If you peek at the answer choices before writing down a BOSS solution, your BOSS solution will be influenced by the answer choices (most of which are, of course, incorrect). In addition, if you read the answer choices first, then you will likely get confused, because all of the answer choices might sound good if you do not have a BOSS solution to which to compare them. Do your best to avoid peeking at the answer choices before writing down a BOSS solution.

Ignoring Answer Choices Takes Discipline

While taking the old paper-and-pencil version of the SAT, it was easy to avoid looking at the answer choices. Students could simply cover the answer choices with their hand.

The digital version of the SAT makes ignoring answer choices much more difficult. You cannot easily cover the answer choices on the screen with your hand and simultaneously write down a BOSS solution on the scratch paper. Therefore, you need to be *disciplined* to avoid looking at the answer choices before writing down your BOSS solution.

Ignore Answer Choices to maximize your SAT Reading score.

PREP EXPERT EXAMPLE

Consider the following *Prep Expert Example.*

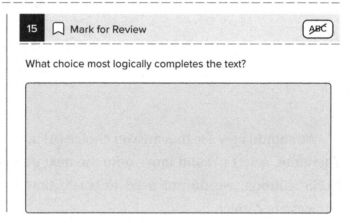

In 2009, political scientist Elinor Ostrom became the first woman to receive the prestigious Nobel Memorial Prize in Economic Sciences for her work on economic governance. It was long unanimously held among economists that natural resources that were collectively used by their users would be overexploited and destroyed in the long term. Elinor Ostrom disproved this idea by conducting field studies on how people in small, local communities manage shared natural resources, such as pastures, fishing waters, and forests. She showed that when natural resources are jointly used by their users, _____

15 ☐ Mark for Review   ⬭ABĆ

What choice most logically completes the text?

Do you notice anything different about the image above? I have manually covered the answer choices with a gray box. The gray box represents how you should *Ignore Answer Choices* on SAT Reading questions. Of course, you cannot actually place a gray box over the answer choices during your Digital SAT. But you should pretend that the answer choices are literally not there.

Only after you create a BOSS solution should you actually look at the answer choices. In this case, let's say that you read the passage and created a BOSS solution that is the following:

People share resources well

Once you have created a BOSS solution, you should look back at the answer choices. To illustrate in this example, I will now remove the gray box that previously covered the answer choices.

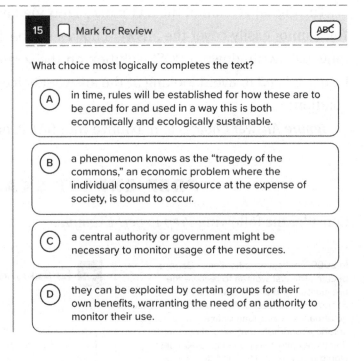

In 2009, political scientist Elinor Ostrom became the first woman to receive the prestigious Nobel Memorial Prize in Economic Sciences for her work on economic governance. It was long unanimously held among economists that natural resources that were collectively used by their users would be overexploited and destroyed in the long term. Elinor Ostrom disproved this idea by conducting field studies on how people in small, local communities manage shared natural resources, such as pastures, fishing waters, and forests. She showed that when natural resources are jointly used by their users, _____

15 ☐ Mark for Review

What choice most logically completes the text?

A) in time, rules will be established for how these are to be cared for and used in a way this is both economically and ecologically sustainable.

B) a phenomenon knows as the "tragedy of the commons," an economic problem where the individual consumes a resource at the expense of society, is bound to occur.

C) a central authority or government might be necessary to monitor usage of the resources.

D) they can be exploited by certain groups for their own benefits, warranting the need of an authority to monitor their use.

We should now see that answer choice (A) most closely matches our BOSS solution. Therefore, select (A) and move onto the next question. Because we created a specific BOSS solution, we do not need to waste time debating whether the other answer choices are correct.

When answering SAT Reading questions, pretend the answer choices are covered by a gray box. This will help you *Ignore Answer Choices* until after you have written down a BOSS solution on your scratch paper.

PREP EXPERT PRACTICE

Try applying this *Prep Expert Strategy* yourself to the following SAT practice questions:

## 51

Climate scientists are certain that human activities are increasing global temperatures, leading to climate change. *However, they are less confident about the specific rate at which global temperatures will rise in the future, as this depends on various factors that are not fully understood.* Environmental scientist Dr. Laura Sanchez and her team recently conducted a study to see if changes in atmospheric methane concentrations could help predict temperature rise, but their research concluded that this method was insufficient to provide an accurate forecast.

Which choice best describes the function of the second sentence in the overall structure of the text?

A) It outlines the primary argument against the findings of Dr. Sanchez and her team.

B) It introduces the key discovery made by Dr. Sanchez and her team.

C) It establishes the challenge that Dr. Sanchez and her team aimed to address but could not.

D) It highlights a fundamental flaw in the approach used by Dr. Sanchez and her team.

## 52

Although individuals with a background in finance constitute a small portion of the overall workforce, they occupy a significantly higher proportion of positions in the banking industry. One possible explanation for this disproportionate representation is that finance education and experience provide individuals with specialized knowledge and skills that are highly valued in the banking sector, leading to their increased _____

Which choice most logically completes the text?

A) desirability among banking employers.

B) inclination to pursue careers in other industries.

C) influence on hiring practices in non-financial sectors.

D) impact on the overall composition of the workforce.

The answers to these SAT practice questions can be found in the back of this book.

PREP EXPERT REVIEW

Key Takeaways

- **Prep Expert Reading Strategy #6—*Ignore Answer Choices*:** Avoid looking at the given answer choices before writing down a BOSS solution to avoid getting influenced by them. Most answer choices are designed to be misleading.

- **Write first:** Write down your BOSS solution on the provided scratch paper before looking at the given answer choices to prevent bias.

- **Digital versus paper:** The Digital SAT format makes it harder to avoid peeking at answer choices. With the old paper version of the SAT, you could simply physically cover the answer choices with your hand. Given that this is no longer the case with the SAT being on a digital screen, you must have discipline to avoid peeking at the answer choices.

- **Discipline needed:** Discipline is crucial to resist viewing the given answer choices on the Digital SAT before writing down your own BOSS solution.

PREPEXPERT

READING STRATEGY #7

CHALLENGE ANSWER CHOICES

PREP EXPERT STRATEGY

75% of All SAT Reading Answer Choices Are INCORRECT

You should challenge every word of the answer choices on SAT Reading questions. You should spend more time justifying why answer choices are *incorrect*. Do not spend time justifying why answer choices are *correct*. Why? Because 75% of answer choices are *incorrect*.

If you are currently attempting to justify why answer choices are correct, then your SAT score is likely suffering. Since most answer choices are incorrect, you will get frustrated. Do not try to justify why answer choices are correct. Instead, you should assume that answer choices are incorrect—do not give them the benefit of the doubt.

Do Not Let Answer Choices Get Away with False Statements

Many students give test-question writers the benefit of the doubt when going through SAT Reading answer choices. Students often think the following when reading answer choices:

"Oh, I guess the passage could be saying that"

or

"Oh, I suppose that actually is in the passage"

Thought processes like these are attempting to justify answer choices. Instead, you should think the following when reading answer choices:

"The passage is definitely not saying that"

or

"That phrase is certainly not in the passage"

Thought processes like these are attempting to *Challenge Answer Choices*.

Every Answer Choice Is "Guilty until Proven Innocent"

In the United States criminal justice system, an accused party is "innocent until proven guilty." However, you should have the exact opposite mindset when it comes to SAT Reading answer choices.

An answer choice is "guilty until proven innocent." This means that you should assume every answer choice is incorrect. Try to challenge every answer choice to find its flaws. This shift in mindset from justifying answer choices to challenging answer choices will boost your SAT Reading score.

Students Struggle with SAT Reading Because They Justify Answer Choices

Students often doubt themselves and think, *"Maybe I just don't fully understand the passage."* Here are some more examples of attempts to justify answer choices:

"Oh, I suppose the author could have been trying to say…"

or

"I guess that could be in the passage…"

or

"Maybe the author was trying to convey…"

Trying to justify incorrect answer choices in this way is detrimental to your SAT Reading score.

To Avoid Justification, You Must Demand Perfect Answer Choices

Every word of a correct answer choice must be 100% correct. If the answer choice is not 100% correct, then it is 100% incorrect. You must scrutinize every word of every answer choice. Demand perfect answer choices.

Challenge Answer Choices to maximize your SAT Reading score.

PREP EXPERT EXAMPLE

Consider the following *Prep Expert Example*. Let's *Challenge Answer Choices* together on an SAT Reading question.

Step 1: Read the Question

Ex

Which choice most logically completes the text?

Step 2: Read the Passage and Ignore Answer Choices

Ex

Researchers studying the civilization of Ancestral Puebloans found that turkey remains at Mesa Verde, a village in southern Colorado, were genetically linked to modern turkey populations in the Rio Grande Valley of north central New Mexico. These genetic markers only appeared after 1280, suggesting that _____

Step 3: Write Down Your BOSS Solution on Scratch Paper

For our BOSS solution, let's write down the following on our scratch paper:

Turkeys: Colorado → New Mexico

The passage describes how turkey populations may have migrated from Colorado to New Mexico after the year 1280. Of course, we don't need to write all of that down on our scratch paper. Instead, we can simply write down "*Turkeys: Colorado → New Mexico*." This gives us a specific BOSS solution to which to compare the answer choices.

Prep Expert
Reading Strategies

Ex

A) Mesa Verde was the original breeding ground for turkeys in the region.

B) **the Ancestral Puebloans of Mesa Verde introduced turkey cultivation to the Rio Grande Valley.**

C) the Ancestral Puebloans of Mesa Verde primarily relied on turkey farming for their sustenance.

D) turkey populations in the Rio Grande Valley were on the brink of extinction before the 1280s.

Remember, our BOSS solution was *"Turkeys: Colorado → New Mexico."* This most closely matches answer choice (B).

As we read the answer choices, we should also *Challenge Answer Choices*:

- **Answer choice (A)**: *Challenge Answer Choices*. Challenge the phrase "the original breeding ground." There is no evidence in the passage text to support this statement.

- **Answer choice (B)**: *Challenge Answer Choices*. There is no phrase in this answer choice that lacks evidence from the passage text.

- **Answer choice (C)**: *Challenge Answer Choices*. Challenge the phrase "primarily relied on turkey farming for their sustenance." There is no evidence in the passage text to support this statement.

- **Answer choice (D)**: *Challenge Answer Choices*. Challenge the phrase "brink of extinction before the 1280s." There is no evidence in the passage text to support this statement.

PREP EXPERT PRACTICE

Try applying this *Prep Expert Strategy* yourself to the following SAT practice questions:

## 53

Among mammals that display complex social interactions, such as dolphins, elephants, and humans, there seems to be a universal preference for symmetry, seen in things like mate selection and aesthetic appreciation. Susan Gonzalez and her team used a series of images of symmetrical and asymmetrical patterns to test whether this trait is also present in solitary red foxes, which have limited social interactions. They found that fox pups showed a significant preference for the symmetrical patterns, suggesting that _____

Which choice most logically completes the text?

A) symmetry is likely perceived as appealing by mammals that have complex social interactions but as uninteresting by solitary animals.

B) researchers should not assume that an innate preference for symmetry is necessarily an adaptation related to social interaction or mate selection.

C) researchers can assume that the preference for symmetry that is seen in social mammals is learned rather than innate.

D) young red foxes show a stronger preference for symmetrical patterns than adult red foxes do.

## 54

Many astronomers rely on their expertise and experience to identify celestial objects based on their observed characteristics. However, a group of researchers recently developed a machine learning algorithm trained on vast amounts of astronomical data. They claim that this algorithm can accurately identify celestial objects as well as human astronomers can. Some astronomers have expressed concern that their role may be diminished by such algorithms, but the researchers argue against this possibility.

Which finding, if true, would most directly support the researchers' claim?

A) In the researchers' study, the algorithm was able to identify celestial objects much faster than human astronomers.

B) In the researchers' study, neither the algorithm nor the human astronomers were able to accurately identify all the celestial objects in the data set.

C) A survey of astronomers showed that identifying celestial objects leaves them with limited time to conduct other critical tasks that require human expertise.

D) A survey of astronomers showed that few of them received specialized training in identifying celestial objects based on observed characteristics.

The answers to these SAT practice questions can be found in the back of this book.

PREP EXPERT REVIEW

Key Takeaways

- **Prep Expert Reading Strategy #7—*Challenge Answer Choices***: Challenge every word of SAT Reading answer choices; 75% of given answer choices are incorrect. Therefore, spend more time disproving than proving the validity of answer choices.

- **False statements**: Do not rationalize answer choices by trying to make them fit the passage. Instead, reject false statements outright without giving them the benefit of the doubt.

- **A common pitfall**: Students often hurt their SAT scores by trying to justify incorrect answer choices instead of recognizing their flaws.

- **Guilty by default**: Treat every answer choice as though it is incorrect until proven otherwise. Flip your mindset from justifying answer choices to challenging them.

- **Demand perfection**: Only accept answer choices in which every word is 100% correct. If any small part of an answer choice is incorrect, cross out the entire answer choice as incorrect.

PREP**EXPERT**
READING STRATEGY #8

USE EVIDENCE FROM THE TEXT

PREP EXPERT STRATEGY

Every Correct Answer Must Be Supported by Evidence from the Text

When answering SAT Reading questions, you must be able to point to the exact word or sentence in the passage that supports your answer. If you cannot point to evidence from the text that supports the answer you selected, you are choosing an incorrect answer.

Why does every correct answer need to be supported by evidence from the text? Because the SAT is a standardized test. This means that there cannot be any questions that are open to interpretation. There can be one, and only one, correct answer per question—without any debate.

If students challenge the validity of a question, the test-question writers must be able to defend the question. They must provide evidence from the text that supports why the correct answer is correct. If the test-question writers cannot provide evidence from the text that supports the correct answer, then it is not a valid SAT Reading question. Test-question writers almost never make such a mistake—do not bet on it. Instead, make sure you can find evidence in the text to support your answers.

Many Students Believe the SAT Reading Section Is Subjective

Many students think that the *subjective* nature of SAT Reading causes them to answer questions incorrectly. If the SAT Reading section were *subjective*, then there would be multiple correct answer choices to every question. The SAT would no longer be a valid standardized test.

This is not true.

The SAT Reading section is just as *objective* as the SAT Math section. This means that there is one, and only one, correct answer to every question. There is only one answer that can be supported by *objective* evidence from the text.

The truth is that the SAT Reading section is black-and-white. There are correct answers supported by evidence from the text. And there are incorrect answers that are not supported by evidence from the text. There is no gray area in SAT Reading passages, questions, or answer choices.

Use Evidence From The Text to maximize your SAT Reading score.

PREP EXPERT EXAMPLE

Consider the following *Prep Expert Example.* Let's *Use Evidence From The Text* together on an SAT Reading question.

Step 1: Read the Question

> **Ex**
>
> Which choice most logically completes the text?

Step 2: Read the Passage and Ignore Answer Choices

> **Ex**
>
> With over 100 countries in agreement, the Green Energy Accord aims to promote renewable energy adoption globally. However, some critics point out a potential flaw in the accord. For instance, it allows member countries to set their own renewable energy targets, which might result in a lack of transparency and accountability in tracking progress toward global renewable energy goals. This could hinder collaborative efforts and lead to _____.

Step 3: Write Down Your BOSS Solution on Scratch Paper

For our BOSS solution, let's write down the following on our scratch paper:

No responsibility

The passage describes how countries will lack responsibility because they can set their own renewable energy goals. Of course, we don't need to write all of that down on our scratch paper. Instead, we can simply write down "*No responsibility.*" This gives us a specific BOSS solution to which to compare the answer choices.

Step 4: Compare Your BOSS Solution to the Answer Choices

Ex

A) a lack of transparency and accountability in tracking progress toward global renewable energy goals.
B) an increase in greenhouse gas emissions due to excessive reliance on fossil fuels.
C) an unfair advantage for certain countries in accessing renewable energy technology.
D) difficulties in enforcing penalties for countries that fail to meet their renewable energy targets.

Remember, our BOSS solution was "*No responsibility.*" This most closely matches answer choice (A). As we are reading the answer choices, we should also *Use Evidence From The Text*.

- **Answer choice (A):** *Use Evidence From The Text*. The phrase "lack of transparency and accountability" is valid. There is clear evidence in the passage text to support this statement.

- **Answer choice (B):** *Use Evidence From The Text*. The phrases "greenhouse gas emissions" and "fossil fuels" are invalid. There is no evidence in the passage text to support these statements.

- **Answer choice (C):** *Use Evidence From The Text*. The phrase "unfair advantage" and the word "technology" are invalid. There is no evidence in the passage text to support these statements.

- **Answer choice (D)**: *Use Evidence From The Text*. The word "penalties" is invalid. There is no evidence in the passage text to support this statement.

PREP EXPERT PRACTICE

Try applying this *Prep Expert Strategy* yourself to the following SAT practice questions:

55

The following text is adapted from Frances Hodgson Burnett's 1911 novel *The Secret Garden*.

> Mary was not so contrary as she used to be. She was beginning to like people and to interest herself in their doings. She laughed till she cried over the little stories Sharpe told her about his quarrels with his wife and his troubles with his mother-in-law. She began to find the dullness of the invalids' society less dull than it had seemed to her at first. And she did not always prefer the society of the moorland boys to that of the girls who lived in fine houses. She began to make plans for the improvement of the village, to be interested in the welfare of the people...

According to the text, what is true about Mary?

A) She is bored with the society of the invalids.
B) She is still very contrary.
C) She is no longer interested in the boys who live on the moor.
D) She is becoming more interested in people and their lives.

56

In the late nineteenth century, researchers began to compile African American spirituals, but they did not always agree about these spirituals' origins. Scholars like George Pullen Jackson argued that African American spirituals were primarily derived from European hymns brought to America by white settlers. Scholars such as Zora Neale Hurston, however, contended that while some European influence is undeniable, African American spirituals are mainly the product of the ongoing interactions of various cultures in America, with significant influences from African traditions.

Which finding, if true, would most directly support Hurston's argument?

A) The spirituals that the researchers compiled included several songs written in the form of hymns, a type of song prevalent in European religious practices.

B) Much of the spirituals that the researchers compiled had similar elements from region to region.

C) Most of the spirituals that the researchers compiled were previously unknown to scholars.

D) Most of the spirituals that the researchers compiled consisted of work songs and field hollers—forms of song tied to the experiences of enslaved Africans in America—of a clearly recent origin.

The answers to these SAT practice questions can be found in the back of this book.

PREP EXPERT REVIEW

Key Takeaways

- **Prep Expert Reading Strategy #8—*Use Evidence From The Text***: For every question on the SAT Reading section, specific evidence from the passage must directly support the correct answer.

- **Standardization**: The SAT demands a single, indisputable, correct answer for every question. The correct answer must be backed by evidence in the text. This eliminates subjectivity and ensures standardization across all SAT Reading questions.

- **Objective, not subjective**: Contrary to what many students believe, the SAT Reading section is objective. This means that the SAT Reading section requires objective evidence for all correct answers just like the SAT Math section.

- **Black-and-white**: The SAT Reading section is clear-cut, with answers either supported by the text (correct) or not (incorrect). The SAT Reading questions are black-and-white; there is no room for gray areas.

PREPEXPERT
READING STRATEGY #9

DON'T SAY THE TEXT "COULD BE..."

PREP EXPERT STRATEGY

"Could Be"

"Could be" is the worst phrase that you can say in your head while considering SAT Reading answer choices. This phrase signals that you are justifying answer choices. As we previously learned, you never want to justify answer choices on SAT Reading.

If you say the text "could be" intending to say this or that, then you are questioning your own comprehension of the passage. You will begin to confuse yourself because you are letting the answer choices lead you down the wrong path.

Avoiding the phrase "could be" as you tackle answer choices is a concrete way to avoid justification. Avoiding the phrase "could be" will help you shift your mindset to begin challenging answer choices. This is exactly what we want to do while going through SAT Reading answer choices.

Do Not Trust the Answer Choices

If you say the text "could be" meaning this or that, then you are also starting to trust the answer choices instead of trusting yourself. Remember: 75% of the answer choices are incorrect, so you should not trust the given answer choices.

Monitor Your Thoughts

This strategy requires you to be conscious of your thoughts as you are reading answer choices. If you catch yourself thinking the phrase "could be" as you are reading the answer choices, you need to quickly reverse your mindset. You must get back into the correct frame of mind to challenge answer choices.

Don't Say The Text "Could Be..." to maximize your SAT Reading score.

PREP EXPERT EXAMPLE

Consider the following Prep Expert Example. Let's use the strategy *Don't Say The Text "Could Be..."* together on an SAT Reading question.

Step 1: Read the Question

> Ex

Which choice most logically completes the text?

Step 2: Read the Passage and Ignore Answer Choices

> Ex

The domestic mango (*Mangifera indica*) has its origins in Southeast Asia. However, it is now widely cultivated in various regions, including East Africa, the Caribbean, and South America. Research conducted by botanist Maria Hernandez and her team involved analyzing the genetic makeup of mango varieties from different parts of the world. Surprisingly, they found that some East African mango varieties share a closer genetic relationship with Southeast Asian ones than with other East African varieties. Given that mango cultivation in East Africa has been established for several centuries and there were no known recent introductions of mangoes from Southeast Asia, the team concluded that _____

Step 3: Write Down Your BOSS Solution on Scratch Paper

For our BOSS solution, let's write down the following on our scratch paper:

Mangoes Asia → Africa long time ago

The passage describes how mangoes from Asia must have been introduced to Africa a long time ago. Of course, we don't need to write all of that down on our scratch paper. Instead, we can simply write down *"Mangoes Asia → Africa long time ago."* This gives us a specific BOSS solution to which to compare the answer choices.

Step 4: Compare Your BOSS Solution To The Answer Choices

Ex

A) mango cultivation in Southeast Asia is relatively recent and traces back to East African origins.

B) East African mango varieties are not suitable for cultivation and must be replaced with Southeast Asian varieties.

C) Southeast Asian mango varieties have undergone significant genetic changes when introduced to East African climates.

D) **ancient trading routes likely facilitated the early introduction of mangoes from Southeast Asia to East Africa.**

Remember, our BOSS solution was *"Mangoes Asia → Africa long time ago."* This most closely matches answer choice (D). As you read the answer choices, *Don't Say The Text "Could Be..."*

- **Answer choice (A)**: *Don't Say The Text "Could Be"* referring to how "mango cultivation in Southeast Asia is relatively recent." There is no evidence in the passage to support this statement.

- **Answer choice (B)**: *Don't Say The Text "Could Be"* referring to how African mangoes "must be replaced with Southeast Asian varieties." There is no evidence in the passage to support this statement.

- **Answer choice (C)**: *Don't Say The Text "Could Be"* referring to how mangoes have "undergone significant genetic changes." There is no evidence in the passage to support this statement.

- **Answer choice (D)**: The phrase "early introduction of mangoes from Southeast Asia to East Africa" matches our BOSS solution. There is clear evidence in the passage to support this statement.

PREP EXPERT PRACTICE

Try applying this *Prep Expert Strategy* yourself to the following SAT practice questions:

57

In 2018, a team of scientists embarked on a mission to study the ocean floor in the Mariana Trench, the deepest part of the world's oceans. They used a specially designed submarine to withstand the extreme pressure at such depths. The submarine's structure was reinforced with high-strength materials and equipped with advanced technology. The scientists found that a regular submarine would not be able to reach such depths due to the immense pressure.

According to the text, why would a regular submarine not be able to reach the depths of the Mariana Trench?

A) Because the Mariana Trench is too wide for a regular submarine to navigate

B) Because the pressure at the depths of the Mariana Trench would exceed the limits of a regular submarine

C) Because the water temperature at the depths of the Mariana Trench is too cold for a regular submarine's equipment

D) Because the ocean currents in the Mariana Trench are too strong for a regular submarine to withstand

58

Scholars have acknowledged the significant influence of Pablo Picasso's artistic career on the art world, but many fail to recognize the contributions of his partner, Fernande Olivier. Fernande, herself an artist, played a crucial role in shaping Picasso's artistic development and even inspired several of his renowned works. Thus, those who primarily attribute Picasso's success solely to his own genius _____

Which choice most logically completes the text?

A) underestimate the impact of other artists on Picasso's artistic evolution.

B) overlook the artistic achievements and influence of Fernande Olivier.

C) may misinterpret the motivations behind Picasso's choice of subjects.

D) tend to view Picasso's artworks in isolation from the broader art movement.

The answers to these SAT practice questions can be found in the back of this book.

PREP EXPERT REVIEW

Key Takeaways

- **Prep Expert Reading Strategy #9—*Don't Say The Text "Could Be..."*:** Dismiss the phrase "could be" in your mind when reading through SAT Reading answer choices to avoid unnecessary self-doubt.

- **Question comprehension:** Using "could be" is a red flag that you are questioning your understanding of the passage. This leads to confusion by encouraging you to consider incorrect, misleading answer choices.

- **Challenge, don't trust:** Shift your approach from justifying answer choices to actively challenging them. Remember, the majority of answer choices on the SAT are incorrect. Do not trust them.

- **Self-trust over answer-choice trust:** Rely on your own understanding rather than the plausibility of the answer choices. Acknowledge the high likelihood of each answer choice being wrong.

- **Thought awareness:** Be conscious of your thought processes and correct any inclination toward "could be" reasoning in your mind. Maintain a critical mindset toward all answer choices throughout the SAT.

 **PREP**EXPERT

READING STRATEGY #10

ASK "DOES THE TEXT MENTION _____?"

PREP EXPERT STRATEGY

"Does the Text Mention _____?"

This is the key question that will unlock the SAT Reading section for you. It is the best question to ask yourself when reading through SAT Reading answer choices. As you are working through the SAT Reading questions, you should constantly ask yourself this question.

Every answer choice should be put to the test by asking yourself the question:

"Does the text mention _____?"

You should fill in that blank with any word, phrase, or sentence that you would like to challenge in a particular answer choice. Asking yourself this key question is a concrete way to *Challenge Answer Choices*.

Forces You to Look for Evidence in the Text

When you *Ask "Does The Text Mention _____?"*, it forces you to search for evidence in the text. Every correct answer on SAT Reading must have supporting evidence in the associated passage.

While reading an answer choice, ask yourself the question, "Does the text mention _____?"

- If the answer is **No**, it is likely an **incorrect** answer (this happens often).
- If the answer is **Yes**, it is likely a **correct** answer (this does not happen often).

Remember that 75% of answer choices on the SAT are incorrect. Thus, most of the time, the passage will not mention the word, phrase, or sentence that you are challenging in a particular answer choice. Eliminate incorrect answer choices on SAT Reading by asking yourself this simple question.

Ask "Does The Text Mention _____?" to maximize your SAT Reading score.

PREP EXPERT EXAMPLE

Consider the following *Prep Expert Example*. Let's *Ask "Does The Text Mention _____?"* together on an SAT Reading question.

Step 1: Read the Question

Ex

Which choice best describes the overall structure of the text?

Step 2: Read the Passage and Ignore Answer Choices

Ex

The following text is adapted from Jane Austen's novel *Sense and Sensibility*, Chapter XIX. Elinor is visiting Mr. Palmer's home and reflecting on her observations of his behavior and character during her visit.

Elinor had seen so little of Mr. Palmer, and in that little had seen so much variety in his address to her sister and herself, that she knew not what to expect to find him in his own family. She found him, however, perfectly the gentleman in his behaviour to all his visitors, and only occasionally rude to his wife and her mother; she found him very capable of being a pleasant companion, and only prevented from being so always, by too great an aptitude to fancy himself as much more ill-used, and therefore, as much more in want of companions than he really was. For the rest of his character and habits, they were marked, as far as Elinor could perceive. He was nice in his eating, uncertain in his hours; fond of his child, though affecting to slight it; and idled away the mornings at billiards, which ought to have been devoted to business. She liked him, however, upon the whole, much better than she had expected.

Step 3: Write Down Your BOSS Solution on Scratch Paper

For our BOSS solution, let's write down the following on our scratch paper:

Elinor observes Mr. Palmer.

The passage describes how Elinor is watching the actions of Mr. Palmer. Of course, we don't need to write all of that down on our scratch paper. Instead, we can simply write down "*Elinor observes Mr. Palmer.*" This gives us a specific BOSS solution to which to compare the answer choices.

Step 4: Compare Your BOSS Solution to the Answer Choices

Ex

A) **It describes Elinor's expectations about Mr. Palmer based on her limited interactions with him, and then details her actual observations of him during her visit to his home**.

B) It establishes Mr. Palmer's character and habits, and then contrasts them with Edward's more admirable traits.

C) It presents Mr. Palmer's behavior in his own family and toward visitors, and then analyzes his personality traits, which are typical for his sex and time of life.

D) It reveals Elinor's initial impressions of Mr. Palmer and her ultimate realization that she cannot like him any more due to his negative qualities.

Remember, our BOSS solution was *"Elinor observes Mr. Palmer."* This most closely matches answer choice (A). As we read the answer choices, we should also *Ask "Does The Text Mention _____?"*

- **Answer choice (A)**: *Ask Does The Text Mention* "Elinor's expectations about Mr. Palmer based on her limited interactions with him"? Yes!

- **Answer choice (B)**: *Ask Does The Text Mention* "Edward's more admirable traits"? No.

- **Answer choice (C)**: *Ask Does The Text Mention* "typical for his sex and time of life"? No.

- **Answer choice (D)**: *Ask Does The Text Mention* a "realization that she cannot like him"? No.

PREP EXPERT PRACTICE

Try applying this *Prep Expert Strategy* yourself to the following SAT practice questions:

59

The following text is adapted from Charlotte Brontë's 1847 novel *Jane Eyre*. Jane, an orphan, lives with her wealthy aunt and cousins, the Reeds.

Jane, a young girl of ten, possessed an intelligence and resilience beyond her years. Despite her tender age, she often found herself taking on the role of the peacekeeper in the Reed household, mediating disputes and offering sound advice. Her aunt, Mrs. Reed, though well-intentioned, often succumbed to her own prejudices and impulsive nature. Jane's ability to remain level-headed and composed in such situations proved invaluable, as she frequently managed to temper the conflicts and prevent them from escalating. Her compassion and strong moral compass were qualities that set her apart from her peers, and it was evident that she possessed a maturity well beyond her age.

According to the text, what is true about Jane?

A) Jane is often caught up in disputes and arguments with her cousins.

B) Jane is quick to judge and lacks compassion for others.

C) Jane's aunt, Mrs. Reed, is a positive role model for her.

D) Jane demonstrates maturity and resilience beyond her years.

## 60

According to historian Sarah Thompson, African American musicians played a significant role in shaping the development of jazz music during the early 20th century. Many of these <u>musicians migrated to cities like New Orleans and Chicago, where they found opportunities to perform and collaborate in a vibrant and diverse musical scene</u>. Their innovative styles and contributions led to the emergence of a distinctly American art form.

Which choice best describes the function of the underlined portion in the text as a whole?

A) It provides historical context for the migration patterns of African American musicians during the early 20th century.

B) It offers a counterargument to the claim made earlier in the text about African American musicians' role in shaping jazz.

C) It highlights the challenges faced by African American musicians in their pursuit of opportunities in the music industry.

D) It explains the cultural significance and impact of African American musicians on the development of jazz music.

The answers to these SAT practice questions can be found in the back of this book.

PREP EXPERT REVIEW

Key Takeaways

- **Prep Expert Reading Strategy #10—*Ask "Does The Text Mention _____?"*:** This is the key question that will help you answer many SAT Reading questions correctly.

- **Actively challenge answer choices**: This strategy is powerful because it forces you to actively challenge the answer choices. When you *Ask "Does The*

Text Mention _____?", you are requiring the SAT to provide you with direct evidence from the text.

- **Evidence-based approach**: The method operates on the principle that every correct answer must be supported by the text. If a phrase in the answer choice is not mentioned in the passage, then the answer choice is wrong.

- **Elimination process**: Remember that 75% of answer choices are incorrect. Therefore, most of the phrases you challenge will certainly *not* be in the text.

- **Ruthless scrutiny**: This approach aims to eliminate incorrect options by closely scrutinizing the passage for references to the phrases found in the answer choices.

PREPEXPERT

READING STRATEGY #11

AVOID EXTREME ANSWERS

PREP EXPERT STRATEGY

Extreme Answers Are Incorrect on SAT Reading

Answer choices that contain extreme words will not usually be correct on the SAT Reading section. An extreme word is a word that is especially strong or emphatic. For example, "always" is an extreme word because it implies an infinite presence of something. The infinite presence of something is rarely possible, accurate, or true. Therefore, answer choices that contain the extreme word "always" are incorrect.

Test-Question Writers Must Be Able to Defend Correct Answers

The job of test-question writers is to create questions for which they can defend why the correct answers are objectively correct. Answer choices containing extreme language are difficult to defend because students can often find at least one exception to an absolute statement.

Therefore, answer choices with extreme words are incorrect. Answer choices using milder language are easier to defend, so they are more often correct. Examples of words that indicate milder language include "may" or "suggests."

You must read everything literally on the SAT Reading section.

Example statement: "All the children are four feet tall."

In everyday language, we would likely recognize that the above statement just means that most of the children are about this height.

On the SAT, however, this statement literally means that every single child on the planet is this exact height.

You must take every statement you read on the SAT Reading section literally. Do not cut the SAT test-question writers any slack. If there is an extreme word such as "all" in the example statement above, it means literally every single possible version of it on the planet.

Avoid Extreme Answers to maximize your SAT Reading score.

PREP EXPERT EXAMPLE

Consider the following *Prep Expert Examples*.

Extreme Words That Indicate Totality or Completeness

Avoid answer choices that contain extreme words that indicate totality or completeness. The table below presents examples of such words to avoid on SAT Reading:

Extreme Words (Totality or Completeness)

all	fail
entire	perfect
every	throughout (history, her life, the ages, etc.)
everyone	totally
everything	whole

Extreme Words That Indicate Frequency

Avoid answer choices that contain extreme words that indicate frequency. The table below presents examples of such words to avoid on SAT Reading:

Extreme Words (Frequency)

always	never	only
every day/everyday	none	perpetually
forever	many	

Prep Expert Tip: The word "many" is typically not considered to be a particularly "extreme" word. However, incorrect SAT Reading answer choices often contain the word "many."

Extreme Words That Indicate Uniqueness or Singularity

Avoid answer choices that contain extreme words that indicate uniqueness or singularity. The table below presents examples of such words to avoid on SAT Reading:

Extreme Words (Uniqueness or Singularity)

completely	only	total
distinct	same	unique
identical	singular/sole	

PREP EXPERT PRACTICE

Try applying this *Prep Expert Strategy* yourself to the following SAT practice questions:

61

In Native American tribes, storytellers have traditionally played a vital role in preserving cultural heritage and passing down tribal knowledge. They have been responsible for recounting legends, myths, and historical events to educate and entertain the community. Although modern forms of communication have emerged, storytellers continue to be highly valued for their unique ability to preserve and transmit their tribe's cultural stories.

Which choice best states the main idea of the text?

A) Despite advancements in communication technology, storytellers remain integral in preserving and transmitting Native American cultural stories.

B) Storytellers have always been highly regarded for their ability to entertain and educate their community.

C) Native American tribes have relied on storytellers as the sole means of passing down cultural knowledge for centuries.

D) Technology has diminished the significance of storytellers in preserving cultural heritage among Native American tribes.

62

Publication Output of Authors A, B, C, and D

Individual	Years Active	Number of Published Works Known and Commonly Credited
Author A	1980–1995	25 (novels), 10 (short stories), 5 (essays)
Author B	1970–1990	20 (novels), 15 (short stories), 7 (essays)
Author C	1990–2010	30 (novels), 20 (short stories), 10 (essays)
Author D	1985–2005	35 (novels), 25 (short stories), 15 (essays)

Some literary researchers studying the prolific writers of the late 20th century have turned their attention to Authors A, B, C, and D. In fact, so many works and associated records for this era have been lost that counts of these four authors' output should be taken as bare minimums rather than totals; it's entirely possible, for example, that _____

Which choice most effectively uses data from the table to complete the example?

A) Author B published fewer novels than Author C, who is credited with 30 novels.

B) Author C's 30 credited novels include only works written after 2010.

C) Author D wrote far more than 35 novels and Author A published more than 5 essays.

D) Author A actually published 25 novels and wrote only 10 short stories.

The answers to these SAT practice questions can be found in the back of this book.

PREP EXPERT REVIEW

Key Takeaways

- **Prep Expert Reading Strategy #11—*Avoid Extreme Answers***: Avoid answer choices containing extreme words like "always" or "all" on the SAT Reading section. These extreme words imply totality or completeness that is rarely accurate.

- **Milder language preference**: Choose answer choices that contain milder, less absolute language, such as "may" or "suggests." These answer choices are easier for test-question writers to defend as correct options. Thus, they are more likely to be correct.

- **Literal interpretation**: Interpret statements on the SAT Reading section literally. Do not assume any flexibility in the intended meaning of the text.

PREPEXPERT

READING STRATEGY #12

AVOID EXTREME "-LY" ADVERBS IN ANSWERS

PREP EXPERT STRATEGY

Answers with Extreme Adverbs Are Incorrect on SAT Reading

An adverb is a part of speech that modifies or describes a verb, an adjective, or another adverb. Typically, adverbs end in the suffix "-ly." "Extreme adverbs" are adverbs that indicate a significant degree or extent of something. SAT Reading answer choices that contain extreme adverbs are often incorrect.

Extreme adverbs indicate a significant degree or intensity of an action or quality. They include words such as "completely," "perfectly," and "absolutely." These adverbs create a sense of totality or absoluteness. This is often at odds with the nuanced passages presented in the SAT Reading section. Such language can be too categorical to represent the subtleties typically found in SAT passages.

SAT Reading is designed to assess a student's ability to comprehend nuanced passages. As such, answers that are too generalizing may not capture the precise meaning the question demands. When an answer choice on the SAT Reading section contains an extreme adverb, approach it with caution. The test-question writers often include these kinds of answer choices to distract students from the correct answer, which is usually more moderate.

However, while an extreme adverb can be a helpful indicator of a potentially incorrect answer, this is not an absolute rule. There may be instances in which the passage's content does align with an extreme adverb's intensity, so it is crucial that you judge the answer in the context of the passage.

Avoid Extreme "-ly" Adverbs In Answers to maximize your SAT Reading score.

PREP EXPERT EXAMPLE

Consider the following *Prep Expert Examples.*

Extreme "-ly" Adverbs

Avoid answer choices containing extreme adverbs that state a significant degree of something. The table below presents examples of such words to avoid on SAT Reading.

Extreme "-ly" Adverbs

broadly	elaborately	largely	significantly
closely	extensively	overly	substantially
considerably	greatly	profoundly	vastly
deeply	heavily	severely	widely

PREP EXPERT PRACTICE

Try applying this *Prep Expert Strategy* yourself to the following SAT practice questions:

63

Text 1
In a study, researchers discovered that giving people compliments about their abilities and talents can actually increase their performance in the future. This is known as the "compliment effect," and it is thought to work by boosting people's confidence and motivation.

Text 2
While the "compliment effect" is certainly an interesting phenomenon, researchers caution that it is not a universal truth. In some cases, too many compliments can actually backfire and make people less motivated.

Additionally, the type of compliment matters—a compliment on a person's effort is more effective than a compliment on their inherent abilities.

Based on the texts, what would the author of Text 2 most likely say about Text 1's characterization of the "compliment effect"?

A) It is overly simplistic given the complexities of human motivation.
B) It is accurate, but lacks the nuance of certain limitations.
C) It is substantially exaggerated, with too much emphasis on the positive effects of compliments.
D) It is broadly misleading, with no mention of the negative effects of compliments.

## 64

Scientists studying the decline in the population of sea otters along the western coast of North America have proposed a hypothesis that connects their decline to an increase in the population of sea urchins. Sea otters are known to feed on sea urchins, which are responsible for damaging kelp forests. Kelp forests provide a critical habitat for numerous marine species.

Which finding, if true, would most directly support the scientists' hypothesis?

A) The population of other sea otter prey, such as crabs and clams, has remained considerably stable over the same time period.
B) Kelp forests have experienced a decline in overall health and biomass coinciding with the decline in sea otter population.
C) Sea urchin abundance tends to be higher in areas with thriving kelp forests than in areas where kelp forests have severely declined.
D) The population of predatory fish that feed on sea otters has greatly increased in the absence of a robust sea otter population.

The answers to these SAT practice questions can be found in the back of this book.

PREP EXPERT REVIEW

Key Takeaways

- **Prep Expert Reading Strategy #12—*Avoid Extreme "-ly" Adverbs In Answers***: On the SAT Reading section, answers with extreme adverbs (words ending in "-ly" that suggest a high degree of something) are typically incorrect.

- **Nuance versus extremity**: Extreme adverbs such as "completely," "perfectly," and "absolutely" are often too strong to accurately represent the nuances of SAT Reading passages.

- **Contextual judgment**: While extreme adverbs can be red flags for wrong answers, they are not universally incorrect. Each answer choice must be evaluated within the context of the passage.

PREPEXPERT

READING STRATEGY #13

AVOID VERBATIM ANSWERS

PREP EXPERT STRATEGY

Verbatim Answers Are Incorrect on SAT Reading

Answer choices that copy phrases verbatim from the associated passage are typically incorrect. You should avoid answer choices that duplicate key phrases or words directly from the passage.

On the surface, answer choices containing verbatim language appear to agree with the original passage. But in reality, these verbatim answers often contain underlying concepts that make them incorrect.

WHY ARE VERBATIM ANSWERS INCORRECT ON SAT READING?

The College Board's test-question writers want students to read the passage. However, many students will choose to skip reading the passage altogether.

Can test-question writers punish students who do not read the passage? Well, they can't stand behind students during the exam and force them to read the passages. But they can trick students who do not read the passage. Test-question writers know that students who do not read the passage will choose answer choices that look similar to the passage.

If you had no idea what a passage is about because you skipped reading it altogether, wouldn't you just choose an answer that has similar words to the passage? Most likely. Therefore, test-question writers create *incorrect answer choices* containing phrases that are identical to phrases in the original passage.

You Must Understand the Passage

To avoid falling for the trap of selecting answer choices with verbatim words and phrases, you must understand the passage. Students who comprehend the underlying concepts of the passage can tell that verbatim answers do not actually agree with the passage.

In other words, the College Board rewards students who take the time to read the passages. And it punishes students who think they can game the system by skipping reading the passage.

Of course, sometimes there will be correct answers with a couple words that are exactly the same as the words in the associated passage. But more often than not, correct SAT answer choices will summarize the underlying concepts of the passage. Correct answers rarely copy the exact same phrases out of the passage word for word.

Avoid Verbatim Answers to maximize your SAT Reading score.

PREP EXPERT EXAMPLE

Consider the following *Prep Expert Example*. Let's *Avoid Verbatim Answers* together on an SAT Reading question.

Step 1: Read the Question

> **Ex**
>
> Which choice best states the main idea of the text?

Step 2: Read the Passage and Ignore Answer Choices

Renowned nutritionist Dr. Elaine Summers has proposed a diet that is based on the principle that eating foods in their raw state can lead to better digestion and nutrient absorption. She cites a study where participants who followed a raw food diet for six months experienced notable improvements in their digestive health and energy levels.

Step 3: Write Down Your BOSS Solution on Scratch Paper

For our BOSS solution, let's write down the following on our scratch paper:

Raw food = good

The passage describes how following a raw food diet for six months can lead to an improvement in health. Of course, we don't need to write all of that down on our scratch paper. Instead, we can simply write down "*Raw food = good*." This gives us a specific BOSS solution to which to compare the answer choices.

Step 4: Compare Your BOSS Solution to the Answer Choices

A) Dr. Elaine Summers has proposed a diet that is based on eating foods in their raw state, as it has been shown to improve digestion and nutrient absorption for six months.

B) Eating foods in their raw state, according to Dr. Summers' principle, is the only way to ensure better digestion and nutrient absorption.

C) **While it may seem unconventional, Dr. Summers' principle suggests that a raw food diet can result in better overall health.**

D) Participants who followed a raw food diet, as per Dr. Summers' study, experienced improvements only in their energy levels and not their overall health.

Remember, our BOSS solution was "*Raw food = good.*" This most closely matches answer choice (C). As we read the answer choices, we should also observe any answers that contain identical phrases to those of the passage.

- **Answer choice (A)**: *Avoid Verbatim Answers.* The phrase "Dr. Elaine Summers has proposed a diet that is based on" is taken verbatim from the original passage, so this answer choice is likely attempting to trick students who did not read or fully understand the passage.

- **Answer choice (B)**: *Avoid Verbatim Answers.* The phrase "eating foods in their raw state" is taken verbatim from the original passage, so this answer choice is likely attempting to trick students who did not read or fully understand the passage.

- **Answer choice (C)**: There are no significant verbatim phrases in this answer choice. It succinctly summarizes the main idea of the passage.

- **Answer choice (D)**: *Avoid Verbatim Answers.* The phrase "participants who followed a raw food diet" is taken verbatim from the original passage, so this answer choice is likely attempting to trick students who did not read or fully understand the passage.

PREP EXPERT PRACTICE

Try applying this *Prep Expert Strategy* yourself to the following SAT practice questions:

## 65

Archaeologist Dr. Priya Singh and her team conducted a study on ancient pottery in the Mediterranean region. By analyzing the residue found on pottery fragments from different time periods, they determined that certain types of pottery were used exclusively for storing olive oil. They also discovered that the presence of specific chemical compounds in the residue indicated the use of olive oil. The team concluded that olive oil played a significant role in the Mediterranean diet during ancient times.

Which finding, if true, would most strongly support the team's conclusion?

A) The chemical compounds found in the residue were also present in pottery fragments used for storing wine.

B) The analysis of pottery from other regions showed a similar pattern of olive oil usage.

C) The pottery fragments used for storing olive oil were found exclusively in coastal areas.

D) The study revealed that the residue found on pottery fragments dated back to a period before the cultivation of olives in the Mediterranean region.

## 66

Researchers studying ancient bird fossils have discovered evidence that supports the theory that some species of ancient birds were capable of long-distance migrations. Anna Rodriguez, Carlos Martinez, and Julia Thompson analyzed stable isotopes in the feathers of fossilized birds from the Late Cretaceous period, approximately 70 million to 66 million years ago. By comparing the isotopic composition of the feathers to that of modern birds with known migration patterns, the researchers were able to infer the potential migratory behavior of the ancient birds. Rodriguez, Martinez, and Thompson propose that these ancient birds undertook long-distance migrations, similar to their modern counterparts.

Which finding, if true, would most directly support Rodriguez, Martinez, and Thompson's claim?

A) The isotopic composition of the feathers in the ancient bird fossils closely matches that of nonmigratory modern birds.

B) Fossilized bird footprints have been found in various locations along the routes of modern birds with known migration patterns.

C) Several ancient bird fossils have been discovered in regions far from their breeding grounds, indicating their propensity for long-distance travel.

D) The average body size of the ancient birds is larger than that of modern migratory birds with similar feeding

habits.

The answers to these SAT practice questions can be found in the back of this book.

PREP EXPERT REVIEW

Key Takeaways

- **Prep Expert Reading Strategy #13—*Avoid Verbatim Answers***: Test creators deliberately include verbatim phrases in answer choices to trap students who avoid reading the entire passage.

- **Comprehension focus**: Students who are successful on SAT Reading fully understand each passage. Answer choices that copy the passage word for word are frequently incorrect.

- **Paraphrasing versus quoting**: Correct answers often paraphrase the content of a passage. This suggests a grasp of the underlying ideas instead of a reliance on carbon-copy text.

- **The SAT incentivizes reading**: The SAT rewards students who invest time in understanding the passages. It disapproves of attempts to game the system by students who try to skip reading the passages.

- **Answer selection strategy**: Avoid answer choices that contain verbatim phrases from the passage to improve the accuracy of your answers on SAT Reading questions.

PREPEXPERT

READING
STRATEGY #14

AVOID OVERQUALIFIED ANSWERS

PREP EXPERT STRATEGY

Overqualified Answers Are Incorrect on SAT Reading

To understand what an "overqualified" answer is, you must first understand what a qualification is. A qualification is a modification that narrows the scope of a phrase.

- **Original statement**: *Students* spend time on social media.
- **Additional qualification**: *High school students* spend time on social media.
- **Additional qualification**: *High school students who are studying for the SAT* spend time on social media.

Notice how each additional qualification makes the statement more specific. The more specific an SAT Reading answer choice is, the more content you have to challenge. The more content you have to challenge, the more likely an answer choice is incorrect.

Look out for "overqualified" answer choices on SAT Reading questions. The more qualifications an answer choice has, the more evidence the passage must provide to support that answer, which is more challenging for test-question writers.

Overqualified answers tend to be traps for unwary test-takers. When an answer choice adds several layers of specificity, it demands a higher level of detailed evidence from the passage to be correct. This level of precision can misrepresent the underlying concepts in a passage.

Typically, SAT Reading prefers more general answers compared to overqualified answers. General answers are more often correct than specific answers that have many qualifications.

Red Flag Qualifier: "Very"

The qualifier "very" is a red flag on the SAT. The word "very" is typically used to intensify or exaggerate a claim, potentially making an answer choice too strong or absolute. SAT Reading prefers answers that are supported by the passage and don't extend beyond the scope of what the author has written.

In most cases, the correct answer will mirror the tone and degree of the assertions made in the passage, so you should be wary of answer choices that include the word "very." "Very" introduces a degree of certainty or emphasis that often exceeds the scope of the text.

Avoid Overqualified Answers to maximize your SAT Reading score.

PREP EXPERT EXAMPLE

Consider the following *Prep Expert Example*. Let's *Avoid Overqualified Answers* together on an SAT Reading question.

Step 1: Read the Question

> Ex

Which choice most logically completes the text?

Step 2: Read the Passage and Ignore Answer Choices

> Ex

In the mid-20th century, despite there being minimal direct contact between Southeast Asian cuisines and West African kitchens, many similarities in the use of spices and flavor profiles can be identified. Assuming that chefs from these distinct regions had not visited each others' countries, these observations most strongly suggest that _____

Step 3: Write Down Your BOSS Solution on Scratch Paper

For our BOSS solution, let's write down the following on our scratch paper:

Shared spices

The passage describes how, despite a lack of contact between the two continents, Asian and African cuisines share similar flavor profiles, so they must have used similar spices. Of course, we don't need to write all of that down on our scratch paper. Instead, we can simply write down *"Shared spices."* This gives us a specific BOSS solution to which to compare the answer choices.

Step 4: Compare Your BOSS Solution to the Answer Choices

Ex

A) **culinary experts from both regions shared a common historical source of spices due to ancient trade routes**.

B) Southeast Asian and West African cuisines developed their use of spices in complete isolation from each other, as confirmed by numerous historical accounts detailing culinary traditions.

C) the spice trade was not significant in shaping the culinary practices of the 20th century, according to a comprehensive analysis of global culinary trends and their socioeconomic influences.

D) chefs in Southeast Asia began to adopt West African spices only after the mid-20th century, as indicated by recipes published in a series of influential cookbooks during that era.

Remember, our BOSS solution was *"Shared spices."* This most closely matches answer choice (A). As we read the answer choices, we should also *Avoid Overqualified Answers*:

- **Answer choice (A):** There are no significant overqualified phrases in this answer choice. It describes how both regions shared the same spices.

- **Answer choice (B):** *Avoid Overqualified Answers.* "As confirmed by numerous historical accounts detailing culinary traditions" is an overqualified phrase that is too specific. In addition, this answer choice is not supported by evidence from the passage.

- **Answer choice (C)**: *Avoid Overqualified Answers.* "According to a comprehensive analysis of global culinary trends and their socioeconomic influences" is an overqualified phrase that is too specific. In addition, this answer choice is not supported by evidence from the passage.

- **Answer choice (D)**: *Avoid Overqualified Answers.* "As indicated by recipes published in a series of influential cookbooks during that era" is an overqualified phrase that is too specific. In addition, this answer choice is likely attempting to trick students who did not read or fully understand the passage.

PREP EXPERT PRACTICE

Try applying this *Prep Expert Strategy* yourself to the following SAT practice questions:

67

Born in 1902 in a small village in Mexico, María Izquierdo is now considered one of the most important figures in Mexican modern art. In a paper for an art history class, a student claims that Izquierdo's paintings provide valuable insights into rural Mexican culture and traditions—in her work, Izquierdo was able to vividly portray various aspects of rural life, infusing her subjects with respect and genuineness.

Which finding, if true, would most directly support the student's claim?

A) Izquierdo painted numerous works meticulously depicting the everyday life, festivals, and traditions of rural Mexican communities.

B) Izquierdo's paintings demonstrate an impressive level of artistic skill, as seen in her effective use of color to evoke emotion and symbolism.

C) During her lifetime, Izquierdo was recognized and acclaimed both within and outside her native Mexico, with her work exhibited in places like the United States, France, and Argentina.

D) Some of the rural scenes and characters Izquierdo painted had long been very popular subjects among Mexican artists.

68

In the early 20th century, the invention of the assembly line revolutionized automobile production by significantly reducing manufacturing costs.

However, the assembly line primarily affected the efficiency of the production process itself, while the stages of design and engineering remained relatively unaffected. This indicates that during the early 20th century, _____

Which choice most logically completes the text?

A) automakers focused more on streamlining the design and engineering phases of automobile production.

B) the costs of designing and engineering automobiles were not significantly impacted by the implementation of assembly line techniques.

C) customers experienced a decline in the quality of automobiles due to the increased emphasis on cost reduction in the production process.

D) the invention of the assembly line allowed automakers to produce a greater variety of automobile models to cater to very diverse customer preferences.

The answers to these SAT practice questions can be found in the back of this book.

PREP EXPERT REVIEW

Key Takeaways

- **Prep Expert Reading Strategy #14—*Avoid Overqualified Answers*:** Qualifications to an answer choice narrow its scope. "Overqualified" answers are often too specific to be correct.

- **Overqualified answers require more evidence:** Because overqualified answers demand more evidence from the passage, they are less likely to be correct.

- **General versus specific:** On the SAT Reading section, general answers are usually preferable to answers that are very specific due to multiple qualifications.

- **"Very" is a red flag:** The word "very" is a qualification that often signifies an exaggerated claim. Typically, an SAT Reading answer choice qualified by the word "very" is incorrect.

 **PREP**EXPERT

READING
STRATEGY #15

INTERPRET DATA

PREP EXPERT STRATEGY

Quantitative Evidence Questions

The SAT Reading section will present you with quantitative data in the form of an informational graphic, such as a graph, table, or chart. The College Board refers to these questions as *Command of Quantitative Evidence Questions*. The question writers are testing your ability to appropriately support, weaken, or illustrate a specified claim based on an informational graphic.

Most Common Question Types

Here are the three most common question types that the SAT may ask you when including graphs, tables, or charts:

- **Support questions**: Which choice best describes data from the table/graph/chart that *support* the claim/conclusion/hypothesis?

- **Weaken questions**: Which choice best describes data from the table/graph/chart that *weaken* the claim/conclusion/hypothesis?

- **Example questions**: Which choice most effectively uses data from the table/graph/chart to complete the *example/statement*?

Standardized Approach to Informational Graphics

To effectively understand graphics associated with these questions, you must use a consistent approach. Here is the standardized approach we recommend to *Interpret Data* on the SAT:

- **Step 1**: Read the title of the informational graphic
- **Step 2**: Read the column and row headers (*if table*) or the titles of the axes (*if graph*)
- **Step 3**: Interpret one row (*if table*) or one data point or bar (*if graph*)

Regarding Step 3, it is particularly important to interpret at least one row of data (if the graphic is a table) or at least one data point or bar (if it is a graph). If you can interpret one line or item of data, then you can interpret the entire informational graphic and fully understand it.

Using the standardized approach above will ensure that you understand every graphic on SAT Reading.

Conceptual Understanding

To interpret data effectively, you must do more than read titles and headers. You must critically analyze the data, compare it with the associated text, and discern patterns or discrepancies. This deeper analysis helps you understand the context and the implications of the data. All of this is essential to answering data-related questions correctly.

Interpret Data to maximize your SAT Reading score.

PREP EXPERT EXAMPLE

Consider the following *Prep Expert Example*. Let's *Interpret Data* together on an SAT Reading question.

Step 1: Read the Question

Which choice best describes data from the table that support Harding and Levine's suggestion?

Step 2: Read the Passage & Ignore Answer Choices

The largest Cretaceous theropods, a group of bipedal carnivorous dinosaurs including species like Giganotosaurus and Spinosaurus, are believed to have been among the fastest land animals of their time. However, estimating the running speed of extinct animals is challenging, and paleontologists Sarah Harding and James Levine have suggested that the estimated speed of these dinosaurs may vary significantly based on the methodology employed in the estimation.

Step 3: Interpret Data on Informational Graphics

Estimated Running Speeds of Cretaceous Theropods

Study	Year	Estimation Method	Approximate Running Speed (km/h)
Smith and Jones	2023	Biomechanical modeling	45–50
Lee et al.	2018	Fossil track analysis	30–40
Nguyen and Patel	2020	Comparative anatomy	55–60
Harris and Clark	2021	Biomechanical modeling	40–45

- Step 1: Read the title of the informational graphic
  - *Estimated Running Speeds of Cretaceous Theropods*

- Step 2: Read the column and row headers
  - Column Headers: *Study, Year, Estimation Method, Approximate Running Speed*

- Row Headers: *Smith and Jones, Lee et al., Nguyen and Patel, Harris and Clark*

- Step 3: Interpret one row
  - In 2023, authors Smith and Jones did a study in which they estimated that the running speed of Cretaceous theropods was between 45 and 50 kilometers per hour.

Step 4: Write Down Your BOSS Solution on Scratch Paper

For our BOSS solution, let's write down the following on our scratch paper:

Hugely varied running speeds based on method

The passage describes how Harding and Levine believe Cretaceous theropod running speed estimates change significantly depending on the methodology used for the estimate. The table supports this claim because the various studies used different methods to estimate running speed, and many of the studies had different estimations of running speed. Of course, we don't need to write all of that down on our scratch paper. Instead, we can simply write down *"Hugely varied running speeds based on method."* This gives us a specific BOSS solution to which to compare the answer choices.

Step 5: Compare Your BOSS Solution to the Answer Choices

Ex

A) Smith and Jones's study, which employed biomechanical modeling, estimated the highest running speed range for the Cretaceous theropods.

B) **The estimates of running speed by Lee et al. using fossil track analysis and Nguyen and Patel using comparative anatomy varied significantly, with each study presenting different ranges**.

C) Both Smith and Jones and Harris and Clark used biomechanical modeling, yet their estimated speed ranges were similar.

D) Nguyen and Patel's estimate using comparative anatomy yielded a maximum speed that was higher than those estimated using biomechanical modeling.

Remember, our BOSS solution was *"Hugely varied running speeds based on method."* This most closely matches answer choice (B).

PREP EXPERT PRACTICE

Try applying this *Prep Expert Strategy* yourself to the following SAT practice questions:

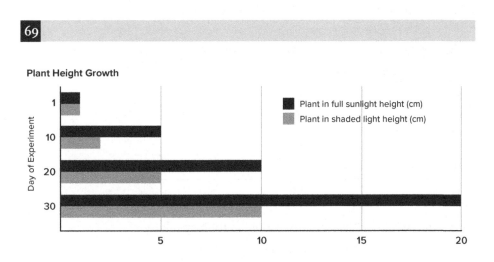
69

To investigate the effect of varying light levels on plant growth, a student in a biology class placed plants in two different light conditions: one with full sunlight and one with shaded light. The student measured the height of the plants in both conditions over 30 days. The student concluded that the increased growth in plant height in the full sunlight condition by day 30 was entirely due to the higher light levels.

Which choice best describes data from the graph that weaken the student's conclusion?

A) The plant height was the same in both light conditions on day 1.
B) The plant height also substantially increased by day 30 in the shaded light condition.
C) The most significant growth in plant height in the full sunlight condition occurred from day 1 to day 10.
D) The plant height on day 30 was taller in the full sunlight condition than in the shaded light condition.

## 70

A group of researchers conducted a study to determine the rates at which different Asian languages are typically spoken and how much information they can effectively convey. The table below presents the data collected, showing the rate of speech (measured in characters per second) and the rate of information conveyed (also measured in characters per second) for five languages: Japanese, Chinese, Korean, Thai, and Vietnamese.

Language	Rate of speech (characters per second)	Rate of information conveyed (characters per second)
Japanese	10	80
Chinese	7	85
Korean	12	80
Thai	8	90
Vietnamese	11	78

The researchers found that while languages vary widely in their speaking rates, the amount of information conveyed tends to vary much less. Consequently, they claim that two languages with very different speaking rates can still convey the same amount of information in a given amount of time.

Based on the data provided in the table, which choice best describes the information that supports the researchers' claim?

A) Among the five languages in the table, Thai and Vietnamese have the lowest rates of speech and the lowest rates of information conveyed.

B) Chinese conveys information at approximately the same rate as Korean, despite being spoken at a slower rate.

C) Among the five languages in the table, the language that is spoken the fastest is also the language that conveys information the fastest.

D) Japanese and Thai are spoken at approximately the same rate, but Japanese conveys information faster than Thai does.

The answers to these SAT practice questions can be found in the back of this book.

PREP EXPERT REVIEW

Key Takeaways

- **Prep Expert Reading Strategy #15—*Interpret Data*:** The SAT Reading section includes *Command of Quantitative Evidence Questions*, which test your ability to interpret data from graphs, tables, or charts.

- **Common question types:** The most common types of questions are support questions (data supporting a claim), weaken questions (data weakening a claim), and example questions (data used to complete an example or statement).

- **Standardized approach to interpret data:** Prep Expert's recommended approach to data questions involves three steps: (1) Read the title of the graphic, (2) Understand column/row headers or axes titles, and (3) Interpret at least one row or data point. Once you can interpret one row or data point, you will be able to interpret the entire graph, table, or chart.

READING STRATEGY #16
HIGHLIGHT THE CLAIM

PREP EXPERT STRATEGY

Textual Evidence Questions

The SAT Reading section will present you with textual evidence in the form of a claim, hypothesis, or argument. The College Board refers to these questions as *Command of Textual Evidence* questions. The question writers are testing your ability to appropriately support, weaken, or illustrate a claim based on textual evidence from the passage.

Most Common Question Types

Here are the three most common question types that the SAT may ask you regarding questions related to textual evidence:

- **Support questions**: Which finding, if true, would most directly *support* the claim, hypothesis, or argument?

- **Weaken questions**: Which finding, if true, would most directly *weaken or undermine* the claim, hypothesis, or argument?

- **Illustrate questions**: Which quotation most effectively *illustrates* the claim, hypothesis, or argument?

Highlight the Claim

To effectively answer *Textual Evidence* questions, you must *Highlight The Claim*. While reading a passage, if you do not know what the claim, hypothesis, or argument is, then it is impossible to correctly answer these *Command of Textual Evidence* questions.

Highlighting the claim the question is referring to will help you ignore the passage's extraneous content so you can focus on what you will need to support, weaken, or illustrate with your answer.

This is the *one time* on the Digital SAT that we recommend using the highlighter tool.

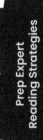

Annotate Button

The College Board's Bluebook app does not have a "highlighter tool" button. Instead, it has an "Annotate" button that allows you to highlight text.

Here is the standardized approach we recommend to *Highlight The Claim* on Digital SAT Reading questions:

- **Step 1**: Identify the passage's claim, hypothesis, or argument
- **Step 2**: Highlight the claim with your mouse
- **Step 3**: Click the "Annotate" button in the upper right-hand corner of the screen
- **Step 4**: Click "Save"

Highlight The Claim to maximize your SAT Reading score.

PREP EXPERT EXAMPLE

Consider the following *Prep Expert Example*. Let's *Highlight The Claim* together on an SAT Reading question.

Step 1: Read the Question

Ex

Which quotation from *Catcher in the Rye* most effectively illustrates the claim?

Step 2: Read the Passage and Ignore Answer Choices

Ex

> *The Catcher in the Rye* is a 1951 novel written by J. D. Salinger. In the story, the protagonist Holden Caulfield encounters various people with whom he often finds fault. Holden has a critical attitude toward others. This is evident when he describes a character, saying, "_____.

Step 3: Highlight the Claim

- **Step 1**: Identify the claim in the passage
  - *Holden has a critical attitude toward others.*

- **Step 2**: Highlight the claim with your mouse
  - *The Catcher in the Rye* is a 1951 novel written by J. D. Salinger. In the story, the protagonist Holden Caulfield encounters various people with whom he often finds fault. Holden has a critical attitude toward others. This is evident when he describes a character, saying, "_____.

- **Step 3**: Click the "Annotate" button in the upper right-hand corner of the screen (this is assuming you are taking the Digital SAT in the Bluebook app)

- **Step 4**: Click "Save" (this is assuming you are taking the Digital SAT in the Bluebook app)

Step 4: Write Down Your BOSS Solution on Scratch Paper

For our BOSS solution, let's write down the following on our scratch paper:

Fault-finder

The claim is that "Holden has a critical attitude toward others." Per the original question, we will need to find a quotation that supports this claim. Of course, we do not need to guess what that quotation is. Instead, we can simply write down that the quote will need to be something related to Holden being a *"Fault-finder."* This gives us a specific BOSS solution to which to compare the answer choices.

Ex

A) **"That guy Morrow was about as sensitive as a toilet seat."**

B) "Boy, I hate it when somebody yells 'Good luck!' at me."

C) "They're nice and all."

D) "I don't care if it's a sad good-by or a bad good-by, but when I leave a place I like to know I'm leaving it."

Remember, our BOSS solution was *"Fault-finder."* This most closely matches answer choice (A).

PREP EXPERT PRACTICE

Try applying this *Prep Expert Strategy* yourself to the following SAT practice questions:

71

Music bands, like the UK-based band The Rolling Stones or US's The Eagles, are groups of musicians who agree to create music together: perhaps for similar taste in music, to convey certain shared messages, or to leverage the synergy of their musical skills. Regardless of the reasons, music bands always involve some level of collaboration among the members. Based on a recent series of interviews with various bands, a music journalist claims that this can be challenging for musicians who are often used to having complete control over their compositions.

Which quotation from the interviews best illustrates the journalist's claim?

A) "The first band I joined had many exceptionally skilled musicians, and we all got along well, but because we struggled with sharing the limelight and attributing the songs, the band didn't stick together."

B) "We create music together, but that doesn't mean all songs are equally the work of all of us. Many of our songs are primarily driven by whoever initially brought the idea to the group."

C) "Having been a band member for several years, it's sometimes hard to remember what it was like to create music alone without the band's support. But that support enhances my personal creativity rather than restricting it."

D) "Sometimes an external musician will choose to collaborate with us on a piece, but all of those pieces fall within the broader themes of the work the band creates independently."

## 72

Political scientists have long debated the impact of negative campaign advertisements on voter attitudes. To investigate this, researchers conducted a study during a local election campaign. They divided participants into two groups: Group A was exposed to a series of negative campaign ads targeting a candidate, while Group B was not exposed to any campaign ads. The researchers then assessed the participants' attitudes toward the targeted candidate immediately after the election.

Which finding from the study, if true, would most directly weaken the claim made by those who argue that negative campaign ads have no impact on voter attitudes?

A) Participants in Group A, who were exposed to negative campaign ads, held more negative attitudes toward the targeted candidate immediately after the election compared to their attitudes prior to the campaign.

B) Participants in Group B, who were not exposed to any campaign ads, held similar attitudes toward the targeted candidate immediately after the election as they held prior to the campaign.

C) Participants who reported being undecided at the start of the study were equally likely to develop positive or negative attitudes toward the targeted candidate, regardless of exposure to negative campaign ads.

D) Participants who reported being strong supporters of the targeted candidate prior to the study held even more positive attitudes toward the candidate immediately after exposure to negative campaign ads.

The answers to these SAT practice questions can be found in the back of this book.

PREP EXPERT REVIEW

Key Takeaways

- **Prep Expert Reading Strategy #16—*Highlight The Claim***: The SAT Reading section includes *Command of Textual Evidence* questions, which test the ability to use textual evidence from a passage to support, weaken, or illustrate a claim.

- **Common question types**: The main question types include support questions (support the claim), weaken questions (weaken the claim), and illustrate questions (illustrate the claim).

- **Highlighting the claim**: A key strategy is to highlight the claim, hypothesis, or argument in the passage. This helps you to focus on the relevant parts of the text and ignore extraneous content.

- **Using digital tools**: Highlighting the claim makes it easier to find evidence to support, weaken, or illustrate the claim. You should use the "Annotate" button in the College Board's Bluebook app for highlighting.

 **PREPEXPERT**

READING STRATEGY #17
FAKE INTEREST

PREP EXPERT STRATEGY

SAT Reading Passages Are Boring

Let's face it: SAT Reading passages are boring. One reason many students score poorly on SAT Reading passages is their lack of interest. When you aren't interested in what you are reading, you won't comprehend the meaning of the passage. Lack of comprehension leads to lower SAT Reading scores.

When you are not interested in what you are reading, you will spend more time reading the passage because you will have to repeatedly reread the passage to comprehend it. This also leads to lower SAT Reading scores.

Interest versus Lack of Interest

- **When you read material that interests you**, you tend to remember the details of what you just read. In addition, you typically read material that interests you at a faster pace. Think of the last article you read on a topic that interests you... do you remember the details? Did you read the article quickly or slowly?

    versus

- **When you read material that does not interest you,** you tend not to remember the details of what you just read. In addition, you typically read material that does not interest you at a slower pace. Think of the last SAT passage you read on a topic that does not interest you...do you remember the details? Did you read that SAT passage quickly or slowly?

Increase Your Interest Level

It is difficult to comprehend a passage or read it quickly if you are not interested in the material. To increase your comprehension and speed, you must increase your interest level in SAT Reading passages. Of course, you cannot force yourself to be interested in topics that don't naturally hold your attention. SAT passages often focus on history, literary works, science, and social studies. If you are not already interested in these topics, you cannot suddenly become interested.

Therefore, you must *Fake Interest* in the SAT Reading topics. How can you *Fake Interest*? Read with curiosity, enthusiasm, and engagement, no matter the topic of the passage.

The Benefits of Faking Interest

When you read SAT Reading passages with interest, you increase your comprehension and reading speed. Even if you are faking interest in the passage topic, you will be amazed at how much better you comprehend the text. When you read with interest, you are engaged with the passage. The more engaged you are, the better you comprehend it. When you read with interest, you are also able to read passages at a quicker pace. This will save you time and help you finish SAT Reading and Writing modules faster than you ever thought possible.

Fake Interest to maximize your SAT Reading score.

PREP EXPERT EXAMPLE

Consider the following *Prep Expert Example*: We have reproduced a sample SAT Reading passage below. Many students would find the passage below "boring." Try reading the passage as most students would. In other words, read the passage as quickly as possible, as monotone as possible, and with no interest at all.

At the heart of every galaxy lies a supermassive black hole, a cosmic enigma of staggering proportions. These black holes, millions to billions of times the mass of our Sun, exert a gravitational pull so strong that not even light can escape. Around them, stars orbit at incredible speeds, and matter is often drawn into a whirlpool-like structure known as an accretion disk. These enigmatic phenomena challenge our understanding of physics, bending space and time and potentially holding keys to unraveling the mysteries of the universe. The study of supermassive black holes not only fascinates astronomers but also offers crucial insights into the formation and evolution of galaxies.

Evaluate how much you actually comprehended from reading the passage with no interest. Now try reading the same passage again. However, this time *Fake Interest* in the passage. I have bolded certain words in the passage that you may want to emphasize in your head as you read. In other words, read the passage as enthusiastically as possible, as engaged as possible, and *Fake Interest* in the topic.

At the heart of every galaxy lies a **supermassive black hole**, a cosmic **enigma of staggering proportions**. These black holes, **millions to billions of times** the mass of our Sun, exert a **gravitational pull so strong** that not even **light** can escape. Around them, **stars orbit at incredible speeds**, and matter is often drawn into a **whirlpool-like structure** known as an **accretion disk**. These enigmatic phenomena challenge our understanding of physics, **bending space and time** and potentially holding keys to **unraveling the mysteries of the universe**. The study of supermassive black holes not only fascinates astronomers but also offers crucial insights into the **formation and evolution of galaxies**.

Evaluate how much you actually comprehended from reading the passage by faking interest.

One tangible method to *Fake Interest* in a passage is to be curious. Be curious about the passage's content as if you really care. Below are a few questions you may have been curious about as you were reading. These questions should have been running through your head:

- *What exactly is a supermassive black hole?*
- *Why can't even light escape from a black hole?*

- *What is an accretion disk?*
- *How does it bend space and time?*
- *Which mysteries of the universe could be unraveled?*

I bet you understood the passage better when you read with interest, curiosity, and engagement. Stay interested, curious, and engaged with all the passages you read on the SAT.

PREP EXPERT PRACTICE

Try applying this *Prep Expert Strategy* yourself to the following SAT practice questions:

73

The following text is adapted from Jane Austen's 1813 novel *Pride and Prejudice*. Elizabeth Bennet and her sisters attend a ball at Netherfield, the home of Mr. Bingley.

> Elizabeth was delighted. She had never seen a place where nature had done more, or where natural beauty had been so little counteracted by an awkward taste. They were all of them warm in their admiration; and at that moment she felt that to be mistress of Pemberley might be something!

Based on the text, which of the following statements best describes Elizabeth's reaction to Netherfield?

A) She finds the natural beauty of Netherfield overwhelming.
B) She thinks that the people of Netherfield have good taste.
C) She feels indifferent toward Netherfield.
D) She would prefer to be the mistress of Netherfield over Pemberley.

74

In many animal species, the size and quality of ornaments, such as elaborate antlers or vibrant plumage, are believed to serve as honest signals of an individual's genetic quality or overall fitness. However, recent research conducted by biologist Sanjay Patel and his team has revealed that in a certain species of deer, individuals can manipulate the

appearance of their antlers through postural adjustments and grooming behaviors, creating the illusion of larger, more impressive antlers. These findings suggest that _____

Which choice most logically completes the text?

A) the size and quality of antlers may not accurately reflect an individual's genetic quality or overall fitness in this species.

B) the mating preferences of female deer in this species are unrelated to the size or appearance of antlers.

C) antler size and quality have no influence on the social dominance of male deer in this species.

D) the manipulation of antler appearance is a common strategy across all species of deer.

The answers to these SAT practice questions can be found in the back of this book.

PREP EXPERT REVIEW

Key Takeaways

- **Prep Expert Reading Strategy #17—*Fake Interest***: Students often find SAT Reading passages to be boring. This leads to a lack of interest, poor comprehension, and lower SAT Reading scores.

- **Interest versus comprehension**: Students comprehend material more quickly when they are interested in it. If you read material you are not interested in, you will likely read it more slowly and not comprehend it well.

- **Faking interest**: To improve reading comprehension and speed, students should *Fake Interest* in SAT Reading passages. Even if the topic does not naturally engage you, you should still try to take an interest in the subject matter.

- **Engagement techniques**: Reading with curiosity and engagement, even artificially, can significantly enhance your comprehension and reading pace.

- **Be curious and enthusiastic**: Experiment with different reading approaches, such as asking curious questions and being enthusiastic as you read.

 **PREP**EXPERT

IMPROVE PASSAGE-READING SPEED

Prep Expert Reading Strategies

PREP EXPERT STRATEGY

The "Slow" Reader Myth

Many students believe that the reason that they score poorly on SAT Reading is because they are "slow" readers. I have good news for you! If you are a "slow" reader, you can still score high on the SAT Reading section.

Contrary to popular belief, the majority of the time that students spend on the SAT Reading section is actually *not* spent reading passages. Instead, the majority of the time students spend on the SAT Reading section is spent answering questions and deciding between answer choices.

It is actually not all that important if you are a fast or slow reader. It is more important that you are able to answer questions efficiently and accurately. Nevertheless, there are a few key techniques you can use to improve your passage-reading speed.

Passage Speed Technique #1: Practice a Passage a Day

Practice reading at least one SAT passage a day to improve your reading speed. Do not waste time reading newspapers or books to improve your reading speed. I know this

---

is the advice that the College Board, Khan Academy, and many other test prep companies give to students. However, reading newspapers and books will not significantly improve your SAT Reading score. Go straight to the source. Practice with a real SAT passage daily to familiarize yourself with the test's passage types, question types, and speed of reading.

Passage Speed Technique #2: Don't Get Caught Up in Details

Students often get too caught up in the details of an SAT Reading passage. Details like dates, times, names, etc. are all easy to refer back to the passage for. Do not focus on the details. Instead, focus on the passage's main ideas, underlying concepts, and author assertions. These key themes are important to understand. Understanding a passage's main idea will earn you far more points on SAT Reading than remembering specific details about that passage.

Passage Speed Technique #3: Don't Sacrifice Comprehension

Don't read so fast that you are only skimming the passage. Many students like to brag that they can read fast. I remember a high school classmate of mine used to boast that she could read an entire page of a novel in seven seconds. Even if this was true, I am sure she did not comprehend much of it. You must understand the passage content to answer questions correctly. If you read too fast, you will end up having to reread parts of each passage over and over to understand it. This will ultimately slow you down. Do not sacrifice passage comprehension for speed.

Improve Passage-Reading Speed to maximize your SAT Reading score.

PREP EXPERT EXAMPLE

Consider the following *Prep Expert Example*: We have reproduced a sample SAT Reading passage below. Read the passage using all the passage speed techniques that we just reviewed:

- **Passage speed technique #1:** Practice a passage a day (this can be your passage for today)
- **Passage speed technique #2:** Don't get caught up in details
- **Passage speed technique #3:** Don't sacrifice comprehension

Example Passage:

A group of geneticists led by Maria Gomez, Rajiv K. Khajuria, and Lin Tao delved into the genetic basis of drought resistance in the model plant species, *Sorghum bicolor* (sorghum). They introduced a gene encoding a novel transcription factor from the xerophyte *Ziziphus jujuba* (jujube) into the sorghum plants. This transcription factor is known to confer enhanced drought tolerance in jujube. When examining the transgenic sorghum plants under controlled drought conditions, the team found that the unaltered sorghum plants exhibited signs of stress and stunted growth, whereas the genetically modified plants maintained robust growth and vigor. This contrast underscored the role of the jujube transcription factor in imparting drought resilience, potentially opening new avenues for developing drought-resistant crops.

Were you able to read the passage faster and comprehend it more fully? If so, continue using the three passage-reading speed techniques. If not, keep practicing with SAT Reading passages until you find the right balance of speed and comprehension.

You want to read quickly enough that you finish SAT Reading and Writing modules on time, but slowly enough that you still fully comprehend the passages. This is a delicate balance you need to practice regularly.

PREP EXPERT PRACTICE

Try applying this *Prep Expert Strategy* yourself to the following SAT practice questions:

75

The following text is adapted from a research article on the benefits of exercise for mental health.

> In a study conducted by Dr. Smith and Dr. Johnson, they examined the effects of regular exercise on mental well-being. The results showed that individuals who engaged in consistent physical activity experienced reduced symptoms of anxiety and depression. The researchers concluded that exercise plays a crucial role in promoting mental health.

Which finding from Smith and Johnson's study, if true, would most directly support their conclusion?

A) Participants who exercised regularly reported no changes in their mental well-being compared to those who did not engage in physical activity.

B) Individuals who engaged in consistent physical activity experienced a significant increase in symptoms of anxiety and depression.

C) The study found a correlation between the duration of exercise sessions and the reduction in symptoms of anxiety and depression.

D) Participants who engaged in physical activity only once a week reported the same reduction in symptoms of anxiety and depression as those who exercised five times a week.

76

Average Number and Duration of Torpor Bouts and Arousal Episodes for Alaska Marmots and Arctic Ground Squirrels, 2008–2011

Feature	Alaska Marmots	Arctic Ground Squirrels
Torpor bouts	15	13.5
Duration per bout	16.81 days	19.77 days
Arousal episodes	14	12.5
Duration per episode	24.2 hours	17.2 hours

When hibernating, Alaska marmots and Arctic ground squirrels enter a state called *torpor*, which minimizes the energy their bodies need to function. Often a hibernating animal will temporarily come out of torpor (called an *arousal episode*) and its metabolic rate will rise, burning more of the precious energy the animal needs to survive the winter. Alaska marmots hibernate in groups and therefore burn less energy, keeping warm during these episodes than they would if they were alone. A researcher hypothesized that because Arctic ground squirrels hibernate alone, they would likely exhibit longer bouts of torpor and shorter arousal episodes than Alaska marmots.

Which choice best describes data from the table that support the researcher's hypothesis?

A) The Alaska marmots' arousal episodes lasted for days, while the Arctic ground squirrels' arousal episodes lasted less than a day.

B) The Alaska marmots and the Arctic ground squirrels both maintained torpor for several consecutive days per bout, on average.

C) The Alaska marmots had shorter torpor bouts and longer arousal episodes than the Arctic ground squirrels did.

D) The Alaska marmots had more torpor bouts than arousal episodes, but their arousal episodes were much shorter than their torpor bouts.

The answers to these SAT practice questions can be found in the back of this book.

PREP EXPERT REVIEW

Key Takeaways

- **Prep Expert Reading Strategy #18—*Improve Passage-Reading Speed***: The three key techniques to increasing passage-reading speed are: (1) Practice one passage per day, (2) Don't get caught up in details, and (3) Don't sacrifice comprehension.

- **Daily SAT passage practice**: Improve reading speed by practicing with real SAT passages daily, rather than by reading newspapers or books, to familiarize yourself with the types of passages and questions on the SAT.

- **Main ideas over details**: Concentrate on understanding the main ideas and assertions in the passages rather than trying to memorize details. Remember, you can always refer back to the passage if needed.

- **Balance speed with comprehension**: Avoid reading so fast that you sacrifice comprehension. Understanding the content is crucial to answer questions correctly without having to reread.

- **Question-answering speed**: Scoring high on the SAT Reading section is more about answering questions efficiently than it is about reading quickly. Most students spend the majority of their time debating the given answer choices rather than reading passages.

PREPEXPERT

READING STRATEGY #19

SIMPLIFY THE OTHER PASSAGE'S RESPONSE

PREP EXPERT STRATEGY

Cross-Text Connections Questions

The SAT Reading section includes a specific question type called *Cross-Text Connections*. These questions test your ability to draw reasonable connections between two texts on related topics. You will be presented with at least two to three *Cross-Text Connections* questions on the SAT Reading and Writing modules.

Most Common Question Types

Below are the two most common types of *Cross-Text Connections* questions:

- **Text 2 response to Text 1**: Based on the texts, how would the author of Text 2 most likely respond to the argument in Text 1?
- **Text 1 response to Text 2**: Based on the texts, how would the author of Text 1 most likely respond to the argument in Text 2?

Simplify the Other Passage's Response

To correctly answer *Cross-Text Connections*, *Simplify The Other Passage's Response*. *Cross-Text Connections* questions almost always ask about one passage's response to the other. Therefore, you should simplify the response in your own words. This will create a powerful BOSS solution to compare the answer choices against.

Here is the standardized approach we recommend to *Simplify The Other Passage's Response* on *Cross-Text Connections* questions:

- **Step 1:** Read the question.
- **Step 2:** Read Text 1.
- **Step 3:** Read Text 2.
- **Step 4:** Simplify the other passage's response (this creates a BOSS solution).

If the question is asking about Text 2's response, Text 2's response should be the one you are simplifying to create a BOSS solution. If the question is asking about Text 1's response, Text 1's response should be the one you are simplifying to create a BOSS solution.

Simplify The Other Passage's Response to maximize your SAT Reading score.

PREP EXPERT EXAMPLE

Consider the following *Prep Expert Example*. Let's *Simplify The Other Passage's Response* together on an SAT Reading question.

Step 1: Read the Question

> Ex
>
> Based on the texts, how would Dr. Lydia Zheng and her team (Text 2) most likely respond to the debate about Planet Nine discussed in Text 1?

Step 2: Read the Passage and Ignore Answer Choices

> Ex
>
> **Text 1**
> Astronomers have long debated the existence of Planet Nine, a hypothetical planet in our solar system beyond Neptune. Some suggest it explains the

peculiar orbits of distant objects in the Kuiper Belt. Others argue that these orbital anomalies can be accounted for without invoking a new planet. This ongoing debate has yet to reach a consensus in the scientific community.

Text 2

Astronomer Dr. Lydia Zheng and her team have proposed a different explanation for the orbital irregularities of Kuiper Belt objects. They argue that these anomalies are the result of gravitational interactions with passing stars and the galactic tide, rather than the presence of a ninth planet. Zheng's team suggests that these external gravitational forces are often underestimated in their impact on distant objects in the solar system.

Step 3: Simplify the Other Passage's Response

Dr. Lydia Zheng and her team have a different explanation for the orbital anomalies presented in Text 1. They believe the anomalies are due to "gravitational interactions with passing stars."

Step 4: Write Down Your BOSS Solution on Scratch Paper

For our BOSS solution, let's write down the following on our scratch paper:

Gravitational forces from stars

This gives us a specific BOSS solution to compare the answer choices to.

Step 5: Compare Your BOSS Solution to the Answer Choices

Ex

A) By supporting the theory that a ninth planet is responsible for the orbital anomalies in the Kuiper Belt

B) By suggesting that the debate is irrelevant since the Kuiper Belt objects are influenced by factors other than a ninth planet

C) **By arguing that the orbital patterns of Kuiper Belt objects can be better explained by the influence of external gravitational forces**

D) By recommending that astronomers should focus more on the study of Neptune's influence on the Kuiper Belt rather than a hypothetical ninth planet

Remember, our BOSS solution was "*Gravitational forces from stars*." This most closely matches answer choice (C).

PREP EXPERT PRACTICE

Try applying this *Prep Expert Strategy* yourself to the following SAT practice questions:

Text 1

When pharmaceutical companies seek to acquire smaller biotech firms, they often argue that the acquisition will accelerate drug development and benefit patients. However, researcher James Frazier examined this claim by analyzing a series of past acquisitions and concluded that drug development actually slows down after such acquisitions.

Text 2

Business analysts Carol Grant and Mark Sutton contend that studies on the impact of acquisitions on drug development often overlook long-term effects, which can be beneficial. Using the case of the biotech sector in Germany, they demonstrated that over an extended period (more than five years in their study), the resources of larger pharmaceutical companies can expedite drug development.

Based on the texts, how would Grant and Sutton (Text 2) most likely respond to Frazier's findings (Text 1)?

A) They would suggest that the financial dynamics of the pharmaceutical industry negate the benefits of acquisitions.

B) They would propose that Frazier compare the near-term effect of acquisitions on drug development with the effect of similar acquisitions in another industry.

C) They would recommend Frazier investigate whether the projected effect on drug development persists over an extended period.

D) They would argue that acquisitions have a different impact on drug development in the biotech industry than in other industries.

Text 1

Psychologists have long debated the nature versus nurture question: whether human behavior is primarily influenced by genetics or environmental factors. The debate centers around determining which factor plays a more significant role in shaping an individual's traits and behaviors. Despite extensive research, a conclusive answer has remained elusive.

Text 2

In their recent study, researchers Mark Johnson and Sarah Chen shed light on the nature versus nurture debate by examining the interplay between genetics and environment in the development of intelligence. They argue that both factors are crucial and interact with each other rather than operating independently. Their findings suggest that genetic predispositions can influence how individuals respond to environmental factors and how these interactions shape intelligence.

Based on the texts, how would Johnson and Chen (Text 2) most likely respond to the ongoing debate discussed in Text 1?

A) By proposing that nature and nurture are not mutually exclusive and interact in shaping human behavior

B) By asserting that genetics play a negligible role compared to environmental factors in determining human behavior

C) By suggesting that the question of nature versus nurture is no longer relevant in modern psychology

D) By recommending further research to conclusively determine whether genetics or environment has a greater impact on human behavior

The answers to these SAT practice questions can be found in the back of this book.

PREP EXPERT REVIEW

Key Takeaways

- **Prep Expert Reading Strategy #19—*Simplify The Other Passage's Response*:** Simplify the other passage's response to create a powerful BOSS solution for comparison with the answer choices.

- *Cross-Text Connections* **questions**: These questions test the ability to draw connections between two texts on related topics.

- **Common types of questions**: These include determining what the author of Text 2 would likely say about Text 1 and vice versa.

- **Standardized approach**: The Prep Expert approach involves reading the question, reading both texts, and then simplifying the response of the text that the question is asking about. The text to simplify depends on which author's response is being questioned.

PREPEXPERT

READING STRATEGY #20

AVOID THESE 5 KISS OF DEATH WORDS ON SAT READING

PREP EXPERT STRATEGY

The Five Words That Are Always Incorrect on SAT Reading Questions

There are five words that are always incorrect on the SAT Reading section. If you see any of these five words in an SAT Reading answer choice, then you can automatically cross that answer choice out. I refer to these five words as delivering the "kiss of death" to any SAT Reading answer choice.

KISS OF DEATH WORD #1: "ALWAYS"

Always indicates that something happens at all times or on all occasions, without exception. An answer choice that contains the word "always" is incorrect because it is an absolute term that is too extreme and inflexible.

KISS OF DEATH WORD #2: "EVERY-" PREFIX ("EVERYONE," "EVERYTHING," ETC.)

The **every- prefix** means "each and all" or "all the members of a group." It forms words indicating that something includes all the individuals in a group or every instance of a particular thing. An answer choice that contains the prefix "every" is incorrect because it presents an absolute statement not supported by the text. The use of the "every" prefix creates an impression of universality or completeness that is rarely accurate.

KISS OF DEATH WORD #3: ONLY

Only refers to the sole or exclusive thing in a given context. It can also indicate that there are no other alternatives or possibilities. An answer choice that contains the word "only" is incorrect because it indicates that there is no other similar item or action in the entire universe, which is difficult to prove.

KISS OF DEATH WORD #4: SAME

Same indicates that two or more things are identical, meaning that they are not different in any way. An answer choice that contains the word "same" is incorrect because it indicates that two items are completely identical, which is difficult to prove.

KISS OF DEATH WORD #5: UNIQUE

Unique indicates that something is unlike anything else in its category and is distinguished by its singularity. An answer choice that contains the word "unique" is incorrect because it indicates that something is one of a kind, which is difficult to prove.

Avoid These 5 Kiss Of Death Words On SAT Reading to maximize your SAT Reading score.

PREP EXPERT EXAMPLE

The table below presents the 5 Kiss of Death Words on SAT Reading.

5 Kiss of Death Words
always
every- prefix (everyone, everything, everywhere, etc.)
only
same
unique

Note that these words make answer choices only on *passage-based* SAT Reading questions incorrect. These questions are located in the first half of an SAT Reading and Writing module.

The 5 Kiss of Death Words for SAT Reading do not make answer choices on *grammar-based* SAT Writing questions incorrect. These questions are located in the second half of an SAT Reading and Writing module.

PREP EXPERT PRACTICE

Try applying this *Prep Expert Strategy* yourself to the following SAT practice questions:

Archaeologists studying the evolution of ancient civilizations have found that certain civilizations, such as those in Mesopotamia and Egypt, developed complex systems of writing and recordkeeping around the same time that they began constructing monumental architecture. Some researchers have hypothesized that the two phenomena are related, with writing being necessary to coordinate the construction of large public works. However, there is no evidence to suggest that writing was a precondition for the construction of monumental architecture, as some civilizations constructed massive structures without a system of writing. This suggests that _____.

Which choice most logically completes the text?

A) monumental architecture is a necessary unique precursor to the development of a system of writing

B) the development of monumental architecture and writing were coincidental and unrelated phenomena

C) monumental architecture was only possible in regions with a preexisting system of writing

D) the connection between the development of writing and monumental architecture will always be unclear

In a study of a particular species of plant, researchers found that the roots of the plant were covered in fine, hair-like structures that secreted an acid. They hypothesized that the plant used this acid to dissolve and absorb nutrients in the soil. To test this hypothesis, the researchers placed the plant in a solution of nutrients and measured the plant's growth rate. They then repeated the experiment, but added an alkaline substance to the solution to neutralize the acid secreted by the plant.

Which finding would most directly support the researchers' hypothesis?

A) The plant grows at a faster rate in the solution with the alkaline substance than in the solution without it.

B) The plant grows at the same rate in both solutions.

C) The plant grows at a slower rate in the solution with the alkaline substance than in the solution without it.

D) The unique plant does not grow in either solution.

The answers to these SAT practice questions can be found in the back of this book.

PREP EXPERT REVIEW

Key Takeaways

- **Prep Expert Reading Strategy #20—*Avoid These 5 Kiss Of Death Words On SAT Reading***: The "Kiss of Death" words on SAT Reading are "always," the "every-" prefix, "only," "same," and "unique." The presence of any of these words indicates that an SAT Reading answer choice is incorrect.

- **Reason for incorrectness**: These words make SAT Reading answers wrong due to their absolute nature. The extreme nature of these words rarely aligns with the nuanced information that SAT Reading passages convey.

- **Nature of words**: Answer choices with these words are too inflexible. These words often imply universality or identicalness that is not typically supported by the evidence in the text.

Prep Expert
Reading Strategies

- **Applicable sections of the SAT**: These five "kiss of death" words apply to passage-based questions in the first half of the SAT Reading and Writing module, not to the grammar-based questions in the second half.

SAT MATH
INTRODUCTION

*"Mathematics is the poetry
of logical ideas."*

—ALBERT EINSTEIN

DIGITAL SAT MATH OVERVIEW

Let's discuss the SAT Math section. There are two SAT Math modules on the Digital SAT.

DIGITAL SAT MATH FORMAT

Section	Questions	Time
SAT Math Module 1	22 questions	35 minutes
SAT Math Module 2	22 questions	35 minutes
TOTAL SAT MATH	44 QUESTIONS	70 MINUTES

Digital SAT Math Format

The first two modules on the Digital SAT are Reading and Writing modules. After you complete these modules, you will be presented with two SAT Math modules.

Therefore, the third module overall on the Digital SAT will be the first SAT Math module that contains 22 questions in 35 minutes. The fourth (and final) module overall on the Digital SAT will be the second SAT Math module, which also contains 22 questions in 35 minutes.

The Digital SAT Math modules contain two question types: multiple-choice questions and student-produced response questions. Multiple-choice questions require students to choose an answer from four given options (A, B, C, or D). There can be only one correct answer to a multiple-choice question. Multiple-choice questions make up approximately 75% of all of the questions on SAT Math modules.

Student-produced response questions require students to fill in their own answer. There can be more than one correct answer to student-produced response questions. However, students need to fill in only one of the correct answers to receive full credit. Student-produced response questions make up approximately 25% of all of the questions on SAT Math modules.

The SAT Math modules are organized by order of difficulty. Typically, questions that appear at the beginning of the module are easy, questions that appear in the middle of the module are a medium level of difficulty, and questions that appear at the end of the module are hard.

In addition, the SAT Math modules are adaptive. This means that if you answer most of the questions correctly on the first SAT Math module, you will be presented with harder questions in the second SAT Math module. This gives you the opportunity to achieve a higher SAT Math score overall. However, if you answer many of the questions incorrectly on the first SAT Math module, you will be presented with easier questions on the second SAT Math module. This will limit your ability to achieve a higher SAT Math score overall.

You should attempt to answer as many questions as possible correctly in the first SAT Math module so that the Digital SAT's adaptive algorithm recognizes that you are a strong math student. The adaptive Digital SAT will then present you with a more difficult second SAT Math module. Although it may seem like punishment for scoring well on the first SAT Math module, seeing harder questions on the second SAT Math module is actually what you want. This is the only way to maximize your SAT Math score.

Digital SAT Math Content

The SAT tests the following math skills and knowledge areas:

SAT MATH CONTENT

Domain	Knowledge Testing Points	# Of Questions	%
Algebra	• Linear equations in one variable • Linear equations in two variables • Linear functions and systems of two linear equations in two variables • Linear inequalities in one or two variables	13–15 questions	~35%

Advanced Math	• Equivalent expressions • Nonlinear equations in one variable • Systems of equations in two variables • Nonlinear functions	13–15 questions	~35%
Problem-Solving and Data Analysis	• Ratios, rates, proportional relationships, and units • Percentages • One-variable data: distributions and measures of center and spread • Two-variable data: models and scatter plots • Probability and conditional probability • Inference from sample statistics and margin of error • Evaluating statistical claims: observational studies and experiments	5–7 questions	~15%
Geometry and Trigonometry	• Area and volume • Lines, angles, and triangles • Right triangles and trigonometry • Circles	5–7 questions	~15%

The first domain is *Algebra*, which includes 13 to 15 questions on the SAT. This makes up about 35% of all questions on the SAT Math modules. The knowledge testing points within this domain include *Linear equations in one variable*; *Linear equations in two variables*; *Linear functions and systems of two linear equations in two variables*; and *Linear inequalities in one or two variables*.

The second domain is *Advanced Math*, which includes 13 to 15 questions on the SAT. This makes up about 35% of all questions on the SAT Math modules. The knowledge testing points within this domain include *Equivalent expressions*; *Nonlinear equations in one variable*; *Systems of equations in two variables*; and *Nonlinear functions*.

The third domain is *Problem-Solving and Data Analysis*, which includes 5 to 7 questions on the SAT. This makes up about 15% of all questions on the SAT Math modules. The knowledge testing points within this domain include *Ratios, rates, proportional relationships, and units*; *Percentages*; *One-variable data: distributions and measures of center and spread*; *Two-variable data: models and scatter plots*; *Probability and conditional probability*; *Inference from sample statistics and margin of error*; and *Evaluating statistical claims: observational studies and experiments*.

The fourth domain is *Geometry and Trigonometry*, which includes 5 to 7 questions on the SAT. This makes up about 15% of all questions on the SAT Math modules. The knowledge testing points within this domain include *Area and volume*; *Lines, angles, and triangles*; *Right triangles and trigonometry*; and *Circles*.

It is not all that important to understand what each of these knowledge testing points are right now. We will discuss them in more detail as we cover *Prep Expert Math Strategies*. For now, know that these knowledge testing points test various math concepts. We will teach you *Prep Expert Math Strategies* to ace all of these math concepts.

SAT Math
Introduction

PREPEXPERT
MATH STRATEGIES

"Mathematics, rightly viewed, possesses not only truth, but supreme beauty."

—BERTRAND RUSSELL

PREP EXPERT MATH STRATEGIES OVERVIEW

Prep Expert Math Strategies are a collection of techniques designed to improve your SAT Math score. These strategies will teach you all of the math concepts tested on the SAT, including *Algebra*; *Advanced Math*; *Problem-Solving and Data Analysis*; and *Geometry and Trigonometry*.

In addition, you will learn problem-solving techniques that are not typically taught in high school math classes. *Prep Expert Math Strategies* offer innovative approaches such as how to use the multiple-choice nature of the SAT to your advantage.

Prep Expert Math Strategies are adaptable, which makes them an ideal resource for students at all levels of proficiency. Whether you are struggling with math basics or looking to refine your math expertise, these strategies will address your goals.

The foundation of Prep Expert's approach to SAT Math is practice. Applying these strategies to actual SAT questions will help you develop habits to master math calculations.

These math skills will also set you up for academic and professional success. If you aspire to pursue a career that is math related in the future (e.g., engineering, finance, etc.), mastering these strategies is a key step on your journey.

Personally, I still use math on a daily basis as an entrepreneur and as a doctor. As an entrepreneur, I use math to understand financial statements, calculate return on investment, and determine future budget analysis. As a doctor, I use math to calculate medication dosages and evaluate lab results. Even if you do not plan to pursue a math-related career, it is important that you master math for your personal finances in the future. You will need to understand interest rates, budget and save appropriately, invest wisely, pay taxes, and manage debt. Therefore, you should master mathematics now for your own future success!

Prep Expert Math Strategies pave the path to SAT Math excellence. By integrating these strategies into your preparation, you can elevate your math skills. They are a road map to success on SAT Math.

Master and apply all of the *Prep Expert Math Strategies* to maximize your SAT Math score.

 **PREP**EXPERT

MATH STRATEGY #1
PLUG IN NUMBERS (PIN)

PREP EXPERT STRATEGY

Plug In Numbers (PIN)

Plug In Numbers (PIN) is the key to solving many SAT Math questions easily. Our brains prefer to work with tangible numbers rather than with abstract variables. On SAT Math, try plugging in your own numbers rather than using the given abstract variables in the problem. This works on many types of problems (i.e., algebra, geometry, graphs, etc.).

Of course, you can do algebra or geometry problems using traditional methods. However, you should still learn the PIN method. Why? It is an alternative method to solve an SAT Math problem when you cannot figure out how to solve it using traditional methods.

In addition, PIN will often make problems much easier and less time consuming. You will bypass many steps that you would normally have to do using traditional methods. As you practice this method more, using PIN will become second nature. Eventually, you will actually prefer this method over traditional methods that you have learned in high school math classes.

Can You Plug in Any Number?

Yes! Typically, you can plug in any number that you would like. Why? Because algebraic expressions must be valid for all numbers. Therefore, it does not matter what number you choose to plug in. For example, you could plug in any of the following for x in an algebra problem:

$$x = 1,000,000$$
$$x = 1,000$$
$$x = -57$$

Or any other number that you would like to plug in for x! Usually, the algebraic equation will still work no matter what number you plug in.

However, I typically recommend plugging in numbers that are small and easy to work with. Alternatively, you should plug in a number that fits easily within the given algebraic expression, geometry problem, graphing problem, etc.

What Is the Best Number to Plug In?

The following number should be your go-to number to plug into SAT Math problems:

$$x = 2$$

I like to plug in the number 2 for x in many algebra questions on the SAT. Why is 2 such a good number to plug in? Because it is a small and easy number to work with. Plugging in the number 2 often makes the math simple to do on your scratch paper.

Why not plug in 0 or 1? Because when you multiply or divide by 0 or 1, you will often get the same number. This will result in multiple answer choices that end up being the same. When you plug a number into an SAT Math problem, you want all of the answer choices to give you different values. This way, you can quickly identify the correct answer choice that matches the original expression in the problem.

High School Math

Most high school math teachers do not teach the *Plug in Numbers* method. Why? Your high school math teacher wants you to learn how to do traditional algebra, geometry, problem-solving, etc. In fact, your teacher wants you to show your work. Your teacher does not want you to bypass the algebra, geometry, or any other traditional math method by plugging in easy numbers.

At Prep Expert, we want to provide you with the most effective and efficient methods to solve problems. PIN is a powerful technique that will help you solve many questions more quickly and accurately on the SAT.

Plug In Numbers (PIN) to maximize your SAT Math score.

PREP EXPERT EXAMPLE

Consider the following *Prep Expert Example.*

Step 1: Read the Question

Ex

The expression $\dfrac{3x+2}{x-4}$ is equivalent to which of the following?

A) $\dfrac{3+2x}{-4}$

B) $3 - \dfrac{2x+4}{4}$

C) $3 + \dfrac{6}{(x-4)}$

D) $3 + \dfrac{14}{(x-4)}$

Step 2: Plug in Numbers

You could solve this question using traditional algebraic methods. However, I am going to show you how to solve it using *Prep Expert Math Strategy #1—Plug In Numbers (PIN).*

Let's try plugging in my favorite number, 2, into the original expression.

$$\frac{3x+2}{x-4} \;\rightarrow\; \frac{3(2)+2}{2-4} \;\rightarrow\; \frac{8}{-2} \;\rightarrow\; -4$$

In this case, now we know that when x is equal to 2, the original expression is equivalent to −4.

Next, plug 2 into answer choices (A) through (D) to determine which one gives you −4 when $x = 2$.

A) $\dfrac{3 + 2x}{-4}$ $\rightarrow$ $\dfrac{3 + 2(2)}{-4}$ $\rightarrow$ $\dfrac{7}{-4}$

B) $3 - \dfrac{2x + 4}{4}$ $\rightarrow$ $3 - \dfrac{2(2) + 4}{4}$ $\rightarrow$ $3 - \dfrac{4 + 4}{4}$ $\rightarrow$ 1

C) $3 + \dfrac{6}{(x - 4)}$ $\rightarrow$ $3 + \dfrac{6}{(2 - 4)}$ $\rightarrow$ $3 + \dfrac{6}{-2}$ $\rightarrow$ 0

D) $3 + \dfrac{14}{(x - 4)}$ $\rightarrow$ $3 + \dfrac{14}{(2 - 4)}$ $\rightarrow$ $3 + \dfrac{14}{-2}$ $\rightarrow$ -4

Step 3: Select Answer

Select answer choice (D). Answer choice (D) is the only one that results in −4 when $x = 2$.

Now you might be thinking: this method takes longer than simply doing the traditional algebra! That is true when you have to write out all of your work, as I just did for this book. However, on the SAT Math section, you will be doing math *quickly* either on your scratch paper or in your head. Therefore, you should be able to *quickly* realize that answer choices (A), (B), and (C) do not give you −4 when $x = 2$. And you won't need to write everything out step by step like I just did. I needed to write out each step above so that everyone reading this book can understand the methodology. But feel free to go much *faster* when you are actually using this strategy on the SAT Math section.

You might also be thinking: What would happen if you did not choose $x = 2$? You would still arrive at the same answer! No matter what number you plug in, you will find that the original expression always matches answer choice (D). Feel free to try $x = 1$, $x = 3$, or $x =$ any number you choose. That is the real magic of PIN!

PREP EXPERT PRACTICE

Try applying this *Prep Expert Strategy* yourself to the following SAT practice questions:

Circle *X* has a radius of 4*m* and circle *Y* has a radius of 120*m*, where *m* is a positive constant. The area of circle *Y* is how many times the area of circle *X*?

A) 30

B) 60

C) 90

D) 900

One gallon of paint will cover 300 square feet of a surface. A deck has a total area of *d* square feet. Which equation represents the total amount of paint, *P*, in gallons, needed to apply three coats of paint to the deck?

A) $P = \dfrac{d}{100}$

B) $P = 900d$

C) $P = \dfrac{d}{300}$

D) $P = 300d$

The answers to these SAT practice questions can be found in the back of this book.

PREP EXPERT REVIEW

Key Takeaways

- **Prep Expert Math Strategy #1—*Plug In Numbers (PIN)*:** Plug in your own numbers instead of using the given abstract variables. This method is applicable to various problem types, including algebra, geometry, and graphs.

- **Advantages of PIN:** PIN simplifies and speeds up problem-solving. With practice, plugging in numbers becomes second nature. It is often faster and easier than traditional high school math methods.

- **Recommended numbers to plug in:** While you could plug in any number you want, we recommend using small numbers that are easy to work with. The number 2 is particularly useful due to its simplicity in calculations. It also avoids the confusing results that can occur if you plug in 0 or 1.

- **High school math versus SAT prep:** High school math typically focuses on traditional methods of algebra, geometry, and problem-solving. Prep Expert SAT Math strategies like *PIN* offer new, efficient ways to solve problems quickly and accurately.

 **PREP**EXPERT

MATH
STRATEGY #2

TEST ANSWER
CHOICES (TAC)

PREP EXPERT STRATEGY

Test Answer Choices (TAC)

Test Answer Choices (TAC) means to substitute the given answer choices back into the original problem. Test each answer choice with the original algebraic expression, geometric figure, or other given item in the problem. Test to see which answer choice works!

TAC is the sister strategy to the last strategy, *Plug In Numbers (PIN)*. In other words, the first two *Prep Expert Math Strategies* are PIN and TAC. What is the difference between PIN and TAC?

- **PIN** involves *plugging in your own numbers* that you choose into the problem.
    - PIN is typically used when variables are in the original problem and variables are in the answer choices.

- **TAC** involves *plugging in the given answer choices* back into the problem.
    - TAC is typically used when variables are in the original problem and real numbers are in the answer choices.

Prep Expert
Math Strategies

Most high school exams, especially algebra exams, are not multiple-choice. Why don't algebra teachers tend to give multiple-choice exams? Because, for many multiple-choice questions, you would be able to skip doing the actual algebra altogether—you could simply test to see which of the answer choices works in the original problem.

Guess what? Almost 80% of the questions on SAT Math are multiple-choice. This means that the vast majority of the time, the answers are right in front of you! You just need to test the answer choices back into the original problem to see which one works.

Of course, PIN and TAC will not work on every question in the SAT Math section. The test-question writers have devised clever ways to prevent students from using these methods alone.

However, you'll be surprised at how often PIN and TAC do in fact work on SAT Math questions. That's why your gut instinct should be to *Plug in Numbers* or *Test Answer Choices* on SAT Math. Using these two *Prep Expert Math Strategies*, you will often find you can answer SAT Math questions more accurately and with less effort. Sometimes you will even find that you can solve the hardest SAT Math problems in seconds! Of course, if these methods do not work, you can always revert back to the traditional algebra, geometry, problem-solving, etc.

Test Answer Choices (TAC) to maximize your SAT Math score.

PREP EXPERT EXAMPLE

Consider the following *Prep Expert Example*.

Step 1: Read the Question

Ex	

x	$f(x)$
0	−96
1	−72
2	−48

For the linear function f, the table shows three values of x and their corresponding values of $f(x)$. Function f is defined by $f(x) = cx + d$, where c and d are constants. What is the value of $c - d$?

A) –96

B) 24

C) 72

D) 120

Step 2: Test Answer Choices

You could solve this question using traditional algebraic methods. However, I am going to show you how to solve it using *Prep Expert Math Strategy #2—Test Answer Choices*.

But I am not going to demonstrate the standard *Test Answer Choices* method. Instead, I want to show you an advanced version of *Test Answer Choices*. In this example, I am not going to plug the given answer choices (A) through (D) back into the original expression. Instead, I am going to plug the values in the table back into the original expression.

Advanced TAC table method: Anytime there is a table of values on SAT Math, try plugging the values in the table back into the original problem. You will often find that doing so will help you solve difficult SAT Math problems with ease.

Let's try plugging the values in the table back into the original problem:

x	$f(x)$
0	–96
1	–72
2	–48

First, let's try plugging in the first row of values, $x = 0$ and $f(x) = -96$, into the original problem.

$$f(x) = cx + d \quad \rightarrow \quad -96 = c(0) + d \quad \rightarrow \quad -96 = d$$

Now we know that $d = -96$. Let's try plugging in the second row of values: $x = 1$ and $f(x) = -72$. Because we know $d = -96$, we can plug that in too.

$$f(x) = cx + d \quad \rightarrow \quad -72 = c(1) + d \quad \rightarrow \quad -72 = c + -96 \quad \rightarrow \quad 24 = c$$

Now that we know $c = 24$ and $d = -96$, we can solve for what the original problem was asking for: $c - d$.

$$c - d \quad \rightarrow \quad 24 - (-96) \quad \rightarrow \quad 120$$

Step 3: Select Answer
Select answer choice (D).

PREP EXPERT PRACTICE

Try applying this *Prep Expert Strategy* yourself to the following SAT practice questions:

 83

$$2x^2 + 6x = 20$$

What is the positive solution to the given equation?

A) $\dfrac{2}{5}$

B) $\dfrac{5}{2}$

C) 2

D) 5

 84

A rectangle has a length of y units and a width of $(y + 12)$ units. If the rectangle has an area of 108 square units, what is the value of y?

A) 6

B) 9

C) 12

D) 18

The answers to these SAT practice questions can be found in the back of this book.

PREP EXPERT REVIEW

Key Takeaways
- **Prep Expert Math Strategy #2—*Test Answer Choices (TAC)*:** The TAC method involves substituting the given answer choices back into the original problem to see which one works. It often works well when the original problem has variables, and the given answer choices have real numbers.

- **Comparison with Plug In Numbers (PIN):** PIN involves substituting your own chosen numbers into the problem, usually when both the problem and answer choices have variables. With TAC, on the other hand, you use the given answer choices as the substitutions.

- **Application to SAT Math:** While TAC and PIN may not work for every question on SAT Math, they are often effective strategies. These methods can lead to quicker and more accurate answers.

- **Advanced TAC table method:** An advanced form of TAC involves using values from a given table in the problem, rather than using the answer choices directly. This method can simplify solving complex table problems on SAT Math.

 **PREP**EXPERT

MATH
STRATEGY #3

ACE EQUATIONS &
INEQUALITIES

PREP EXPERT STRATEGY + EXAMPLE

Ace Equations & Inequalities

To perform well on SAT Math, you must *Ace Equations & Inequalities*. Below are the most important key concepts to master this topic for the SAT. In this section as well as the SAT Math chapters that follow, I will present the *Prep Expert Strategy* and *Prep Expert Example* together. This will help you understand abstract math concepts using examples that immediately follow.

Definition of Terms

1. **Linear equation**: An equation that represents a straight line on a graph. It is a mathematical statement that expresses the relationship between two variables, typically x and y. The exponent on x is 1 in a linear equation. An example of a linear equation would be $y = 2x + 4$.

2. **Nonlinear equation**: An equation that does not represent a straight line on a graph (i.e., a curve). The exponent on x is not 1 in a nonlinear equation. An example of a nonlinear equation would be $y = 2x^4 + 4$.

---

3. **Inequality**: A statement that compares two values, expressing that one is greater than, less than, or equal to the other. Inequalities use the following symbols: < (less than), > (greater than), ≤ (less than or equal to), ≥ (greater than or equal to), and ≠ (not equal to). An example of an inequality would be $2x + 3 < 7$.

Key Concepts

KEY CONCEPT #1: SOLVING ONE-VARIABLE EQUATIONS

Solve a linear equation with one variable by finding the value of the variable that makes the equation true.

Prep Expert Strategy
1. Simplify the equation as much as possible.
2. Use the basic operations of addition, subtraction, multiplication, and division to isolate the variable on one side of the equation.
3. Check your answer by substituting the solution back into the original equation.

Prep Expert Example
- **Question**: What is the solution to the following one-variable equation?

$$\frac{1}{3}x + 11 = 20$$

- **Answer**:

$$\frac{1}{3}x + 11 = 20 \quad \rightarrow \quad \frac{1}{3}x = 9 \quad \rightarrow \quad x = 27$$

KEY CONCEPT #2: SOLVING TWO-VARIABLE EQUATIONS

Solve a linear equation with two variables by finding the values of both variables that make the equation true. Typically, you need at least two equations to solve for the values of two variables. We will cover how to do this using elimination or substitution methods later. However, the SAT will sometimes present you with only one equation with two variables and ask you for the value of a new equation. While this might seem like an impossible task, follow the steps below to solve these problems.

Prep Expert
Math Strategies

Prep Expert Strategy

1. Recognize if the SAT presents you with only one equation, but two variables.
2. Compare the original equation with the new equation.
3. Determine if there is a simple multiplication, division, or other manipulation that could be done to the original equation to find the value of the new equation.

Prep Expert Example

- **Question**: If $\frac{1}{8}x + \frac{1}{4}y = 10$, what is the value of $2x + 4y$?

- **Answer**: Recognize that to get from ⅛ to 2 or ¼ to 4, you must multiply by 16.

$$(16)[\frac{1}{8}x + \frac{1}{4}y] = (10)(16) \quad \rightarrow \quad 2x + 4y = 160$$

KEY CONCEPT #3: SOLVING NONLINEAR EQUATIONS

Solve a nonlinear equation with one variable by finding the value of the variable that makes the nonlinear equation true.

Prep Expert Strategy

1. Recognize that the equation is nonlinear.
2. Use specific techniques for solving nonlinear equations, such as exponent rules, factoring, the quadratic formula, etc.
3. Check your solution(s) by substituting the answer back into the original equation.

Prep Expert Example

- **Question**: What is the solution to the following nonlinear equation?

$$2x^3 = 128$$

- **Answer**:

$$2x^3 = 128 \quad \rightarrow \quad x^3 = 64 \quad \rightarrow \quad x = 4$$

KEY CONCEPT #4: SOLVING ABSOLUTE VALUE EQUATIONS

An absolute value expression always has a non-negative value. Solve absolute value equations by setting the expression inside the absolute value equal to both the positive and negative values.

Prep Expert Strategy

1. Separate the absolute value expression so that it is by itself on one side of the equation.
2. Set the expression inside the absolute value equal to both positive and negative values.
3. Solve each resulting equation.
4. Combine the solutions from both equations and check them by substituting the answers back into the original equation.

Prep Expert Example

- **Question**: What is the solution to the following absolute value equation?

$$|x + 1| = 3$$

- **Answer**:

$$|x + 1| = 3 \quad \rightarrow \quad x + 1 = 3 \ or \ x + 1 = -3 \quad \rightarrow \quad x = 2 \ or \ x = -4$$

KEY CONCEPT #5: SOLVING SINGLE-VARIABLE INEQUALITIES

Solve an inequality with one variable by finding the range of values of the variable that make the inequality true.

Prep Expert Strategy

1. Simplify the inequality as much as possible.
2. Isolate the variable on one side of the inequality.
3. Express the solution as a range of values using interval notation.

Prep Expert Example

- **Question**: What is the solution to the following single-variable inequality?

$$x + 2 \geq 3$$

- **Answer:**

$$x + 2 \geq 3 \quad \rightarrow \quad x \geq 1$$

KEY CONCEPT #6: INEQUALITIES AND NEGATIVE NUMBER OPERATIONS

When multiplying or dividing inequalities by negative numbers, you must reverse the direction of the inequality.

Prep Expert Strategy

1. Determine whether the number you are multiplying or dividing by is positive or negative.
2. Multiply or divide both sides of the inequality by the number.
3. Flip the inequality sign if the number is negative.

Prep Expert Example

- **Question:** What happens to the following inequality when you multiply it by −2?

$$x + 2 \geq 3$$

- **Answer:**

$$(-2)(x + 2) \geq (3)(-2) \quad \rightarrow \quad -2x - 4 \leq -6 \quad \rightarrow \quad -2x \leq -2 \quad \rightarrow \quad x \geq 1$$

KEY CONCEPT #7: GRAPHING TWO-VARIABLE INEQUALITIES

Graph an inequality with two variables by representing the solution on a coordinate plane. The solution consists of all the points that satisfy the inequality.

Prep Expert Strategy

1. Convert the inequality to slope-intercept form if possible.
2. Identify the boundary line by changing the inequality sign to an equal sign.
3. Shade the region that satisfies the inequality.
4. Test a few points in each region to confirm the shading.

Prep Expert Example

- **Question:** What is the graph of $y < x + 4$?

- **Answer:**

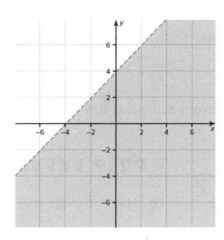

Any (x, y) value that lands in the shaded portion of the graph is a possible solution to the inequality. For example, $(2, 2)$ is a solution, but $(0, 6)$ is not a solution. The dotted line indicates that the points on the line are not possible solutions.

KEY CONCEPT #8: CONVERTING WORD PROBLEMS TO INEQUALITIES

SAT word problems often involve translating real-world situations into mathematical expressions using inequalities.

Prep Expert Strategy

1. Carefully read the word problem and identify the key information.
2. Define the variables involved in the problem.
3. Translate the given information into mathematical expressions.
4. Identify key terms such as "at least," "at most," "to meet or exceed," "maximum," etc.
5. Set up the inequality based on the problem's constraints.

Prep Expert Example

- **Question:** How would you convert the following word problem to an inequality?

  A banana has 98 calories. An apple has 77 calories. The daily recommended calories from fruits is 400 calories. Write an inequality that represents the possible number of bananas (b) and number of apples (a) to meet or exceed the recommended daily fruit calorie intake.

- **Answer:**

$$98b + 77a \geq 400$$

Ace Equations & Inequalities to maximize your SAT Math score.

PREP EXPERT PRACTICE

Try applying this *Prep Expert Strategy* yourself to the following SAT practice questions:

85

The total cost, in dollars, to attend a theme park consists of an entrance fee of $40 and a $15 per-ride fee. A person intends to spend a maximum of $100 to attend the theme park. Which inequality represents this situation?

A) $15x \leq 100$
B) $15 + 40x \leq 100$
C) $40x \leq 100$
D) $40 + 15x \leq 100$

86

If $|2x - 3| = 60$, what is the positive value of $3x + 4$?

The answers to these SAT practice questions can be found in the back of this book.

PREP EXPERT REVIEW

Key Takeaways

- **Prep Expert Math Strategy #3—*Ace Equations & Inequalities*:** Understand linear equations (straight lines), nonlinear equations (curves), and inequalities (comparative expressions).

- **Single-variable equations:** Solve single-variable equations by isolating the variable and checking solutions through substitution.

- **Two-variable equations**: For equations with two variables, use multiplication, division, or other manipulations to find values of new equations.

- **Nonlinear equations**: Use specific techniques such as exponent rules or the quadratic formula.

- **Absolute value equations**: Set the expression inside absolute value to both positive and negative values, and solve.

- **Graphing inequalities**: Convert to slope-intercept form, identify boundary lines, and shade the appropriate regions on a graph.

- **Word problems**: Translate real-world verbal descriptions into mathematical expressions, or vice versa.

PREPEXPERT

MATH
STRATEGY #4

ACE EXPRESSIONS
& POLYNOMIALS

PREP EXPERT STRATEGY + EXAMPLE

Ace Expressions & Polynomials

To perform well on SAT Math, you must *Ace Expressions & Polynomials*. Below are the most important concepts to master this topic for the SAT.

Definition of Terms

1. **Expression**: A combination of numbers, variables, and mathematical operations. An example of an expression would be $x + 4$.

2. **Expression versus equation**: The difference between an equation and an expression is that an equation has an equal sign, but an expression does not have an equal sign. An example of an equation that contains multiple expressions would be $x + 4 = y + 7$.

3. **Polynomial**: An expression consisting of variables and coefficients, combined using addition, subtraction, and multiplication. Polynomials are usually written in standard form, with the terms arranged in descending order of

Prep Expert
Math Strategies

degree. The degree of a polynomial is the highest power of the variable that appears in the expression. For example, the polynomial $3x^2 - 2x + 1$ is a quadratic polynomial of degree 2, while the polynomial $4x^3 + 2x^2 - x + 3$ is a cubic polynomial of degree 3.

Key Concepts

KEY CONCEPT #1: AVOIDING SIGN ERRORS IN EXPRESSION SIMPLIFICATION

Sign errors are one of the main reasons that students answer questions incorrectly on the SAT Math section. Follow the steps below to reduce sign errors.

Prep Expert Strategy

1. If an expression contains subtraction, change the subtraction to the addition of a negative.
2. If an expression contains multiplication of a negative, multiply and distribute that negative throughout the whole expression.
3. Double-check your work to ensure that all signs are correct.

Prep Expert Example

*   **Question**: How would you avoid sign errors when simplifying the following expression?

$$2 + -3(4x + 5)$$

*   **Answer**:

$$2 + -3(4x + 5) \quad \rightarrow \quad 2 + -12x + -15 \quad \rightarrow \quad -12x + (2 + -15) \quad \rightarrow$$
$$-12x + -13 \quad \rightarrow \quad -12x - 13$$

KEY CONCEPT #2: COMBINING LIKE TERMS IN POLYNOMIAL ARITHMETIC

"Like terms" are terms that have the same variables and exponents. Combine like terms by adding or subtracting the coefficients of like terms.

Prep Expert Strategy

1. Identify like terms with the same variables and exponents (i.e., x^2, x, or constant terms).
2. Add or subtract the coefficients of like terms.
3. Simplify complex polynomials by grouping and combining like terms to reduce them to their simplest forms.

Prep Expert Example

- **Question:** How would you simplify the following polynomial equation?

$$x^3y^2 + 6y^3 - 10x^2y^3 = 2x^3y^2 + 6x^2y^3 + 6y^3$$

- **Answer:**

$$x^3y^2 + 6y^3 - 10x^2y^3 = 2x^3y^2 + 6x^2y^3 + 6y^3$$
$$(x^3y^2 - 2x^3y^2) = (6x^2y^3 + 10x^2y^3) + (6y^3 - 6y^3)$$
$$(x^3y^2 + -2x^3y^2) = (16x^2y^3) + (0)$$
$$-x^3y^2 = 16x^2y^3$$
$$0 = x^3y^2 + 16x^2y^3$$
$$0 = x^2y^2(x + 16y)$$

KEY CONCEPT #3: MULTIPLYING POLYNOMIALS USING FOIL

The FOIL method is a mnemonic device for multiplying polynomials that stands for **F**irst, **O**uter, **I**nner, **L**ast. It helps you keep track of the products of corresponding terms from each polynomial.

Prep Expert Strategy

1. Write each polynomial factor separately.
2. Identify the corresponding terms from each polynomial using the FOIL pattern: First, Outer, Inner, Last.
3. Multiply the corresponding terms and add the products together.
4. Simplify the expression by removing any remaining terms with zero coefficients.

Prep Expert Example

- **Question:** How would you use the FOIL method to multiply the following polynomials?

$$(x^2 + 10y^3) \times (2x^3 - 6y^2)$$

- **Answer:**

$$(x^2 + 10y^3) \times (2x^3 - 6y^2)$$
$$(x^2)(2x^3) + (x^2)(6y^2) + (10y^3)(2x^3) + -(10y^3)(6y^2)$$
$$2x^5 + 6x^2y^2 + 20x^3y^3 + -60y^5$$

KEY CONCEPT #4: EFFICIENT SUBSTITUTION
FOR EXPRESSIONS AND POLYNOMIALS

Substitute expressions and polynomials efficiently by systematically replacing variables with their corresponding values.

Prep Expert Strategy

1. Carefully read the problem and identify the expression or polynomial to be substituted.
2. Determine the values to substitute for the variables.
3. Replace each variable in the expression or polynomial with its corresponding value.
4. Simplify the resulting expression or polynomial.

Prep Expert Example

- **Question:** If $y = x^3 - 5x + 2$ and $z = x^3 + 10x - 6$ what is $z + 2y$?
- **Answer:**

$$z + 2y$$
$$(x^3 + 10x - 6) + 2(x^3 - 5x + 2)$$
$$x^3 + 10x - 6 + 2x^3 - 10x + 4$$
$$3x^3 - 2$$

Ace Expressions & Polynomials to maximize your SAT Math score.

PREP EXPERT PRACTICE

Try applying this *Prep Expert Strategy* yourself to the following SAT practice questions:

<table>
<tr><td>87</td><td>88</td></tr>
</table>

87

$$(4x^2 + 3x) - (2x^2 + 5x)$$

Which expression is equivalent to the given expression?

A) $2x^2 - 2x$
B) $2x^2 - 8x$
C) $6x^2 + 2x$
D) $6x^2 + 8x$

88

Which expression is equivalent to

$\dfrac{5y(y - 3) - 2(y - 3)}{y - 3}$, where $y \neq 3$?

A) $5y$
B) $5y - 2$
C) $5y^2 - 2y - 15$
D) $5y^2 - 2y + 1$

The answers to these SAT practice questions can be found in the back of this book.

PREP EXPERT REVIEW

Key Takeaways

- **Prep Expert Math Strategy #4—*Ace Expressions & Polynomials*:** Expressions are combinations of numbers and operations without an equal sign, while equations include an equal sign. Polynomials are expressions with variables and coefficients, using addition, subtraction, and multiplication, arranged in descending order of degree.

- **Reduce sign errors:** Three methods that work well to avoid sign errors when simplifying expressions include the following: (1) Change subtraction to addition of a negative, (2) Multiply and distribute negatives through the expression, and (3) Double-check all signs.

- **Combine like terms in polynomials:** Identify terms with the same variables and exponents, then add or subtract their coefficients. Simplify complex polynomials by grouping and combining like terms.

- **Use FOIL for multiplying polynomials:** Apply the FOIL (First, Outer, Inner, Last) method for multiplying polynomials. This method involves multiplying corresponding terms from each polynomial and simplifying the expression.

- **Efficient substitution in expressions and polynomials:** For efficient substitution, first identify the expression or polynomial that needs to be substituted. Then determine the values to replace the variables with. Finally, simplify the resulting expression or polynomial after the substitution.

 **PREP**EXPERT

MATH STRATEGY #5

ACE FRACTIONS & EXPONENTS

PREP EXPERT STRATEGY + EXAMPLE

Ace Fractions & Exponents

To perform well on SAT Math, you must *Ace Fractions & Exponents*. Below are the most important concepts to master this topic for the SAT.

Definition of Terms

1. **Fraction**: A way of representing a division of one quantity by another. Fractions are represented as two numbers separated by a horizontal or diagonal line. The number above the line is called the *numerator* and the number below the line is called the *denominator* (example: in ¾, 3 is the numerator and 4 is the denominator).

2. **Exponent**: An exponent is a number that indicates the power to which another number, called the base, is raised. The exponent is usually written as a small superscript number to the right of the base. For example, in the expression 3^4, the number 4 is the exponent, and 3 is the base.

Key Concepts

KEY CONCEPT #1: ADDING AND SUBTRACTING LIKE FRACTIONS

"Like fractions" have common denominators. Simply add or subtract the numerators while keeping the denominator the same.

Prep Expert Strategy
1. Identify the fractions that have the same denominator.
2. Add or subtract the numerators of the fractions.
3. Keep the denominator the same.

Prep Expert Example
- **Question**: How would you add the following like fractions?

$$\frac{2}{4} + \frac{1}{4}$$

- **Answer**:

$$\frac{2}{4} + \frac{1}{4} \;\rightarrow\; \frac{3}{4}$$

KEY CONCEPT #2: ADDING AND SUBTRACTING UNLIKE FRACTIONS

Unlike fractions have different denominators. To add or subtract unlike fractions, you must first find their lowest common denominator (LCD). The LCD is the smallest common multiple of the two denominators. Once you have found the LCD, you can rewrite each fraction using the LCD as the denominator. Then you can add or subtract the fractions.

Prep Expert Strategy
1. Identify the fractions that have different denominators.
2. Find the lowest common denominator (LCD) of the denominators.
3. Rewrite each fraction using the LCD as the denominator.
4. Add or subtract the numerators of the fractions.

Prep Expert Example
- **Question**: How would you add the following unlike fractions?

$$\frac{2}{4} + \frac{1}{8}$$

- **Answer:**

$$\frac{2}{4} + \frac{1}{8} \quad \rightarrow \quad \frac{4}{8} + \frac{1}{8} \quad \rightarrow \quad \frac{5}{8}$$

KEY CONCEPT #3: ADDING AND SUBTRACTING FRACTIONS WITH ALGEBRAIC EXPRESSIONS

When adding or subtracting fractions with denominators that contain different algebraic expressions, use the product of the two expressions as the lowest common denominator. The product of the two expressions will contain all of the factors necessary to rewrite each fraction using the same denominator.

Prep Expert Strategy

1. Identify the fractions that have different algebraic expressions in their denominators.
2. Find the product of the two algebraic expressions.
3. Rewrite each fraction using the product of the two expressions as the denominator.
4. Add or subtract the numerators of the fractions.

Prep Expert Example

- **Question:** How would you add the following fractions with different algebraic expressions in their denominators?

$$\frac{2}{(x+2)} + \frac{1}{(x-2)}$$

- **Answer:**

$$\frac{2}{(x+2)} + \frac{1}{(x-2)} \quad \rightarrow \quad \frac{2(x-2)}{(x+2)(x-2)} + \frac{1(x+2)}{(x-2)(x+2)} \quad \rightarrow$$

$$\frac{2x-4}{(x+2)(x-2)} + \frac{x+2}{(x-2)(x+2)} \quad \rightarrow \quad \frac{3x-2}{(x+2)(x-2)} \quad \rightarrow \quad \frac{3x-2}{(x^2-2x+2x-4)} \quad \rightarrow$$

$$\frac{3x-2}{x^2-4}$$

KEY CONCEPT #4: RATIONALIZING RADICAL DENOMINATORS

Rationalize a fraction with a radical in the denominator by multiplying the numerator and denominator by a conjugate of the denominator. A conjugate is an expression that is identical to the original expression except that the sign of the radical term is reversed. Rationalizing the fraction simplifies the expression and makes it easier to work with.

Prep Expert Strategy
1. Identify the fraction with a radical in the denominator.
2. Find the conjugate of the denominator.
3. Multiply the numerator and denominator of the fraction by the conjugate.
4. Simplify the resulting expression.

Prep Expert Example
- **Question**: How would you rationalize the following fraction with a radical in the denominator?

$$\frac{3}{(x - \sqrt{2})}$$

- **Answer**:

$$\frac{3}{(x - \sqrt{2})} \rightarrow \frac{3}{(x - \sqrt{2})} \times \frac{(x + \sqrt{2})}{(x + \sqrt{2})} \rightarrow \frac{3(x + \sqrt{2})}{(x - \sqrt{2})(x + \sqrt{2})} \rightarrow$$

$$\frac{3x + 3\sqrt{2}}{(x^2 + x\sqrt{2} - x\sqrt{2} - 2)} \rightarrow \frac{3x + 3\sqrt{2}}{(x^2 - 2)}$$

KEY CONCEPT #5: WORKING WITH POSITIVE EXPONENTS

A positive exponent indicates how many times a number (the base) is multiplied by itself.

Prep Expert Strategy
1. Identify the expression with a positive exponent.
2. Multiply the base by itself the number of times indicated by the positive exponent.

Prep Expert Example

- **Question:** How would you simplify the following expression with a positive exponent?

$$9^2$$

- **Answer:**

$$9^2 \rightarrow 81$$

KEY CONCEPT #6: WORKING WITH NEGATIVE EXPONENTS

A negative exponent indicates to take the reciprocal of the base and then raise to the positive exponent.

Prep Expert Strategy

1. Identify the expression with a negative exponent.
2. Take the reciprocal of the base.
3. Raise the denominator to the positive exponent (absolute value of negative exponent).

Prep Expert Example

- **Question:** How would you simplify the following expression with a negative exponent?

$$9^{-2}$$

- **Answer:**

$$9^{-2} \rightarrow \frac{1}{9^2} \rightarrow \frac{1}{81}$$

KEY CONCEPT #7: CONVERTING FRACTIONAL EXPONENTS TO RADICALS

Convert a fractional exponent to a radical by making the denominator the root of the radical and making the numerator the power of the base that is now under the radical sign.

Prep Expert Strategy

1. Identify the expression with a fractional exponent.
2. Make the denominator the root of the radical.
3. Make the numerator the power of the base that is now under the radical sign.

Prep Expert
Math Strategies

Prep Expert Example

- **Question:** How would you convert the following expression with a fractional exponent to a radical?

$$9^{\frac{1}{2}}$$

- **Answer:**

$$9^{\frac{1}{2}} \;\rightarrow\; \sqrt[2]{9^1} \;\rightarrow\; 3$$

KEY CONCEPT #8: CONVERTING RADICALS TO FRACTIONAL EXPONENTS

Convert a radical to a fractional exponent by determining the root of the base. Make the root of the radical the denominator of the fractional exponent. Make the power of the base the numerator of the fractional exponent.

Prep Expert Strategy

1. Identify the expression with a radical.
2. Determine the root of the radical.
3. Make the root of the radical the denominator of the fractional exponent.
4. Make the power of the base the numerator of the fractional exponent.

Prep Expert Example

- **Question:** How would you convert the following radical to an expression with a fractional exponent?

$$\sqrt[3]{x^2}$$

- **Answer:**

$$\sqrt[3]{x^2} \;\rightarrow\; x^{\frac{2}{3}}$$

KEY CONCEPT #9: MULTIPLYING COMMON BASES WITH EXPONENTS

When multiplying expressions with the same base, the exponents are added. This principle stems from the property of exponents that states $a^m \times a^n = a^{(m+n)}$.

Prep Expert Strategy

1. Identify the expressions with the same base.
2. Determine the exponents of each expression.

3. Add the exponents to obtain the new exponent.
4. Combine the bases and write the new exponent.

Prep Expert Example
- **Question**: How would you multiply the following expression with common bases?

$$3^5 \times 3^2$$

- **Answer**:

$$3^5 \times 3^2 \quad \rightarrow \quad 3^7 \quad \rightarrow \quad 2{,}187$$

KEY CONCEPT #10: DIVIDING COMMON BASES WITH EXPONENTS

When dividing expressions with the same base, the exponents are subtracted. This principle stems from the property of exponents that states $a^m \div a^n = a^{(m-n)}$.

Prep Expert Strategy
1. Identify the expressions with the same base.
2. Determine the exponents of each expression.
3. Subtract the exponents to obtain the new exponent.
4. Combine the bases and write the new exponent.

Prep Expert Example
- **Question**: How would you divide the following expression with common bases?

$$3^5 \div 3^2$$

- **Answer**:

$$3^5 \div 3^2 \quad \rightarrow \quad 3^3 \quad \rightarrow \quad 27$$

KEY CONCEPT #11: POWER OF A POWER IN EXPONENTS

When you raise an exponent to another exponent, you multiply the exponents. This principle stems from the property of exponents that states $(a^m)^n = a^{(m \times n)}$.

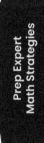

Prep Expert Strategy
1. Identify the expression with the exponent raised to another exponent.
2. Determine the base and the exponents.
3. Multiply the exponents to obtain the new exponent.
4. Leave the base unchanged and write down the resulting exponent.

Prep Expert Example

- **Question:** How would you simplify the following expression with an exponent raised to another exponent?

$$(3^5)^2$$

- **Answer:**

$$(3^5)^2 \;\rightarrow\; 3^{10} \;\rightarrow\; 59{,}049$$

KEY CONCEPT #12: APPLYING EXPONENT RULES TO VARIABLES

All of the exponent rules also apply to algebraic variables. The variables may be in the exponents or in the bases.

Prep Expert Strategy

1. Apply the rules of exponents if there are variables in the exponents.
2. Apply the rules of exponents if there are variables in the bases.

Prep Expert Example

- **Question:** How would you apply the same exponent rules to expressions with algebraic variables?

- **Answer:** See the examples below.

$3^x \times 3^y$	$3^x \div 3^y$	$(3^x)^y$
3^{x+y}	3^{x-y}	(3^{xy})
$x^3 \times x^2$	$x^3 \div x^2$	$(x^2)^3$
x^5	x^1	(x^6)

KEY CONCEPT #13: COMMON BASE FACTORIZATION IN EXPONENTS

Common base factorization is used in algebra to simplify expressions that have the same base raised to different powers. This concept requires identifying the greatest common exponent among terms with the same base. Once identified, you factor out this base raised to the lowest exponent from all terms.

1. Identify the terms in the expression that have the same base raised to different exponents.

2. Look for the smallest exponent among those terms (the exponent you will factor out).

3. Rewrite the expression by factoring out the common base raised to the lowest exponent.

4. Simplify the remaining expression inside the parentheses.

Prep Expert Example

- **Question:** How would you factor the following expression with exponents?

$$x^4 + 2x^3 - 3x^2$$

- **Answer:**

$$x^4 + 2x^3 - 3x^2 \quad \rightarrow \quad x^2(x^2 + 2x - 3)$$

KEY CONCEPT #14: COMMON SAT EXPONENTS

Familiarize yourself with common exponents that appear frequently on the SAT.

Prep Expert Strategy

1. Make sure that you know all of the squares, cubes, and exponents of 2 in the table below.

Prep Expert Example

Squares			Cubes	Exponents of 2
$1^2 = 1$	$7^2 = 49$	$13^2 = 169$	$1^3 = 1$	$2^1 = 2$
$2^2 = 4$	$8^2 = 64$	$14^2 = 196$	$2^3 = 8$	$2^2 = 4$
$3^2 = 9$	$9^2 = 81$	$15^2 = 225$	$3^3 = 27$	$2^3 = 8$
$4^2 = 16$	$10^2 = 100$		$4^3 = 64$	$2^4 = 16$
$5^2 = 25$	$11^2 = 121$		$5^3 = 125$	$2^5 = 32$
$6^2 = 36$	$12^2 = 144$		$6^3 = 216$	$2^6 = 64$

Prep Expert
Math Strategies

KEY CONCEPT #15: RECOGNIZING PERFECT SQUARES AND CUBES

Perfect squares involve raising a number to the power of 2, while perfect cubes involve raising a number to the power of 3. You can gain a significant advantage on the SAT by quickly recognizing and factoring perfect squares and cubes.

Prep Expert Strategy

1. Identify numbers that are raised to the power of 2 or 3.
2. Recognize these numbers as perfect squares or cubes.
3. Apply factoring techniques to deconstruct perfect squares and cubes.

Prep Expert Example

- **Question**: How would you rewrite the following expression as perfect squares and cubes?

$$\frac{27}{100}$$

- **Answer**:

$$\frac{27}{100} \rightarrow \frac{3^3}{10^2}$$

Ace Fractions & Exponents to maximize your SAT Math score.

PREP EXPERT PRACTICE

Try applying this *Prep Expert Strategy* yourself to the following SAT practice questions:

89

Which expression is equivalent to $4x^7y^3 + 8x^3y^3$?

A) $4x^3y^3(x^4 + 2)$
B) $4x^3y^3(x^2)$
C) $4x^3y^3(x^4 + 1)$
D) $4x^3y^3(x^2 + 2)$

90

Which expression is equivalent to $a^{\frac{7}{8}}$, where $a > 0$?

A) $\sqrt[8]{a^{56}}$
B) $\sqrt[64]{a^{56}}$
C) $\sqrt[49]{a^{56}}$
D) $\sqrt[7]{a^{56}}$

The answers to these SAT practice questions can be found in the back of this book.

PREP EXPERT REVIEW

Key Takeaways

- **Prep Expert Math Strategy #5—*Ace Fractions & Exponents*:** This section covered key concepts for mastering fractions and exponents on SAT Math.

- **Key concepts related to fractions:** You must know how to add and subtract like and unlike fractions, work with fractions with algebraic expressions in the denominator, and rationalize radical denominators.

- **Key concepts related to exponents:** You must know how to work with positive and negative exponents, convert between fractional exponents and radicals, multiply and divide common bases with exponents, and find the power of a power in exponents.

- **Application to SAT prep:** Exponent rules are also applicable to algebraic variables. Learn how to do common base factorization. And recognize common perfect squares and cubes for a significant advantage on SAT Math.

PREPEXPERT

MATH STRATEGY #6

ACE QUADRATICS & PARABOLAS

PREP EXPERT STRATEGY + EXAMPLE

Ace Quadratics & Parabolas

To perform well on SAT Math, you must *Ace Quadratics & Parabolas*. Below are the most important concepts to master this topic for the SAT.

Definition of Terms

1. **Quadratic:** An expression, equation, or function that involves the square of a variable. Specifically, a quadratic is a second-degree polynomial, which means it has a highest-degree term that is a square of a variable. The standard form of a quadratic can be written as $ax^2 + bx + c$.

2. **Parabola:** The graph of a quadratic. It is a U-shaped curve that is symmetrical on either side of a vertical line called the axis of symmetry. The vertex is the point where the function has its minimum or maximum value, depending on whether the parabola opens upward or downward.

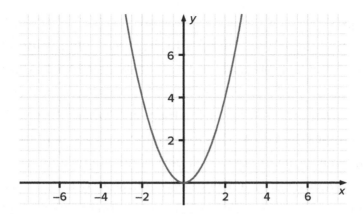

Key Concepts

KEY CONCEPT #1: FACTORING QUADRATICS

It is important to use the standard form of a quadratic, $ax^2 + bx + c$. Factoring quadratics involves finding two numbers that add up to the coefficient of the x term (b) and multiply together to the constant term (c). You can do this by listing out the factors of the constant term (c) and then finding two factors that add up to the coefficient of x (b).

Prep Expert Strategy

1. Find two numbers that multiply to the constant term and add to the coefficient of the x term.
2. Rewrite the equation as $ax^2 + bx + c = (x + m)(x + n)$
3. Make sure that $m \times n = c$
4. Make sure that $m + n = b$

Prep Expert Example

- **Question:** How would you factor the following quadratic?

$$x^2 - 7x + 12$$

- **Answer:**

$$x^2 - 7x + 12 \quad \rightarrow \quad (x - 3)(x - 4)$$

KEY CONCEPT #2: INTERPRETING SOLUTIONS OF QUADRATICS

Solutions, roots, zeros, and x-intercepts are terms used interchangeably to describe the x-values that solve the quadratic equation $ax^2 + bx + c = 0$. These solutions are where the graph of the quadratic function crosses the x-axis.

Prep Expert Strategy

1. Recognize that these terms all refer to the same thing. Solutions, roots, zeros, and x-intercepts all represent the x-values that make a quadratic equation equivalent to 0.

2. Understand that the x-intercepts are the points where the graph of the quadratic equation crosses the x-axis. This means that the y-value of these points is 0.

3. Remember that the solutions, roots, zeros, and x-intercepts can be found by setting the quadratic equation equal to 0 and solving for x. There may be one or two solutions, or even no solutions, depending on the specific quadratic equation.

Prep Expert Example

- **Question**: How would you find the solutions, roots, zeros, and x-intercepts of the following quadratic?

$$x^2 - 7x + 12$$

- **Answer**:

$$x^2 - 7x + 12 = 0 \quad \rightarrow \quad (x - 3)(x - 4) = 0$$

Solution/roots/zeros/x-intercepts: $x = 3$ *or* $x = 4$

KEY CONCEPT #3: INTERPRETING FACTORS OF QUADRATICS

Factors of a quadratic equation are binomial expressions that yield the quadratic equation when multiplied together. Each factor corresponds to a root of the equation. Setting each factor equal to zero gives the solutions to the equation.

Prep Expert Strategy

1. A factor is an expression that divides a quadratic equation without leaving a remainder.

2. Factors can be used to rewrite a quadratic equation in a more simplified form. This can be helpful for understanding the properties of the quadratic equation.

3. Factors can be used to solve quadratic equations. By setting each factor equal to 0, you can find the solutions of the quadratic equation.

Prep Expert Example

- **Question**: How would you find the factors of the following quadratic?

$$x^2 - 7x + 12$$

- **Answer:**

$$x^2 - 7x + 12 = 0 \quad \rightarrow \quad (x - 3)(x - 4)$$
$$\text{Factors: } (x - 3) \text{ or } (x - 4)$$

KEY CONCEPT #4: FINDING QUADRATIC FACTORS WITH TABLES

The SAT will sometimes present you with a table of the x-values and y-values for a particular quadratic. The test-question writers will then ask you to determine the factors of the quadratic from just the table of values. To do this, follow the steps below.

Prep Expert Strategy

1. Look at the y-values in the table. Determine when the y-value is equal to 0.
2. Look at the x-values in the table. Determine the corresponding x-value when the y-value is equal to 0.
3. This x-value is the solution to the quadratic (remember that the solutions, roots, zeros, and x-intercepts occur when the y-value equals 0).
4. To create a "factor," write an expression that subtracts this value from x itself.

Prep Expert Example

- **Question:** Given the table below, what would be a factor of the quadratic function $f(x)$?

x-value	f(x) (y-value)
1	10
2	6
3	0
4	−2

- **Answer:** When the y-value is equal to 0, the x-value is equal to 3. Therefore, 3 is a solution to the quadratic function above. The expression **(x – 3)** would evenly divide $f(x)$. **(x – 3)** is a factor of the $f(x)$ quadratic function.

KEY CONCEPT #5: SIMPLIFYING PERFECT SQUARE QUADRATICS

Perfect square quadratics are special quadratic equations that factor into identical binomial factors. They can be simplified to $(ax + b)^2$, which indicates the square of a binomial.

Prep Expert Strategy

1. Recognize perfect square quadratics (*Hint*: they often have a constant term that is a square).
2. Write the quadratic as $(ax + b)(ax + b)$.
3. Write the quadratic as $(ax + b)^2$.

Prep Expert Example

- **Question**: How would you simplify the following perfect square quadratic?

$$4x^2 - 20x + 25$$

- **Answer**:

$$4x^2 - 20x + 25 \quad \rightarrow \quad (2x - 5)(2x - 5) \quad \rightarrow \quad (2x - 5)^2$$

KEY CONCEPT #6: QUADRATIC EXPRESSIONS AS VARIABLES

Sometimes, an expression within a quadratic equation can be treated as a single variable to make solving it simpler. This substitution is particularly helpful when dealing with complex or nested quadratic forms.

Prep Expert Strategy

1. Look for a portion of the quadratic that you can substitute with a single variable.
2. Solve the simplified equation.
3. Replace the substituted variable back into the original equation.

Prep Expert Example

- **Question**: In the following equation, how would you treat the expression $(x - 2)$ like you would x in a regular quadratic equation?

$$(x - 2)^2 - 6(x - 2) + 8 = 0$$

- **Answer**:

$$(x - 2)^2 - 6(x - 2) + 8 = 0$$
$$[(x - 2) - 4] \times [(x - 2) - 2] = 0$$
$$[(x - 6)] \times [(x - 4)] = 0$$
$$x = 6 \ \ or \ \ x = 4$$

KEY CONCEPT #7: QUADRATIC FORMULA

The quadratic formula, $x = \frac{-b \pm \sqrt{b^2 - 4ac}}{2a}$, is used to solve for x in the standard quadratic equation $ax^2 + bx + c = 0$. The formula provides both solutions for x, accounting for both the positive and negative square roots.

Prep Expert Strategy

1. Write down the quadratic formula: $x = \frac{-b \pm \sqrt{b^2 - 4ac}}{2a}$
2. Plug the coefficients of your quadratic equation into the formula.
3. Calculate to find the two possible values for x.

Prep Expert Example

- **Question**: How would you solve the following quadratic using the quadratic equation?

$$x^2 - 3x = 17$$

- **Answer**:

$$x^2 - 3x = 17 \quad \rightarrow \quad x^2 - 3x - 17 = 0$$

$$x = \frac{-b \pm \sqrt{b^2 - 4ac}}{2a} \quad \rightarrow \quad x = \frac{-(-3) \pm \sqrt{(-3)^2 - 4(1)(-17)}}{2(1)} \quad \rightarrow \quad x = \frac{3 \pm \sqrt{9 + 68}}{2} \quad \rightarrow$$

$$x = \frac{3 \pm \sqrt{77}}{2} \quad \rightarrow \quad x = \frac{3 + \sqrt{77}}{2} \quad or \quad x = \frac{3 - \sqrt{77}}{2}$$

KEY CONCEPT #8: DISCRIMINANT OF THE QUADRATIC FORMULA

The discriminant ($b^2 - 4ac$) located under the square root in the quadratic formula determines the nature of the solutions of the quadratic equation. If the discriminant is positive, there are two real solutions. If the discriminant is zero, there is one real solution. And if the discriminant is negative, there are no real solutions.

Prep Expert Strategy

1. Identify the discriminant as $b^2 - 4ac$ within the quadratic formula.
2. Calculate the discriminant to determine the nature of the solutions (roots).
3. Use the discriminant to predict the number of solutions or x-intercepts on the graph.

Prep Expert Example

- **Question:** How many times does the graph of $x^2 + 4x + 4 = 0$ intersect the x-axis?

- **Answer:**

$$b^2 - 4ac \quad \rightarrow \quad 4^2 - 4(1)(4) \quad \rightarrow \quad 0$$

The discriminant is equal to 0. Therefore, we know the quadratic has **one solution** and only intersects the x-axis once.

KEY CONCEPT #9: ORIENTATION OF PARABOLAS

The coefficient a when a quadratic is written in the standard form $ax^2 + bx + c$ determines the direction of the parabola's opening. A positive coefficient a indicates that the parabola opens upward. A negative coefficient a indicates that the parabola opens downward.

Prep Expert Strategy

1. Write the quadratic in the standard form $ax^2 + bx + c$.
2. Determine the sign of the coefficient a in the standard-form quadratic.
3. If a is positive, the parabola opens upward. If a is negative, the parabola opens downward.
4. Sketch the parabola to see the orientation.

Prep Expert Example

- **Question:** Does the graph of $y = x^2 + 2x - 8$ open upward or downward?
- **Answer:** The parabola opens upward because a is positive 1.

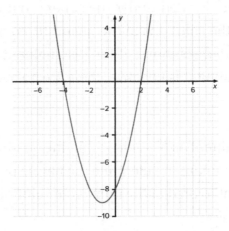

KEY CONCEPT #10: LINE OF SYMMETRY IN PARABOLAS

The line of symmetry in a parabola is a vertical line that passes through the vertex, dividing the parabola into two mirror-image halves.

Prep Expert Strategy

1. On the graph of a parabola, draw an imaginary line that runs vertically through the vertex.
2. This line divides the parabola into two symmetrical halves.

Prep Expert Example

- **Question**: Where is the line of symmetry in the graph of $y = x^2 + 2x - 8$?

- **Answer**: See the dotted line below.

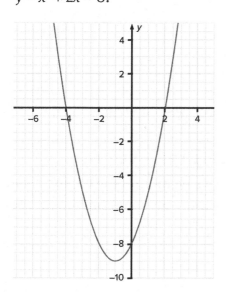

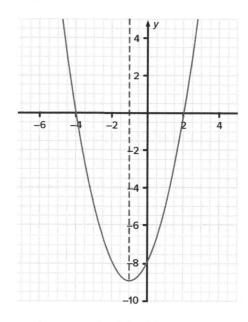

KEY CONCEPT #11: X-INTERCEPTS OF PARABOLAS

The *x*-intercepts of a parabola are the points where the graph intersects the *x*-axis. These intercepts correspond to the solutions of the quadratic equation when the output value $f(x)$ is set to zero.

Prep Expert Strategy

1. To find *x*-intercepts using a quadratic equation, set it equal to 0 and solve for *x*.
2. To find *x*-intercepts using the graph of a parabola, identify where the parabola crosses the *x*-axis.

- **Question:** What are the *x*-intercepts of the equation $y = x^2 + 2x - 8$ using the graph of the parabola below?

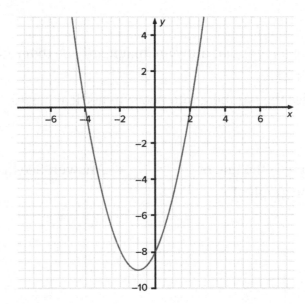

- **Answer:** The two *x*-intercepts for this parabola are (–4, 0) and (2, 0).

KEY CONCEPT #12: EQUIDISTANT X-INTERCEPTS FROM VERTEX

The *x*-intercepts of a parabola are symmetrically spaced around the vertex. If you find one *x*-intercept, you can locate the other by measuring an equal horizontal distance from the vertex's *x*-coordinate in the opposite direction.

Prep Expert Strategy

1. Calculate the horizontal distance from the vertex to one *x*-intercept.
2. Measure the same horizontal distance from the vertex to the opposite side to find the other *x*-intercept.
3. Ensure that both *x*-intercepts are equidistant horizontally from the vertex. By definition, both *x*-intercepts will always have a *y*-coordinate of 0 (*x*-intercepts intersect the *x*-axis, which means their *y*-value must be 0).

Prep Expert Example

- **Question:** If you are given that one *x*-intercept of a quadratic is located at (5, 0), and you know the vertex is located at (3, –2), what are the coordinates of the other *x*-intercept? *Hint*: *x*-intercepts are always horizontally equidistant from the *x*-value of the vertex.

- **Answer**: The horizontal distance between 5 and 3 is 2. This means that the given *x*-intercept is 2 units to the right of the vertex. Therefore, the other *x*-intercept must be 2 units to the left of the vertex at an ***x*-coordinate of 1** (3 – 2). Thus, the second *x*-intercept must be **(1, 0)**.

KEY CONCEPT #13: VERTEX OF A PARABOLA

The vertex of a parabola represents the maximum or minimum point of the function, which occurs at the peak or the trough of the curve. Whether the vertex is a maximum or minimum depends on whether the parabola opens upward or downward.

Prep Expert Strategy
1. On the graph of a parabola, identify the maximum or minimum point.
2. The coordinates of this point represent the vertex.

Prep Expert Example
- **Question**: Where is the vertex in the graph of $y = x^2 + 2x - 8$?

- **Answer**: The vertex is located at the point (–1, –9) in the parabola.

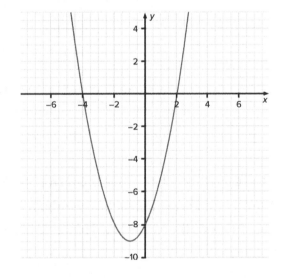

KEY CONCEPT #14: X-COORDINATE OF VERTEX FORMULA

You can calculate the *x*-coordinate of a parabola's vertex using the formula $x = -\dfrac{b}{2a}$ for a quadratic in standard form. Finding the *x*-coordinate is often the first step in identifying the complete coordinates of the vertex.

Prep Expert Strategy

1. Use the formula $x = -\dfrac{b}{2a}$ to calculate the *x*-coordinate of the vertex.

2. Substitute the *x*-coordinate back into the equation to find the *y*-coordinate.

3. The point (x, y) is the vertex of the parabola.

4. If *a* (the coefficient on x^2) is *positive*, then the vertex represents the *minimum* (because this means the parabola opens upward).

5. If *a* (the coefficient on x^2) is *negative*, then the vertex represents the *maximum* (because this means the parabola opens downward).

Prep Expert Example

- **Question**: What is the minimum value for the graph $y = x^2 + 8x + 4$?

  Hint: When the SAT asks for the "minimum" or "maximum" value, it is asking for the *y*-coordinate, not the *x*-coordinate.

- **Answer**: In the original equation, a (the coefficient of x^2) is positive. Therefore, the vertex represents the minimum.

$$\frac{-b}{2a} \;\rightarrow\; \frac{-8}{2(1)} \;\rightarrow\; \frac{-8}{2}$$

$-4 \;\rightarrow\;$ *x*-coordinate of the vertex of the parabola

$y = x^2 + 8x + 4 \;\rightarrow\; y = (-4)^2 + 8(-4) + 4 \;\rightarrow\; y = 16 + -32 + 4$

$y = -12 \;\rightarrow\;$ *y*-coordinate of the vertex of the parabola *(minimum of the parabola)*

KEY CONCEPT #15: HORIZONTAL INTERSECTION AT THE VERTEX

A horizontal line intersects a parabola at exactly one point if and only if it intersects at the vertex of the parabola. This point is where the parabola's maximum or minimum value lies.

Prep Expert Strategy

1. The only time a horizontal line can intersect a parabola at only one point is at the vertex.

2. The SAT may state that a horizontal line (y = constant) intersects a parabola at only one point. If so, you should know to find the vertex of the parabola.

3. As we just reviewed, the first step to find the vertex of a parabola is to use the formula $x = -\dfrac{b}{2a}$ to find the x-value of the vertex.

Prep Expert Example

- **Question:** The line $y = -2$ intersects $y = x^2 - 4x + 2$ at just one point. What are the coordinates of this point?

- **Answer:**

$$\frac{-b}{2a} \quad \rightarrow \quad \frac{+4}{2(1)} \quad \rightarrow \quad \frac{4}{2}$$

$$2 \rightarrow x\text{-coordinate of the vertex of the parabola}$$
$$y = x^2 - 4x + 2 \quad \rightarrow \quad y = (2)^2 - 4(2) + 2 \quad \rightarrow \quad y = 4 - 8 + 2$$
$$y = -2 \rightarrow y\text{-coordinate of the vertex of the parabola}$$
$$\text{Vertex coordinates: } \textbf{(2, --2)}$$

Ace Quadratics & Parabolas to maximize your SAT Math score.

PREP EXPERT PRACTICE

Try applying this *Prep Expert Strategy* yourself to the following SAT practice questions:

91

$$h(x) = -2x^2 + 40$$

What is the maximum value of the given function?

A) −40

B) 0

C) 40

D) There is no maximum value

92

In the xy-plane, the graph of the equation $y = 2x^2 - 5x + 12$ intersects the line $y = c$ at exactly one point. What is the value of c?

A) $\dfrac{3}{8}$

B) $\dfrac{9}{8}$

C) $\dfrac{12}{8}$

D) $\dfrac{71}{8}$

The answers to these SAT practice questions can be found in the back of this book.

PREP EXPERT REVIEW

Key Takeaways

- **Prep Expert Math Strategy #6—*Ace Quadratics & Parabolas***: This section covered key concepts for mastering quadratics and parabolas on SAT Math.

- **Quadratics and parabolas**: A quadratic is a second-degree polynomial ($ax^2 + bx + c$). A parabola is a U-shaped graph of a quadratic that is symmetrical.

- **Factoring and solutions**: Factoring involves finding numbers that *add* up to b and *multiply* to c in the quadratic's standard form. Solutions, roots, zeros, and x-intercepts of quadratics are the x-values where the quadratic is equal to zero.

- **Quadratic formula and discriminant**: The quadratic formula ($x = \dfrac{-b \pm \sqrt{b^2 - 4ac}}{2a}$), is used for finding solutions. The discriminant ($b^2 - 4ac$) indicates the nature of these solutions.

- **Characteristics of parabolas**: The coefficient of x^2 in a quadratic determines the parabola's opening direction. The line of symmetry runs through the vertex of a parabola and divides it into two equal halves.

- **Vertex and x-intercepts**: The vertex represents the maximum or minimum point of the parabola. Use the formula $x = -\dfrac{b}{2a}$ to calculate the x-intercept of the vertex of a parabola. x-intercepts are the points where the parabola crosses the x-axis and are horizontally equidistant from the vertex.

 **PREP**EXPERT

MATH STRATEGY #7

ACE EXPONENTIAL GROWTH & DECAY

PREP EXPERT STRATEGY + EXAMPLE

Ace Exponential Growth & Decay

To perform well on SAT Math, you must *Ace Exponential Growth & Decay*. Below are the most important concepts to master this topic for the SAT.

Definition of Terms

1. **Exponential growth**: When a quantity grows at an increasingly faster rate over time (example: increasing by 50% per year).

2. **Linear growth**: When a quantity grows at a constant rate over time (example: increasing by 50 units per year).

3. **Exponential decay**: When a quantity decreases at an increasingly fast rate over time (example: decreasing by 50% per year).

4. **Linear decay**: When a quantity decreases at a constant rate over time (example: decreasing by 50 units per year).

Key Concepts

KEY CONCEPT #1: EXPONENTIAL GROWTH FORMULA

Exponential growth involves quantities increasing over time, described by the formula $A = P(1 + r)^t$. Understanding this involves recognizing how changes in the initial amount, growth rate, and time affect the final value. This concept is essential to understanding real-world phenomena such as investment growth.

Prep Expert Strategy

1. Familiarize yourself with the standard exponential growth formula:

$$A = P(1 + r)^t$$

A = the value after time t, P = the initial value,
r = the growth rate, t = time elapsed

Prep Expert Example

- **Question**: Assuming t is in years, what are A, P, r, and t in the following exponential growth equation?

$$A = 100(1 + 0.5)^2$$

- **Answer**:

$$A = 100(1 + 0.5)^2$$
$A = 100(1.5)^2 = 100(2.25) = 225$ (represents the value after 2 years)
$P = 100$ (represents the initial value)
$r = +0.5$ (represents a positive 50% growth rate)
$t = 2$ (represents that 2 years have elapsed)

KEY CONCEPT #2: EXPONENTIAL DECAY FORMULA

Exponential decay involves quantities decreasing over time, described by the formula $A = P(1 - r)^t$. Mastery of this concept requires understanding how different decay rates and time periods influence the final amount. This formula is crucial to understanding phenomena such as asset depreciation.

Prep Expert Strategy

1. Familiarize yourself with the standard exponential decay formula:

$$A = P(1 - r)^t$$
A = the value after time t, P = the initial value,
r = the growth rate, t = time elapsed

Prep Expert Example

- **Question**: Assuming t is in years, what are A, P, r, and t in the following exponential decay equation?

$$A = 20(1 - 0.3)^4$$

- **Answer**:

$$A = 20(1 - 0.3)^4$$
$$A = 20(0.7)^4 = 20(0.2401) = 4.802 \text{ (represents the value after 4 years)}$$
$$P = 20 \text{ (represents the initial value)}$$
$$r = -0.3 \text{ (represents a negative 30\% growth rate)}$$
$$t = 4 \text{ (represents that 4 years have elapsed)}$$

KEY CONCEPT #3: GRAPHS OF EXPONENTIAL GROWTH & DECAY

Graphing exponential growth and decay illustrates how values change over time. Key features include the curve's steep rise or fall and its approach toward an asymptote.

Prep Expert Strategy

1. Exponential growth graphs are characterized by rapid growth that quickly approaches infinity ($y \to \infty$).
2. Exponential decay graphs are characterized by rapid decline that quickly approaches 0 ($y \to 0$).

Prep Expert Example

- **Exponential Growth Graph Example**: The graph of $y = 2^t$ quickly approaches infinity as time elapses (t increases).

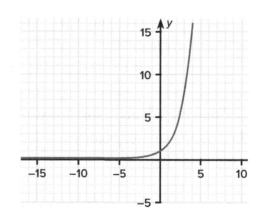

- **Exponential Decay Graph Example**: The graph of $y = (\frac{1}{2})^t$ quickly approaches 0 as time elapses (t increases).

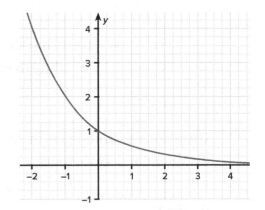

KEY CONCEPT #4: SIMPLE INTEREST VERSUS COMPOUND INTEREST

Understanding simple and compound interest is crucial in finance. Simple interest grows in a linear fashion and can be calculated using $A = P(1 + rt)$. Compound interest grows exponentially and can be calculated using $A = P(1 + r)^t$.

Prep Expert Strategy

1. **Simple interest** is an example of *linear growth*. In other words, money grows at a constant rate, or by a fixed amount, over time.
2. **Compound interest** is an example of *exponential growth*. In other words, money grows at an exponential rate, or by a percentage, over time.

Prep Expert Example

- **Question**: After 10 years, how much more money would a compound interest savings account that grows at 10% a year have than a simple interest savings account that grows at $10 per year? Assume both accounts started with $1,000.

- **Answer**:
  Compound Interest:
  $$A = P(1 + r)^t = 1,000(1 + 0.1)^{10} = 1,000(1.1)^{10} = 1,000(2.59374) = \$2,593.74$$
  Simple Interest:
  $$A = P(1 + rt) = 1,000(1 + (0.01)(10)) = 1,000(1 + 0.1) = \$1,100.00$$

You can calculate the growth rate, r, in the simple interest equation by taking the amount that the account is increasing per year ($10) and dividing it by the initial amount ($1,000) $\rightarrow$ 10 ÷ 1,000 = 0.01.

Difference: $2,593.74 − $1,100.00 = $1,493.74

Prep Expert
Math Strategies

KEY CONCEPT #5: APPLY PIN TO EXPONENTIAL GROWTH & DECAY SAT PROBLEMS

On the SAT, many exponential growth and decay problems can be solved using *Prep Expert Math Strategy #1—Plug In Numbers (PIN)*. You can replace variables with real numbers. This approach simplifies complex problems, making them more manageable.

Prep Expert Strategy

1. Many exponential growth and decay problems do not require the use of formulas at all on the SAT.
2. Instead, solve them using *Plug in Numbers (PIN)*.
3. Rather than thinking about abstract exponential growth or decay, try plugging in a real number for the time (either that you choose or from a table the SAT gives you).
4. Then determine what value the quantity should be at that time.

Prep Expert Example

- **Question:** Daniel opened a savings account at a credit union. The table shows the exponential relationship between the time t, in years, since Daniel opened the account and the total amount n, in dollars, in the account. If Daniel made no additional deposits or withdrawals, which of the following equations best represents the relationship between t and n?

Time (years)	Total amount (dollars)
0	1,000.00
1	1,010.00
2	1,020.10

A) $n = (1 + 1,000)^t$
B) $n = (1 + 0.01)^t$
C) $n = 1,000(1 + 0.01)^t$
D) $n = 0.01(1 + 1,000)^t$

- **Answer:**
  1. The first row of the table shows that when $t = 0$, the total amount should be $1,000.

2. Plug in $t = 0$ into the various equations in answer choices (A), (B), (C), and (D).

3. Only answer choice (C) results in $1,000 when $t = 0$. Therefore, (C) is the answer.

Ace Exponential Growth & Decay to maximize your SAT Math score.

PREP EXPERT PRACTICE

Try applying this *Prep Expert Strategy* yourself to the following SAT practice questions:

93

The population of a city grows exponentially with a growth factor of 1.05 per year. The initial population of the city is 100,000. Which equation represents the population, *P*, of the city *t* years after the initial population?

A) $P = \dfrac{1}{1.05}(100{,}000)^t$

B) $P = 1.05(100{,}000)^t$

C) $P = 100{,}000(\dfrac{1}{1.05})^t$

D) $P = 100{,}000(1.05)^t$

94

$$g(t) = 500(0.8)^t$$

The given function *g* models the population of a city *t* years after 2010, where *t* is a non-negative integer. If $y = g(t)$ is graphed in the *ty*-plane, which of the following is the best interpretation of the *y*-intercept of the graph in this context?

A) The estimated population of the city in 2010 was 500.

B) The estimated population of the city in *t* years was 500.

C) The minimum estimated population of the city during the given time period was 500.

D) The maximum estimated population of the city during the given time period was 500.

The answers to these SAT practice questions can be found in the back of this book.

PREP EXPERT REVIEW

Key Takeaways

- **Prep Expert Math Strategy #7—Ace Exponential Growth & Decay**: This section covered key concepts for mastering exponential growth and decay on SAT Math.

- **Exponential growth and decay formulas**: The exponential growth formula is $A = P(1 + r)^t$. The exponential decay formula is $A = P(1 - r)^t$. A is the final amount, P is the initial amount, r is the growth rate, and t is the time elapsed.

- **Graphical representation**: Exponential growth graphs show a rapid rise, approaching infinity as time passes. Exponential decay graphs depict a rapid decline, approaching zero over time.

- **Simple versus compound interest**: Simple interest represents a value growing linearly over time and is given by the formula $A = P(1 + rt)$. Compound interest represents a value growing exponentially over time and is given by the formula $A = P(1 + r)^t$.

- **Applying *Plug in Numbers (PIN)***: Many exponential growth and decay problems on the SAT can be solved by plugging in numbers for the variables. This simplifies abstract equations and makes them easier to solve.

Prep Expert
Math Strategies

PREPEXPERT

MATH
STRATEGY #8

ACE SYSTEM OF EQUATIONS

PREP EXPERT STRATEGY + EXAMPLE

Ace System Of Equations

To perform well on SAT Math, you must *Ace System Of Equations*. Below are the most important concepts to master this topic for the SAT.

Definition of Terms

1. **System of equations**: A set of two or more equations that must be solved together in order to find the values of the variables that satisfy all the equations.

2. **System of linear equations**: A system of linear equations in two variables represents two straight lines in the *x-y* coordinate plane. The point where the two lines intersect is the solution to the system of equations.

Key Concepts

KEY CONCEPT #1: SUBSTITUTION METHOD IN
SOLVING SYSTEM OF EQUATIONS

The substitution method solves a system of equations by isolating one variable in one equation and substituting its expression into the other equation. This step simplifies the system to one equation. You solve to find one variable's value and then substitute it back to find the other.

Prep Expert Strategy
1. Choose one of the equations that is easiest to solve for one variable.
2. Isolate this one variable in the equation.
3. Substitute the expression for this variable into the other equation.
4. Solve this new equation for the single variable.
5. Substitute this value back into one of the original equations to find the value of the other variable.

Prep Expert Example
- **Question**: How would you solve the following system of equations using the substitution method? *Hint*: It is often easiest to solve for a variable that has a 1 or a −1 coefficient.

$$2x + 2y = 18$$
$$x - y = 1$$

- **Answer**:

$$x - y = 1 \quad \rightarrow \quad x = y + 1$$

Now, substitute x back into the other equation to solve for y.

$$2x + 2y = 18 \quad \rightarrow \quad 2(y + 1) + 2y = 18 \quad \rightarrow \quad 2y + 2 + 2y = 18 \quad \rightarrow \quad 4y = 16 \quad \rightarrow \quad y = 4$$

Now, substitute y back into either equation to solve for x.

$$x - y = 1 \quad \rightarrow \quad x - 4 = 1 \quad \rightarrow \quad x = 5$$

The final solution to the system of equations is (5, 4).

KEY CONCEPT #2: ELIMINATION METHOD IN SOLVING SYSTEM OF EQUATIONS

The elimination method solves systems of equations by adding or subtracting the equations to eliminate one variable. Adjusting the equations, if necessary, allows you to cancel out one variable. This makes it possible to solve for the other variable, and then back-solve for the first.

Prep Expert Strategy

1. Write the equations in standard form ($Ax + By = C$) and align them vertically.
2. Multiply one or both equations by necessary values to get the coefficients of one variable to be the same or opposite.
3. Eliminate one variable by adding or subtracting the equations.
4. Solve the resulting equation for the remaining variable.
5. Substitute this value back into one of the original equations to find the value of the other variable.

Prep Expert Example

- **Question**: How would you solve the following system of equations using the elimination method? *Hint*: Multiply the first equation by 2 to get a +4 coefficient of *y*. This is the opposite of the −4 coefficient of *y* in the second equation, which will make it easy to eliminate!

$$3x + 2y = 8$$
$$2x - 4y = -2$$

- **Answer**:

$$2\,[3x + 2y = 8] \quad \rightarrow \quad 6x + 4y = 16$$

Now, align the two equations vertically and add together to eliminate *y*.

$$6x + 4y = 16$$
$$+\ 2x - 4y = -2$$
$$\overline{}$$
$$8x = 14 \quad \rightarrow \quad x = \frac{14}{8} \quad \rightarrow \quad x = \frac{7}{4}$$

Now, substitute *x* back into either equation to solve for *y*.

$$2x - 4y = -2 \quad \rightarrow \quad 2\left(\frac{7}{4}\right) - 4y = -2 \quad \rightarrow \quad \left(\frac{14}{4}\right) - 4y = -\left(\frac{8}{4}\right) \quad \rightarrow$$

$$-4y = -\frac{22}{4} \quad \rightarrow \quad y = \frac{22}{16} \quad \rightarrow \quad y = \frac{11}{8}$$

The final solution to the system of equations is $\left(\frac{7}{4}, \frac{11}{8}\right)$.

KEY CONCEPT #3: INTERSECTION OF LINES = ONE SOLUTION OF LINEAR SYSTEM OF EQUATIONS

A solution to a linear system of equations is the intersection point of two lines represented by the equations. This point satisfies both equations. If the lines intersect at one point, the system has one unique solution.

Prep Expert
Math Strategies

1. Plot both equations on a graph.
2. Look for the point where the two lines intersect on a graph. The coordinates of the intersection point are the solution to the system of equations.

Prep Expert Example

- **Question**: What is the solution to the system of equations below?

$$y = -x + 4$$

$$y = \frac{1}{2}x + 4$$

- **Answer**: The final solution to the system of equations is (0, 4).

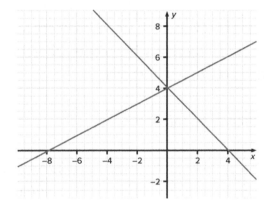

KEY CONCEPT #4: PARALLEL LINES =
NO SOLUTION OF LINEAR SYSTEM OF EQUATIONS

A linear system of equations has no solution when it represents two parallel lines, which never intersect. This occurs when the lines have the *same* slope but *different* y-intercepts.

Prep Expert Strategy

1. Parallel lines never intersect and, thus, represent a system of equations with no solution.
2. Check if both lines have the same slope but different y-intercepts.
3. To algebraically identify a system of equations with no solution, rewrite both equations in slope-intercept form ($y = mx + b$). Then determine if the slopes are identical and the y-intercepts are *different*.

4. To graphically identify a system of equations with no solution, determine whether the two lines are parallel on the graph.

Prep Expert Example

- **Question**: What is the solution to the following system of equations?

$$x + 2y = 5$$
$$2x + 4y = 8$$

- **Answer**:

Algebraic identification of no solution:

$$\text{Equation 1: } x + 2y = 5 \quad \rightarrow \quad 2y = -x + 5 \quad \rightarrow \quad y = -\frac{1}{2}x + \frac{5}{2}$$

$$\text{Equation 2: } 2x + 4y = 8 \quad \rightarrow \quad 4y = -2x + 8 \quad \rightarrow \quad y = -\frac{1}{2}x + 2$$

When the two equations are rewritten in slope-intercept form ($y = mx + b$), it is clear they have the same slope, but different y-intercepts. Therefore, the two linear equations must be parallel lines that do not intersect.

Graphical identification of no solution:

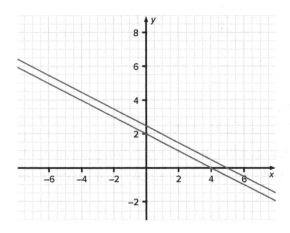

The solution to the system of equations is **no solution**.

KEY CONCEPT #6: SAME LINE = INFINITE SOLUTIONS OF LINEAR SYSTEM OF EQUATIONS

A linear system of equations has infinite solutions when it represents two of the same line that overlap with each other. This occurs when the lines have the *same* slope and the *same* y-intercepts.

1. When two of the same lines overlap, they represent a system with infinite solutions.
2. Check if both lines have the same slope and the same *y*-intercepts.
3. To algebraically identify a system of equations with infinite solutions, rewrite both equations in slope-intercept form ($y = mx + b$). Then determine if the slopes are identical and the *y*-intercepts are *identical.*
4. To graphically identify a system of equations with infinite solutions, determine whether the two lines overlap on the graph.

Prep Expert Example

-   **Question**: What is the solution to the system of equations below?

$$x + 3y = 6$$
$$2x + 6y = 12$$

-   **Answer**:

Algebraic identification of no solution:

$$\text{Equation 1: } x + 3y = 6 \quad \rightarrow \quad 3y = -x + 6 \quad \rightarrow \quad y = -\frac{1}{3}x + 2$$

$$\text{Equation 2: } 2x + 6y = 12 \quad \rightarrow \quad 6y = -2x + 12 \quad \rightarrow \quad y = -\frac{1}{3}x + 2$$

When the two equations are rewritten in slope-intercept form ($y = mx + b$), it is clear that they have the same slope and the same *y*-intercepts. Therefore, the two linear equations are the same lines that intersect an infinite number of times.

Graphical identification of infinite solutions:

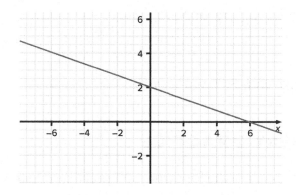

The solution to the system of equations is **infinite solutions**.

On the SAT, many system of equations problems can be solved using *Prep Expert Math Strategy #2—Test Answer Choices (TAC)*. TAC involves plugging the given answer choices into the system of equations to identify the correct solution. This strategy is useful for SAT Math multiple-choice questions. TAC can be quicker than traditional algebraic methods.

Prep Expert Strategy

1. Many systems of equations problems on the SAT do not require you to use algebra at all.
2. Instead, solve them using *Test Answer Choices (TAC)*.
3. Rather than thinking about abstract algebra, try plugging in the answer choices. Then determine which answer choice works with the system of equations.

Prep Expert Example

- **Question:** Which ordered pair (x, y) is a solution to the given system of equations?

$$2x - 5 = 7$$
$$(2x - 5)^2 = y$$

A) $(6, 144)$
B) $(6, 36)$
C) $(6, 49)$
D) $(6, 85)$

- **Answer:**
  1. All of the answer choices have 6 as the x-value.
  2. Test $x = 6$ into the first equation. It clearly works!
  3. Test $x = 6$ into the second equation. It results in $y = 49$.
  4. Only answer choice (C) has 49 as the y-value. Therefore, (C) is the answer.

Ace System Of Equations to maximize your SAT Math score.

PREP EXPERT PRACTICE

Try applying this *Prep Expert Strategy* yourself to the following SAT practice questions:

$$54x - 36y = 18y + 12$$

$$ry = \frac{1}{9} - 15x$$

In the given system of equations, r is a constant. If the system has no solution, what is the value of r?

$$3x + 5y = 11$$
$$2x + 4y = 8$$

The solution to the given system of equations is (x, y). What is the value of y?

A) 1

B) 2

C) 3

D) 4

The answers to these SAT practice questions can be found in the back of this book.

PREP EXPERT REVIEW

Key Takeaways

- **Prep Expert Math Strategy #8—*Ace System Of Equations***: This section covered key concepts for mastering systems of equations on SAT Math.

- **Types of systems of equations**: A system of equations is a set of two or more equations with variables that need to be solved together. A system of linear equations represents two lines in the xy-plane. The intersection point of these two lines is the solution.

- **Substitution method**: Isolate one variable in one equation, substitute its expression into the other equation, solve for one variable, and then back-substitute to find the other variable.

- **Elimination method**: Align two equations vertically, adjust them to cancel out one variable, and solve for the other. Then back-solve for the first variable.

- **Characteristics of solutions**: If two lines intersect at one point, there is a unique solution. Parallel lines (which have the same slope but different y-intercepts) indicate that there is no solution. Identical lines (same slope and y-intercept) indicate that there are infinite solutions.

Prep Expert
Math Strategies

- **Applying *Test Answer Choices (TAC)*:** You can often test the given answer choices on multiple-choice system of equations questions on the SAT Math section to find the correct solution. This removes the need to do traditional algebra.

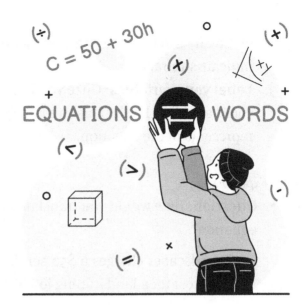

PREPEXPERT

MATH STRATEGY #9

TRANSLATE EQUATIONS ACCURATELY

PREP EXPERT STRATEGY + EXAMPLE

Translate Equations Accurately

To perform well on SAT Math, you must *Translate Equations Accurately*. Below are the most important concepts to master this topic for the SAT.

Key Concepts

KEY CONCEPT #1: TRANSLATING WORDS INTO EQUATIONS

You must be able to convert verbal descriptions into mathematical equations. This requires you to understand how common language translates into mathematical operations.

Prep Expert Strategy

1. **Identify the unknowns:** Determine what the problem is asking you to solve for. These are typically the variables in the equation.

2. **Use keywords to identify mathematical operations:** Look for keywords that indicate which mathematical operations to use. For example, "sum," "total,"

or "in all" can indicate addition, while "difference" or "decrease by" can indicate subtraction.

3. **Label your variables**: Once you have written the equation in words, label your variables clearly. This can help you to keep track of what each variable represents in the equation.

Prep Expert Example
- **Question**: How would you translate the following verbal description into an equation?

   A landscaper charges a $50 service fee plus $30 per hour for labor. The total cost for a landscaping job is based on the number of hours of labor.

- **Answer**:
   1. The unknowns present are the number of hours of labor and total cost of the job.
   2. The keywords to identify mathematical operations are "plus" (indicates addition) and "per hour" (indicates multiplication).
   3. I would label the variable for "number of **h**ours of labor" as h and the "total **c**ost of the job" as C.
   4. Translate words into equation: $C = 50 + 30h$

KEY CONCEPT #2: TRANSLATING EQUATIONS INTO WORDS

You must be able to convert mathematical equations into verbal descriptions. This requires interpreting and articulating the relationships and scenarios depicted by equations into everyday language.

Prep Expert Strategy
1. **Identify the variables**: Look at the equation and identify the variables that are present. These are the quantities that the equation is describing.
2. **Identify the mathematical operations**: Look at the equation and identify the mathematical operations that are present. These operations describe the variables' relationship to one another.
3. **Be accurate**: When translating an equation into a verbal description, make sure that your description accurately represents the meaning of the equation. Double-check your work to make sure that you haven't made any mistakes.

Prep Expert Example
- **Question**: The equation for a car traveling at 30 miles per hour is given by $C = 30x$. What is the interpretation of x in this context?

- **Answer**:
  1. The variables present are C and x.
  2. The mathematical operation in this equation is x being multiplied by 30.
  3. Given that 30 is the speed (in miles per hour), then x must be *the time the car has traveled* (in hours). C is the distance the car has traveled after x time has elapsed.

KEY CONCEPT #3: DECODING MATHEMATICAL OPERATIONS

Prep Expert Strategy
1. Make sure you understand the table below that translates the most common words and phrases in verbal descriptions into mathematical operations.

Prep Expert Example

Mathematical Operation	Common Words or Phrases
addition (+)	plus, more, sum, total, in all, combine, increased (by)
subtraction (−)	minus, less, difference, reduce (by), decreased (by)
multiplication (×)	times, product (of), percent (of), of (in fractions), per (in rates)
division (÷)	divided (by), out (of), proportion (of), per (in unit conversions)
equals (=)	is, equal (to), yields, results (in)
greater than (>)	greater than, more than, over, exceeds
less than (<)	less than, fewer than, below, under

Translate Equations Accurately to maximize your SAT Math score.

PREP EXPERT PRACTICE

Try applying this *Prep Expert Strategy* yourself to the following SAT practice questions:

## 97

In a city, there is a 4-hectare public garden and a 20-hectare commercial area. The total number of flowers in the city is 1,800. The equation $4x + 20y = 1,800$ represents this situation. Which of the following is the best interpretation of x in this context?

A) The average number of flowers per hectare in the public garden
B) The average number of flowers per hectare in the commercial area
C) The total number of flowers in the public garden
D) The total number of flowers in the commercial area

## 98

For groups of 20 or more people, a theme park charges $25 per person for the first 20 people and $18 for each additional person. Which function g gives the total charge, in dollars, for a tour group with m people, where $m \geq 20$?

A) $g(m) = 18m + 180$
B) $g(m) = 18m + 500$
C) $g(m) = 25m - 400$
D) $g(m) = 18m + 25$

The answers to these SAT practice questions can be found in the back of this book.

PREP EXPERT REVIEW

Key Takeaways

- **Prep Expert Math Strategy #9—*Translate Equations Accurately***: This section covered key concepts for translating equations on SAT Math.

- **Translating words into equations**: Understand how to convert verbal descriptions into mathematical equations. To do this effectively, identify unknowns and use keywords to determine the appropriate mathematical operations.

- **Translating equations into words**: Understand how to convert mathematical expressions into verbal descriptions. To do this effectively, focus on identifying variables and their relationships.

- **Decoding mathematical operations**: Familiarize yourself with the table of common words and phrases that signify mathematical operations to accurately decode verbal descriptions.

 PREPEXPERT

MATH STRATEGY #10

LOOK AT THE BIGGER PICTURE

PREP EXPERT STRATEGY · EXAMPLE

Look At The Bigger Picture

To perform well on SAT Math, you must *Look At The Bigger Picture*. Below are the most important concepts to master this topic for the SAT.

Key Concepts

KEY CONCEPT #1: THE SAT REWARDS STUDENTS WHO NOTICE THE BIGGER PICTURE

High school math is formulaic: you are presented with a problem, and you solve that problem using a traditional method. On the SAT Math, the traditional high school methods used to solve problems can often take longer and require more effort than necessary. Instead, SAT Math test-question writers reward students who look at the bigger picture.

What Does Looking At the Bigger Picture Mean?
Looking at the bigger picture can mean you are doing a variety of things when you approach an SAT Math problem, including these:

- Noticing patterns
- Identifying similarities or differences
- Analyzing the overall problem
- Paying attention to commonalities

Looking at the bigger picture will increase your SAT Math score.

How Do the SAT Math Test-Question Writers Reward Students?
When you *Look At The Bigger Picture*, you will often find simpler and faster solutions to solve SAT Math problems. These are solutions that often go unnoticed by students who are solving the question using traditional high school math methods.

Shift your approach from traditional, formulaic methods commonly taught in high school classrooms. Instead, use a broader, more strategic approach. The SAT challenges you to recognize patterns, draw parallels, and analyze problems holistically.

In summary, do not immediately jump into the traditional methods of high school math to solve SAT math problems. Instead, take a step back to *Look At The Bigger Picture*. Determine if there is a simpler solution to the problem. If so, the test-question writers are likely rewarding the few students who notice it.

Prep Expert Example
- **Question:** If $7(x - 1) = 6(x - 1) + 10$, what is the value of $x - 1$?

- **Answer:**
  1. *Do not* immediately start doing traditional algebra and solve for x.
  2. *Look at the bigger picture!* If you simply subtract $6(x - 1)$ from both sides, you will immediately find the value of $x - 1$.

$$\begin{aligned} 7(x - 1) &= 6(x - 1) + 10 \\ -6(x - 1) \quad &-6(x - 1) \\ (x - 1) &= 10 \end{aligned}$$

Look At The Bigger Picture to maximize your SAT Math score.

PREP EXPERT PRACTICE

Try applying this *Prep Expert Strategy* yourself to the following SAT practice questions:

99

If $3(x - 2) = 2(x - 2) + 15$, what is the value of $x - 2$?

A) -5
B) 3
C) 5
D) 15

100

The expression $\dfrac{40}{10y + 80}$ is equivalent to $\dfrac{4}{y + c}$, where c is a constant and $y > 0$. What is the value of c?

A) 5
B) 8
C) 10
D) 80

The answers to these SAT practice questions can be found in the back of this book.

PREP EXPERT REVIEW

Key Takeaways

- **Prep Expert Math Strategy #10—*Look At The Bigger Picture***: This section covered key concepts to look at the bigger picture on SAT Math.

- **Strategic problem-solving**: The SAT Math section rewards students who look at the bigger picture. This means noticing patterns, identifying similarities or differences, and analyzing the overall problem to find simpler and faster solutions.

- **Efficiency over tradition**: Traditional high school math methods may not be the most efficient for SAT Math. Instead, a broader, more strategic approach that focuses on overall problem analysis and pattern recognition leads to higher scores.

- **Rewards from test-question writers**: SAT test-question writers will often reward students who see the bigger picture and notice a more straightforward solution to the problem.

Prep Expert
Math Strategies

PREPEXPERT

MATH
STRATEGY #11
ACE GRAPHS

PREP EXPERT STRATEGY + EXAMPLE

Ace Graphs

To perform well on SAT Math, you must *Ace Graphs*. Below are the most important concepts to master this topic for the SAT.

Definition of Terms

1. **Linear function graph**: A straight line that represents a linear function in which the rate of change is constant. The equation of a linear function is $y = mx + b$, where m is the slope of the line and b is the y-intercept.

2. **Quadratic function graph**: A parabola for which the rate of change is not constant, but is instead a quadratic rate. The equation of a quadratic function is $y = ax^2 + bx + c$.

3. **Exponential function graph**: A curve that represents an exponential function. The equation of an exponential function is $y = ab^x$.

4. **Slope**: A measure of the steepness of a line, defined as the change in the *y*-coordinate divided by the change in the *x*-coordinate between any two points on a line.

Key Concepts

KEY CONCEPT #1: GRAPH QUADRANTS

The *x*-axis and *y*-axis divide a graph into four quadrants, creating a coordinate plane. Each quadrant is determined by the sign of the *x* and *y* coordinates.

Prep Expert Strategy

1. Quadrant I (*x* positive, *y* positive)
2. Quadrant II (*x* negative, *y* positive)
3. Quadrant III (*x* negative, *y* negative)
4. Quadrant IV (*x* positive, *y* negative)

Prep Expert Example

- **Question**: Which graph quadrants do the points (2, 2), (–2, 2), (– 2, –2), and (2, –2) fall into on a coordinate plane, respectively?

- **Answer**:

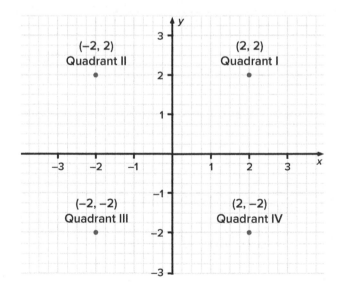

(2, 2) is in Quadrant I
(–2, 2) is in Quadrant II
(–2, –2) is in Quadrant III
(2, –2) is in Quadrant IV

KEY CONCEPT #2: THE SLOPE-INTERCEPT FORM OF LINEAR EQUATIONS

The slope-intercept form of a linear equation is expressed as $y = mx + b$, where m represents the slope, and b is the y-intercept. This form provides a straightforward way to identify the slope and the point at which the line crosses the y-axis for any linear equation.

Prep Expert Strategy

1. The slope-intercept formula for a linear equation is $y = mx + b$. In this formula, m represents the slope and b represents the y-intercept.
2. Practice identifying m and b in different linear equations.

Prep Expert Example

- **Question**: What is the slope-intercept form of the graph below? *Hint*: A line that passes through the origin has a y-intercept equal to 0 ($b = 0$).

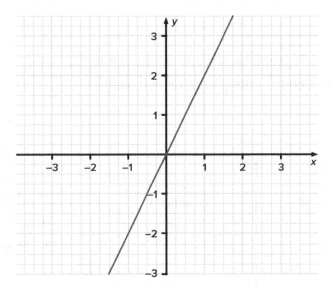

- **Answer**:

$$\text{Slope} = \frac{rise}{run} = \frac{+2}{+1} = 2 \qquad y\text{-intercept} = 0$$

$$y = mx + b \quad \rightarrow \quad y = (2)x + 0 \quad \rightarrow \quad y = 2x$$

KEY CONCEPT #3: CALCULATING THE SLOPE OF A LINEAR GRAPH

The slope of a linear graph measures the rate of change of the y-coordinate with respect to the x-coordinate. It is calculated as the ratio of the change in y (vertical change) to the change in x (horizontal change), often noted as $\frac{\Delta y}{\Delta x}$. A positive slope indicates an upward trend, while a negative slope indicates a downward trend.

Prep Expert Strategy

1. Slope is the ratio of the change in *y* to the change in *x*:

$$\frac{\Delta y}{\Delta x} = \frac{(\text{change in } y)}{(\text{change in } x)} = \frac{(y_2 - y_1)}{(x_2 - x_1)}$$

2. Pick two points on a line and calculate the vertical change (Δy) and horizontal change (Δx) between them.

3. Divide the vertical change by the horizontal change to find the slope.

Prep Expert Example

- **Question**: What is the rate of change of the graph below? *Hint*: The slope of a line represents the **rate of change**.

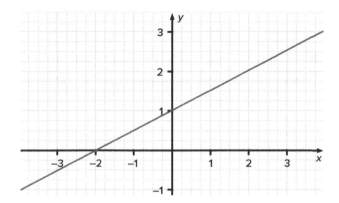

- **Answer**: Choose any two points on the line, such as (–2, 0) and (0, 1).

$$\text{Slope} = \frac{\Delta y}{\Delta x} = \frac{(\text{change in } y)}{(\text{change in } x)} = \frac{(y_2 - y_1)}{(x_2 - x_1)} = \frac{(0 - 1)}{(-2 - 0)} = \frac{-1}{-2} = \frac{1}{2}$$

KEY CONCEPT #4: UNDERSTANDING SLOPE MAGNITUDE

The "magnitude" of a slope indicates how steep a line is, regardless of its direction. It is always a positive value, representing the absolute value of the slope.

Prep Expert Strategy

1. The magnitude of a slope is its absolute value, which is always positive.

2. To find the magnitude of a slope, calculate the absolute value of the slope.

Prep Expert Example

- **Question**: Which line has greater magnitude?

$$\text{Line 1: } y = 2x - 3$$
$$\text{Line 2: } y = -5x + 7$$

- **Answer**:

Line 1 slope: 2 → *Line 1 slope magnitude*: +2
Line 2 slope: −5 → *Line 2 slope magnitude*: +5

Line 2 has a greater magnitude than Line 1 (Line 2 is steeper than Line 1).

KEY CONCEPT #5: PARALLEL LINE SLOPES

Parallel lines do not intersect. These lines always have equal slopes, meaning they rise and run at the same rate. Understanding this property allows you to identify parallel relationships in linear equations.

Prep Expert Strategy

1. Parallel lines never intersect and always have equal slopes.
2. Practice identifying parallel lines in graphs and equations.

Prep Expert Example

- **Question**: The lines on the graph below are parallel. What is the slope of each line?

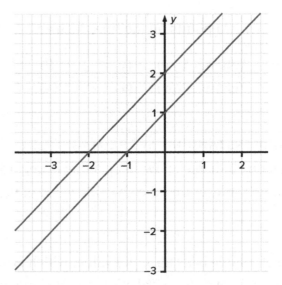

- **Answer**: Choose any two points on either line, such as (–1, 0) and (0, 1).

$$\text{Slope} = \frac{\Delta y}{\Delta x} = \frac{(\text{change in } y)}{(\text{change in } x)} = \frac{(y_2 - y_1)}{(x_2 - x_1)} = \frac{(0 - 1)}{(-1 - 0)} = \frac{-1}{-1} = 1$$

The slope of the bottom line is 1. Because the two lines are parallel, the slope of the top line is also 1.

KEY CONCEPT #6: PERPENDICULAR LINE SLOPES

Two perpendicular lines intersect at a 90-degree angle. Their slopes have a specific relationship: they are opposite reciprocals of each other. This means if one line has a slope of m, the perpendicular line will have a slope of $\frac{-1}{m}$.

Prep Expert Strategy

1. The slopes of perpendicular lines are opposite reciprocals.
2. To find the opposite of a number, reverse its sign (e.g., positive becomes negative).
3. To find the reciprocal of a number, find its inverse (e.g., flip the fraction upside down).

Prep Expert Example

- **Question**: The lines on the graph below are perpendicular. What is the slope of each line?

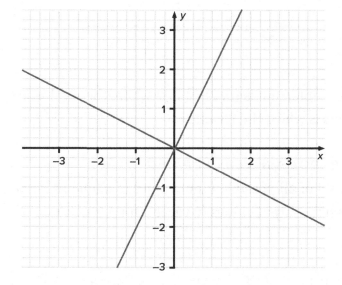

- **Answer:** Choose any two points on either line, such as (0, 0) and (1, 2).

$$\text{Slope} = \frac{\Delta y}{\Delta x} = \frac{(\text{change in } y)}{(\text{change in } x)} = \frac{(y_2 - y_1)}{(x_2 - x_1)} = \frac{(2 - 0)}{(1 - 0)} = \frac{2}{1} = 2$$

The slope of the positive line is 2. Because the two lines are perpendicular, the slope of the negative line is $-\frac{1}{2}$.

KEY CONCEPT #7: GRAPH INTERCEPTS (X-AXIS AND Y-AXIS)

Intercepts are points where the graph crosses the axes.

Prep Expert Strategy

1. The x-intercept is where the graph crosses the x-axis ($y = 0$).
2. The y-intercept is where the graph crosses the y-axis ($x = 0$).
3. Practice finding intercepts from equations by setting y to 0 to find x-intercepts and x to 0 to find y-intercepts.

Prep Expert Example

- **Question:** What are the intercepts of the graph below?

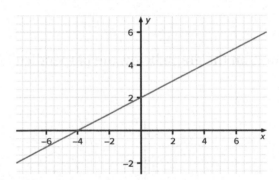

- **Answer:** The y-intercept is (0, 2). This is where the x-value is 0. The x-intercept is (−4, 0). This is where the y-value is 0.

KEY CONCEPT #8: DOMAIN VERSUS RANGE

The domain is the set of all possible input values (x-values) for a function. The range is the set of all possible output values (y-values) for a function.

Prep Expert Strategy

1. **Domain** refers to all of the possible *x-values* for a particular graph.

2. **Range** refers to all of the possible *y-values* for a particular graph.
3. Use graphs to visualize the domain and range of functions.

Prep Expert Example
- **Question**: What is the domain and range of $y = x^2$?
- **Answer**:

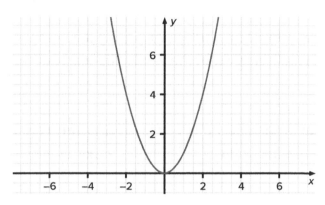

Domain: $(-\infty, \infty)$ **Range**: $[0, \infty)$

Looking at the graph, you can see that *y* can never be a negative number. Therefore, the minimum for the range is 0 (inclusive).

KEY CONCEPT #9: GRAPH ASYMPTOTES

An asymptote is a line or curve that a function approaches but never touches.

Prep Expert Strategy
1. A vertical asymptote is a vertical line that a graph approaches but never touches.
2. A horizontal asymptote is a horizontal line that a graph approaches but never touches.
3. Use graphs to visualize the asymptotes of functions.

Prep Expert Example
- **Question**: What are the vertical and horizontal asymptotes of the graph?

- **Answer**: The vertical asymptote is the line $x = 2$. The horizontal asymptote is the line $y = 0$.

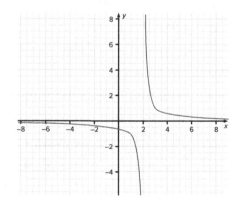

KEY CONCEPT #10: GRAPH REFLECTIONS

Graph reflections occur when a graph is flipped over a line, such as the *x*-axis or *y*-axis. This transformation changes the graph's orientation while maintaining its shape and size.

Prep Expert Strategy

1. When a graph is reflected about the *x*-axis, flip it across the *x*-axis.
2. When a graph is reflected about the *y*-axis, flip it across the *y*-axis.

Prep Expert Example

- **Question**: What is the reflection of the graph below about the *x*-axis?

- **Answer**: Flip the graph across the *x*-axis as seen below.

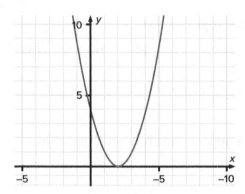

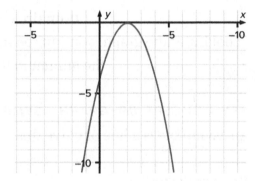

KEY CONCEPT #11: EVEN VERSUS ODD FUNCTIONS

Even and odd functions have specific symmetry properties. An even function is symmetric about the *y*-axis, meaning $f(x) = f(-x)$. An odd function is symmetric about the origin, meaning $f(-x) = -f(x)$.

Prep Expert Strategy

1. Even functions are symmetric across the *y*-axis. Common examples of even functions include x^2, x^4, and $cos(x)$.
2. Odd functions are symmetric across the origin. Common examples of odd functions include x^3, x^4, and $sin(x)$.

Prep Expert Example
- Example of an Even Function:

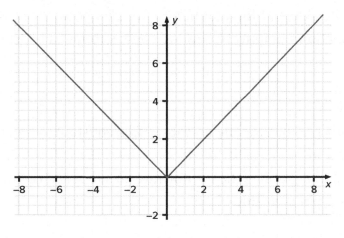

$$y = |x|$$
The graph of $y = |x|$ is symmetric across the y-axis.

- Example of an Odd Function:

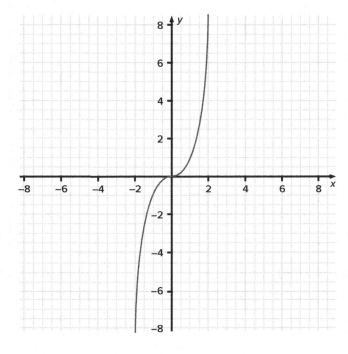

$$y = x^3$$
The graph of $y = x^3$ is symmetric across the origin.

Prep Expert
Math Strategies

KEY CONCEPT #12: VERTICAL GRAPH SHIFTS

Vertical graph shifts involve moving the graph up or down along the y-axis. This shift does not change the shape of the graph, but alters its position. Upward shifts add a constant to the function's output. Downward shifts subtract a constant from the function's output.

Prep Expert Strategy

1. **Up**: To shift a graph vertically upward, *add* a constant to the function's output ("outside of x").
2. **Down**: To shift a graph vertically downward, *subtract* a constant from the function's output ("outside of x").

Prep Expert Example

- Example of a Vertical Graph Shift—*Upward*:

- Example of a Vertical Graph Shift—*Downward*:

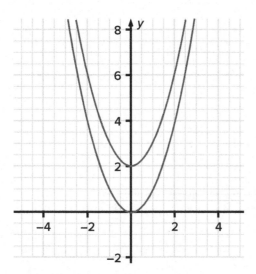

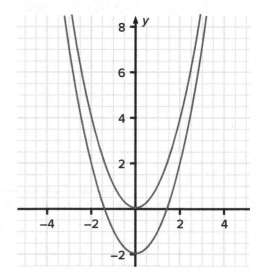

Original (bottom line): $y = x^2$
Vertically shifted *up 2 units*
(top line): $y = x^2 + 2$

Original (top line): $y = x^2$
Vertically shifted *down 2 units*
(bottom line): $y = x^2 - 2$

KEY CONCEPT #13: HORIZONTAL GRAPH SHIFTS

Horizontal graph shifts move the graph left or right along the x-axis. Like vertical shifts, they do not alter the graph's shape, but instead reposition it horizontally. A leftward

Prep Expert
Math Strategies

shift involves subtracting a constant from the *x*-values. A rightward shift involves adding a constant to the *x*-values.

Prep Expert Strategy

1. **Left**: To shift a graph horizontally left, *add* a constant to the *x*-value ("inside of *x*").
2. **Right**: To shift a graph horizontally right, *subtract* a constant from the *x*-value ("inside of *x*").

Prep Expert Example

- Example of a Horizontal Graph Shift—*Left*:

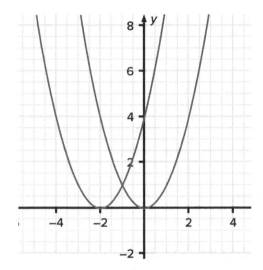

Original (right line): $y = x^2$
Horizontally shifted *left 2 units*
(left line): $y = (x + 2)^2$

- Example of a Horizontal Graph Shift—*Right*:

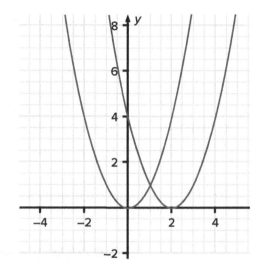

Original (left line): $y = x^2$
Horizontally shifted *right 2 units*
(right line): $y = (x - 2)^2$

KEY CONCEPT #14: ROOTS AND X-INTERCEPTS

The zeros of a graph, also known as the roots or *x*-intercepts, are the *x*-values where the graph intersects the *x*-axis ($y = 0$).

Prep Expert Strategy

1. The zeros of a graph are also known as the roots or *x*-intercepts.

2. The zeros of a graph are the values of x for which the graph intersects the x-axis.

3. The zeros of a graph occur when $y = 0$.

Prep Expert Example

- **Question**: How many distinct zeros does the following graph have?

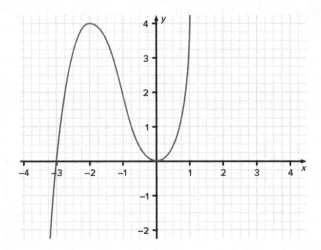

- **Answer**: The graph intersects the x-axis twice. The points of intersection are $(-3, 0)$ and $(0, 0)$. Therefore, the graph has two distinct zeros.

Ace Graphs to maximize your SAT Math score.

PREP EXPERT PRACTICE

Try applying this *Prep Expert Strategy* yourself to the following SAT practice questions:

| 101 |

The function g is defined by $g(x) = 3x - 15$. The graph of $y = g(x)$ in the xy-plane has an x-intercept at $(a, 0)$ and a y-intercept at $(0, b)$, where a and b are constants. What is the value of $a + b$?

A) −10

B) 5

C) 15

D) 20

x	y
15	100
20	140
25	180

For line p, the table shows three values of x and their corresponding values of y. Line q is the result of translating line p up 10 units in the xy-plane. What is the x-intercept of line q?

A) $(-\frac{16}{3}, 0)$

B) $(-\frac{8}{5}, 0)$

C) $(-\frac{7}{2}, 0)$

D) $(\frac{5}{4}, 0)$

The answers to these SAT practice questions can be found in the back of this book.

PREP EXPERT REVIEW

KEY TAKEAWAYS

- **Prep Expert Math Strategy #11—*Ace Graphs***: This section covered key concepts for mastering graphs on SAT Math.

- **SAT graphs**: Key concepts include understanding graph quadrants, the slope-intercept form of linear equations, calculating and comparing slopes, and recognizing the properties of parallel and perpendicular lines.

- **Graph characteristics**: Knowledge of graph intercepts (x- and y-axis), domain versus range, graph asymptotes, and reflections is vital. This includes identifying graph shifts both vertically and horizontally, and understanding x-intercepts.

- **Graph transformations**: Understand how graphs are transformed through reflections and shifts (both vertical and horizontal). Recognize even and odd function properties and their graphical symmetries.

Prep Expert
Math Strategies

PREPEXPERT

MATH STRATEGY #12

ACE DATA ANALYSIS

PREP EXPERT STRATEGY + EXAMPLE

Ace Data Analysis

To perform well on SAT Math, you must *Ace Data Analysis*. Below are the most important concepts to master this topic for the SAT.

Key Concepts

KEY CONCEPT #1: FREQUENCY IN DATA SETS

Frequency indicates how often a value appears in a data set. Identifying a value's frequency involves interpreting data from charts or graphs.

Prep Expert Strategy

1. Frequency is the number of times that a particular value or category occurs in a data set.
2. Learn to read frequency tables, which display how often each value occurs.

Prep Expert Example

- **Question:** What is the frequency of 15-year-olds in the data set below?

Age	Frequency (Number of People)
13 years old	5
14 years old	10
15 years old	15
16 years old	20
17 years old	10
18 years old	5

- **Answer:** The frequency of people who are 15 years old in the data set is **15 people**.

KEY CONCEPT #2: MAXIMUM VALUE IN DATA SETS

The maximum value is the largest number in a data set.

Prep Expert Strategy

1. The maximum is the largest value in a data set.
2. Find the maximum in simple lists of numbers, bar charts, and line graphs.

Prep Expert Example

- **Question:** What is the maximum in the data set below?

Age	Frequency (Number of People)
13 years old	5
14 years old	10
15 years old	15
16 years old	20
17 years old	10
18 years old	5

- **Answer:** The maximum in the data set is **18 years old**.

KEY CONCEPT #3: MINIMUM VALUE IN DATA SETS

The minimum value is the smallest number in a data set.

Prep Expert Strategy

1. The minimum is the smallest value in a data set.
2. Find the minimum in simple lists of numbers, bar charts, and line graphs.

Prep Expert Example

- **Question**: What is the minimum in the data set below?

Age	Frequency (Number of People)
13 years old	5
14 years old	10
15 years old	15
16 years old	20
17 years old	10
18 years old	5

- **Answer**: The minimum in the data set is **13 years old**.

KEY CONCEPT #4: RANGE IN DATA SETS

The range is the difference between the maximum and minimum values in a data set, indicating its spread. Understanding the concept of range is key to analyzing data's variability and consistency.

Prep Expert Strategy

1. The range is the difference between the largest and smallest values in a data set.
2. Find the maximum and minimum values and calculate the range between the two.

Prep Expert Example

- **Question**: What is the range of the data set below?

Age	Frequency (Number of People)
13 years old	5
14 years old	10
15 years old	15
16 years old	20
17 years old	10
18 years old	5

- **Answer:** The range of the data set is **5 years** (18 years old – 13 years old).

KEY CONCEPT #5: INTERPRETING SCATTERPLOTS

Scatterplots show relationships between two data sets. Interpreting scatterplots involves identifying correlations and drawing conclusions about the relationship between variables.

Prep Expert Strategy

1. In a scatterplot, the distribution of data points provides information about correlation.
2. Distinguish between positive, negative, and no correlation.
3. Identify patterns and trends in scatterplots.

Prep Expert Example

- **Positive correlation:**   - **Negative correlation:**

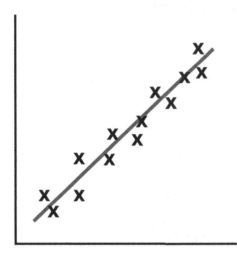   

The distribution in the scatterplot shows a strong positive correlation. The data points are clustered around a line that slopes upward.

The distribution in the scatterplot shows a strong negative correlation. The data points are clustered around a line that slopes downward.

- **No correlation**: The distribution in the scatterplot shows no correlation. The data points are not clustered in any identifiable pattern and show no trend.

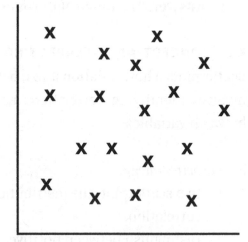

KEY CONCEPT #6: CALCULATING MEAN

The mean is the average value of a set of numbers. Calculate the mean by adding up all the values in the data set and then dividing the total by the number of values. The mean is a single value that represents the center of the data.

Prep Expert Strategy

1. Add up all the numbers in the data set.
2. Count the number of values in the data set.
3. Divide the sum by the number of values.

Prep Expert Example

- **Question**: What is the mean for the data set below?

$$3, 5, 6, 6, 7, 8, 8, 8, 12$$

- **Answer**:
  1. $3 + 5 + 6 + 6 + 7 + 8 + 8 + 8 + 12 = 63$ sum
  2. There are 9 values
  3. $63 \div 9 = 7$

KEY CONCEPT #7: CALCULATING MEDIAN

The median is the middle value in a data set when the data is arranged in order from smallest to largest. The median is particularly useful when the data is skewed by outliers, since it is not as affected by extreme values as the mean is.

Prep Expert
Math Strategies

Prep Expert Strategy

1. Arrange the data points in numerical order.
2. If the data set has an odd number of values, the median is the middle number.
3. If the data set has an even number of values, the median is the average of the two middle numbers.

Prep Expert Example

- **Question:** What is the median for the data set below?

$$3, 5, 6, 6, 7, 8, 8, 8, 12$$

- **Answer:**
  1. The data points are already arranged from smallest to largest.
  2. The data set contains an odd number of values: 9 values
  3. The median is the middle number: **7**

KEY CONCEPT #8: CALCULATING MODE

The mode of a data set is the value that appears most frequently. A data set may have one mode, more than one mode, or no mode at all if no number repeats.

Prep Expert Strategy

1. List all values in the data set.
2. Count the frequency of each value.
3. The value(s) with the highest frequency is the mode.

Prep Expert Example

- **Question:** What is the mode of the data set below?

$$3, 5, 6, 6, 7, 8, 8, 8, 12$$

- **Answer:** The value 8 appears three times—more than any other number—so **8** is the mode.

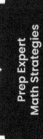

Prep Expert
Math Strategies

KEY CONCEPT #9: IDENTIFYING OUTLIERS

An outlier is a data point that differs significantly from other data points in a set. Outliers can be very high or low values that stand out from the rest of the data. In a normal distribution of data, the mean is equal to the median. However, if there are outliers, the mean will be pulled in the direction of the outlier.

Prep Expert Strategy

1. Normal distribution: mean = median
   - Large outlier: mean > median
   - Small outlier: mean < median
2. Outliers mainly impact mean and have minimal to no impact on median or mode.

Prep Expert Example

$$3, 5, 6, 6, 7, 8, 8, 8, 12$$

- **Normal distribution**: For the data set above, the mean is equal to the median (both are 7). Therefore, the data set has a "normal" distribution.

$$3, 5, 6, 6, 7, 8, 8, 8, 97$$

- **Large outlier**: For the data set above, the mean is greater than the median. Why? Because there is a large outlier (97) that increases the mean without affecting the median (7).

$$-65, 5, 6, 6, 7, 8, 8, 8, 12$$

- **Small outlier**: For the data set above, the mean is less than the median. Why? There is a small outlier (−65) that decreases the mean without affecting the median (7).

KEY CONCEPT #10: STANDARD DEVIATION

Standard deviation is a measure of the amount of variability in a set of data. It is a measure of how far the individual data points are from the mean of the data. A high standard deviation indicates that the values are spread out over a wider range. A low standard deviation indicates that the values tend to be close to the mean.

Prep Expert Strategy

1. *High* **standard deviation**: data points are *spread out* over a wide range of values.
2. *Low* **standard deviation**: data points are *tightly clustered* around the mean.
3. The SAT *will not* require you to calculate standard deviation using the standard deviation formula, so don't waste your time memorizing it.

Prep Expert Example
- **Question**: Which of the two data sets below has a larger standard deviation?

    Set A: [1, 2, 3, 3, 4, 5]
    Set B: [1, 2, 3, 97, 98, 99]

- **Answer**: The mean of Set A is 3 (18 ÷ 6 values). The mean of Set B is 50 (300 ÷ 6 values). The values in Set B are spread out further from its mean (50). Therefore, **Set B** has the larger standard deviation.

KEY CONCEPT #11: MARGIN OF ERROR

Margin of error is a statistic expressing the amount of random sampling error in a survey's results. It describes how far off the mean of a survey sample is, compared to the true mean of the larger population.

Prep Expert Strategy
1. **Example**: A survey of 100 high school students from Clark High School (a high school with 3,000 students) found that on average Clark students get 7 hours of sleep +/−1 hour.
    - The margin of error in the above example is 1 hour.
2. **Increase margin of error**: The larger the *standard deviation*, the larger the margin of error.
3. **Decrease margin of error**: The larger the *sample size*, the smaller the margin of error.

Prep Expert Example
- **Question**: Which of the two data sets below has a larger margin of error?

    Set A: [1, 2, 3, 3, 4, 5]
    Set B: [1, 2, 3, 97, 98, 99]

- **Answer**: As we covered previously, Set B has a larger standard deviation. Any data set that has a larger standard deviation will have a larger margin of error. Therefore, **Set B** has the larger margin of error.

KEY CONCEPT #12: CONFIDENCE INTERVAL

Confidence intervals estimate the range within which a population parameter lies, based on sample data. Confidence intervals describe the range of values within which the true population mean is likely to fall with a given level of confidence.

Prep Expert Strategy

1. **Example**: A survey of 100 high school students from Clark High School (a high school with 3,000 students) found that on average Clark students get 7 hours of sleep +/−1 hour.
   - The confidence interval in the above example is 6 hours–8 hours.
2. **Increase confidence interval**: The larger the *standard deviation*, the larger the confidence interval.
3. **Decrease confidence interval**: The larger the *sample size*, the smaller the confidence interval.

Prep Expert Example

- **Question**: Which of the two data sets below has a larger confidence interval?

  Set A: [1, 2, 3, 3, 4, 5]
  Set B: [1, 2, 3, 97, 98, 99]

- **Answer**: As we covered previously, Set B has a larger standard deviation. Any data set that has a larger standard deviation will have a larger confidence interval. Therefore, **Set B** has the larger confidence interval.

Key Concept #13: Total Sum

"Total sum" is a Prep Expert term used to describe the number you get when you add up all of the values in a data set. To calculate the total sum, you could simply add up all of the values in a data set. However, on the SAT, the test-question writers do not always give you all of the values in a data set. In this case, calculate the total sum by multiplying the mean of the data set by the number of values in the set. Total sum is a useful tool to solve many SAT problems.

Prep Expert Strategy

1. Identify the mean of a data set.
2. Identify the number of values in that data set.

3. Multiply the mean by the number of values in the data set.
4. The result is the total sum of that data set.

Prep Expert Example
- **Question**: What is the last value in a set of 10 numbers that has a mean of 20, if the other 9 numbers are as follows?

$$1, 2, 3, 4, 5, 6, 7, 8, 9$$

- **Answer**:
  1. The problem states that the mean of the final data set is 20.
  2. The number of values in the final data set is 10.
  3. The total sum of the final data set is $20 \times 10 = 200$.
  4. The total sum of the current data set with 9 values is 45.
  5. Therefore, the last value in the final data set is $200 - 45 = $ **155**.

KEY CONCEPT #14: COMBINING DATA SETS TO FIND A NEW MEAN

The SAT will often ask you to calculate the mean when you add two different data sets together. To calculate the new mean of the combined data set, add together the total sum of both sets. Then divide the total sum by the total number of values in the combined data set.

Prep Expert Strategy
  1. Calculate the total sum of each individual data set.
  2. Add these total sums together.
  3. Determine the total number of values in the combined data set.
  4. Divide the combined total sum by this total number of values.
  5. The result is the new mean of the combined data set.

Prep Expert Example
- **Question**: The mean number of hours of sleep for 10 boys is 10 hours. The mean number of hours of sleep for 20 girls is 7 hours. What is the mean for both groups combined?

- **Answer:**
  1. The total sum for the boys is 10 hours (mean) × 10 boys (number of values) = 100.
  2. The total sum for the girls is 7 hours (mean) × 20 girls (number of values) = 140.
  3. The combined total sum is 100 + 140 = 240.
  4. The total values in the combined data set is 10 boys + 20 girls = 30.
  5. Divide the combined total sum by the total number of values: 240 ÷ 30 = 8.
  6. Therefore, the mean number of hours slept for both groups is **8 hours**.

Ace Data Analysis to maximize your SAT Math score.

PREP EXPERT PRACTICE

Try applying this *Prep Expert Strategy* yourself to the following SAT practice questions:

103

From a population of 100,000 people, 2,000 were chosen at random and surveyed about a new local policy. Based on the survey, it is estimated that 25% of people in the population support the policy, with an associated margin of error of 4%. Based on these results, which of the following is a plausible value for the total number of people in the population who support the new policy?

A) 10,000
B) 20,000
C) 24,000
D) 30,000

104

Data set B consists of 8 positive integers less than 50. The list shown gives 7 of the integers from data set B:

$$35, 42, 38, 45, 41, 39, 40$$

The mean of these 7 integers is 40. If the mean of data set B is an integer that is greater than 40, what is the value of the largest integer from data set B?

The answers to these SAT practice questions can be found in the back of this book.

PREP EXPERT REVIEW

Key Takeaways

- **Prep Expert Math Strategy #12—*Ace Data Analysis***: This section covered key concepts for mastering data analysis on SAT Math.

- **Frequency analysis:** Learn to read frequency tables, interpret charts, and identify patterns in data sets.

- **Value extremes:** Understand how to find the maximum and minimum values in data, which assess the upper and lower limits.

- **Data range:** Calculate the range of a data set, which is the difference between the maximum and minimum values. Understand data spread and variability.

- **Scatterplot interpretation:** Analyze scatterplots to identify positive correlation, negative correlation, or no correlation. Be able to draw conclusions about relationships based on these correlations.

- **Calculating central tendencies:** Understand how to calculate mean, median, and mode. Mean is the average, median is the middle value when values are ordered from smallest to largest, and mode is the most frequent value.

- **Identifying outliers:** Outliers are values that differ significantly from the rest of the data set. Outliers affect the mean but have little impact on the median or mode.

- **Understanding variability:** Understand standard deviation and margin of error. Standard deviation measures how spread out data points are from the mean. Margin of error indicates the potential error range in survey results.

- **Confidence intervals:** Understand confidence intervals, which estimate the range of a population parameter based on a sample.

- **Total sum:** It is important that you learn to calculate the total sum of a data set. Master the technique of calculating a new mean when combining different data sets.

Prep Expert
Math Strategies

PREPEXPERT

MATH
STRATEGY #13

DO THE FIRST STEP
ON SCRATCH PAPER

PREP EXPERT STRATEGY

Do The First Step On Scratch Paper

Many students approach the SAT Math section in the wrong way.

- *Wrong way*: **Start each math problem in your head (or on the calculator).** This is the incorrect approach to SAT Math. You will end up storing many unnecessary details in your head. This will clog your working memory and reduce your ability to think critically.

- *Correct way*: **Do the first step of each math problem on the provided scratch paper.** The correct approach to SAT Math is to write the first step of the problem on your scratch paper. This will free up your working memory and critical thinking ability. By keeping your pencil glued to the scratch paper during the SAT Math section, you will immediately boost your score!

What Does "First Step" Really Mean?

The first step is simply the most intuitive problem-solving technique to do first, even if you don't know how to solve the whole problem yet. Here are some examples of the first step:

- If the problem has an equation that is not simplified, simplify the equation.
- If the problem has a description of a graph, draw out the graph.
- If the problem has a description of a triangle, draw out the triangle.
- If the problem has an "*x*" in it, try plugging in a number for *x*.

Many students think they need to know how to solve an *entire math problem* before getting started on the problem. This is not true. Just do the first step!

Even if you do the wrong first step...doing *any first step* will get your brain juices flowing. This will often lead you to the correct answer.

The Magic of the First Step

Even if you have no idea how to solve an SAT Math problem, do the first step on scratch paper.

→ The first step will lead to the second step
→ The second step will lead to the third step
→ More steps...
→ *Answer*!

Eventually, you will discover that you have solved the problem that you initially thought you did not know how to solve. This is the magic of doing the first step on scratch paper!

This strategy works because the answer to many SAT math problems is not immediately apparent. But once you do the first step, the subsequent steps often reveal themselves. Eventually, the answer is right there in front of you.

Long (or Detailed) Math Problems Can Be Intimidating

Some SAT Math problems are long word problems or contain many details. This can cause some students to freeze up, not knowing where to start. Doing the first step on scratch paper is an especially powerful strategy in this scenario.

When an SAT Math problem is a long word problem (or has many details), just get the problem started. *Do The First Step On Scratch Paper*. You will discover that what you originally thought was a complex problem is often easy to solve. You just need to do the first step and get the problem started.

Label Everything on Your Scratch Paper

As you are working through the steps of an SAT Math problem on your scratch paper, make sure you label everything:

- If you draw a triangle, label everything about that triangle.
- If you sketch a graph, label everything about the graph.
- If you write down a variable, label what the variable represents.

Labeling everything on your scratch paper will help you stay organized and make fewer mathematical errors. Labeling everything will also free up your working memory by getting details out of your head. Your mind can then think critically about each step of the problem.

If the SAT has given you a diagram, sketch it out on your scratch paper. Have the foresight to label everything you can on it, even if it may not seem important. For example, if the SAT has a diagram of a triangle, over-label it by writing in items such as the height of the triangle. Even if the problem has not specifically asked about the height, over-labeling will often help you solve the problem.

Avoid Math Mistakes by Doing the First Step on Scratch Paper

Another benefit of doing the first step on scratch paper is that it will help you avoid mental math mistakes. When your pencil is glued to the scratch paper, it will help you work out simple math on paper instead of in your head.

Doing math on paper generally leads to fewer mistakes. When we do mental math, we all sometimes make silly mistakes. For example, it's better to simply write out that $6 \times 5 = 30$ than make a mental mistake in your head that 6×5 is equal to 35. You might think that you wouldn't make such a mistake, but even the most mathematically gifted students can commit these small errors with mental math under the pressure of the SAT.

When Do You Check Your Work on an SAT Math Section?

If you are like most students, you probably check your work at the end, after you have finished all problems on an SAT Math section. However, no student in the history of the SAT has ever found a mistake after they have completely finished an SAT Math section.

Okay, that's a bit dramatic! But you probably won't find an error after you have completed all the problems on an SAT Math section. The reason students do not find errors after they have completed an SAT Math section is that they are often just confirming their answers.

Confirming answers is different than looking for errors. When you are done with an SAT Math section, you are likely only reviewing your work. Rarely do you dive deep enough back into the details of a problem to find an error in your work.

Verify Each Step on Your Scratch Paper as You Go

If checking your work at the end does not work, what does? Checking your work as you work through each problem. As you are solving a problem on your scratch paper, you should verify each step. For example, you should verify that 3×12 actually does equal 36, or confirm that the formula for the area of a triangle really is $\frac{1}{2}bh$.

Verifying each step as you go is a much more effective way to check your work because you are fully engrossed in a problem. You will not have to review the details of a particular question because you are already knee-deep in those details.

Verifying each step as you go will also prevent frustration, such as when a small arithmetic error causes your answer to be slightly off. Don't be afraid to verify even the smallest steps so that you don't make small mistakes. Small mistakes can cause big drops in SAT Math scores. Verify each step as you go to avoid all mistakes, big and small.

Do The First Step On Scratch Paper to maximize your SAT Math score.

PREP EXPERT EXAMPLE

Consider the following *Prep Expert Example*.

Step 1: Read the Question

> Ex
>
> A line passes through the points (2, 3) and (4, 7). Write the equation of the line in slope-intercept form.
>
> A) $y = 2x + 1$
> B) $y = 2x - 1$
> C) $y = x + 5$
> D) $y = x + 1$

Step 2: Do The First Step On Scratch Paper

You could try to solve this question in your head using mental math. However, you may make a mistake under the time pressure of the SAT. I am going to show you how to solve it using *Prep Expert Math Strategy #13—Do The First Step On Scratch Paper*.

Let's get the problem started by completing the first step of finding the slope of the line.

$$\text{Slope} = \frac{(y_2 - y_1)}{(x_2 - x_1)} = \frac{(7 - 3)}{(4 - 2)} = \frac{4}{2} = 2$$

Now we know that the slope is equal to 2. This eliminates answer choices (C) and (D). Plug in 2 as the slope into the slope-intercept equation of a line.

$$y = mx + b \quad \rightarrow \quad y = (2)x + b$$

Now, plug in one of the given points to determine what the *b* value (*y*-intercept) is.

$$3 = (2)2 + b \quad \rightarrow \quad 3 = 4 + b \quad \rightarrow \quad b = -1$$

Therefore, the final equation of the line in slope-intercept form is the following:

$$y = mx + b \quad \rightarrow \quad y = 2x - 1$$

Step 3: Select Answer

Select answer choice (B). Answer choice (B) is the only one that matches our answer.

Notice how *Doing The First Step On Scratch Paper* led to the second step, which led to the third step, which eventually got us to the correct answer. While this might seem like it takes longer, it is actually very quick when you are working through problems on your own during the SAT. In addition, working through SAT Math problems on scratch paper will help you avoid mental math mistakes that can cost you big points.

PREP EXPERT PRACTICE

Try applying this *Prep Expert Strategy* yourself to the following SAT practice questions:

## 105

When the quadratic function g is graphed in the xy-plane, where $y = g(x)$, its vertex is $(2, -3)$. One of the x-intercepts of this graph is $(\frac{5}{2}, 0)$. What is the other x-intercept of the graph?

A) $(-\frac{1}{2}, 0)$

B) $(\frac{3}{2}, 0)$

C) $(\frac{9}{2}, 0)$

D) $(\frac{13}{2}, 0)$

x	$g(x)$
1	4
2	8
3	12

For the linear function g, the table shows three values of x and their corresponding values of $g(x)$. Function g is defined by $g(x) = cx + d$, where c and d are constants. What is the value of $c - d$?

A) -8

B) 4

C) 10

D) 16

The answers to these SAT practice questions can be found in the back of this book.

PREP EXPERT REVIEW

Key Takeaways

- **Prep Expert Math Strategy #13—*Do The First Step On Scratch Paper***: Begin each SAT Math problem by writing down the first step on scratch paper, rather than trying to solve it in your head or on a calculator. This frees up your working memory and improves critical thinking ability.

- **First-step approach**: The "first step" refers to the first logical action, like simplifying an equation or sketching a graph. It kick-starts problem-solving, even without a complete solution in mind.

- **Progression through steps**: Starting with the first step on paper will lead to the subsequent steps, gradually revealing the solution to a problem that initially seemed unsolvable.

Prep Expert Math Strategies

- **Error reduction**: Label every detail on scratch paper as you work through a problem. This keeps you organized, minimizes errors, and off-loads details from your working memory onto paper.

- **Verify as you go**: Rather than checking your work at the end, verify each step as you go. This approach is more effective in catching and preventing mistakes, therefore improving your overall performance on the SAT Math modules.

 **PREP**EXPERT

MATH
STRATEGY #14

ACE PERCENTAGES
& RATIOS

PREP EXPERT STRATEGY + EXAMPLE

Ace Percentages & Ratios

To perform well on SAT Math, you must *Ace Percentages & Ratios*. Below are the most important concepts to master this topic for the SAT.

Definition of Terms

1. **Percentage**: A way of expressing a fraction or a proportion as a number out of 100.

2. **Ratio**: A comparison of two or more quantities expressed as a fraction or a division.

Key Concepts

KEY CONCEPT #1: BASIC PERCENTAGE CALCULATION FORMULA

This formula is used to find the percentage of a number. It involves dividing the part by the whole and then multiplying by 100.

Prep Expert Strategy

Use the formula below to calculate a percentage:

$$\text{Percentage} = \frac{\text{part}}{\text{whole}} \times 100$$

Prep Expert Example

- **Question:** A student answered 42 out of 50 questions correctly on a test. What percentage of questions did the student answer correctly?

- **Answer:**

$$\text{Percentage} = \frac{\text{part}}{\text{whole}} \times 100$$

$$\text{Percentage} = \frac{42}{50} \times 100 = (0.84) \times 100 = 84\%$$

KEY CONCEPT #2: CONVERTING PERCENTAGES TO DECIMALS

To convert a percentage to a decimal, divide it by 100. You can do this by moving the decimal point two places to the left.

Prep Expert Strategy

Use the formula below to convert a percentage to a decimal:

$$\text{Decimal} = \left(\frac{\text{percentage}}{100}\right)$$

Prep Expert Example

- **Question:** What is 108% expressed as a decimal?

- **Answer:**

$$\text{Decimal} = \left(\frac{\text{percentage}}{100}\right) = \left(\frac{108}{100}\right) = 1.08$$

KEY CONCEPT #3: PERCENT CHANGE CALCULATION

This calculation is used to determine the percentage increase or decrease from one value to another. It is calculated by subtracting the original value from the new value, dividing the result by the original value, and multiplying by 100. This gives you the percent change.

Prep Expert Strategy
Use the formula below to calculate percent change:

$$\text{Percent Change} = (\frac{\text{New Value} - \text{Old Value}}{\text{Old Value}}) \times 100\%$$

Prep Expert Example
- **Question**: If a stock value increased in value from $80 to $90, by what percent did its value change?

- **Answer**:

$$\text{Percent Change} = (\frac{\text{New Value} - \text{Old Value}}{\text{Old Value}}) \times 100\%$$

$$\text{Percent Change} = (\frac{90 - 80}{80}) \times 100\% = (\frac{10}{80}) \times 100\% = 0.125 \times 100\% = 12.5\%$$

KEY CONCEPT #4: CALCULATING TOTAL PRICE WITH PERCENTAGE FEES

The SAT will often present you with a price that includes fees. You can solve these questions by using the formula below.

Prep Expert Strategy
Use the equation below to solve what the original price of an item is (*x*) when you are given the price including the fee:

$$\text{Price Including The Fee} = 1.[\ ][\ ]x$$
$$x = price\ without\ the\ fee$$
$$[\ ] = fee\ percentage\ expressed\ as\ a\ decimal$$

Prep Expert Example
- **Question**: If $10 represents the price that includes an 8% fee, what is the price without the fee?

- **Answer:**

$$\text{Price Including The Fee} = 1.[\ ][\ ]x \quad \rightarrow \quad 10 = 1.08x \quad \rightarrow \quad x = 9.26$$

The price without the 8% fee is **$9.26**.

KEY CONCEPT #5: APPLYING SAMPLE PROPORTIONS TO FULL DATA SETS

This concept involves extrapolating data from a sample to make predictions about a larger population. If you are given a sample of data, multiply the sample proportion percentage by the new quantity in the full data set. Make sure to identify the correct sample proportion percentage and new quantity to use.

Prep Expert Strategy

Use the formula below to apply sample proportion percentage to a full data set:

$$\text{Sample Proportion Percentage} \times \text{New Quantity}$$

Prep Expert Example

- **Question:** In a survey of 200 people, 120 people rated a new movie as "excellent" and 80 rated it as "good." There were no other ratings besides these "excellent" and "good" ratings. Based on this survey data, what is the estimated total number of people overall who are likely to have rated the movie as "excellent"?
    - Total number of people who left a rating: 25,000
    - Total number of people who did not leave a rating: 150,000

- **Answer:**

    120 out of 200 people rated the movie as "excellent."

    $$\text{Sample proportion percentage} = \left(\frac{120}{200}\right) = 0.60 = 60\%.$$

    The total number of people who left a rating is 25,000.

    $$\text{Sample Proportion Percentage} \times \text{New Quantity}$$
    $$60\% \times 25{,}000 = 15{,}000$$

KEY CONCEPT #6: BASIC RATIO CALCULATION FORMULA

A ratio is a comparison of two quantities. The basic formula to find a ratio involves dividing one quantity by another quantity.

Prep Expert Strategy

Use the formula below to calculate a ratio:

$$\text{Ratio} = (\frac{\text{Quantity 1}}{\text{Quantity 2}})$$

Prep Expert Example

- **Question**: If there are 5 boys and 6 girls in a class, what is the ratio of boys to girls?

- **Answer**:

$$\text{Ratio} = (\frac{\text{Quantity 1}}{\text{Quantity 2}}) = (\frac{5}{6})$$

The ratio of boys to girls can be expressed as $\frac{5}{6}$ or 5:6.

KEY CONCEPT #7: CALCULATING QUANTITIES IN CONSTANT RATIOS

If a ratio is constant, new quantities must scale up or down proportionally.

Prep Expert Strategy

Use the formula below to calculate old or new quantities when the ratio stays the same:

$$(\frac{\text{Old Quantity 1}}{\text{Old Quantity 2}}) = (\frac{\text{New Quantity 1}}{\text{New Quantity 2}})$$

Prep Expert Example

- **Question**: The ratio of lengths of two roads is 3 miles to 5 miles. If the length of the smaller road increases by 57 miles, by what number must the length of the larger road increase to maintain the same ratio?

- **Answer:**

$$\left(\frac{\text{Old Quantity 1}}{\text{Old Quantity 2}}\right) = \left(\frac{\text{New Quantity 1}}{\text{New Quantity 2}}\right) \;\rightarrow\; \left(\frac{3}{5}\right) = \left(\frac{60}{\text{New Quantity 2}}\right) \;\rightarrow$$

$$\text{New Quantity 2} = 60 \times \left(\frac{5}{3}\right) = 100$$

The larger road will have a final length of 100 miles, and it is currently 5 miles long. Therefore, the length of the larger road must increase by **95 miles** (100 miles – 5 miles) to maintain the same ratio to the length of the smaller road.

KEY CONCEPT #8: TOTAL RATIO PARTS

"Total ratio parts" is a Prep Expert term used to describe the total number of equal parts in a ratio. To calculate the total ratio parts, add up the number of parts in each quantity in the ratio. You can then use the total ratio parts to multiply or divide by. This will help you correctly answer many SAT ratio problems.

Prep Expert Strategy
Use the formula below to find the total ratio parts.

Total Ratio Parts = (# of Parts in Quantity 1) + (# of Parts in Quantity 2)

Prep Expert Example
- **Question:** If the ratio of the number of boys to the number of girls in a class is 3:4, and there are 28 students in the class, how many girls are in the class?

- **Answer:**

Total Ratio Parts = (# of Parts in Quantity 1) + (# of Parts in Quantity 2)
Total Ratio Parts = 3 + 4 = 7

Divide the total number of students in the class (28)
by the total ratio parts (7).
$28 \div 7 = 4$

This means that each ratio part is equivalent to 4 students.
Girls represent 3 ratio parts.
$4 \times 3 = 12$
There are **12 girls** in the class.

On the SAT, many percentage problems can be solved using *Prep Expert Math Strategy #2—Test Answer Choices (TAC)*. TAC involves plugging the given answer choices into the problem to identify the correct solution.

Prep Expert Strategy

1. Many percentage problems do not require you to use algebra at all on the SAT.
2. Instead, solve them using *Test Answer Choices (TAC)*.
3. Rather than thinking about abstract algebra, try plugging in the answer choices. Then determine which answer choice works for the percentage problem.

Prep Expert Example

- **Question**: A restaurant manager needs to buy new tables for the dining area and has decided to purchase identical tables for each of the 50 spaces. The total budget for the tables is $20,000, which includes a 5% sales tax. What is the closest to the highest possible price per table, before sales tax, that the manager could pay based on this budget?

  A) $380.95
  B) $399.05
  C) $418.10
  D) $437.15

- **Answer**:
  1. Test $380.95: $380.95 × 50 tables × 1.05 = $19,999.88
  2. That is about as close to $20,000 as you can get!
  3. **Select (A)**. Notice how we did not have to do any algebra to find the answer!

Ace Percentages & Ratios to maximize your SAT Math score.

PREP EXPERT PRACTICE

Try applying this *Prep Expert Strategy* yourself to the following SAT practice questions:

107

For a certain rectangular region, the ratio of its length to its width is 45 to 15. If the width of the rectangular region increases by 10 units, how must the length change to maintain this ratio?

A) It must decrease by 30 units.
B) It must increase by 30 units.
C) It must decrease by 10 units.
D) It must increase by 10 units.

108

A company has a total budget of $20,000 to purchase the same model of laptop for each of their 120 employees. This budget includes a 9% sales tax. What is the closest value to the maximum possible price per laptop, before sales tax, the company could pay based on this budget?

A) $142.86
B) $152.90
C) $167.58
D) $179.92

The answers to these SAT practice questions can be found in the back of this book.

PREP EXPERT REVIEW

Key Takeaways

- **Prep Expert Math Strategy #14—*Ace Percentages & Ratios***: This section covered key concepts for mastering percentages and ratios on SAT Math.

- **Key concepts for percentages and ratios**: Understand the basic calculation formulas for percentages and ratios and how to convert percentages to decimals.

- **Applying concepts with formulas**: Use standardized formulas to calculate percentages, convert percentages to decimals, determine percent change, and handle total price calculations with percentage fees.

- **SAT Math application**: For SAT Math problem-solving, understand how to extrapolate sample proportions to larger data sets for estimation, maintain constant ratios when scaling quantities, and determine the total parts in a ratio.

- **Applying *Test Answer Choices (TAC)***: You can often simply test the given answer choices in percentage and ratio problems to find the correct solution. Doing so eliminates the need for traditional algebra.

Prep Expert Math Strategies

 **PREP**EXPERT

MATH
STRATEGY #15

ACE UNIT
CONVERSIONS & RATES

PREP EXPERT STRATEGY • EXAMPLE

Ace Unit Conversions & Rates

To perform well on SAT Math, you must *Ace Unit Conversions & Rates*. Below are the most important concepts to master this topic for the SAT.

Definition of Terms

1. **Unit conversions**: The process of converting a quantity expressed in one unit of measurement to another unit of measurement.

2. **Rate**: How much of one quantity is associated with one unit of another quantity. For example, speed is the rate of the *distance* traveled to the *time* it takes to travel that distance.

Key Concepts

KEY CONCEPT #1: BASIC PRINCIPLES OF UNIT CONVERSION

The foundational formula for unit conversion transforms one unit into another unit.

Prep Expert Strategy

Use the formula below to convert units:

Quantity in Old Unit × Conversion Factor* = Quantity in New Unit
The conversion factor is the ratio of the old unit to the new unit.

Prep Expert Example
- **Question:** How many feet are in 100 meters? Note that 1 meter = 3.28 feet (conversion factor).

- **Answer:**

    Quantity in Old Unit × Conversion Factor = Quantity in New Unit

    $$100 \text{ meters} \times 3.28 \left(\frac{\text{feet}}{\text{meters}} \right) = 328 \text{ feet}$$

KEY CONCEPT #2: CONSISTENCY IN UNIT CONVERSIONS

When performing unit conversions, it is important to keep track of units. Ensure that the units cancel out correctly. Use consistent units throughout the conversion process.

Prep Expert Strategy
1. You must meticulously track units to ensure they cancel out correctly.
2. This prevents errors due to incompatible unit mix-ups.

Prep Expert Example
- **Question:** How many inches are in 1 yard?

- **Answer:**

    $$1 \text{ yard} \times \frac{3 \text{ feet}}{1 \text{ yard}} \times \frac{12 \text{ inches}}{1 \text{ foot}} = 36 \text{ inches}$$

KEY CONCEPT #3: SQUARING AREA UNITS

A common mistake in unit conversions is forgetting to square the conversion factor when converting area units. Be careful when converting area units—make sure to square them.

1. Double check whether you are dealing with *area* units.

2. If so, do not forget to *square* everything!

Prep Expert Example

*   **Question**: How many square inches are in 1 square yard?

*   **Answer**:

$$1 \text{ yard}^2 \times \frac{3^2 \text{ feet}^2}{1^2 \text{ yard}^2} \times \frac{12^2 \text{ inches}^2}{1^2 \text{ foot}^2} =$$

$$1 \text{ yard}^2 \times \frac{9 \text{ feet}^2}{1 \text{ yard}^2} \times \frac{144 \text{ inches}^2}{1 \text{ foot}^2} = 1296 \text{ inches}^2$$

KEY CONCEPT #4: POPULATION DENSITY

Population density describes the relationship between a region's population and its area.

Prep Expert Strategy

Use the formula below to calculate population density:

$$\text{Population Density} = (\frac{\text{Total Population}}{\text{Total Area}})$$

Prep Expert Example

*   **Question**: City A has a population density of 100 people per square kilometer and an area of 10 square kilometers. City B has a population density of 50 people per square kilometer and an area of 40 square kilometers. What is the population density of City A and City B combined?

*   **Answer**:

$$\text{City A Population Density} = (\frac{\text{City A Total Population}}{\text{City A Total Area}})$$

$$100 = (\frac{\text{City A Total Population}}{10 \text{ km}^2})$$

City A Total Population = 1,000 people

$$\text{City B Population Density} = \left(\frac{\text{City B Total Population}}{\text{City B Total Area}}\right)$$

$$50 = \left(\frac{\text{City B Total Population}}{40 \text{ km}^2}\right)$$

$$\text{City B Total Population} = 2{,}000 \text{ people}$$

$$\text{City A \& B Population Density} = \left(\frac{\text{City A \& B Total Population}}{\text{City A \& B Total Area}}\right)$$

$$\text{City A \& B Population Density} = \left(\frac{1{,}000 + 2{,}000 \text{ people}}{10 + 40 \text{ km}^2}\right)$$

$$\text{City A \& B Population Density} = \left(\frac{3{,}000 \text{ people}}{50 \text{ km}^2}\right) = 60 \text{ people per square kilometer}$$

KEY CONCEPT #5: CALCULATING RATES

Understand how to calculate rates. Rates describe the relationship between two different quantities over time. Understanding rates is essential for understanding how one variable changes relative to another variable.

Prep Expert Strategy

Use the formula below to calculate rates:

$$\text{Rate} = \left(\frac{\text{Quantity}}{\text{Time}}\right)$$

Prep Expert Example

- **Question:** A car travels 200 miles in 4 hours. What is the speed of the car in miles per hour?

- **Answer:**
$$\text{Rate} = \left(\frac{\text{Quantity}}{\text{Time}}\right) = \left(\frac{200 \text{ miles}}{4 \text{ hours}}\right) = 50 \text{ miles per hour}$$

KEY CONCEPT #6: CALCULATING THE AVERAGE
RATE OF TWO DIFFERENT RATES

To calculate an average rate from two different rates, add the quantities and times separately and then divide the total quantity by the total time.

Prep Expert Strategy

To calculate the average rate between two different rates, follow the steps below:

1. Add the two quantities (often distances) together. Make the numerator the total quantity.
2. Calculate the time of each rate separately. Add the two times together. Make the denominator the total time.
3. Divide the total quantity by the total time.

$$\text{Average Rate} = \left(\frac{\text{Total Quantity}}{\text{Total Time}}\right)$$

Prep Expert Example

- **Question**: Car A travels a distance of 300 miles at a rate of 50 miles per hour, and Car B travels the same distance of 300 miles at a rate of 60 miles per hour. What is the average rate of the two cars over the entire distance? (*Hint*: It is not 55 miles per hour.)

- **Answer**:

    Total Quantity = 300 miles + 300 miles = 600 miles

    Car A Time = 300 miles / 50 miles per hour = 6 hours

    Car B Time = 300 miles / 60 miles per hour = 5 hours

    Total Time = 6 hours + 5 hours = 11 hours

$$\text{Average Rate} = \left(\frac{\text{Total Quantity}}{\text{Total Time}}\right) = \left(\frac{600 \text{ miles}}{11 \text{ hours}}\right) = 54.55 \text{ miles per hour}$$

Ace Unit Conversions & Rates to maximize your SAT Math score.

PREP EXPERT PRACTICE

Try applying this *Prep Expert Strategy* yourself to the following SAT practice questions:

A factory produces widgets at a constant rate 30 of widgets per minute. At what rate, in widgets per <u>hour</u>, does the factory produce the widgets?

A certain park has an area of 8,000,000 square yards. What is the area, in <u>square miles</u>, of this park? (1 mile = 1,760 yards)

A) 0.26
B) 2.58
C) 25.83
D) 258.26

The answers to these SAT practice questions can be found in the back of this book.

PREP EXPERT REVIEW

Key Takeaways

- **Prep Expert Math Strategy #15—*Ace Unit Conversions & Rates***: This section covered key concepts for mastering unit conversions and rates on SAT Math.

- **Mastering unit conversions**: Understand the formula for unit conversion, using the conversion factor to transform one unit into another.

- **Consistency in unit conversions**: It is crucial to keep track of and consistently cancel out units during conversions.

- **Squaring in area unit conversions**: Remember to square the conversion factor when dealing with square units to ensure accurate area conversions.

- **Calculating population density**: Learn to calculate population density by relating the total population of a region to its area using the formula for population density.

- **Understanding average rates**: Understand how to calculate rates by correlating two different quantities and how to compute the average rate from different rates. This involves adding up both quantities and both times before dividing.

Prep Expert
Math Strategies

 **PREPEXPERT**

MATH STRATEGY #16

ACE PROBABILITY

PREP EXPERT STRATEGY + EXAMPLE

Ace Probability

To perform well on SAT Math, you must *Ace Probability*. Below are the most important concepts to master this topic for the SAT.

Definition of Terms

1. **Classical probability**: This type of probability is based on the assumption that all outcomes in a sample space are equally likely. For example, if you roll a fair 6-sided die, the probability of getting any particular number (1, 2, 3, 4, 5, or 6) is 1/6.

2. **Conditional probability**: This type of probability is the likelihood of an event occurring after another event has already occurred. For example, if you know that a card drawn from a deck is a heart, the probability that the next card drawn will also be a heart is different than if you did not have any information about the first card.

Key Concepts

KEY CONCEPT #1: CLASSICAL PROBABILITY

Classical probability is the ratio of the number of favorable outcomes to the total number of possible outcomes in a sample space. Classical probability is useful when dealing with equally likely outcomes, such as flipping a coin.

Prep Expert Strategy

1. Classical probability calculates the likelihood of an event by dividing the number of favorable outcomes by the total number of possible outcomes.
2. Identify the total number of equally likely outcomes.
3. Determine the number of favorable outcomes for the event of interest.

Prep Expert Example

- **Question**: If you roll a fair 6-sided die, what is the probability of rolling an even number?

- **Answer**:
$$\text{Probability} = \frac{\text{\# of Favorable Outcomes}}{\text{\# of Possible Outcomes}} = \frac{3}{6} = 0.5 \ or \ 50\%$$

KEY CONCEPT #2: CONDITIONAL PROBABILITY

Conditional probability is the likelihood of an event occurring after another event has already occurred. Conditional probability is useful when dealing with outcomes that change based on previous outcomes, such as selecting cards from a deck.

Prep Expert Strategy

1. Conditional probability calculates the likelihood of an event after another event has already occurred.
2. Identify the two events involved and understand how they are related.
3. Calculate the probability of the first event occurring.
4. Calculate the probability of the second event occurring.

Prep Expert Example

- **Question**: A bag has 5 red marbles and 3 blue marbles. You draw one marble at random from the bag without looking. The first marble you draw is blue, and it is removed from the bag. What is the probability that you draw a red marble on your second attempt?

- **Answer:**

$$\text{Probability} = \frac{\text{\# of Favorable Outcomes}}{\text{\# of Possible Outcomes}}$$

$$\text{Probability (first attempt of drawing a red marble)} = \frac{5}{8}$$

Even if a question does not specifically ask for it, it is often useful to calculate the probability of the first attempt. Doing so will help you understand the number of favorable and possible outcomes on the second attempt.

$$\text{Probability (second attempt of drawing a red marble)} = \frac{5}{7}$$

In this example, the second attempt did not create a change in favorable outcomes (5) since you did not select a red marble on the first attempt (it was a blue marble). However, the second attempt did produce a change in possible outcomes (from 8 to 7) since you removed one blue marble after the first attempt. Therefore, the conditional probability of selecting a red marble on the second attempt is 5/7 or 0.714.

KEY CONCEPT #3: COMPLEMENTARY PROBABILITY

Complementary probability is the probability of the complement of an event. This is usually the probability that the event *does not happen*. Complementary probability is useful when it is easier to calculate the probability of an event not happening than the probability of an event happening.

Prep Expert Strategy
1. Understand that complementary probability is the likelihood of an event *not* happening.
2. Calculate the probability of the event occurring.
3. Subtract this probability from 1 to find the probability of the event *not* occurring.

Prep Expert Example

- **Question:** A jar contains 20 marbles, of which 8 are red, 5 are green, and 7 are blue. If one marble is chosen at random from the jar, what is the probability that it is *not* red?

- **Answer:**

$$\text{Complementary Probability} = 1 - \frac{\text{\# of Favorable Outcomes}}{\text{\# of Possible Outcomes}}$$

$$\text{Complementary Probability} = 1 - \frac{8}{20} = \frac{12}{20} = \frac{3}{5} \text{ or } 0.6 \text{ or } 60\%$$

KEY CONCEPT #4: ADDITION RULE FOR MUTUALLY EXCLUSIVE EVENTS

Use the addition rule for mutually exclusive events when you have two or more events that cannot happen at the same time. The probability of either event occurring is the sum of the probabilities of each event occurring separately.

Prep Expert Strategy

1. Understand that this rule applies to events that cannot happen at the same time.
2. Identify the mutually exclusive events.
3. Calculate the probability of each event occurring separately.
4. Add these probabilities together.

Prep Expert Example

- **Question:** A store sells three types of fruit: apples, oranges, and bananas. On a certain day, the store sells 150 apples, 100 oranges, and 50 bananas. If a customer selects a fruit at random, what is the probability that it is either an apple *or* an orange? *Hint:* Use the addition rule when you see the word "or" in a probability problem.

- **Answer:**

$$\text{Probability}_{\text{apple}} = \frac{\text{\# of Favorable Outcomes}}{\text{\# of Possible Outcomes}} = \frac{150}{300}$$

$$\text{Probability}_{\text{orange}} = \frac{\text{\# of Favorable Outcomes}}{\text{\# of Possible Outcomes}} = \frac{100}{300}$$

$$\text{Probability}_{\text{apple or orange}} = \frac{150}{300} + \frac{100}{300} = \frac{250}{300} = \frac{5}{6} \text{ or } 0.83 \text{ or } 83\%$$

KEY CONCEPT #5: MULTIPLICATION RULE FOR INDEPENDENT EVENTS

Use the multiplication rule for independent events when there are two or more independent events occurring in sequence. The probability of all events occurring is the product of their individual probabilities.

Prep Expert Strategy

1. Understand that this rule applies to two or more independent events occurring in sequence.
2. Identify the independent events.
3. Calculate the probability of each event occurring.
4. Multiply these probabilities together.

Prep Expert Example

- **Question**: A club has 12 members, of whom 5 are women and 7 are men. If two members are selected at random to attend a conference, what is the probability that both members are men?
  - *Hint 1*: Use the multiplication rule when you see the word "and" or "both" in a probability problem.
  - *Hint 2*: Don't forget that the probability of picking the second man changes because this is a case of conditional probability.

- **Answer**:

$$\text{Probability}_{\text{1st man}} = \frac{\text{\# of Favorable Outcomes}}{\text{\# of Possible Outcomes}} = \frac{7}{12}$$

$$\text{Probability}_{\text{2nd man}} = \frac{\text{\# of Favorable Outcomes}}{\text{\# of Possible Outcomes}} = \frac{6}{11}$$

$$\text{Probability}_{\text{1st man and 2nd man}} = \frac{7}{12} \times \frac{6}{11} = \frac{42}{132} = \frac{7}{22} \text{ or } 0.32 \text{ or } 32\%$$

Ace Probability to maximize your SAT Math score.

PREP EXPERT PRACTICE

Try applying this *Prep Expert Strategy* yourself to the following SAT practice questions:

111

Each face of a fair 10-sided die is labeled with a number from 1 through 10, with a different number appearing on each face. If the die is rolled one time, what is the probability of rolling a 7?

A) $\frac{1}{10}$

B) $\frac{2}{10}$

C) $\frac{5}{10}$

D) $\frac{7}{10}$

112

The table summarizes the distribution of size and shape for 120 balls of equal volume.

	Small	Medium	Large	Total
Round	20	30	25	75
Square	15	20	10	45
Total	35	50	35	120

If one of these balls is selected at random, what is the probability of selecting a medium-sized ball? (Express your answer as a decimal or fraction, not as a percent.)

The answers to these SAT practice questions can be found in the back of this book.

PREP EXPERT REVIEW

Key Takeaways

- **Prep Expert Math Strategy #16—*Ace Probability***: This section covered key concepts for mastering probability on SAT Math.

- **Classical probability**: Focus on the ratio of favorable outcomes to total outcomes in scenarios with equally likely outcomes.

- **Conditional probability**: Understand the likelihood of an event given a prior event. This is crucial in scenarios in which outcomes are interdependent, like drawing cards from a deck.

- **Complementary probability**: This is useful in scenarios in which it is easier to calculate the probability of an event *not* happening. Calculate the probability of an event and then subtract it from 1 to find its complement.

- **Addition rule for mutually exclusive events**: Apply this rule when dealing with events that cannot occur simultaneously. Practice identifying mutually exclusive events and calculating their separate probabilities before adding them together.

- **Multiplication rule for independent events**: Apply this rule when dealing with sequences of independent events. Practice identifying independent events and calculating the product of their individual probabilities. Remember the first event could change the probability of the second event (i.e., conditional probability).

PREPEXPERT

MATH STRATEGY #17
ACE LINES & ANGLES

PREP EXPERT STRATEGY + EXAMPLE

Ace Lines & Angles

To perform well on SAT Math, you must *Ace Lines & Angles*. Below are the most important concepts to master this topic for the SAT.

Key Concepts

KEY CONCEPT #1: PARALLEL LINES

Parallel lines maintain the same distance apart and never intersect. Parallel lines have equal slopes.

Prep Expert Strategy

1. Parallel lines are two lines that are always the same distance apart and never intersect.
2. Parallel lines have the same slope.

Prep Expert Example

- **Question:** If lines A and B are parallel, and the slope of line A is 2, what is the slope of line B?

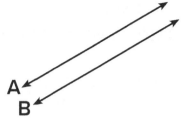

- **Answer:** 2

KEY CONCEPT #2: PERPENDICULAR LINES

Perpendicular lines are two lines that intersect at a right angle, forming a 90° intersection. Perpendicular lines have a unique slope relationship in which the slope of one line is the negative reciprocal of the other.

Prep Expert Strategy

1. Perpendicular lines are two lines that intersect at a right angle (90°).
2. The slopes of perpendicular lines are negative reciprocals of each other.

Prep Expert Example

- **Question:** If the slope of line A is 8, what is the slope of line B?

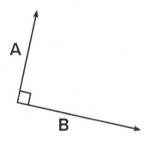

- **Answer:** $-\dfrac{1}{8}$

KEY CONCEPT #3: COMPLEMENTARY ANGLES

Complementary angles are pairs of angles that together total 90°. These angles are a fundamental aspect of geometric shapes, particularly in right-angled triangles.

Prep Expert Strategy

1. Complementary angles are two angles that add up to 90°.

Prep Expert Example

- **Question:** If angles A and B are complementary, and angle A is equal to 40°, what is the measure of angle B?

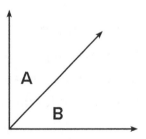

- **Answer:** 50°

KEY CONCEPT #4: SUPPLEMENTARY ANGLES

Supplementary angles are two angles that total 180° and form a linear pair.

Prep Expert Strategy

1. Supplementary angles are two angles that add up to 180°.

Prep Expert Example

- **Question**: If angles A and B are supplementary, and angle A is equal to 150°, what is the measure of angle B?

- **Answer**: 30°

KEY CONCEPT #5: VERTICAL ANGLES

Vertical angles are two angles that are opposite to each other when two lines intersect. Vertical angles are always equal in degree measure.

Prep Expert Strategy

1. When two lines intersect, the angles that are opposite each other (across the intersection) are called vertical angles.
2. Vertical angles are equal to each other.

Prep Expert Example

- **Question**: If angles A and B above are vertical angles, and angle A is equal to 30°, what is the measure of angle B?

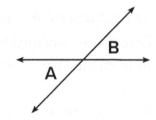

- **Answer**: 30°

KEY CONCEPT #6: CORRESPONDING ANGLES

Corresponding angles are angles formed when a transversal intersects two parallel lines. This creates equal angles in corresponding positions on each line. This property is important for determining parallelism and calculating unknown angles.

Prep Expert Strategy

1. A corresponding angle is a pair of angles formed by a line (called a transversal) intersecting two parallel lines.
2. Angles that are on the same side of the transversal and in corresponding positions are called corresponding angles.
3. Corresponding angles are equal to each other.

Prep Expert Example

- **Question**: If angles A and B are corresponding angles, and angle A is equal to 130°, what is the measure of angle B?

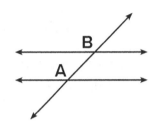

- **Answer**: 130°

KEY CONCEPT #7: CONVERTING DEGREES TO RADIANS

Radians are an alternative to degrees for measuring angles, based on the radius of a circle.

Prep Expert Strategy

1. Radians are a unit of measurement for angles similar to degrees.
2. To convert radians to degrees, use the following formula below.

$$\pi = 180°$$

Prep Expert Example

- **Question**: How many degrees are in an angle if it measures ³⁄₈π radians?

- **Answer**:

$$\frac{3}{8}\pi \quad \rightarrow \quad \frac{3}{8}(180°) \quad \rightarrow \quad 67.5°$$

Ace Lines & Angles to maximize your SAT Math score.

PREP EXPERT PRACTICE

Try applying this *Prep Expert Strategy* yourself to the following SAT practice questions:

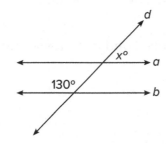

Note: Figure not drawn to scale

In the figure shown, line *d* intersects parallel lines *a* and *b*. What is the value of *x*?

The measure of angle *X* is $\frac{\pi}{6}$ radians. The measure of angle *Y* is $\frac{2\pi}{3}$ radians greater than the measure of angle *X*. What is the measure of angle *Y*, in degrees?

A) 60

B) 90

C) 120

D) 150

The answers to these SAT practice questions can be found in the back of this book.

PREP EXPERT REVIEW

Key Takeaways

- **Prep Expert Math Strategy #17—*Ace Lines & Angles***: This section covered key concepts for mastering lines and angles on SAT Math.

- **Parallel lines**: Parallel lines never intersect and always have identical slopes.

- **Perpendicular lines**: Perpendicular lines intersect at a right angle (90°) and have slopes that are negative reciprocals of each other.

- **Complementary angles**: Complementary angles are a pair of angles that add up to 90°.

- **Supplementary angles**: Supplementary angles are a pair of angles that add up to 180°.

- **Vertical angles**: Vertical angles are opposite angles at line intersections, and are always equal in measure.

- **Corresponding angles**: Corresponding angles are formed when a transversal intersects parallel lines and are equal in corresponding positions.

- **Converting degrees to radians**: Radians measure angles based on circle radius. Use the following formula to convert between radians and degrees: $\pi = 180°$.

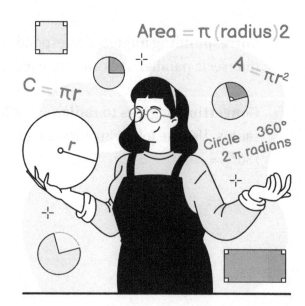

Area = π (radius)2

$A = \pi r^2$

$C = \pi r$

r

Circle 360°
2 π radians

PREP**EXPERT**

MATH STRATEGY #18

ACE RECTANGLES & CIRCLES

Prep Expert
Math Strategies

PREP EXPERT STRATEGY + EXAMPLE

Ace Rectangles & Circles

To perform well on SAT Math, you must *Ace Rectangles & Circles*. Below are the most important concepts to master this topic for the SAT.

Key Concepts

KEY CONCEPT #1: RECTANGLES

Rectangles are four-sided polygons with right angles at each corner. This shape's opposite sides are both equal in length and parallel to each other.

Prep Expert Strategy

1. A rectangle is a four-sided polygon in which each of the four angles is a right angle (90°).

- **Question:** The perimeter of a rectangle is 70 inches, and its length is 5 inches more than twice its width. What are the dimensions of the rectangle?

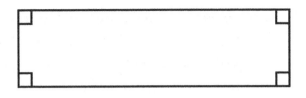

- **Answer:**

$$\text{Perimeter} = 2\,(length) + 2\,(width)$$
$$70 = 2\,(2w + 5) + 2\,(w)$$
$$70 = 4w + 10 + 2w$$
$$60 = 6w$$
$$w = 10 \text{ inches}$$
$$l = 2w + 5 = 2(10) + 5 = 25 \text{ inches}$$

KEY CONCEPT #2: SQUARES

A square is a specific type of rectangle in which all four sides are of equal length. All four angles of a square are also right angles.

Prep Expert Strategy

A square is a special type of rectangle in which all four sides are equal in length.

Prep Expert Example

- **Question:** A square has an area of 36 square inches. What is the length of each side of the square?

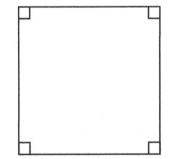

- **Answer:**

$$\text{Area} = length^2$$
$$36 = (l)^2$$
$$l = 6 \text{ inches}$$

KEY CONCEPT #3: CIRCLES

A circle is made up of all points in a plane that are equidistant from a central point, known as the center. The distance from the center to any point on the circle is the radius. The distance across the entire circle, passing through the center, is the diameter.

1. A circle is a closed shape consisting of all the points in a plane that are equidistant from a fixed point called the center.
2. The distance from the center to any point on the circle is the radius (r).
3. The distance across the circle passing through the center is the diameter (D).

$$D = 2r$$

Prep Expert Example

- **Question:** The radius of the circle is 6 units. What is the length of the diameter?

- **Answer:**
$$Diameter = 2\,(radius)$$
$$D = 2\,(6)$$
$$D = 12 \text{ units}$$

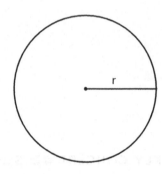

KEY CONCEPT #4: CIRCLE CIRCUMFERENCE

The circumference of a circle is the total length of its edge. It is calculated using the formula $C = 2\pi r$ or $C = \pi d$, where C is the circumference, r is the radius, and d is the diameter of the circle.

Prep Expert Strategy

1. The circumference of a circle is the distance around the edge of the circle.
2. Here is the formula for calculating the circumference of a circle:

$$C = 2\pi r$$

Prep Expert Example

- **Question:** The radius of the circle is 6 units. What is the circumference?

- **Answer:**
$$Circumference = 2\pi\,(radius)$$
$$C = 2\pi(6)$$
$$C = 12\pi \text{ units}$$

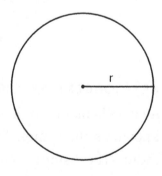

KEY CONCEPT #5: CIRCLE AREA

The area of a circle is the space contained within its circumference. It is calculated using the formula $A = \pi r^2$, where A is the area and r is the radius.

Prep Expert Strategy

1. The area of a circle is the space enclosed inside the circle.
2. Here is the formula for calculating the area of a circle:

$$A = \pi r^2$$

Prep Expert Example

- **Question:** The radius of the circle is 6 units. What is the area of the circle?

- **Answer:**

$$Area = \pi(radius)^2$$
$$A = \pi(6)^2 \quad \rightarrow \quad A = 36\pi \text{ square units}$$

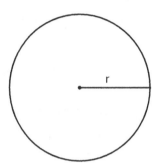

KEY CONCEPT #6: CIRCLE ANGLE MEASURE

A circle encompasses a total of 360° or 2π radians.

Prep Expert Strategy

1. A circle is made up of 360° or 2π radians.

$$Circle = 360^\circ = 2\,\pi\ radians$$

Prep Expert Example

- **Question:** What is the measure, in radians, of the central angle inscribed by ⅓ of a circle?

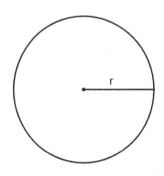

- **Answer:**

$$\frac{1}{3}Circle = \frac{1}{3}(360^\circ) = 120^\circ$$

Remember the formula for converting degrees to radians: π = 180°

$$\frac{120^\circ}{180^\circ}\pi \quad \rightarrow \quad \frac{2}{3}\pi\ radians$$

KEY CONCEPT #7: CENTRAL ANGLES, ARCS, AND SECTORS IN CIRCLES

Central angles in a circle are formed by two radii creating an angle at the center. Arcs are segments of the circle's circumference. Sectors are the areas enclosed by two radii and an arc.

Prep Expert Strategy

1. A central angle in a circle is an angle whose vertex is the center of the circle. A central angle's rays (or sides) intersect the circle at two distinct points on its circumference.
2. An arc is a portion of the circle's circumference that is bounded by two points.
3. A sector is a region bounded by two radii and an arc of the circle between them.

Prep Expert Example

- **Question:** If the central angle is equal to 90° and the radius is 6 units, what is the length of the arc?

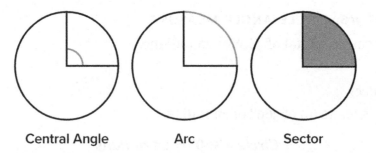

| Central Angle | Arc | Sector |

- **Answer:** The central angle is 90°, which is ¼ of the entire circle of 360°. Therefore, the arc will be ¼ of the circle's circumference.

$$C = 2\pi(6) = 12\pi$$
$$\text{Arc length} = ¼ \times 12\pi = \textbf{3π units}$$

KEY CONCEPT #8: PROPORTIONAL RATIOS OF CENTRAL ANGLES, ARCS, AND SECTORS

The sizes of central angles, arcs, and sectors in a circle are proportionally related. The length of an arc and the area of a sector can be determined using the central angle.

1. Central angles, arcs, and sectors can be related using the following ratios:

$$\frac{\textbf{Central Angle}}{\textbf{360}^{\textbf{o}}} = \frac{\textbf{Arc Length}}{\textbf{Circumference}} = \frac{\textbf{Sector Area}}{\textbf{Circle Area}}$$

Prep Expert Example

- **Question**: If the central angle is equal to 90° and the radius is 6 units, what is the area of the sector?

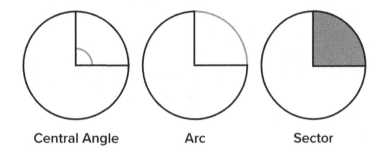

| Central Angle | Arc | Sector |

- **Answer**:

$$\frac{\text{Central Angle}}{360^{o}} = \frac{\text{Sector Area}}{\text{Circle Area}} \quad \rightarrow \quad \frac{90^{o}}{360^{o}} = \frac{\text{Sector Area}}{36\pi}$$

$$\text{Sector Area} = \frac{90^{o}}{360^{o}}(36\pi) = 9\pi \text{ units}^{2}$$

KEY CONCEPT #9: INSCRIBED ANGLES IN CIRCLES

Inscribed angles are formed by two intersecting chords with a vertex on the circle's circumference. The measure of an inscribed angle is always half that of the central angle that intercepts the same arc.

Prep Expert Strategy

1. An inscribed angle in a circle is an angle formed by two intersecting chords of the circle.
2. The vertex of an inscribed angle is on the circumference of the circle.
3. The measure of an inscribed angle is equal to half the measure of the central angle of the arc that it intercepts.

$$\textbf{Inscribed Angle} = \frac{1}{2} \textbf{(Central Angle)}$$

- **Question:** What is the measure, in degrees, of the inscribed angle BCD, if the measure of the central angle of arc BD is equivalent to 90º?

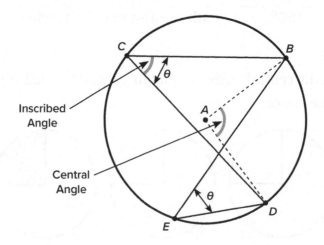

- **Answer:**

$$\text{Inscribed Angle} = \frac{1}{2}(\text{Central Angle}) = \frac{1}{2}(90º) = 45º$$

KEY CONCEPT #10: CIRCLE EQUATION

The equation of a circle in a coordinate plane describes all points of the circle in terms of its center and radius. It is represented as $(x - h)^2 + (y - k)^2 = r^2$, where (h, k) is the center of the circle and r is the radius.

Prep Expert Strategy

1. The circle equation is as follows:

$$(x - h)^2 + (y - k)^2 = r^2$$

Prep Expert Example

- **Question:** What is the equation of a circle with center $(2, -3)$ and radius 4?

- **Answer:**

$$(x - h)^2 + (y - k)^2 = r^2$$
$$(x - 2)^2 + (y + 3)^2 = 4^2$$
$$(x - 2)^2 + (y + 3)^2 = 16$$

KEY CONCEPT #11: CIRCLE EQUATION GRAPH SHIFTS AND RADIUS CHANGES

Shifting a circle's equation on a coordinate plane involves altering the coordinates of its center. Moving the circle up or down changes the *y*-coordinate, while moving it left or right changes the *x*-coordinate. Additionally, changing the radius of the circle requires adjustments to the formula.

Prep Expert Strategy

1. Circle equation graph shifts are typically the opposite of what you would expect of most other graph shifts. See below.
   - **Shift up**: Subtract from the *y*
   - **Shift down**: Add to the *y*
   - **Shift right**: Subtract from the *x*
   - **Shift left**: Add to the *x*
   - **Change radius**: Do not forget, too, that the radius is squared

Prep Expert Example

- **Question**: How would you rewrite the following equation for a circle to shift it 2 units downward, 3 units to the right, and change the radius to 1?

$$(x - 2)^2 + (y + 4)^2 = 9$$

- **Answer**:

$$(x - 2)^2 + (y + 4)^2 = 9 \quad \rightarrow \quad (x - 5)^2 + (y + 6)^2 = 1$$

Ace Rectangles & Circles to maximize your SAT Math score.

PREP EXPERT PRACTICE

Try applying this *Prep Expert Strategy* yourself to the following SAT practice questions:

Note: Figure not drawn to scale.

The circle shown has center O, circumference 192π, and diameters $\overline{KM}$ and $\overline{LN}$. The length of arc KN is twice the length of arc KL. What is the length of arc LM?

A) 32π

B) 64π

C) 96π

D) 128π

A circle in the xy-plane has a diameter with endpoints (6, 8) and (6, 18). An equation of this circle is $(x - 6)^2 + (y - 13)^2 = r^2$, where r is a positive constant. What is the value of r?

The answers to these SAT practice questions can be found in the back of this book.

PREP EXPERT REVIEW

Key Takeaways

- **Prep Expert Math Strategy #18—*Ace Rectangles & Circles***: This section covered key concepts for mastering rectangles and circles on SAT Math.

- **Rectangles and squares**: A rectangle is a four-sided polygon with all right angles, and its opposite sides are both equal in length and parallel. A square is a special type of rectangle in which all four sides are equal.

- **Circles**: A circle is made up of points that are all equidistant from a fixed center. The radius connects the center to any point on the circle. The diameter is twice the radius.

- **Central angles, arcs, and sectors**: Central angles form at the circle's center, while arcs are portions of the circumference, and sectors are areas enclosed by radii and arcs. Their measurements are proportionally interrelated, allowing you to calculate arc lengths and sector areas based on the central angle.

- **Circle equation**: The standard circle equation is $(x - h)^2 + (y - k)^2 = r^2$, where (h, k) is the center of the circle and r is the radius.

- **Circle equation graph shifts**: Circle graph shifts include moving up, down, right, or left, each requiring specific adjustments to the equation of a circle. Changing the radius also requires you to remember to adjust for the square in the equation. Be aware of the differences in circle graph shifts compared to other kinds of graph shifts.

PREPEXPERT

MATH STRATEGY #19

ACE TRIANGLES

PREP EXPERT STRATEGY • EXAMPLE

Ace Triangles

To perform well on SAT Math, you must *Ace Triangles*. Below are the most important concepts to master this topic for the SAT.

Key Concepts

KEY CONCEPT #1: TRIANGLE BASICS

A triangle is a two-dimensional shape consisting of three straight sides and three interior angles. The sum of these angles always equals 180°.

Prep Expert Strategy

1. A triangle is a closed two-dimensional figure with three straight sides and three angles.
2. The sum of the interior angles in a triangle always adds up to 180°.

Prep Expert Example

- **Question**: If angle A is equal to 70° and angle B is equal to 70°, what is the measure of angle C? *Note*: figure not drawn to scale.

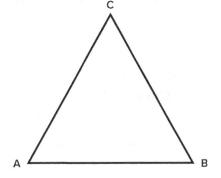

- **Answer**:

$$\angle A + \angle B + \angle C = 180°$$
$$70° + 70° + \angle C = 180° \quad \rightarrow \quad \angle C = 40°$$

KEY CONCEPT #2: TRIANGLE AREA

The area of a triangle is determined by the formula $A = \frac{1}{2}bh$, where *A* is the area, *b* is the base, and *h* is the height. The base is the length of the base of the triangle. The height is the perpendicular height from the base to the opposite vertex. This formula calculates the space within the triangle.

Prep Expert Strategy

1. Here is the formula for calculating the area of a triangle:

$$\text{Area} = \frac{1}{2}bh$$

Prep Expert Example

- **Question**: If the base of a triangle is equal to 6 and the height of a triangle is equal to 8, what is the area of the triangle?

- **Answer**:

$$\text{Area} = \frac{1}{2}bh = \frac{1}{2}(6)(8) = 24$$

KEY CONCEPT #3: EQUILATERAL TRIANGLES

All three sides of equilateral triangles are equal in length, and all three angles are of equal measure (each is 60°).

Prep Expert Strategy

1. An equilateral triangle is a type of triangle in which all three sides are of equal length.

Prep Expert
Math Strategies

2. All three angles in an equilateral triangle are also of equal measure, each measuring 60°.

Prep Expert Example

- **Question**: If the perimeter of an equilateral triangle is 24 units, what is the length of one of its sides?

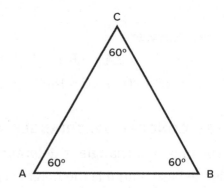

- **Answer**:

    Perimeter = 3 × Equal Sides

    24 = 3 × Equal Sides

    Equal Sides = 8 units (each)

KEY CONCEPT #4: ISOSCELES TRIANGLES

An isosceles triangle has two sides of equal length and, opposite each of the equal sides, two angles of equal measure.

Prep Expert Strategy

1. An isosceles triangle is a type of triangle in which two sides are of equal length.

2. The two angles opposite the equal sides are also equal in an isosceles triangle.

Prep Expert Example

- **Question**: In the isosceles triangle ABC, AC = BC, and the measure of angle B is 70°. What is the measure of angle C?

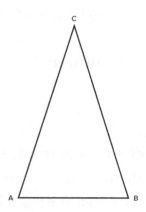

- **Answer**:

    $$\angle A + \angle B + \angle C = 180°$$
    $$70° + 70° + \angle C = 180° \quad \rightarrow \quad \angle C = 40°$$

KEY CONCEPT #5: SIMILAR TRIANGLES

Similar triangles are the same shape but may vary in size. The corresponding angles of these triangles are equal. The corresponding sides of similar triangles are also in proportion.

Prep Expert Strategy

1. Similar triangles are triangles that are the same shape but not necessarily the same size.
2. Corresponding **angles** of two similar triangles are **equal** in measure.
3. Corresponding **sides** are **proportional** in length.

Prep Expert Example

- **Question**: In the diagram, triangles ABC and DEF are similar. If the length of AB is 10, the length of DE is 5, and the length of EF 7, what is the length of BC?

- **Answer**:
    - If the two triangles are similar, then we know the corresponding side lengths are proportional.
    - The corresponding side length of AB is double the side length of DE (10 versus 5).
    - Therefore, we know that the corresponding side length of BC is double the side length of EF.
    - Since we know that the side length of EF is 7, then the side length of BC is **14**.

KEY CONCEPT #6: RIGHT TRIANGLES

A right triangle is characterized by one angle measuring 90°, known as the right angle. The side opposite the right angle is its longest side, called the hypotenuse.

Prep Expert Strategy

1. A right triangle has one angle measuring 90°, which is called a right angle.
2. The side opposite the right angle is called the hypotenuse.
3. The other two sides are called legs.

Prep Expert Example

- **Question:** In a right triangle, the angle opposite side length a is equivalent to 35°. What is the measure of the angle opposite side length b?

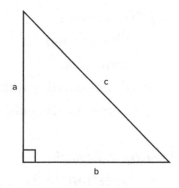

- **Answer:**

$$90° + 35° + \angle(\text{opposite side length } b) = 180°$$
$$\angle(\text{opposite side length } b) = 55°$$

KEY CONCEPT #7: PYTHAGOREAN THEOREM

The Pythagorean theorem states the square of the length of the hypotenuse is equal to the sum of the squares of the other two sides in any right triangle.

Prep Expert Strategy

1. Here is the Pythagorean theorem:

$$a^2 + b^2 = c^2$$

$a \,\&\, b \;\rightarrow\;$ represent the lengths of the legs of a right triangle

$c \;\rightarrow\;$ represents the length of the hypotenuse of a right triangle

Prep Expert Example

- **Question:** In a right triangle, the hypotenuse is 13 and one leg is 5. What is the length of the other leg?

- **Answer:**

$$a^2 + b^2 = c^2$$
$$5^2 + b^2 = 13^2 \;\rightarrow\; 25 + b^2 = 169 \;\rightarrow\; b^2 = 144 \;\rightarrow\; b = 12$$

KEY CONCEPT #8: COMMON PYTHAGOREAN TRIPLES

Pythagorean triples are sets of three integers that satisfy the Pythagorean theorem. Common examples include (3, 4, 5) and (5, 12, 13). Knowing these triples is useful to quickly solve problems involving right triangles.

Prep Expert Strategy

1. Recognize the side lengths of common right triangles below so that you do not need to use the Pythagorean formula on the SAT.

Side Length	Side Length	Hypotenuse
3	4	5
5	12	13
6	8	10
7	24	25
9	12	15
10	24	26

Prep Expert Example

- **Question:** In a right triangle, the hypotenuse is 25 and one leg is 7. What is the length of the other leg?

- **Answer:** 24

KEY CONCEPT #9: 30-60-90 TRIANGLES

In a 30-60-90 triangle, the side lengths of the short side : long side : hypotenuse are in a fixed ratio of 1 : √3 : 2, respectively.

Prep Expert Strategy
1. The College Board will give you the 30-60-90 triangle figure below as part of the SAT Math Reference Sheet on test day.
2. Study 30-60-90 triangles now so that you fully understand the side length proportions before test day.

Prep Expert Example

- **Question:** Triangle ABC is a 30-60-90 triangle. The length of BC is 6. What is the length of AB?

- **Answer:**

    $2x = 6 \rightarrow x = 3$

    The length of AB is **3**.

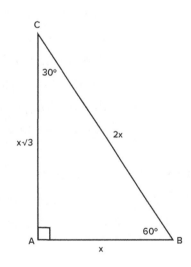

KEY CONCEPT #10: DIVIDING EQUILATERAL TRIANGLES INTO 30-60-90 TRIANGLES

When an equilateral triangle is divided by an altitude (a line from a vertex to the midpoint of the opposite side), it forms two 30-60-90 right triangles.

Prep Expert Strategy
1. Any time there is an equilateral triangle on the SAT, split it into two 30-60-90 triangles.
2. Draw an altitude (a perpendicular line) from one of the vertices of the triangle to the opposite side. Doing so will often help you solve the problem.

Prep Expert Example
- **Question:** If an equilateral triangle has side lengths of 10, what is the length of an altitude of the equilateral triangle?

- **Answer:**

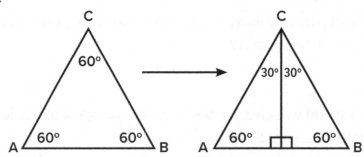

- The equilateral side length of 10 is equivalent to the hypotenuse of the 30-60-90 triangles.
- Therefore, $2x = 10$ (*or x = 5*).
- The altitude of the equilateral triangle is equivalent to the long side of the 30-60-90 triangles. Based on the properties of 30-60-90 triangles, we know that the long side is equivalent to the following: *long side* = $x\sqrt{3}$ = $5\sqrt{3}$
- Therefore, the altitude of the equilateral triangle is **5√3**.

KEY CONCEPT #11: 45-45-90 TRIANGLES

A 45-45-90 triangle is an isosceles right triangle in which the legs are of equal length and the hypotenuse is √2 times the length of each leg.

1. The College Board will give you the 45-45-90 triangle figure below as part of the SAT Math Reference Sheet on test day.

2. Study 45-45-90 triangles now so that you fully understand the side length proportions before test day.

Prep Expert Example

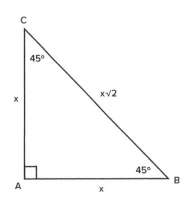

*   **Question**: Triangle ABC is an isosceles right triangle. The length of BC is 6√2. What is the length of AB? *Hint*: A 45-45-90 triangle may also be referred to as an "isosceles right triangle"— do not let this terminology fool you!

*   **Answer**:

    $$BC \ (hypotenuse) = 6\sqrt{2}$$
    $$x\sqrt{2} = 6\sqrt{2} \ \rightarrow \ x = 6$$

    The length of side AB is **6**.

KEY CONCEPT #12: DIVIDING SQUARES INTO 45-45-90 TRIANGLES

When you divide a square along its diagonal, it forms two 45-45-90 triangles.

Prep Expert Strategy

1. Anytime there is a square on the SAT, split it into two 45-45-90 triangles.

2. Draw a straight line from one corner of the square to the opposite corner (a diagonal). Doing so will often help you solve the problem.

Prep Expert Example

*   **Question**: The diagonal of a square is 10√2. What is the length of each side of the square?

*   **Answer**:

    *   The diagonal of a square of 10√2 is equivalent to the hypotenuse of the 45-45-90 triangles.

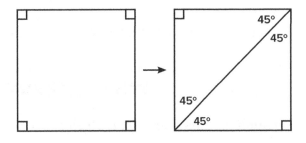

Prep Expert
Math Strategies

- Therefore, $x\sqrt{2} = 10\sqrt{2}$ (or $x = 10$).
- The side lengths of the square are equivalent to the side lengths of the 45-45-90 triangles. Based on the properties of 45-45-90 triangles, we know that the side lengths are equivalent to the following:
  side length = x = 10
- Therefore, the side lengths of the square are **10**.

KEY CONCEPT #13: TRIANGLE INEQUALITY THEOREM

The triangle inequality theorem states that the sum of the lengths of any two sides of a triangle must be greater than the length of the remaining side.

Prep Expert Strategy

1. In other words, the length of the longest side of a triangle cannot be greater than the sum of the lengths of the other two sides.

Prep Expert Example

- **Question:** Two sides of a triangle have the lengths 3 and 4. Which of the following cannot be the perimeter of the triangle?

  A) 9
  B) 11
  C) 13
  D) 15

- **Answer:**
  - The triangle inequality theorem tells us that the length of the third side must be less than 7 (the sum of the other two sides: 3 and 4).
  - Therefore, the perimeter of the triangle cannot be greater than the following: *Maximum triangle perimeter*: 3 + 4 + 7 = 14
  - Select answer choice **(D) 15**.

Ace Triangles to maximize your SAT Math score.

PREP EXPERT PRACTICE

Try applying this *Prep Expert Strategy* yourself to the following SAT practice questions:

An isosceles right triangle has a hypotenuse of 100 inches. What is the perimeter, in inches, of this triangle?

A) $50\sqrt{2}$

B) $100\sqrt{2}$

C) $100 + 50\sqrt{2}$

D) $100 + 100\sqrt{2}$

The perimeter of an equilateral triangle is 60 centimeters. The height of this triangle is $k\sqrt{3}$ centimeters, where k is a constant. What is the value of k?

The answers to these SAT practice questions can be found in the back of this book.

PREP EXPERT REVIEW

Key Takeaways

- **Prep Expert Math Strategy #19—*Ace Triangles*:** This section covered key concepts for mastering triangles on SAT Math.

- **Triangle basics:** Triangles have three straight sides and three angles. The sum of the interior angles of a triangle is always equal to 180°.

- **Triangle area:** Calculate the area of a triangle using the formula $A = \frac{1}{2}bh$, where b is the base and h is the height.

- **Triangle types:** The different types of triangles include equilateral, isosceles, and right triangles.

- **Special triangles:** Recognizing the properties of special triangles, especially 30-60-90 and 45-45-90 triangles, can simplify complex problems.

- **Triangle theorems:** Familiarity with the Pythagorean theorem and the triangle inequality theorem is essential for the SAT.

Prep Expert
Math Strategies

PREPEXPERT

MATH
STRATEGY #20
ACE TRIGONOMETRY

PREP EXPERT STRATEGY • EXAMPLE

Ace Trigonometry

To perform well on SAT Math, you must *Ace Trigonometry*. Below are the most important concepts to master this topic for the SAT.

Important Note

Many students are intimidated by trigonometry on the SAT for one of two reasons:

1. They have not taken trigonometry in high school yet, *or*
2. They find trigonometry to be a difficult subject.

Good news! The SAT does not test all of trigonometry. Instead, the SAT tests students only on a few trigonometry-related concepts. Most of the trigonometry concepts tested on the SAT are related to right triangles.

More good news! The maximum number of trigonometry-related questions you will see on the SAT is three questions. Most students encounter only one or two trigonometry-related questions on the SAT.

Hopefully the good news above eases any worries you may have related to trig-onometry on the SAT. Now, let's teach you everything you need to know related to trigonometry for the SAT.

KEY CONCEPT #1: SINE

The sine function is a fundamental ratio in right triangles. The sine of a given angle in a right triangle is the ratio of the side length opposite that angle to the hypotenuse length.

Prep Expert Strategy

1. The sine formula is given below:

$$\sin(\theta) = \frac{\text{opposite}}{\text{hypotenuse}}$$

Prep Expert Example

*   **Question**: What is sin(60°) in the right triangle shown?

*   **Answer**:

$$\sin(\theta) = \frac{\text{opposite}}{\text{hypotenuse}}$$

$$\sin(60^\circ) = \frac{4\sqrt{3}}{8} = \frac{\sqrt{3}}{2}$$

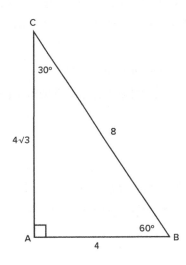

KEY CONCEPT #2: COSINE

The cosine function is a fundamental ratio in right triangles. The cosine of a given angle in a right triangle is the ratio of the side length adjacent to that angle to the hypotenuse length.

Prep Expert Strategy

1. The cosine formula is given below:

$$\cos(\theta) = \frac{\text{adjacent}}{\text{hypotenuse}}$$

Prep Expert Example

- **Question:** What is *cos*(60°) in the right triangle shown?

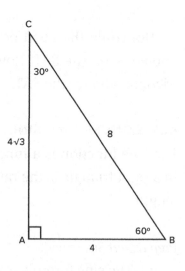

- **Answer:**

$$cos(\theta) = \frac{\text{adjacent}}{\text{hypotenuse}}$$

$$cos(60°) = \frac{4}{8} = \frac{1}{2}$$

KEY CONCEPT #3: TANGENT

The tangent function is a fundamental ratio in right triangles. The tangent of a given angle in a right triangle is the ratio of the side length opposite that angle to the side length adjacent to that angle.

Prep Expert Strategy

1. The tangent formula is given below:

$$tan(\theta) = \frac{\text{opposite}}{\text{adjacent}}$$

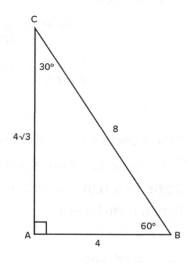

Prep Expert Example

- **Question:** What is tan(60°) in the right triangle shown?

- **Answer:**

$$tan(\theta) = \frac{\text{opposite}}{\text{adjacent}}$$

$$tan(60°) = \frac{4\sqrt{3}}{4} = \sqrt{3}$$

KEY CONCEPT #4: RADIANS AS AN ANGLE MEASUREMENT UNIT

Radians are an alternative to degrees for measuring angles, based on the radius of a circle.

Prep Expert Strategy

1. Radians are a unit of measurement for angles similar to degrees.

2. To convert radians to degrees, use the following formula:

$$\pi = 180^\circ$$

Prep Expert Example

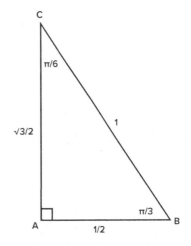

-   **Question**: What is sin(π/3) in the right triangle shown?

-   **Answer**:

$$\sin(\pi/3) = \frac{\text{opposite}}{\text{hypotenuse}}$$

Replace π with 180° to quickly understand the degree measure.

$$\sin(60^\circ) = \frac{\text{opposite}}{\text{hypotenuse}} = \frac{\frac{\sqrt{3}}{2}}{1} = \frac{\sqrt{3}}{2}$$

KEY CONCEPT #5: THE UNIT CIRCLE

The unit circle is a fundamental tool in trigonometry, defined as a circle with a radius of one unit that is centered at the origin of the *x-y* coordinate plane.

Prep Expert Strategy

1. The unit circle is a tool used to create right triangles and calculate trigonometric functions.

2. It is called a *unit* circle because the radius is always 1.

3. Therefore, the hypotenuses of the right triangles formed by the unit circle are always 1.

4. This is important to know when calculating sine, cosine, and tangent of right triangles formed by the unit circle.

Prep Expert Example

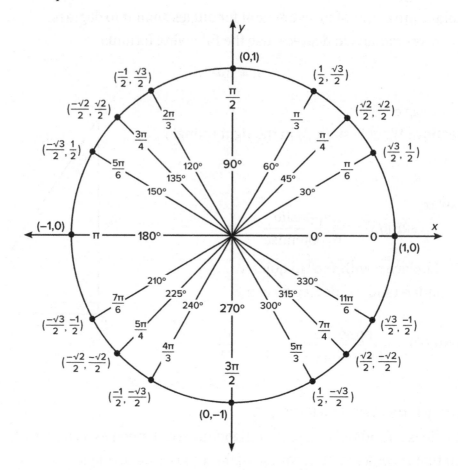

Prep Expert Tip: You do not need to memorize the unit circle, but you do need to understand it.

KEY CONCEPT #6: THE UNIT CIRCLE AND RIGHT TRIANGLES

There are many applications of right triangles within the unit circle. Although it is a unit *circle*, it is more important to pay attention to the *right triangles*.

Prep Expert Strategy

1. The unit circle forms right triangles by drawing a perpendicular line from the *x*-axis to a point on the circumference of the unit circle.

Prep Expert Example

- **Question:** What is cos(30°)?

- **Answer:**

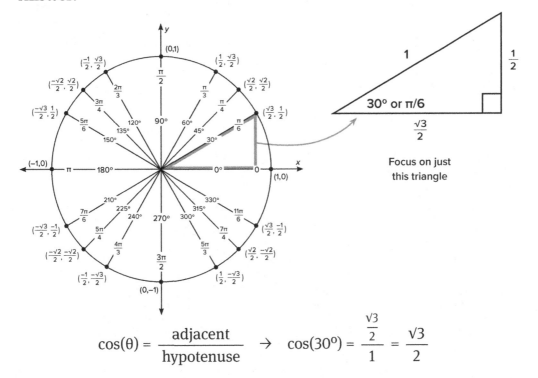

$$\cos(\theta) = \frac{\text{adjacent}}{\text{hypotenuse}} \quad \rightarrow \quad \cos(30°) = \frac{\frac{\sqrt{3}}{2}}{1} = \frac{\sqrt{3}}{2}$$

KEY CONCEPT #7: THREE RIGHT TRIANGLES IN THE UNIT CIRCLE

There are three specific right triangles formed within the unit circle. These triangles are key to simplifying the calculation of trigonometric functions. These three triangles are then repeated in each of the four quadrants of the *x-y* coordinate plane.

Prep Expert Strategy

1. **Triangle 1:** A 30-60-90 triangle with the long side on the *x*-axis and a hypotenuse of 1.
2. **Triangle 2:** A 45-45-90 triangle with a hypotenuse of 1.
3. **Triangle 3:** A 30-60-90 triangle with the short side on the *x*-axis and a hypotenuse of 1.

Prep Expert
Math Strategies

Prep Expert Example

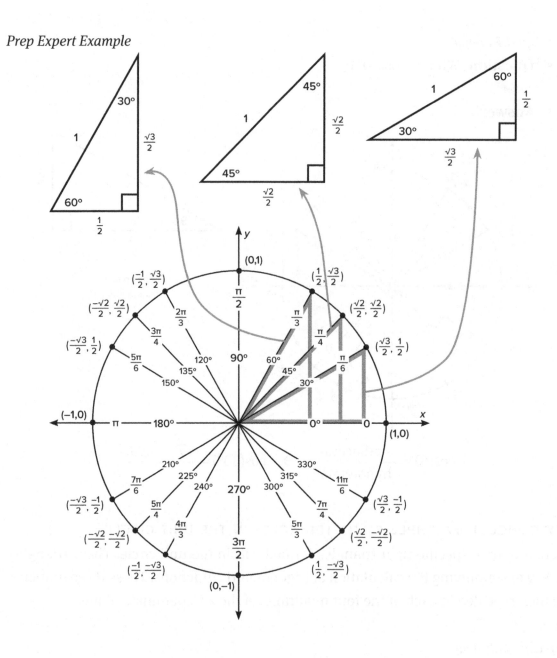

KEY CONCEPT #8: SIGN CHANGES IN THE UNIT CIRCLE

The signs of sine, cosine, and tangent values change in different quadrants of the unit circle. Understanding these sign changes is crucial for solving trigonometric equations.

Prep Expert Strategy

1. Depending on the quadrant of the *x-y* coordinate plane that a right triangle is in, the *x*-value or the *y*-value may be negative.

2. Therefore, the sine, cosine, or tangent may be negative in the unit circle.

Prep Expert Example

- **Question**: What is cos(150°)?

- **Answer**:

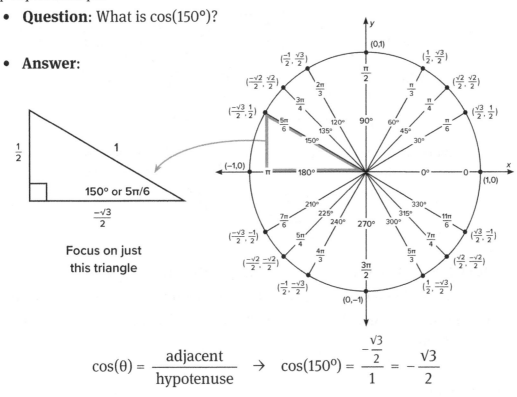

Focus on just
this triangle

$$\cos(\theta) = \frac{\text{adjacent}}{\text{hypotenuse}} \quad \rightarrow \quad \cos(150°) = \frac{-\frac{\sqrt{3}}{2}}{1} = -\frac{\sqrt{3}}{2}$$

KEY CONCEPT #9: CAST RULE IN THE UNIT CIRCLE

The CAST rule is a mnemonic that can help you remember the signs of trigonometric functions in different quadrants of the unit circle.

Prep Expert Strategy

1. Use the CAST rule to remember which ratio (sine, cosine, or tangent) will be positive depending on the quadrant of the unit circle that the right triangle is located in.

   a. **C**osine ratio is positive in Quadrant 4

   b. **A**ll ratios are positive in Quadrant 1

   c. **S**ine ratio is positive in Quadrant 2

   d. **T**angent ratio is positive in Quadrant 3

2. If the trigonometric function is in a different quadrant than the ones listed above, then it will have a negative sign.

Prep Expert Example

Quadrant 2
sine ratio
is positive

Quadrant 1
all ratios are
positive

S   **A**

T   **C**

Quadrant 3
tangent ratio
is positive

Quadrant 4
cosine ratio
is positive

KEY CONCEPT #10: X-VALUES AND Y-VALUES IN THE UNIT CIRCLE

The *x*-value and *y*-value coordinates of points on the unit circle correspond to the cosine and sine values, respectively. This relationship is fundamental to applying trigonometric functions.

Prep Expert Strategy

1. The *x-values* on the unit circle are equal to the *cosine* value of that angle because the hypotenuse is always 1.

2. The *y-values* on the unit circle are equal to the *sine* value of that angle because the hypotenuse is always 1.

Prep Expert Example

- **Question:** What is cos(225°)?

- **Answer:**

$$\cos(\theta) = x - \text{value}$$

$$\cos(225^\circ) = -\frac{\sqrt{2}}{2}$$

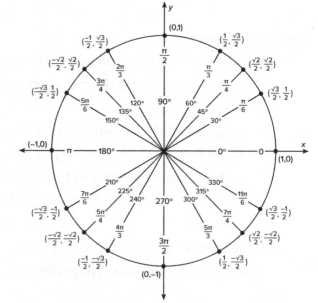

KEY CONCEPT #11: CONVERTING SINE VALUES IN THE UNIT CIRCLE

Sine values are equivalent to *y*-coordinates on the unit circle, so any two sine values with the same *y*-coordinate will be equivalent.

Prep Expert Strategy

1. Two angles with the same sine value will have the same *y*-coordinate on the unit circle.

Prep Expert Example

- **Question:** What other sine value on the unit circle is equivalent to sin(60°)?
- **Answer:**

$$\sin(60^\circ) = y - \text{value}$$

$$\sin(60^\circ) = \frac{\sqrt{3}}{2}$$

The only other sine value that has a *y*-coordinate of $\frac{\sqrt{3}}{2}$ is **sin(120°)**.

$$\sin(60^\circ) = \sin(120^\circ)$$

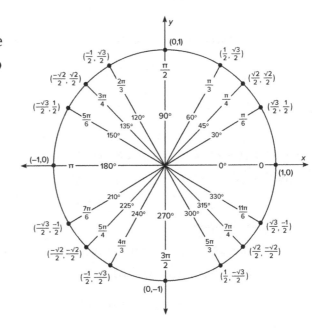

KEY CONCEPT #12: CONVERTING COSINE VALUES IN THE UNIT CIRCLE

Cosine values are equivalent to *x*-coordinates on the unit circle, so any two cosine values with the same *x*-coordinate will be equivalent.

Prep Expert Strategy

1. Two angles with the same cosine value will have the same *x*-coordinate on the unit circle.

Prep Expert Example

- **Question:** What other cosine value on the unit circle is equivalent to *cos*(π/3)?

- **Answer:**

$$cos(\frac{\pi}{3}) = x - \text{value}$$

$$cos(\frac{\pi}{3}) = \frac{1}{2}$$

The only other cosine value that has a x-coordinate of $\frac{1}{2}$ is **cos(5π/3)**.

$$cos(\frac{\pi}{3}) = cos(\frac{5\pi}{3})$$

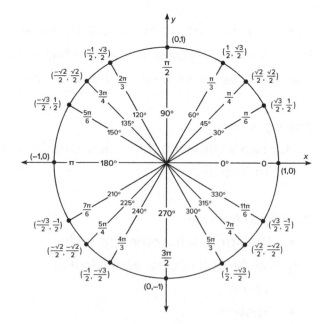

KEY CONCEPT #13: CONVERTING BETWEEN SINE AND COSINE

Convert between sine and cosine values by subtracting the given angle from 90°.

Prep Expert Strategy

1. If the SAT asks you to convert between sine and cosine values, subtract the given angle from 90° (or $\frac{\pi}{2}$).

$$\mathbf{cos(\theta) = sin(90^o - \theta) \quad \rightarrow \quad sin(\theta) = cos(90^o - \theta)}$$

Prep Expert Example

- **Question:** What is the equivalent cosine to sin(60°)?

- **Answer:**

$$sin(60^\circ) = cos(90^\circ - 60^\circ) \quad \rightarrow \quad sin(60^\circ) = cos(30^\circ)$$

KEY CONCEPT #14: COMPLEMENTARY ANGLES— SINE AND COSINE RELATIONSHIP

We just covered that to convert between sine and cosine, you must subtract the given angle from 90°. This also means that the two angles must add up to 90° (i.e., they must be complementary angles).

1. If the cosine and sine values of two angles are equal to each other, the two angles are complementary (add up to 90°).

$$\cos(A^o) = \sin(B^o) \quad \rightarrow \quad A^o + B^o = 90^o$$

Prep Expert Example

*   **Question**: What is the value of *x* in the following equation?

$$\sin(x^o + 20^\circ) = \cos(2x^o + 40^\circ)$$

*   **Answer**:

$$\sin(x^o + 20^\circ) = \cos(2x^o + 40^\circ)$$
$$(x^o + 20^\circ) + (2x^o + 40^\circ) = 90^\circ \quad \rightarrow$$
$$3x^o + 60^\circ = 90^\circ \quad \rightarrow \quad 3x^o = 30^\circ \quad \rightarrow \quad x = 10$$

KEY CONCEPT #15: COMPLEMENTARY ANGLES—SINE AND COSINE EQUALITY

We just covered that equivalent sine and cosine values have complementary angles. This also means that complementary angles have equivalent sine and cosine values.

Prep Expert Strategy

1. If two angles are complementary (add up to 90°), the cosine and sine values of those two angles are equal to each other.

$$A^o + B^o = 90^o \quad \rightarrow \quad \cos(A^o) = \sin(B^o)$$

Prep Expert Example

*   **Question**: In the following right triangle, if $\cos(A^\circ) = 0.8$, what is $\sin(B^\circ)$?

*   **Answer**: Because this is a right triangle, we know that $A^o + B^o = 90^o$. Therefore, $\cos(A^o) = \sin(B^o)$.

    $$\cos(A^o) = 0.8 \quad \sin(B^o) = 0.8$$

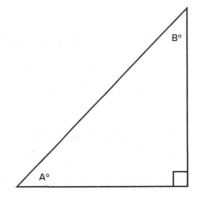

Ace Trigonometry to maximize your SAT Math score.

PREP EXPERT PRACTICE

Try applying this *Prep Expert Strategy* yourself to the following SAT practice questions:

119

Triangle *ABC* is similar to triangle *XYZ*, where angle *A* corresponds to angle *X* and angles *B* and *Y* are right angles. If $cos(A) = \frac{5}{13}$, what is the value of $cos(X)$?

A) $\frac{13}{5}$

B) $\frac{5}{13}$

C) $\frac{12}{5}$

D) $\frac{5}{12}$

120

In triangle *XYZ*, $cos(Y) = \frac{35}{37}$ and angle *X* is a right angle. What is the value of $cos(Z)$?

The answers to these SAT practice questions can be found in the back of this book.

PREP EXPERT REVIEW

Key Takeaways

- **Prep Expert Math Strategy #20—*Ace Trigonometry***: This section covered key concepts for mastering trigonometry on SAT Math.

- **Trigonometry on the SAT**: The SAT tests only a few trigonometry concepts, mostly related to right triangles. Typically, there are no more than three trigonometry-related questions total on the SAT.

- **Fundamental trigonometric ratios**: Understanding sine (opposite/hypotenuse), cosine (adjacent/hypotenuse), and tangent (opposite/adjacent) ratios in right triangles is crucial.

- **The unit circle**: The unit circle, with its radius of one unit, is essential for calculating trigonometric functions.

- **Right triangles in the unit circle**: The unit circle forms specific right triangles (e.g., 30-60-90, 45-45-90) that are useful for simplifying trigonometric calculations.

- **x-values and y-values in the unit circle**: The x- and y-coordinates of points on the unit circle correspond to the cosine and sine values of angles, respectively.

- **Sign changes**: In the unit circle, the signs of sine, cosine, and tangent change in different quadrants, and the CAST rule can help you remember these changes.

- **Complementary angles**: It's important to understand the relationship between complementary angles (which add up to 90°). The sine of one angle equals the cosine of its complementary angle, and vice versa.

25% OFF
PREP EXPERT
SAT & ACT COURSES AND TUTORING

Use the Coupon Code BOOK25 at prepexpert.com

Want to take your SAT score to the next level? Enroll in an online Prep Expert SAT course or tutoring package. Save 25% OFF with the promo code **BOOK25**. Here are some of the benefits:

- **200-Point SAT Score Improvement Guarantee:** We guarantee students who take our 6-Week Flagship SAT Prep Course will improve their official SAT score by at least 200 points or we will refund 100% of your money. Terms and conditions apply.

- **4-Point ACT Score Improvement Guarantee:** We guarantee students who take our 6-Week Flagship ACT Prep Course will improve their official ACT score by at least 4 points or we will refund 100% of your money. Terms and conditions apply.

- **99th Percentile Instructors:** All Prep Expert courses are taught by instructors who have scored in the top 1% of the test that they teach and have significant teaching experience.

- **Course Formats:** We offer a variety of course formats, including live online courses, on-demand video courses, and one-on-one tutoring packages.

- **Course Schedules:** We offer 100+ SAT and ACT course schedules year-round, including 6-week, 7-week, and 8-week courses that start in the summer, fall, winter, and spring.

Scan the QR code or visit
prepexpert.com

PREPEXPERT
SAT VOCAB
WORD LISTS

"Vocabulary is a matter of word-building as well as word-using."

—DAVID CRYSTAL

PREP EXPERT SAT VOCAB WORD LISTS

We have compiled data-driven lists of the most common vocabulary words that appear on SAT Reading. Learning these words will help you comprehend SAT Reading passages, questions, and answer choices better. This is one of the most effective ways to raise your score on SAT Reading.

We recommend memorizing the vocabulary words using *Prep Expert Reading Strategy #5—Use The 7-Repetition Method For Vocab*. But you may memorize the words using any method you prefer. You may want to review the words regularly, create flash cards, or incorporate them into quizzes.

Many of the words may seem straightforward. This is intentional. The Digital SAT does not test as many obscure vocabulary words as the old paper-based SAT did. However, just because you *think* a word is "easy" does not mean that you should skip learning it. Test your knowledge. Cover the synonym/definition and articulate the definition yourself. Many students believe they know what a particular vocabulary word means, but when they are asked to articulate the definition of the word themselves, they are unable to come up with one. If you can't create your own definition of a given vocabulary word, then you do not fully understand the meaning of the word. Therefore, you must learn the given synonym or definition.

The goal is to make sure you understand the meaning of all of the words in these lists prior to your official Digital SAT test day. If you achieve this goal, your SAT Reading score will skyrocket!

#	Word	Synonym	Definition
1	**Memoir**	Autobiography	A historical account or autobiography written from personal knowledge
2	**Dexterity**	Skill	Skill in performing tasks, especially with the hands
3	**Harvest**	Crop or Gather	The process/period of gathering in crops; or to obtain or acquire something, often with effort/skill
4	**Degrade**	Deteriorate	To decline in physical condition; or to humiliate, belittle, or demean someone
5	**Emerge**	Arise	To move out of or away from something and become visible
6	**Divert**	Redirect	To cause someone or something to change course or turn from one direction to another
7	**Retrospect**	Recollection	The act of looking back or reflecting on past events, experiences, or situations
8	**Forge**	Build	To create something strong, enduring, or successful
9	**Inane**	Silly	Silly; stupid
10	**Impudent**	Rude	Not showing due respect for another person; impertinent
11	**Vulgar**	Crude	Lacking refinement or good taste; or offensive or inappropriate
12	**Invigorate**	Energize	To give strength or energy to
13	**Malevolent**	Evil	Having or showing a wish to do evil to others
14	**Disparage**	Belittle	To regard or represent as being of little worth
15	**Impartial**	Fair	To be fair and just in judgment or decision-making, considering all relevant factors objectively
16	**Prosaic**	Mundane	Ordinary, lacking imagination or excitement
17	**Pilgrimage**	Journey	A pilgrim's journey
18	**Ratify**	Approve	To formally approve or confirm something, usually by a vote or signature
19	**Elusive**	Evasive	Difficult to find, catch, or achieve
20	**Subtle**	Slight	Delicate, elusive, or not immediately obvious

Prep Expert SAT Vocab List 2

#	Word	Synonym	Definition
1	**Narrative**	Story	A spoken or written account of connected events; a story
2	**Predatory**	Exploitative	Seeking to exploit or oppress others
3	**Evoke**	Bring Out	To bring or recall a feeling, memory, or image to the conscious mind
4	**Candor**	Honesty	The quality of being open and honest
5	**Ideal**	Perfect	Satisfying one's conception of what is perfect; most suitable
6	**Suppress**	Repress	To prevent the expression or occurrence of something
7	**Renounce**	Relinquish	To formally give up, reject, or disown something, such as a claim, belief, or title
8	**Deviate**	Diverge	Depart from an established course
9	**Pivotal**	Crucial	Of crucial importance in relation to the development or success of something else
10	**Disdain**	Contempt	Consider to be unworthy of one's consideration
11	**Prudent**	Wise	Showing good judgment and caution, especially in practical matters
12	**Domestic**	Homely	Of or relating to the running of a home or to family relations
13	**Abstain**	Refrain	To choose not to do something
14	**Perceptive**	Discerning	Having or showing keen insight, understanding, or awareness
15	**Fortuitous**	Lucky	Fortunately happening by chance or accident rather than design
16	**Overburdened**	Overwhelmed	Loading with too great a burden
17	**Tenuous**	Fragile	Weak, slender, or fragile; lacking strength or substance
18	**Hackneyed**	Trite	Lacking significance through having been overused; unoriginal and trite
19	**Annotate**	Comment	To add notes giving explanation or comment
20	**Effectual**	Effective	Successful in producing a desired or intended result

SAT Vocab
Word Lists

#	Word	Synonym	Definition
1	**Aberration**	Anomaly	A deviation from the normal or typical
2	**Yield**	Surrender or Produce	To surrender to authority; or to produce a result
3	**Frugal**	Thrifty	Living in a simple, thrifty, or sparing manner, often avoiding unnecessary expenses or waste
4	**Peripheral**	Outer	On the edge of something, not centrally important
5	**Replicable**	Duplicable	Capable of being replicated or reproduced, often in a scientific or experimental context
6	**Stimulus**	Trigger	A factor or event that incites activity or development
7	**Monarch**	Ruler	A sovereign head of state, especially a king or queen
8	**Wary**	Cautious	Cautious, watchful, or suspicious of potential danger or problems
9	**Cosmic**	Galactic	Relating to the universe or cosmos
10	**Juvenile**	Youthful	Relating to young people
11	**Tangible**	Concrete	Objects or qualities that are physical, material, or substantial in nature, as opposed to abstract
12	**Stoic**	Unemotional	Being unaffected by or indifferent to pleasure or pain, showing self-control
13	**Rhetoric**	Oratory	The art of using language effectively and persuasively, often with the aim of influencing others
14	**Fanciful**	Imaginative	Overimaginative and unrealistic
15	**Condescending**	Patronizing	Looking down upon others or considering oneself as more knowledgeable or important
16	**Transient**	Temporary	Temporary or passing, not lasting or permanent
17	**Circuitous**	Indirect	Longer than the most direct way
18	**Inexplicable**	Unexplainable	Unable to be explained or accounted for
19	**Censure**	Disapprove	Formal disapproval or criticism
20	**Harbinger**	Precursor	A herald of something to come, often serving as a sign or indication of future events

#	Word	Synonym	Definition
1	**Brazen**	Bold	Bold and without shame
2	**Stately**	Majestic	Dignified and impressive in appearance, manner, or size
3	**Infrastructure**	Framework	Basic physical and organizational structures and facilities (i.e., buildings, roads, etc.)
4	**Nefarious**	Evil	An action or activity that is wicked or criminal
5	**Aide**	Assistant	A person who helps in particular work
6	**Adhere**	Stick	To remain attached or connected to something
7	**Contrite**	Regretful	Feeling or expressing remorse at the recognition that one has done wrong
8	**Entitled**	Privileged	Believing oneself to be inherently deserving of privileges or special treatment
9	**Pretentious**	Showy	Attempting to impress by affecting greater importance or merit than is actually possessed
10	**Abstract**	Conceptual	Existing in thought but not having physical existence
11	**Inhibit**	Stop	To hinder, restrain, or prevent an action or process
12	**Correlate**	Relate	To establish a connection or correspondence between elements, factors, or phenomena
13	**Superficial**	Shallow	Concerned only with surface appearances and lacking depth or substance
14	**Twentieth Century**	1900s	The period from 1901 to 1999
15	**Ascend**	Rise	To go up or climb
16	**Undermine**	Weaken	To weaken, sabotage, or subvert from below or secretly
17	**Adversity**	Hardship	Difficulties or misfortune
18	**Porous**	Permeable	Capable of allowing the passage or diffusion of substances through pores or openings
19	**Dismissive**	Disregardful	Feeling that something is unworthy of consideration
20	**Profound**	Deep	Having deep meaning, significance, or insight

SAT Vocab Word Lists

#	Word	Synonym	Definition
1	**Rudimentary**	Basic	Basic or undeveloped, lacking complexity or sophistication
2	**Cultivate**	Develop	To prepare and use land for crops or gardening; or to promote the growth and development
3	**Capitulate**	Surrender	To cease resisting or fighting; to admit defeat or accept an unfavorable outcome
4	**Dynamic**	Energetic	Characterized by constant change, activity, or progress
5	**Acquire**	Obtain	To buy or obtain an object or asset
6	**Contemplate**	Ponder	To think deeply or carefully about something
7	**Alleviate**	Relieve	To make suffering less severe
8	**Vigor**	Energy	Physical or mental strength, energy, or vitality
9	**Satire**	Mockery	A literary or artistic work that uses irony, humor, or exaggeration to criticize or mock
10	**Colonial**	Settler	Relating to the control exerted by one country over another as a colony
11	**Aboriginal**	Indigenous	Being the first inhabitants of a region
12	**Conceal**	Hide	To hide or keep something or someone from being seen, discovered, or known
13	**Inconsequential**	Trivial	Not important or significant
14	**Whimsical**	Fanciful	Playfully quaint or fanciful, having a sense of unpredictable or fantastical charm
15	**Chronicle**	Record	A factual written account of important events
16	**Foster**	Encourage	To encourage the development of something, especially something desirable
17	**Invasive**	Intrusive	Tending to spread prolifically and harmfully
18	**Infamy**	Disgrace	The state of being well known for some bad quality or deed
19	**Facetious**	Witty	Treating serious issues with deliberately inappropriate humor
20	**Intrigue**	Fascinate	To arouse the curiosity or interest of; fascinate

#	Word	Synonym	Definition
1	**Concede**	Admit	To admit that something is true after first denying or resisting it
2	**Disengage**	Detach	To separate or release from something to which they are attached
3	**Decipher**	Interpret	To convert a text written in code, or a coded signal, into normal language
4	**Ambivalent**	Conflicted	Having mixed feelings or contradictory ideas
5	**Arid**	Dry	Having little or no rain; too dry or barren
6	**Diligent**	Industrious	Having or showing care and conscientiousness in one's work or duties
7	**Surmise**	Speculate	To make an educated guess or inference based on limited evidence or intuition
8	**Hybrid**	Mixed	Made by combining two different elements; a mixture
9	**Institution**	Establishment	An established organization, society, or establishment, typically with a specific purpose
10	**Indigenous**	Native	Originating or occurring naturally in a particular place
11	**Prevail**	Triumph	To prove more powerful or superior; to predominate
12	**Cognitive**	Mental	Relating to mental processes or activities involved in knowing, understanding, and perceiving
13	**Assess**	Evaluate	To evaluate or estimate the nature, ability, or quality
14	**Thwart**	Hinder	To prevent or hinder the accomplishment of something
15	**Adulation**	Flattery	Excessive admiration or praise
16	**Repudiate**	Reject	To reject, disown, or refuse to accept something, often due to disagreement or disapproval
17	**Altruistic**	Selfless	Acting or behaving in a manner that seeks to benefit others
18	**Intrepid**	Fearless	Fearless or courageous in the face of danger, challenges, or difficult situations
19	**Hierarchical**	Ranked	Arranged in order of rank
20	**Passive**	Inactive	Not actively participating or involved in a particular activity

SAT Vocab Word Lists

#	Word	Synonym	Definition
1	**Myriad**	Numerous	A countless or extremely great number
2	**Grapple**	Wrestle	To engage in a close fight or struggle without weapons; wrestle
3	**Insidious**	Stealthy	Proceeding in a gradual, subtle way, but with harmful effects
4	**Concerted**	Collective	Jointly arranged or carried out
5	**Provoke**	Incite	To incite or stimulate a response, often deliberately
6	**Posit**	Postulate	To assume as a fact; put forward as a basis of argument
7	**Vindicate**	Exonerate	To clear from blame, suspicion, or doubt, proving one's innocence or correctness
8	**Conceive**	Imagine	To form a mental representation of; imagine
9	**Recant**	Retract	To officially withdraw or renounce a belief or statement previously made
10	**Materialism**	Consumerism	A tendency to consider material possessions as more important than spiritual values
11	**Underscore**	Emphasize	To emphasize or highlight the importance or significance of something
12	**Refute**	Disprove	To prove a statement, argument, or belief to be false or incorrect
13	**Obfuscate**	Confuse	To render obscure, unclear, or unintelligible
14	**Obscure**	Unclear	Difficult to understand, ambiguous, or vague
15	**Distinct**	Unique	Recognizably different from something else of a similar type
16	**Excavate**	Dig	Make a hole or channel by digging
17	**Fastidious**	Meticulous	Very attentive to and concerned about accuracy and detail
18	**Expend**	Spend	Spend or use up a resource such as money, time, or energy
19	**Linguist**	Language Expert	A person who studies or is skilled in languages, especially the structure, history, and usage
20	**Induce**	Cause	To persuade, influence, or convince someone to do something or adopt a certain course of action

#	Word	Synonym	Definition
1	**Culminate**	Peak	To reach a climax or point of highest development
2	**Disperse**	Scatter	To distribute or spread over a wide area
3	**Refugee**	Exile	A person who has been forced to leave their home country due to war, persecution, or disaster
4	**Oblige**	Require	To make legally or morally bound to do something
5	**Constitute**	Comprise	To be a part of a whole
6	**Laudatory**	Praiseworthy	Expressing praise and commendation
7	**Rebut**	Refute	To offer arguments or evidence in response to a claim or accusation, contradicting or disproving it
8	**Progressive**	Forward-thinking	Characterized by or advocating progress, change, or improvement
9	**Protagonist**	Hero	The main character or hero in a story or play
10	**Immutable**	Unchangeable	Unchanging over time or unable to be changed
11	**Assurance**	Guarantee	A positive declaration intended to give confidence
12	**Credence**	Credibility	Acceptance or belief in the truth, validity, or reliability of something
13	**Anguish**	Sorrow	Severe mental or physical pain or suffering
14	**Fabricate**	Construct	To invent or concoct, typically with deceitful intent
15	**Conceptual**	Theoretical	Based on ideas or concepts
16	**Benign**	Harmless	Not causing harm or injury; not malignant or dangerous
17	**Diminish**	Reduce	To lessen or lower in value, quality, or degree
18	**Civilian**	Nonmilitary	A person not in the armed services
19	**Nebulous**	Vague	In the form of a cloud or haze; hazy
20	**Enigma**	Mystery	A person or thing that is mysterious or difficult to understand

SAT Vocab Word Lists

#	Word	Synonym	Definition
1	Emulate	Imitate	To imitate or copy the actions, behavior, or style of someone or something
2	Imperceptible	Unnoticeable	Impossible to perceive
3	Reign	Rule	Period of time during which a monarch or ruler holds power
4	Ebullient	Enthusiastic	Cheerful and full of energy
5	Artificial	Synthetic	Made or produced by human beings
6	Potency	Strength	The state or quality of being potent, powerful, or strong
7	Atypical	Unusual	Deviating from the usual or typical characteristics or traits
8	Amicable	Friendly	Characterized by friendliness and absence of discord
9	Conform	Obey	To comply with rules, standards, or laws
10	Discern	Perceive	To perceive or recognize
11	Latent	Hidden	Existing but not yet developed or manifest; hidden or concealed
12	Contemporary	Modern	Belonging to the present time or occurring in the same period
13	Nuance	Subtlety	A subtle difference in or shade of meaning, expression, or sound
14	Acquaintance	Associate	A person one knows slightly
15	Conjecture	Hypothesis	An opinion or conclusion formed on the basis of incomplete information
16	Exonerate	Acquit	To absolve someone from blame for a fault or wrongdoing
17	Clairvoyant	Psychic	A person who claims to have a supernatural ability to perceive future events
18	Inherent	Intrinsic	Existing in something as a permanent, essential, or characteristic attribute
19	Lucrative	Profitable	Producing a great deal of profit
20	Explicit	Clear	Stated clearly and in detail, leaving no room for confusion

#	Word	Synonym	Definition
1	**Conspicuous**	Obvious	Standing out so as to be clearly visible
2	**Dormant**	Inactive	In a state of rest or inactivity
3	**Contentious**	Controversial	Causing or likely to cause an argument
4	**Multidisciplinary**	Interdisciplinary	Combining several academic disciplines or professional specializations in an approach
5	**Equanimity**	Composure	Mental calmness, composure, and evenness of temper, especially in a difficult situation
6	**Disconcerting**	Disturbing	Causing one to feel unsettled
7	**Unanimity**	Consensus	Agreement or consensus among all participants
8	**Disposition**	Temperament	A person's inherent qualities of mind and character
9	**Pathogen**	Germ	A bacterium, virus, or other microorganism that can cause disease
10	**Attrition**	Erosion	The process of reducing something's strength through sustained attack
11	**Consolidate**	Merge	To combine or merge separate elements, entities, or parts into a single, unified whole
12	**Linear**	Sequential	Arranged in or extending along a straight line
13	**Foreground**	Front	The part of a view that is nearest to the observer
14	**Preoccupied**	Absorbed	Engrossed in thought; distracted
15	**Encapsulate**	Summarize	Express the essential features of something succinctly
16	**Polarize**	Divide	To divide or cause to divide into two sharply contrasting groups or sets of opinions or beliefs
17	**Decentralized**	Distributed	Organized or structured in a way that disperses or distributes power, authority, or control
18	**Revelation**	Discovery	A surprising or remarkable disclosure or discovery, often bringing new understanding or insight
19	**Emigrate**	Depart	To leave one's own country in order to settle in another
20	**Proponent**	Advocate	A person who advocates a theory, proposal, or action

SAT Vocab Word Lists

SAT PRACTICE QUESTION ANSWERS

*"Practice does not make perfect.
Only perfect practice makes perfect."*

—VINCE LOMBARDI

SAT PRACTICE QUESTION ANSWERS

Below are the answers to the SAT practice questions in this book.

#1	B	#21	D	#41	C	#61	A	#81	D	#101	A
#2	D	#22	D	#42	C	#62	C	#82	A	#102	D
#3	A	#23	B	#43	C	#63	B	#83	C	#103	C
#4	A	#24	B	#44	B	#64	B	#84	A	#104	48
#5	B	#25	C	#45	A	#65	B	#85	D	#105	B
#6	D	#26	A	#46	A	#66	C	#86	98.5	#106	B
#7	B	#27	D	#47	C	#67	A	#87	A	#107	B
#8	C	#28	D	#48	D	#68	B	#88	B	#108	B
#9	D	#29	D	#49	D	#69	B	#89	A	#109	1,800
#10	A	#30	C	#50	D	#70	B	#90	B	#110	B
#11	D	#31	D	#51	C	#71	A	#91	C	#111	A
#12	B	#32	D	#52	A	#72	A	#92	D	#112	5/12 or 0.42
#13	C	#33	A	#53	B	#73	A	#93	D	#113	50
#14	D	#34	A	#54	C	#74	A	#94	A	#114	D
#15	D	#35	A	#55	D	#75	C	#95	−15	#115	B
#16	D	#36	B	#56	D	#76	C	#96	A	#116	5
#17	C	#37	A	#57	B	#77	C	#97	A	#117	D
#18	C	#38	B	#58	B	#78	A	#98	B	#118	10
#19	A	#39	D	#59	D	#79	B	#99	D	#119	B
#20	B	#40	A	#60	A	#80	C	#100	B	#120	12/37 or 0.32

ENJOYED THE BOOK?
LEAVE A REVIEW ON AMAZON.COM

 PREPEXPERT

Direct link to the Amazon book page at prepexpert.com/book

Did you enjoy *Prep Expert Digital SAT Playbook*? Did the book help you improve your SAT score? Or better yet, did the book help you get into college or win scholarships? I would be personally grateful if you left a review on Amazon. Here's what your review can do:

- **SAT Scores:** The more parents and students who see your positive review on Amazon, the more students there will be who improve their own SAT scores.

- **College Admissions:** The more parents and students who see your positive review on Amazon, the more students who will gain admissions into the college of their dreams.

- **$1 Billion Scholarship Mission:** The more parents and students who see your positive review on Amazon, the more students who will win scholarships. You would help Prep Expert achieve its $1 Billion Scholarship Mission.

Your review on Amazon can positively change the lives of other people. It may take you only a few seconds to write a review. But the positive impact you can make could last for years. At Prep Expert, our motto is *Change Your Score, Change Your Life*. If this book has helped change your score, please help us change the lives of more students by spreading the word.

 **Scan the QR code or visit**
prepexpert.com/book

Thank you for reading, and good luck on your SAT!
—Dr. Shaan Patel